Recasting the Disney Princess in an Era of New Media and Social Movements

Recasting the Disney Princess in an Era of New Media and Social Movements

Edited by Shearon Roberts

LEXINGTON BOOKS
Lanham • Boulder • New York • London

Published by Lexington Books
An imprint of The Rowman & Littlefield Publishing Group, Inc.
4501 Forbes Boulevard, Suite 200, Lanham, Maryland 20706
www.rowman.com

6 Tinworth Street, London SE11 5AL, United Kingdom

Copyright © 2020 by The Rowman and Littlefield Publishing Group, Inc.

All rights reserved. No part of this book may be reproduced in any form or by any electronic or mechanical means, including information storage and retrieval systems, without written permission from the publisher, except by a reviewer who may quote passages in a review.

British Library Cataloguing in Publication Information Available

Library of Congress Cataloging-in-Publication Data

Names: Roberts, Shearon, 1984– editor.
Title: Recasting the Disney princess in an era of new media and social movements / edited by Shearon Roberts.
Description: Lanham : Lexington Books, 2020. | Includes bibliographical references and index. | Summary: "This collection analyzes the way that the Walt Disney Company has co-opted contemporary social discourse and studies how the current Disney era reflects changes in a global society where audiences are empowered by new media and social justice movements"— Provided by publisher.
Identifiers: LCCN 2019058673 (print) | LCCN 2019058674 (ebook) | ISBN 9781793604019 (cloth) | ISBN 9781793604033 (paper) | ISBN 9781793604026 (epub)
Subjects: LCSH: Walt Disney Productions. | Girls in motion pictures. | Women in motion pictures. | Heroines in motion pictures. | Motion pictures—Social aspects—United States.
Classification: LCC PN1999.W27 R43 2020 (print) | LCC PN1999.W27 (ebook) | DDC 791.43/652621—dc23
LC record available at https://lccn.loc.gov/2019058673
LC ebook record available at https://lccn.loc.gov/2019058674

∞™ The paper used in this publication meets the minimum requirements of American National Standard for Information Sciences—Permanence of Paper for Printed Library Materials, ANSI/NISO Z39.48-1992.

Contents

Acknowledgments	ix
Prologue: Tiana Turns Ten	xiii

Part I: Rebranding the Disney Princess

1 Recasting the Disney Princess in an Era of New Media
   and Social Movements   3
   Shearon Roberts

2 Diversity Sells: The Dollars and Cents of "Woke" Rebranding   21
   Shaniece B. Bickham and Shearon Roberts

3 *Sofia the First*: A Princess Life Fit for a Preschool Audience   43
   Sarah Maben

4 From Princess to Heroine: Expanding Representations
   of Girls and Women   59
   Jana Thomas and Holly Pate

5 Pop, Hip-Hop, and the "Hamiltonization" of the Disney
   Soundtrack   79
   Daron Roberts and Turon Nicholas

Part II: Diversifying the Disney Princess

6 Elena of Avalor and Mama Coco: Latina Sheroes and
   Knowledge Keepers   99
   Alberto Rodriguez and Veronica Nohemi Duran

7 #NolaBorn: Tiana and the Road Home for New Orleans
Residents 117
Sheryl Kennedy Haydel

8 *Moana*: The Daughter of the Chief and Polynesian
(in)Visibility 129
Jenny Banh

9 #MakeMulanRight: Retracing the Genealogy of Mulan
from Ancient Chinese Tale to Disney Classic 147
Jenny Banh

10 *Pocahontas*: Digital Coloniality, Coercive Fiction, and
"Renewing" Western Hegemonic Power 163
Leece Lee-Oliver

11 A Whole New Worldview: Gender Norms, Islamophobia,
and Orientalism 181
Krystal Ghisyawan

Part III: Deconstructing Princess Narratives

12 Belle: Beyond the Classic Story for the Modern Audience 199
Rebecca Weidman-Winter

13 "Let It Go" as Radical Mantra: Subverting the Princess
Narrative in *Frozen* 211
Susanne R. Hackett

14 Shuri of Wakanda, The People's Princess 227
Charity Clay

15 *Maleficent*: Rape, Wrath, and the Feminine Divine 245
Sarah A. Clunis

Part IV: Embedding Social Discourse around the Disney Heroine

16 Disney's Social Consciousness: Explaining
#BlackLivesMatter through *Zootopia* 263
Ahli Chatters and Shearon Roberts

17 "It's Good to Be Bad": Marginalization and Othering
in the *Descendants* Films 281
Shearon Roberts

18 No Capes Needed: The Plight of Super Moms 295
Alexis Woods Barr

19	The Women of Wakanda: Black Beauty and Casting *Abeo Jackson*	309
20	Culture Wars and the Politics of *Finding Dory* *Prairie Endres-Parnell*	321

Epilogue: Notes from behind the Camera from a Father
   of Two Daughters   339
   Varion Laurent

Index   341

About the Editor and Contributors   345

Acknowledgments

"When I grow up I want to be a racer." My then four-year-old daughter Zoe uttered these words in a packed chapel at her preschool graduation. I was stunned and proud. Why a racer? Because Vanellope von Schweetz sang in "A Place Called Slaughter Race" in Disney's *Ralph Breaks the Internet* (2018) that her dream was to be the ultimate, daredevil racer. It is through the lens of my daughter and her older brother Zachary, eight, that this volume was born.

Our children do not know a world where Disney did not include superheroes or Jedi. Disney-Marvel-Lucasfilm-Pixar-Disney Channels-Disney apps and Disney+—it's all Disney to them. And even for fairy tales, there are new princesses in town, and they are no snowflakes. Their Disney is not my Disney. It's Disney 4.0. My kids and those of the contributors of this volume helped to shape this intellectual work.

As much as our childhoods have been marked by cultural moments created by Disney, for better or worse, so too is the current Disney era shaping childhood memories for a new generation of children. I am extremely proud of the spectrum of voices in this volume that is diverse and interdisciplinary. I thank the contributors to this volume, their children, mentors, research assistants, loved ones, and native communities that inspired their chapters. Our "production babies" also inspired our work and the cover illustration and they are: Alexandra, Maxwell, Olivia, Lindsay, Lauren, RJ, Judah, Ezra, Ora, Chaim, Riya, Clark, Davis, Valentina, Sebastian, Francesca, Sydney, Melody, Mayah, Luna Isabela, Anastasia, Alexandra, Annabelle, Elora, Chelsey, Cherona, and Isabelle.

My sister colleagues at my institution, Sarah Clunis and Charity Clay are always willing to support anything I set my mind to, have my back no matter how impossible the timeline is to our already well-stretched and over-tapped lives. Thank you to my dear friend Tyra Gross, who sent Alexis Woods Barr to me, another super mom in the academy. I am indebted to my fellow mom in the academy Sarah Maben, who has provided me with invaluable professional opportunity and brought both new wonderful colleagues Rebecca Weidman-Winter and Prairie Endres-Parnell to this project. I am grateful to both Holly Pate who graciously brought her colleague Jana Thomas along, which was vital in capturing a specific demographic's voice in this volume.

I had the good fortune of joining a cohort of diverse faculty working in digital ethnic studies in 2018 and through this network, Jenny Banh, Leece Lee-Oliver, and Alberto Rodriguez became a part of my world. Jenny, Leece, and Alberto, you have been a much needed voice to this project, and this volume is enhanced by the work that you all do. I thank Alberto for bringing Veronica Duran to this project.

As much as I was thrilled to collaborate with new colleagues, I got to bring along old ones as well. I thank my former professor Dr. Shaniece Bickham for kindly agreeing to be part of this volume and my dear friend Susanne Hackett whose intellect I admire. I thank Sheryl Kennedy Haydel for her steadfast friendship and support over the last five years. I reconnected with the astounding Krystal Ghisyawan who is doing phenomenal work in Diaspora studies. There is only one "chic" in my mind who can write a chapter on casting and acting and it is my dear childhood friend and actor Abeo Jackson. I thank my dear colleague Varion Laurent for lending his talent to create the cover illustration and his industry insights for the epilogue. I also thank my students Prinsey Walker and Hannah Shareef for your reflections in the prologue, and Ahli Chatters for being one of the earliest inspirations for my research on Disney. Thank you to Kelsey Ray and her mother Pamela Hilliard for contributing to this volume and my life. You all and the Singletarys (Pastor, Jolisa, and Joseph) are the reason New Orleans is my second home.

Last, but by no means least, my siblings Turon Nicholas and Daron Roberts got far more of musical talent than I did. Both of them became accomplished vocalists and musicians, respectively, and because of their professional backgrounds, they were the only ones I wanted to write a chapter about music.

As much as this book was inspired by my two children, my own exposure to Disney came from my mother, Bernadette Roberts. A classically trained pianist, music director, choral arranger, songwriter, and all-around superwoman, my mother instilled a love for the arts and culture in her five children. It was her dream that we could go to Disney World. She is

Acknowledgments

very much the source of my Disney influences growing up, as she taught us, and the many children she taught music to, how to play, sing, and perform Disney classics. More importantly, my ability to thrive as a scholar and a mother today is because of her steadfast and practical support, from reminding me I can do it when I am too tired, her proofing of every line in this manuscript, and watching my kids more times than I can count or tell her thank you for. So thank you mom, again, from the bottom of my heart. I have gotten incredible anonymous feedback from close colleagues on different stages of this work and I thank them for their peer reviews, edits, and proofreading of this volume. Thank you to my acquisition editor Judith Lakamper, assistant editor Shelby Russell, production editor Megan Murray, and the production team at Lexington Books for seeing the value of this work and supporting me through the production process. Finally, I thank my spouse, Nicholas Enarl Ramjattan, for putting up with my exhaustion as I juggle all the balls of being mother, wife, and scholar.

Prologue
Tiana Turns Ten

This prologue marks the ten-year anniversary of *The Princess and the Frog*. In examining Disney's cultural impact, this volume includes younger voices and the three essays below let this generation reflect on popular culture and what it meant for young Black girls in New Orleans to have a Black princess from their city to call their own.

Shearon Roberts

MY TIANA PARTY
Kelsey Ray

When it was my fourth birthday, I asked my mom if I can have a Tiana party. Tiana was my favorite Disney princess. At the time, I was absolutely in love with Princess Tiana. I had never seen a Black princess before, until my mom bought me the movie *The Princess and the Frog*. I can remember wanting to watch the movie over and over. I was so infatuated with Princess Tiana that my mom bought me everything Tiana. I had all of her collectables, which I still have to this day. At my party I can remember looking at Princess Tiana as if she was this Black beautiful magical princess. Her dress was so beautiful to me; all I can remember is seeing her in the movie with this beautiful gown and tiara. I was so excited that day, when she said hello to me, I just stared at her with excitement; she was so beautiful to me.

Tiana was my favorite princess. She was a princess that looked like me, had the same hair texture as me, my color, and she was from New

Orleans. *Princess and the Frog* was a movie that encouraged young Black girls to believe in themselves. Now looking back on those years and relating to a lot of things that happened in the movie, I now know that the struggle, commitment, and determination Tiana had to achieve her goals really paid off.

TIANA AT TEN
Prinsey Walker

Packed in my father's new pickup truck, my family drove to one of the few movie theaters open in the Greater suburban areas of New Orleans in 2009—the only cinema ten minutes away from my home, the AMC Westbank Palace Theater. The lot, packed with cars, belonged to majority Black families. In the ticket line, I stared at little girls in their coats, wearing giant bows, prancing around their families. They fidgeted with excitement to see the magic Disney developed starring a leading lady that looked like them. We all felt butterflies in our stomachs. This moment was special because Tiana was not just a Black princess. Tiana was the first Black Disney princess and she was from our city.

In this moment, this movie felt like one of the elements that revitalized the city, after the destruction of Hurricane Katrina. *The Princess and the Frog* animated the city back to life. Animators returned the color to the streets that seemed to fade from my childhood. I could smell the gumbo Tiana stirred with her mother. I felt the humidity in the swamps. The beignets contained the fluffy white sugar powder, looking rich to the taste.

However, now that the original audience matured, including me, feelings about the first Black princess from New Orleans have aged. As we grew up, as much as we loved the film, we also started to challenge the cultural storytelling of the movie, particularly the choice to associate this story of a frog prince, to a Black girl, who turned into an animal. Despite how conflicted we feel about our first Black princess, she has been, to this date, all we have been given. One Black Disney princess is not enough. Representation matters. New Orleans could be the first to house a Disney princess of color. But it need not be the last.

IN MEMORIAM OF THE WOMAN BEHIND TIANA
Hannah Shareef

Princess Tiana was inspired by the life of Chef Leah Chase who found her passion for cooking while waiting tables in the French Quarters. In that very moment she said to herself, "Why can't I have that for my own people? A fine dining restaurant." In late 2018, I interviewed Chase for *My Nola, My Story* for "A Conversation with Leah Chase." When Disney first set out to develop the character of Tiana, Chase told them then that "it is about time to show little African American children somebody like them." Chase not only used her voice then, but she had done this for decades as a Civil Rights icon who "changed the course of America with a bowl of gumbo," one of her favorite quotes.

As Chase fed leaders of the Civil Rights Movement at her Dooky Chase restaurant, she said "white people attended meetings to show support, they ate what we ate and by doing so it was evident that food brings us together, we are one." In high school, Chase said she remembered standing on the corner with the nuns as she waited for President Franklin D. Roosevelt to pass in a local parade. During that time in 1935, she never thought her culinary skills would allow her to meet presidents in the future. She shared about meeting Presidents George W. Bush and Barack Obama: "I cannot believe I have lived long enough to serve presidents." Chase was more than a gifted chef, she was a woman who knew that there was no "greater calling than feeding people." Throughout the community of New Orleans she encouraged young people to "never play small with your life."

I

REBRANDING THE DISNEY PRINCESS

1

✢

Recasting the Disney Princess in an Era of New Media and Social Movements

Shearon Roberts

RECASTING THE DISNEY PRINCESS

On June 19, 2018, the Walt Disney Studios company named a woman, Jennifer Lee, to one of its highest executive positions: Chief Creative Officer, for Walt Disney Animation Studios. Her role: "creative oversight of all films and associated projects of their respective studios."[1] Lee's career is the story of recasting princesses. Her first role ever with the studio was as co-writer of *Wreck-It Ralph* (2012). She co-created the story of a princess who rejects all attributes of the fairyland, sugarcoated world she is boxed into, both literally and figuratively. Princess Vanellope von Schweetz loves racing fast cars, considers herself one of the guys, dons a hoody and sports a ponytail, and is ostracized for rejecting the status quo. Her very story line of non-conformity—in having a glitch, is what drives her opponents to work to marginalize and ultimately eliminate her from their world. As much as he is also an awkward reject, Ralph aims to be her friend, not her hero or a love interest. She saves him in the end as much as he works to help her.

This was Lee's first work at Disney. She went on to spend the next seven years recasting women and girls at the studio when she followed up *Wreck-It Ralph* by co-writing and co-directing 2013's Oscar-winning *Frozen*. That Disney is shaking things up not only by what stories it tells, but who it hires is not novel. This volume connects our current social climate to the content we consume and concludes that the Walt Disney Company is aiming to keep up with the times.

Over this decade (2009 to 2019) Disney's works, from all its studios, and platforms, have dominated the box office, creating a decade that has put the studio above its competitors. The success of its studios has also allowed the company to expand its revenue streams across attractions, merchandizing, and digital entertainment. As much as the company has now outpaced the industry in profits, it has done so by reimagining its brand and its identity.

The goal of this volume is to account for and critically evaluate what cultural imprint Disney's works have left on society and future generations, from this current second revival.[2] Its first renaissance (1989–1999) saw the proliferation of princess films, and the impact of those portrayals on children, and especially women and girls.[3] Then the studio's success waned in the early 2000s, and the box office went lukewarm, as the studio struggled to determine and understand its audience.[4] Times were changing, and it was not the first time Disney missed the mark on gauging public tastes, as it had experienced a prior slump after Walt Disney's death in 1966.[5]

From 2009 onward, the company began a slow but steady shift to new narratives. What aided this shift, in part, was Disney putting its ears to the ground. Beginning with Disney's *The Princess and the Frog*, the first Black princess, Disney enlisted a brain trust of African American voices and influencers.[6] It's a practice that has extended to the making of 2016's *Moana*.[7] In opening its creative process to the communities whose stories Disney aimed to tell (and also profit from), the studio sought to build rapport and ownership by audiences. The studio coupled its approach with hiring women executives like Jennifer Lee and Kathleen Kennedy (Lucasfilm), with contemporary perspectives and points of view, and consciously hired more diverse producers, directors, writers, cast and crew, across its studios and works in this decade. The studio created programs like the Disney Launchpad,[8] a shorts incubator for diverse filmmakers, and its Executive Incubator and Studios Intern Program to attract diverse talent.[9] The company created the hashtag #WomenBehindTheMagic to showcase women in leadership and creative roles across the company's holdings.[10]

This book seeks to unpack how this expanding diversity from the top-on-down at Disney is recasting and retelling what the studio has singularly been known for, the making of princesses. The volume features contributing authors who take an interdisciplinary look at how the works of the first decade of this second revival reflect current social movements and contemporary social mediated discourse.

GOOD NARRATIVES MAKE GOOD CENTS

In business, "trust drives revenue." A re-purposed Disney may be altruistic, but it has been good for business. As much as this volume aims to critique the works created during Disney's second revival, it also examines the political economy of a major global company and brand. In 2016, Disney set an industry record, earning $7.6 billion from its films. It bested itself in 2019, with a projected haul of over $10 billion.[11] Table 1.1[12] shows how Disney's recent works with female leads and top-billed female co-stars have broken records and the bank for the studio and its holdings. Table 1.1 also demonstrates that in executing Disney's new vision, its works expand into diversity of race/ethnicity and portrayals of gender, receive critical acclaim, and set records that confirm popular reception from audiences and consumers. Even films considered box office bombs, or that received poor or mixed reviews from critics, all grossed over $100 million.

When compared to other studios, few have come close to producing films that grossed over $1 billion. By the end of summer 2019, Disney set several records. It had the most amount of films to gross over $1 billion in a single year. It broke its own 2016 record for total film revenue, earning $7.67 billion by the middle of 2019, with still more films to premiere in the second half of the year. It broke the record for the highest grossing film of all time: *Avengers: Endgame*. Combined with Fox films, it earned 40 percent of the 2019 box office.[13]

Simply associating with Disney franchises have been good for rivals. Marvel Studio's agreement with Sony for the *Spiderman* film franchise earned Sony its first $1 billion film in 2019.[14] Warner Brothers also saw success in both racial and gender diversity for the DC Extended Universe, earning $1.148 billion for the Jason Momoa–led *Aquaman* in 2018. The film became the highest grossing DCEU film and film based on a DC Comics character, surpassing films on Batman. It followed up the success of *Wonder Woman* in 2017 that revitalized the fledgling DCEU franchise. Clearly diversity in race and gender is good business not just for Disney, but for Hollywood across the board. In all genres from horror (*Get Out* and *Us*) to comedy (*Crazy Rich Asians*) diverse-helmed films have been good business for studios. Disney has staked its claim on the diversity bandwagon, and as its 2018 box office returns show in Figure 1.1, it has outpaced its rivals. The 2018 figures in particular are boosted by one of the most groundbreaking films for diversity, Marvel Studios' *Black Panther*.

Disney captured a quarter of the marketplace in 2018 among the Big Six Studios, as shown in Figure 1.1, not counting films that Disney may have distributed from smaller independent studios. It grossed double the amount of revenue than the next studio by only producing a third of the films of its closest competitor in the same year. Each year since 2015, it has been the fastest studio to $1 billion at the box office, and in 2018, the studio earned that total in under 117 days from the start of the year,[15] its fastest billon-dollar haul, thanks to the success of *Black Panther*. No

Table 1.1. Disney Films' Success with Works with Female Leads/Co-Stars, 2009 to 2019.

Year	Film	Studio	Record	Acclaim
2009	The Princess and the Frog	Disney Animation Studios	$270 million	• Nominated for 3 Oscars • Number 1 at box office opening weekend. • Number 1 for 2009 Theater Average
2010	Tangled	Disney Animation Studios	$586 million	• Nominated for an Oscar • Number 8 highest grossing Disney animation • Number 10 highest grossing film of 2010.
2010	Alice in Wonderland	Walt Disney Pictures	$1.025 billion	• Second highest grossing film of 2010. • Won Oscars for Best Art Direction and Costume Design • Was Fifth Highest Grossing Film of All time During Its Run
2012	Marvel's The Avengers	Marvel Studios	$1.518 billion	• Highest grossing film of 2012. • Became third highest grossing film of all time the same year. • Positive reviews from critics and audiences.
2012	Brave	Pixar Animation Studios	$554 million	• Won Oscar for Best Animated Feature • Third Highest Grossing Animation of 2012 • Eighth Highest Grossing Pixar Film
2012	Wreck-It Ralph	Disney Animation Studios	$496 million	• Nominated for Oscar for Best Animated Feature • Number 4 highest grossing animation of 2012
2013	Oz the Great and Powerful	Walt Disney Pictures	$490 million	• Topped the box office its opening weekend. • Number 13 highest grossing film of 2013. • Mila Kunis won 2014 MTV Movie Award for Best Villain for performance as Wicked Witch of the West.
2013	Frozen	Disney Animation Studios	$1.272 billion	• Oscar winner for Best Animated Feature • Highest Grossing Animation of All Time • Highest Grossing Film of 2013

Year	Title	Studio	Gross	Notes
2014	Into the Woods	Walt Disney Pictures	$213 million	• Nominated for 3 Oscars • Release was 4th biggest Christmas Day film
2014	Maleficent	Walt Disney Pictures	$758 million	• Nominated for Oscar for Best Costume Design • 4th Highest Grossing Film of 2014.
2015	Avengers: Age of Ultron	Marvel Studios	$1.405 billion	• Fourth highest grossing film of 2015. • Fifth highest grossing film of all time, at that time. • Positive critic reviews.
2015	Cinderella	Walt Disney Pictures	$534 million	• Nominated for an Oscar • Number 12 highest grossing film of 2015.
2015	Inside Out	Pixar Animation Studios	$857 million	• Won Oscar for Best Animated Feature • Highest opening for an original story at the time. • Seventh highest grossing film of 2015
2015	Descendants	Disney Channel Original Productions	n/a	• Fifth most watched original movie in cable history • 6.6 million viewers for its premiere • 10.5 million viewers for playback
2015	Star Wars: The Force Awakens	Lucasfilm	$2.053 billion	• Highest grossing domestic film of all time • Highest grossing film of 2015 • Highest grossing *Star Wars* franchise film • Third highest grossing film of all time • Won Oscar for Best Visual Effects
2016	Moana	Disney Animation Studios	$637 million	• Nominated for 2 Oscars • Broke records on its opening week • Highest markets in Asia
2016	Rogue One: A Star Wars Story	Lucasfilm	$1.049 billion	• Second highest grossing film of 2016 • Third highest grossing film in *Star Wars* franchise • Nominated for two Oscars

(continued)

Table 1.1. (continued)

Year	Film	Studio	Record	Acclaim
2016	Finding Dory	Pixar Animation Studios	$1.021 billion	• Second Pixar film to cross $1 billion • Third highest grossing film of 2016 • Highest grossing domestic animated film
2016	Alice through the Looking Glass	Walt Disney Pictures	$272 million	• Considered a box office bomb domestically. • In China, was 2nd biggest live-action opening at the time
2016	Zootopia	Walt Disney Animation Studios	$1.021 billion	• Won Academy Award for Best Animated Feature • Fourth Highest Grossing film of 2016. • Became Disney Animation's highest grossing film since Frozen, at the time.
2017	Descendants 2	Disney Channel Original Productions	n/a	• 8.92 million viewers for its premiere • 21 million viewers on playback. • Highest rated cable show for its debut
2017	Coco	Pixar Animation Studios	$798 million	• Won 2 Oscars • Number 11 highest grossing film of 2017 • Number 15 highest grossing animation ever
2017	Star Wars: The Last Jedi	Lucasfilm	$1.316 billion	• Highest grossing film of 2017 • Number 9 highest grossing film of all time • Nominated for 4 Oscars
2017	Beauty and the Beast	Walt Disney Pictures	$1.259 billion	• Highest grossing live-action musical film • Number 14 highest grossing film of all time • Number 10 highest grossing film domestically • Nominated for 2 Oscars
2018	Black Panther	Marvel Studios	$1.348 billion	• 1st ever super hero film nominated for Oscar Best Picture • Number 5 highest grossing worldwide • Highest grossing domestic film of 2018 • Disney's 2nd highest grossing domestic film • Highest scored critics rating

Year	Title	Studio	Box Office	Notes
2018	Avengers: Infinity War	Marvel Studios	$2.048 billion	- First superhero film to gross over $2 billion. - Highest grossing film of 2018. - Fourth highest grossing film of all time, at that time.
2018	The Incredibles 2	Pixar Animation Studios	$1.242 billion	- Highest grossing animated film of 2018 - Highest grossing domestic animated feature - Nominated for 2019 Oscar for Best Animated Feature
2018	A Wrinkle in Time	Walt Disney Pictures	$133 million	- Considered a box office flop - First live-action with a budget over $100 million, directed by a woman of color.
2018	Ant Man and the Wasp	Marvel Studios	$623 million	- Number 11 highest grossing film of 2018
2018	Ralph Breaks the Internet	Disney Animation Studios	$473 million	- Nominated for Oscar for Best Animated Feature - Debuted Number 1 at the box office
2018	Mary Poppins Returns	Walt Disney Pictures	$318 million	- Nominated for 4 Oscars
2018	The Nutcracker and the Four Realms	Walt Disney Pictures	$173 million	- Unfavorable reviews from critics - Considered a box office flop
2019	Captain Marvel	Marvel Studios	$1.128 billion	- Highest grossing film by a woman director.
2019	Dumbo	Walt Disney Pictures	$353 million	- Underperformed at the box office - Mixed critical reviews
2019	Avengers: Endgame	Marvel Studios	$2.797 billion	- Highest grossing film worldwide of all time. - Fastest film to earn $1 billion and $1.5 billion. - Fifth highest grossing all-time, inflation adjusted.
2019	Aladdin	Walt Disney Pictures	$1.051 billion	- Audience score of 91% - Mixed critical reviews - Highest grossing film release in the Middle East of all time - Highest grossing 2019 film in Japan, surpassing Avengers: Endgame

(continued)

Table 1.1. *(continued)*

Year	Film	Studio	Record	Acclaim
2019	Dark Phoenix	Disney-Fox (holdover film from 2019 merger)	$252.4 million	• Described as a box office bomb. • Negatively reviewed by critics. • X-Men franchise to be restructured and relaunched under Marvel Studios
2019	Toy Story 4	Pixar Animation Studios	$1.073 billion	• Had the highest worldwide opening for an animated film until passed by *The Lion King* (2019) • A+ critics and audience approval rating • Won the 2020 Oscar for Animated Feature Film
2019	The Lion King	Walt Disney Pictures	$1.656 billion	• Set record for biggest opening for an animated film. • Mixed critics reviews, A+ review score by audiences. • Became the highest grossing animated film at the time until *Frozen 2*.
2019	Descendants 3	Disney Channel Original Productions	n/a	• Cable's highest rated show since *Descendants 2*. • Premiered with 8.4 million viewers.
2019	Maleficent 2	Walt Disney Pictures	$491 million	• First at the box office in opening week. • Film costume design received several industry awards.
2019	Frozen 2	Disney Animation Studios	$1.438 billion	• Highest grossing animated movie of all time.
2019	Star Wars: The Rise of Skywalker	Lucasfilm	$1.06 billion	• Pre-sale tickets outsold *Avengers-Endgame*. • The third highest opening for a film in December.

Prepared by Shearon Roberts
*n/a (not applicable); N.B. Numbers are unadjusted for inflation and last dated January 2020.

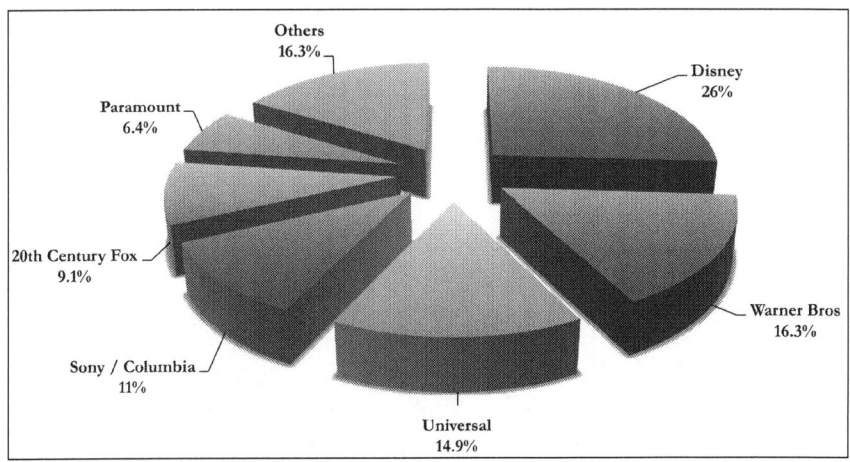

Figure 1.1. Disney's Share of the Marketplace Compared to its Competitors in 2018.
Box Office Mojo, "Studio Market Share, January 1–December 31, 2018," https://www.boxofficemojo.com/studio/?view=company&view2=yearly&yr=2018&p=.htm. Chart created by author.

other studio has come close to Disney to earn a billion dollars thrice in one year, and its acquisition of News Corp's 20th Century Fox Studios, means Disney can potentially break more records in works for young adult and adult audiences, as acquiring Marvel and Lucasfilm has done for the studio within this decade. When Disney+ launched in late 2019, it allowed the Walt Disney Company to enter and compete in the lucrative, subscriber-based, streaming business.

DISNEY'S CULTURAL IMPACT

In 2013, Johnson Cheu's[16] volume outlined Disney's impact on representations of race, ethnicity, gender, sexuality, and disability, and it does so up to 2009's *Up*. This volume focuses on works primarily from 2009 onwards, and works with female and diverse leads, not just in Disney's animations, but live-action films and films in Disney's other studio franchises. Cheu notes that while money and technology solidify power in the industry, what sustains Disney's power is its cultural imprint, globally.[17]

A few other key works have homed in on Disney's cultural impact, particularly during the renaissance period of the nineties.[18] Among them is Janet Wasko's *Understanding Disney*.[19] What scholars in prior works note is that it is difficult to separate Disney's impact from our lives. Even scholars who critically evaluate Disney hold profound memories and schema associated with their own personal development that involves Disney, in some form or the other.[20] In his 2010 work, Henry Giroux concedes that he is both a "cultural critic and concerned father of three children," and both factors inform his study of Disney.[21]

Giroux defines Disney as a "worldwide distributor of a particular kind of politics."[22] And he describes Disney's success as minding a "titanium-clad brand image—synonymous with a notion of childhood innocence and wholesome entertainment."[23] It peddles "youthful fantasies" and targets middle class "conscientious parents" resulting in "lifetime consumers" once these children become parents and transfer Disney iconicity on to another generation.

In the early 2000s, this is the essence of Disney's appeal, and primarily white families and white audiences benefitted most from its conservative view of culture, as Giroux noted. In this book, one small shift is occurring. Families and children of color, for better or worse, are more visible in the works Disney has produced since, and is scheduled to produce. When the full breadth of Disney's culture making is considered, looking at both Marvel and Lucasfilm, it is possible to see even more radical forms of cultural viewpoints in this current decade that work to empower communities of color, than previous works had done before.

It therefore calls on critical voices once again to take a second look at Disney's cultural impact in using its political and economic might to champion discourses that present and confront realities and experiences of women and people of color. This is not to say that Disney always gets it right, as most works on Disney have always noted, and that this book also does. It also means that Disney will now profit significantly from a more diverse, globalized consumer. It also shows how easily entertainment can commodify and appropriate marginalized groups and their cultures, without necessarily directly impacting the well-being of such groups. For now, such representation and visibility is a start.

CONTEMPORARY SOCIAL MOVEMENTS

Hollywood and corporations around the world have had to respond to our current times. Few media alternatives match the power of Disney, but scholars note that the Internet has been tailor-made for global mediated forms of social protest.[24] What activists failed to achieve prior to the 2000s, new media has connected communities across localities, cities, states, and countries. Like-minded causes found allies and community in collective struggle, and social media democratized communication, allowing activists and influencers to supersede traditional media as gatekeepers, allowing for a freer, un-policed flow of information.[25] Injustices and forms of oppression that received less attention in the mainstream could be amplified through digital forms of communication and new media technologies. Social media toward the later part of the 2000s emerged as a digital public sphere, where digital discourse resulted in offline forms of action.[26]

The creation of collective digital communities empowered consumers and audiences in ways that matched the political and economic might of traditional gatekeepers. This power, aided by mediated social movements and its discourse, often championed by digital activism, could have real life, offline results.

Social movements have always needed a mass medium.[27] Getting into the news was a primary way for movements to gain momentum and visibility for awareness to galvanize support for change. New media, particularly social media, have flung the doors wide open for visibility for social movements, and some scholars have cautioned that observers avoid taking a fully "techno-optimistic" view of social media's impact on movements.[28] Scholars note that social media activism consists of weaker ties, and less risk for online allies engaging in movements. In the past, activists could lose their lives for their activities, but social media activism offers less sacrifice for those who participate. Scholars have also noted the habit of slacktivism, where the work of participating in movements has been reduced to joining an online group, or hitting the like button, with no real commitment to more risky activities to further the work of a movement.[29]

While on one end techno-determinists believe that social media can lead to more freedoms, skeptics also concede that "the fact that barely committed actors cannot click their way to a better world does not mean that committed actors cannot use social media effectively."[30]

Therefore, at the very minimum, social media may mean more activists can have more unvetted access to shaping public discourse, and at the worst, spreading propaganda. Still, voices that are marginalized, and that otherwise would be ignored by mainstream gatekeepers, also gain advantages through the access new media provides in bringing injustices to the attention of a wider social consciousness.

This is the contemporary distinction of social movements today, compared to activism prior to the digital age. It allows issues to gain public consciousness faster, that reaches audiences even farther, and this collective digital support can be global. Traditional corporate and political holders of power, therefore, can have its trust eroded in an instance, if digital discourse is unfavorable. Likewise, brands are prompted to consider digital discourse of social movements, with the understanding that its ability to meet and reach its customers, in part, is stipulated by how consumers perceive and view its brands.

In selling entertainment, Disney's primary audience has always been families. Parents serve as gatekeepers for what their children consume, as they have the purchasing power to take kids to the movies, buy product merchandise, and cover the costs of a trip to Disney World. Changing public discourse, through social movements, also impacts what society considers are messages children today should receive. The chapters in this volume further examine how various movements have begun to critique traditional messages aimed at girls, women, children in general, and young adults. For Disney, this means that to appeal to consumer tastes, it must also represent and reflect shifting social norms. In tapping into social media discourse, Disney works to avoid appearing out of touch. The studio is constantly adjusting its position as a cultural force; one that mirrors the current times, providing entertainment and memories that feel authentic to the customers it wishes to serve for decades to come.

DISSECTING A DECADE

While Disney has arguably had works that sought to challenge the status quo in prior eras of its filmmaking history, this book is specifically concerned with its undoing of its princess and heroine narratives of prior eras, with works in its most current era. This is a specific exercise that Disney has embarked on, with a slate of remakes, as well as new works that contrast starkly with previous works where women and girls were the lead characters. This book aims to take a wide view of Disney's current experimenting with discourse around women and girls, with the common entry point, the backdrop of contemporary social movements and their mediated presence. Therefore, this book positions these new works in conversation with contemporary social discourse as a measurement to evaluate the cultural statements Disney is making, as well as to critique how successful these statements can be made within the confines of storytelling for entertainment.

More importantly, the erasure of communities of color in social movements and activism continues even today as white allies often become the preferred faces of social movements.[31] Therefore, this book features the critical examination of Disney's recent works from scholars of color, and women scholars and practitioners, amplifying their voices in the sense-making of cultural products. Scholarship is also rooted in the perspective of the author, and contributors to the volume are also parents and caregivers, who also wrestle with the imprint of Disney's cultural products in their own households and for their loved ones. Disney products are prevalent not just in movies, but on the small screen, in grocery stores, and on mobile devices. The ubiquity of Disney to most households make its impact observable in the daily lives of most consumers, particularly parents.

This book is broken up into four sections that contextualize evolving narratives around women and girls. Firstly, "Rebranding the Disney Princess" examines strategy employed by Disney to position its studio amidst contemporary social discourse. Secondly, "Diversifying the Disney Princess," looks at how Disney's newest takes at diverse women and girls aims to avoid some of the clichés the studio perpetuated with its princess works of the nineties. Thirdly, "Deconstructing Princess Narratives" examines what messages Disney aims to disseminate, specifically about gender, in works that go beyond basic notions of women as princesses. Fourthly, the chapters of "Embedding Social Discourse around the Disney Heroine," examines specific social discourses, and how recent works delve into these debates for teachable lessons for audiences.

All four sections of the book reflect scholarship and insights that aim to identify the potential of the cultural impact of new discourses. At the same time, the contributions in this book are cautious to single out in what instances the works miss the mark, and in other instances, reinforces centuries old tropes about women, girls, and people of color. More importantly, this volume designates its purpose and space for intellectual debates about Disney's cultural impact by scholars and practitioners of color, by women, and from backgrounds that range from the sciences to the arts. Collectively, this volume reflects that increasingly both in our academic and public discourse, women and people of color are striving to break the silence around marginalization of thought, both to educate and transform cultural norms for future generations.

NOTES

1. The Walt Disney Company, "Walt Disney and Pixar Animation Studios Name Chief Creative Officers," June 19, 2018, https://www.thewaltdisneycompany.com/walt-disney-and-pixar-animation-studios-name-chief-creative-officers/.

2. Chris Pallant, *Demystifying Disney: A History of Disney Feature Animation*, (London, UK: Bloomsbury Publishing USA, 2011).

3. Sarah M. Coyne, Jennifer Ruh Linder, Eric E. Rasmussen, David A. Nelson, and Victoria Birkbeck, "Pretty as a Princess: Longitudinal Effects of Engagement with Disney Princesses on Gender Stereotypes, Body Esteem, and Prosocial Behavior in Children," *Child Development* 87, no. 6 (2016): 1909–1925; Dorothy L. Hurley, "Seeing White: Children of Color and the Disney Fairy Tale Princess," *The Journal of Negro Education* (2005): 221–232.

4. Chris Pallant, *Demystifying Disney: A History of Disney Feature Animation*.

5. Ibid.

6. *The Pittsburgh Courier*, "Disney's 'The Princess and the Frog' a Dream Come True for Many," December 17, 2009, https://newpittsburghcourieronline

.com/2009/12/17/disneys-the-princess-and-the-frog-a-dream-come-true-for-many/.

7. Joana Robinson, "How Pacific Islanders Helped Disney's *Moana* Find Its Way," *Vanity Fair*, November 16, 2016, https://www.vanityfair.com/hollywood/2016/11/moana-oceanic-trust-disney-controversy-pacific-islanders-polynesia.

8. The Walt Disney Company, "Disney Launchpad: Shorts Incubator Creates New Opportunities for Filmmakers to Share Diverse Perspectives," June 3, 2019. https://www.thewaltdisneycompany.com/disney-launchpad-shorts-incubator-creates-new-opportunities-for-filmmakers-to-share-diverse-perspectives/.

9. Walt Disney Television, "Walt Disney Television Announces New Programs to Attract and Develop Talent from Underrepresented Backgrounds," July 1, 2019, https://www.thewaltdisneycompany.com/walt-disney-television-announces-new-programs-to-attract-and-develop-talent-from-underrepresented-backgrounds/

10. Disney Parks, @DisneyParks, Twitter Post, July 20, 2019, accessed July 25, 2019, https://twitter.com/DisneyParks/status/1152594047380447233.

11. Pamela McClintock, "Box Office: 'Lion King' Nudges Disney Toward Record Year of $1 B hits," *The Hollywood Reporter*, July 22, 2019, https://www.hollywoodreporter.com/news/lion-king-aladdin-add-fuel-disneys-record-year-1b-hits-1225937.

12. Box Office Mojo, "Disney All Time Box Office Results," accessed August 18, 2019, https://www.boxofficemojo.com/studio/chart/?studio=buenavista.htm&debug=0&view=parent&p=.htm; The Numbers, "All Time Worldwide Box Office for Disney Movies," accessed July 30, 2019, https://www.the-numbers.com/box-office-records/worldwide/all-movies/theatrical-distributors/walt-disney.

13. Travis Clark, "The 5 Disney Movies That Have Made Over $1 Billion at the Box Office in 2019," *Business Insider*, August 16, 2019, https://www.businessinsider.com/disney-movies-with-1-billion-at-box-office-2019-8.

14. Travis Clark, "The 5 Disney Movies That Have Made Over $1 Billion at the Box Office in 2019."

15. Box Office Mojo, "Fastest Studios to $1 Billion in a Given Year," https://www.boxofficemojo.com/alltime/fasteststudios.htm.

16. Johnson Cheu, Ed., *Diversity in Disney Films: Critical Essays on Race, Ethnicity, Gender, Sexuality and Disability*, (Jefferson, NC: McFarland, 2015). Cheu's introduction looks at how globalization influences diverse recasting of Disney films. Since Disney has always been a global cultural force, this volume specifically accounts for how new media and social movements move Disney in new directions, expanding on Cheu's volume.

17. Johnson Cheu, Ed., *Diversity in Disney Films: Critical Essays on Race, Ethnicity, Gender, Sexuality and Disability*, 2.

18. Amy Davis, *Handsome Heroes and Vile Villains: Masculinity in Disney's Feature Films* (Bloomington, IN: Indiana University Press, 2014); *Good Girls and Wicked Witches: Changing Representations of Women in Disney's Feature Animation, 1937–2001* (Bloomington, IN: Indiana University Press, 2007); "The 'Dark Prince' and Dream Women: Walt Disney and Mid-Twentieth Century American Feminism," *Historical Journal of Film, Radio and Television* 25, no. 2 (2005): 213–230; Sean Griffin, *Tinkerbelles and Evil Queens: The Walt Disney Company from the Inside*

Out (New York: NYU Press, 2000); Chris Pallant, *Demystifying Disney: A History of Disney Feature Animation*; Annalee R. Ward, *Mouse Morality: The Rhetoric of Disney Animated Film* (Austin, TX: University of Texas Press, 2002); Janet Wasko, *Understanding Disney: The Manufacture of Fantasy* (Hoboken, NJ: John Wiley & Sons, 2013).

19. Janet Wasko, *Understanding Disney: The Manufacture of Fantasy*.
20. Johnson Cheu, Ed., *Diversity in Disney Films: Critical Essays on Race, Ethnicity, Gender, Sexuality and Disability*, 7.
21. Henry A. Giroux and Grace Pollock, *The Mouse That Roared: Disney and The End of Innocence* (Lanham, MD: Rowman & Littlefield Publishers, 2010), xiv.
22. Henry A. Giroux and Grace Pollock, *The Mouse That Roared: Disney and The End of Innocence*, xiv.
23. Ibid, xiii.
24. Wim Van de Donk, Brian D. Loader, Paul G. Nixon, and Dieter Rucht, *Cyberprotest: New Media, Citizens and Social Movements* (London, UK: Routledge, 2004).
25. Rens Vliegenthart and Stefaan Walgrave, "The Interdependency of Mass Media and Social Movements," In *The Sage Handbook of Political Communication*. London: Sage Publications (2012): 387–398.
26. Christian Fuchs, "Some Reflections on Manuel Castells' Book Networks of Outrage and Hope. Social Movements in the Internet Age," *TripleC: Communication, Capitalism & Critique. Open Access Journal for a Global Sustainable Information Society* 10, no. 2 (2012): 777.
27. Rens Vliegenthart and Stefaan Walgrave, "The Interdependency of Mass Media and Social Movements."
28. Christian Fuchs, "Some Reflections on Manuel Castells' Book Networks of Outrage and Hope. Social Movements in the Internet Age," 777.
29. Christian Fuchs, "Some Reflections on Manuel Castells' Book Networks of Outrage and Hope. Social Movements in the Internet Age," 778.
30. Ibid p. 778; original quote in Clay Shirky, "The Political Power of Social Media," *Foreign Affairs* 90, no. 1 (2011): 38.
31. Diane Goodman, *Promoting Diversity and Social Justice: Educating People from Privileged Groups* (New York: Routledge, 2011).

BIBLIOGRAPHY

Box Office Mojo. "Studio Market Share, January 1–December 31, 2018." Accessed January 7, 2019. https://www.boxofficemojo.com/studio/?view=company&view2=yearly&yr=2018&p=.htm.
———. "Fastest Studios to $1 Billion in a Given Year." Accessed January 7, 2019. https://www.boxofficemojo.com/alltime/fasteststudios.htm.
———. "Disney All Time Box Office Results." Accessed August 18, 2019. https://www.boxofficemojo.com/studio/chart/?studio=buenavista.htm&debug=0&view=parent&p=.htm.

Cheu, Johnson, ed. *Diversity in Disney films: Critical Essays on Race, Ethnicity, Gender, Sexuality and Disability*. Jefferson, NC: McFarland Publishing, 2015.

Clark, Travis. "The 5 Disney Movies That Have Made Over $1 Billion at the Box Office in 2019." *Business Insider*, August 16, 2019. https://www.businessinsider.com/disney-movies-with-1-billion-at-box-office-2019-8.

Coyne, Sarah M., Jennifer Ruh Linder, Eric E. Rasmussen, David A. Nelson, and Victoria Birkbeck. "Pretty as a Princess: Longitudinal Effects of Engagement with Disney Princesses on Gender Stereotypes, Body Esteem, and Prosocial behavior in Children." *Child Development* 87, no. 6 (2016): 1909–1925.

Davis, Amy M. *Handsome Heroes and Vile Villains: Masculinity in Disney's Feature Films*. Bloomington, IN: Indiana University Press, 2014.

———. *Good Girls and Wicked Witches: Changing Representations of Women in Disney's Feature Animation, 1937–2001*. Bloomington, IN: Indiana University Press, 2007.

———. "The 'Dark Prince' and Dream Women: Walt Disney and Mid-Twentieth Century American Feminism." *Historical Journal of Film, Radio and Television* 25, no. 2 (2005): 213–230.

Disney Parks, @DisneyParks, Twitter Post, July 20, 2019, accessed July 25, 2019, https://twitter.com/DisneyParks/status/1152594047380447233.

Fuchs, Christian. "Some Reflections on Manuel Castells' Book Networks of Outrage and Hope. Social Movements in the Internet Age." *TripleC: Communication, Capitalism & Critique. Open Access Journal for a Global Sustainable Information Society* 10, no. 2 (2012): 775–797.

Giroux, Henry A., and Grace Pollock. *The Mouse That Roared: Disney and the End of Innocence*. Lanham, MD: Rowman & Littlefield Publishers, 2010.

Goodman, Diane J. *Promoting Diversity and Social Justice: Educating People from Privileged Groups*. New York: Routledge, 2011.

Griffin, Sean. *Tinker Belles and Evil Queens: The Walt Disney Company from the Inside Out*. New York: NYU Press, 2000.

Hurley, Dorothy L. "Seeing White: Children of Color and the Disney Fairy Tale Princess." *The Journal of Negro Education* (2005): 221–232.

McClintock, Pamela. "Box Office: 'Lion King' Nudges Disney Toward Record Year of $1 B hits," *The Hollywood Reporter*, July 22, 2019. https://www.hollywoodreporter.com/news/lion-king-aladdin-add-fuel-disneys-record-year-1b-hits-1225937.

Pallant, Chris. *Demystifying Disney: A History of Disney Feature Animation*. London, UK: Bloomsbury Publishing USA, 2011.

Robinson, Joana. "How Pacific Islanders Helped Disney's *Moana* Find Its Way," *Vanity Fair*, November 16, 2016, Accessed December 20, 2019. https://www.vanityfair.com/hollywood/2016/11/moana-oceanic-trust-disney-controversy-pacific-islanders-polynesia.

The Numbers. "All Time Worldwide Box Office for Disney Movies." Data as of December 2018. Accessed January 7, 2019. https://www.the-numbers.com/box-office-records/worldwide/all-movies/theatrical-distributors/walt-disney.

The Pittsburgh Courier. "Disney's 'The Princess and the Frog' a Dream Come True for Many." December 17, 2009, Accessed December 20, 2019. https://new

pittsburghcourieronline.com/2009/12/17/disneys-the-princess-and-the-frog-a-dream-come-true-for-many/.

The Walt Disney Company. "Walt Disney and Pixar Animation Studios Name Chief Creative Officers." June 19, 2018. Accessed December 20, 2019. https://www.thewaltdisneycompany.com/walt-disney-and-pixar-animation-studios-name-chief-creative-officers/.

———. "Disney Launchpad: Shorts Incubator Creates New Opportunities for Filmmakers to Share Diverse Perspectives." June 3, 2019. https://www.thewaltdisneycompany.com/disney-launchpad-shorts-incubator-creates-new-opportunities-for-filmmakers-to-share-diverse-perspectives/.

Shirky, Clay. "The Political Power of Social Media." *Foreign Affairs* 90 no. 1 (2011): 28-41.

———. *Here Comes Everybody. The Power of Organizing without Organizations.* London: Allen Lane, 2008.

Van de Donk, Wim, Brian D. Loader, Paul G. Nixon, and Dieter Rucht. *Cyberprotest: New Media, Citizens and Social Movements.* London, UK: Routledge, 2004.

Vliegenthart, Rens, and Stefaan Walgrave. "The Interdependency of Mass Media and Social Movements." *The Sage Handbook of Political Communication.* London: Sage Publications (2012): 387–398.

Walt Disney Television. "Walt Disney Television Announces New Programs to Attract and Develop Talent from Underrepresented Backgrounds." July 1, 2019. https://www.thewaltdisneycompany.com/walt-disney-television-announces-new-programs-to-attract-and-develop-talent-from-underrepresented-backgrounds/.

Ward, Annalee R. *Mouse Morality: The Rhetoric of Disney Animated Film.* Austin, TX: University of Texas Press, 2002.

Wasko, Janet. *Understanding Disney: The Manufacture of Fantasy.* Hoboken, NJ: John Wiley & Sons, 2013.

2

✣

Diversity Sells

The Dollars and Cents of "Woke" Rebranding

Shaniece B. Bickham and Shearon Roberts

BEYOND ENTERTAINMENT: DIVERSITY AND INCLUSION AS ECONOMIC STRATEGY

To some, diversity and inclusion are two terms that might appear to be cliché. Corporations across the world have executives and programs committed to diversity and inclusion, and many have even made concerted efforts to demonstrate their awareness and sensitivity to these issues. The Walt Disney Company (Disney), in particular, is one of the corporations that have publicly expressed commitment to diversity and inclusion. Though diversity and inclusion are two separate terms with distinct definitions, over time they have been presented collectively both in scholarly literature and in corporate job descriptions. Definitions of diversity tend to focus on "the composition of groups and workforces," with emphasis specifically on both observable and non-observable characteristics including but not limited to demographics and cultural differences.[1] Inclusion traditionally refers to the extent in which members from diverse groups are involved and participate in organizations and their decision-making processes.[2]

Disney's commitment to this issue has been echoed among several of its top executives in recent years. Marvel Studios President Kevin Feige spoke about the significance of *Black Panther* during an interview with *NPR* in 2018:

> I've said that *Black Panther* will not be a one-off for us—it will be the beginning of something we believe in very deeply, have always believed in, and

that our bosses at the Walt Disney Company believe in and encourage, which is the movies should represent the world in which they are made, and should be made by people that exist in the world and that bring new stories to it. And boy does *Black Panther* showcase, beyond our wildest dreams, the best of what can happen.³

Just two years prior, Disney's long-time CEO Robert Iger noted that diversity is a "core strategy" for the company.⁴ Alan Horn, chairman of Walt Disney Studios, has also been credited with recognizing the importance of diversity. Horn stated that Disney's goal is to tell inclusive stories. These stories, according to Horn, should be those that are reflective of the world.⁵

The examples of Disney executives' pledge to diversity and inclusion do not end with Igor, Horn, and Feige. Even Kathleen Kennedy, president of Lucasfilm, mentioned the importance of female inclusion in production:⁶ "In the creative community, there's no excuse for not making a more equitable environment. It literally comes down to companies that just aren't trying hard enough."⁷

Though Disney executives often turn to traditional media platforms to express their commitment to diversity and inclusion, company executives have also used social media to make statements about these issues. One example of Disney delving into social media occurred when the Chief Creative Officer at Walt Disney Animation Studios, Jennifer Lee, made her mark in 2018 with the launch of the #DreamBigPrincess initiative. Lee's initiative provides support for young female filmmakers and the creation of work that spotlights female role models.⁸

Lee's #DreamBigPrincess is just one example of a growing trend of companies interacting with their stakeholders and consumers on social media as a means to promote their commitment to social issues. This practice, known as social branding, is an effective way for companies to demonstrate their traditional corporate social responsibility (CSR) messages through modern communication platforms. An early definition of CSR focuses on the actions of companies that extend beyond their primary business interests.⁹ In addition, CSR has traditionally been framed and studied using four main components: economic, legal, ethical and philanthropic, with ethical and philanthropic aspects receiving greater attention.¹⁰

The purpose of this chapter is to examine key principles of CSR along with associated social branding and messaging as part of larger strategic communication goals; evaluate recent trends in "woke" (socially conscious) branding using a case study approach; and explore how Disney's specific strategic communication actions have been used to make this awakening of sorts evident to the corporation's stakeholders. Finally, the chapter will show how Disney's use of CSR strategies through social branding and messaging tactics has positioned the company as one that is cognizant of the importance of diversity and inclusion, social justice, and representation, among other social issues.

PRINCIPLES OF CSR IN RELATION TO SOCIAL BRANDING AND MESSAGING

Corporate communications executives have realized that social media is a vehicle used to not only reach target audiences, but to also interact with them about the issues that matter to these audiences most.[11] Corporations that promote CSR through informal communication strategies using social media are able to gain an understanding of their target audiences' positions on various issues.[12] As a result, the promotion of CSR messages has become part of many corporations' standard strategic communication plan.[13]

Companies committed to CSR integrate their concern for social and environmental issues with their business interactions with stakeholders on a voluntary basis.[14] Based on this definition,[15] interaction with consumers about diversity and inclusion issues fits the mold of what is traditionally considered CSR. This isn't a new trend, however. On the contrary, what is relatively new is the strategic approach used to promote corporations' socially responsible image through social branding and messaging on social media.

RECENT CASE STUDIES IN "WOKE" BRANDING

There are several recent examples of corporations launching their own CSR campaigns that incorporate social branding and messaging about pressing social issues that focus on diversity and inclusion. This portion of the chapter will focus specifically on three corporations' efforts to connect with stakeholders about the #BlackLivesMatter and #MeToo movements.

Social issues involving race relations and the treatment of African American males by police specifically, and in American society in general, have taken the forefront. The #BlackLivesMatter movement launched in 2013 after the acquittal of George Zimmerman for the shooting death of unarmed African American teen Trayvon Martin. It played an instrumental role in organizing supporters to "intervene in violence inflicted on Black communities by the state and vigilantes."[16] What began as a collaboration among three women, Alicia Garza, Patrisse Cullors, and Opal Tometi, has grown into a "member-led global network of 40 chapters."[17]

Another major social issue that has garnered national attention is the #MeToo movement. Though the movement was launched in 2006 by Tarana Burke to educate and provide resources to supporters and advocates about sexual assault and abuse, the movement gained a viral following in 2017—when a top Hollywood executive, Harvey Weinstein, was exposed for sexual assault.[18] The movement was developed initially to support women of color, but has since been embraced by women of several different races and walks of life. At the height of the movement, women across the world shared on social media as much or as little about their experiences with being sexually harassed and/or assaulted. Some posts simply included #MeToo, with no further details posted. In many instances, the hashtag spoke for itself.

Nike's #ImWithKaep

It was during the height of the #BlackLivesMatter movement in 2016 that former NFL quarterback Colin Kaepernick decided to protest in his own way. Kaepernick's initial protests consisted of him remaining seated during the National Anthem prior to the start of San Francisco 49ers games, the team that he played for. Kaepernick expressed that he did not want to "stand up to show pride in a flag for a country that oppresses black people and people of color."[19] His protests then changed to him kneeling during the National Anthem.

In September 2018, Nike launched an advertisement campaign that featured former NFL football player Colin Kaepernick. Celebrating the thirty-year anniversary of Nike's famous "Just Do It" tagline, the corporation's campaign featured other prominent celebrities who have broken barriers in their respective sports. The inclusion of Kaepernick garnered most attention, however, due to Kaepernick's ongoing protest of the unfair treatment of African American males in the United States, which many believe led to him being dismissed from his quarterback position and without a job in the NFL. The Nike campaign sparked both support and disapproval with supporters posting to social media with the hashtag #ImWithKaep and opponents posting with the hashtag #NikeBoycott. Kaepernick's preferred method to protest was by kneeling during the National Anthem at the NFL games, which many people felt was disrespectful to the military and the United States flag.

Though not all of Nike's stakeholders were in agreement with the campaign as evidenced by the #NikeBoycott posts, Nike's advertising campaign was a success. News reports show that Nike's revenue soared.[20] Nike's shares increased almost 5 percent in only a few weeks timespan after the launch of the campaign on Labor Day of 2018.[21] The increase equated to $6 billion in profits.[22] E-commerce research firm Edison Trends estimated a 31 percent increase in Nike's online sales between the Sunday before Labor Day and the Tuesday after.[23] Nike's profit increase is despite efforts from some consumers to boycott the company as a result of the Kaepernick advertisement. Though #BoycottNike and #NikeBoycott did generate some support, it was not substantial enough to negatively impact the Nike brand or profit margin.[24]

Gillette's #MeToo

Just a few weeks ahead of Super Bowl LIII, Gillette thrust itself into the spotlight of the #MeToo movement thanks to the company's "We Believe" advertisement that spoke against "toxic masculinity." The #MeToo movement focuses on bringing awareness to issues of sexual assault and harassment.

The Gillette advertisement encouraged men to be their best selves while holding one another accountable.[25] While some consumers expressed their support of Gillette and happiness about the company stepping forward to take a stand against sexual assault and violence, there were men who found the advertisement offensive.[26] Long-time male consumers of the company expressed on social media that they were not pleased with the advertisement. Others expressed that they understood the importance of the #MeToo movement, but that Gillette's targeting of men gave the impression that all men were guilty of unacceptable and unbecoming behavior.

As part of Gillette's advertising campaign, the company also pledged $1 million for the next three years to non-profits with programs that help men to become better role models.[27] Financially, Gillette's parent company, Procter & Gamble, reported that Gillette's sales did not decrease or increase as a result of its #MeToo advertisement.[28] Procter & Gamble's Chief Financial Officer, Jon Moeller, said that Gillette received "'unprecedented levels' of media coverage and customer engagement" as a result of the advertisement.[29]

Pepsi—CSR and Social Branding Gone Wrong

Pepsi, Co. attempted to express its position on "wokeness" about the #BlackLivesMatter movement in 2017, but their efforts fell flat. The corporation's "Live for Now Moments Anthem" advertisement featured model Kendall Jenner portraying someone who was able to calm heated tensions during a protest simply by offering a police officer a can of Pepsi. The company was immediately blasted for trivializing such an important issue.[30] Many who chose to speak out against the company on social media expressed that the company was attempting to capitalize on the re-enactments of serious protests.[31]

Other opponents to the advertisement simply took issue with the company's choice to feature a supermodel in the campaign.[32] The advertisement's focal point seemed to imitate a defining moment during a protest in Baton Rouge, Louisiana, that involved a standoff between protestor Ieshia Evans and police in July of 2016. The backlash resulted in Pepsi pulling the advertisement and issuing an apology.[33] In its official statement, Pepsi acknowledged that it had "missed the mark" in its efforts to "project a global message of unity, peace and understanding."[34]

Case Study Comparisons

Nike and Gillette are two companies that took a chance with launching advertisement and social media campaigns that would position them as being on the right side of history during a time when being "woke" and cognizant of issues that impact society is important to a large segment of their consumers. Their actions were carried out in spite of the possible alienation of some of their core consumers. The Nike and Gillette campaigns are similar in this way, and though both were successful in demonstrating CSR, there were differences in the execution of the two campaigns.

The first difference is that Nike's #ImWithKaep campaign made a statement with a new and unique hashtag in solidarity with someone who had been publicly shunned in the court of public opinion. Gillette's "We Believe" campaign, however, served as a way to show the company's support of an existent social media movement, #MeToo, that had in many ways already become widely accepted and successful. Next, Nike's campaign expanded beyond social media and into the homes of consumers through television commercials. Gillette's "We Believe" advertisement was limited to online distribution. Finally, Nike's efforts to reach audiences beyond social media users resulted in a positive economic return for the company, as compared to Gillette's strategy, which didn't positively or negatively impact the company's bottom line.

A comparison of Nike's campaign to Pepsi's "Live for Now Moments Anthem" shows that Pepsi also aimed to expand its reach beyond social media through a television commercial. The two campaigns are also similar in that they both addressed issues that were not popular or well-received by mainstream society. And although both companies chose well-known figures to feature in their campaigns, Nike's focus on Kaepernick garnered support for both the company and Kaepernick, while Pepsi's selection of supermodel Kendall Jenner resulted in backlash against the company and Jenner because consumers did not view her as someone well-versed on the #BlackLivesMatter movement.

The successes and failures of recent CSR and social branding strategy presented in the three aforementioned case studies can serve as teaching tools for companies interested in launching their own campaigns around controversial issues of the day. Companies have to demonstrate that they not only have an idea of what these issues are, but that they also understand the complexities of these issues and those who are affected by them. Mastering this trait can result in a positive reputation among consumers in addition to increased profitability for the companies. When this trait isn't mastered, the opposite can occur and could result in a ruined reputation and a negative impact on a company's overall bottom line.

BRANDING WOKENESS THE DISNEY WAY

In its 2015 report to stakeholders, Jay Rasulo, Disney's then Chief Financial Officer stated he was often asked to outline the business argument in support of Disney Citizenship, the company's initiatives that shape its corporate social responsibility. Rasulo responded:

> We believe that our efforts to be a good corporate citizen have direct impact on our financial strength, as well as our reputation as one of the most trusted and admired companies in the world.[35]

Disney's Citizenship Framework outlined two key areas: "Act Responsibly" and "Inspire Others."[36] Under "Act Responsibly—Responsible Content" Disney committed to "create and market responsible, high quality products and entertainment experiences."[37] The company identified "ethical conduct," "environmental stewardship," "civic engagement," "respectful workplaces," and a "responsible supply chain," as other tenants of acting responsibly.[38] Under "Inspire Others—Strengthen Communities" Disney committed to "bring hope, happiness and comfort to kids and families." This second area also emphasized the company's mission to encourage healthier living, conservation of nature, and creative thinking that inspires children to reimagine the future.[39] We examine next how Disney executes its Citizenship Framework in two areas: 1) around Responsible and Inspiring campaigns around race and 2) around Responsible and Inspiring campaigns around gender. We analyze these campaigns both in how they embody Disney's style of content creation, markets Disney's products, and addresses social discourse today.

RESPONSIBLE AND INSPIRING CAMPAIGNS AROUND RACE

The campaign, "Be Inspired. Disney Citizenship," touches on a number of subjects ranging from promoting healthy lifestyles to protecting the environment. It has also focused on celebrating and promoting racial pride. As such, since 2015 "Be Inspired" launched several series of content to mark the following: "Disney Black History Month," "Disney Celebrates Hispanic Heritage Month," and "Disney Asian Pacific American Heritage Month."

These community-based campaigns all had the following four features in common. Firstly, they aired across Disney's channels: the Disney Channel, Disney Junior, and Disney XD. Online, they also appeared as commercials on the Disney NOW app, Disney's websites, and on Disney channel's YouTube channels. In some cases, Disney on Broadway marked the various cultural heritage months.[40] The second feature they shared in common is that they connected Disney's content to the message of the campaigns. This was done in two ways. A) The campaign would feature a young Disney star from a popular Disney channel show, of the specific racial background, as the narrator/host of the segment. B) The campaign would connect a story line from a popular Disney channel show to a story line in the campaign. In essence, these community-focused series connected Disney's creative content to its messaging around race and the celebration of racial identity and pride. For instance, Sofia Carson of the *Descendants* movies on Disney Channel hosted one of the Hispanic Heritage Month featurettes.[41] Karan Brar of *BUNK'D* shared his connection to Asian heritage for an Asian Pacific American Heritage Month featurette.[42]

Thirdly, how does Disney create the non-advertisement, advertisement? These community-focused campaigns consisted of a series of short videos ranging from one to five minutes long. They are not preachy. They do not overtly sell Disney merchandize or products, like inviting families to visit their resorts, or to buy the latest show's toys. They are uplifting in tone. They speak directly to the youngest of audiences as if in a conversation among friends. They feature beloved characters in children and tween's shows. They are placed to run quickly before popular shows; or on apps they run as infomercials. They feel like public service announcements for children, but with all the magical animation, childlike narratives, and Disney soundtrack that would still hold children's attentions rather than have them decide to take a bathroom break.

Lastly, they all feature personalized lessons. These can range from history lessons to culture lessons to current affairs. Like PSAs, there is something to learn, specifically about what makes those cultures unique, and also what connects them to the American and or the global experience. The Black History Month campaign appears to be dated the longest among Disney's "strengthening communities" "Be Inspired" series. This is likely because Black History Month has been more officially recognized, and has a track record of how such celebration takes place. The Hispanic and Asian Pacific American heritage months are relatively newer community celebrations in the United States.[43]

Therefore we analyze next how Disney executed social consciousness, drawing from the sample of featurettes for Black History Month from 2015 to 2019. We demonstrate how Disney executes the four features above in selected featurettes from Disney's celebration of Black History Month. Those featurettes are designated as part of the "Be Inspired" Disney Citizenship campaign, because the logo for the campaign is included in the segment.

DISNEY'S BLACK HISTORY MONTH

Messages for Young Children

For the youngest of audiences and Disney's target audience—girls, Disney produced the "Come Celebrate Black History Month with Doc McStuffins and Real Doctors" series. We retrieved a sample of video featurettes that dated between 2015 to 2017. The series aired on multiple platforms: the Disney Channel, Disney Junior, Disney's website and apps and on Disney's YouTube channels. The host of the featurettes were Doc McStuffins, in animated form. All the doctors featured, were real life African American women physicians. The doctors identify why Doc McStuffins is special, and reflect on what made them become a doctor. Doctor Angela Tucker, a family doctor, praised McStuffins. She said: "The first time I saw Doc on TV, I was so excited. When I was a kid, I wanted to be a doctor because of what I saw on TV. So now how many kids are going to be a doctor because of Doc."[44] Dr. Leah Backhus, a surgeon, echoed Tucker in a different segment:

> The first time I saw Doc McStuffins, I thought wow, here's a little African American girl, whose a great role model . . . Black History is really important, because it's a time when we can all think back about all the contributions people have made before us and all the things we can go on and be inspired to do in the future.[45]

Other segments pay tribute to African American trailblazers. Dr. Leticia Bradford tells Doc McStuffins that Dr. Claudia Thomas is her hero, because when she saw that she was an orthopedic surgeon, she realized she could be one too. She echoed the other doctors and talked about why role models are important.

> When I saw Doc McStuffins for the first time, I thought how exciting to have someone on TV that's a doctor and that looks like me . . . I hope that when they see me, they realize that science can be fun and that medicine is a field for everyone.[46]

Other segments with Doc McStuffins featured conversations between children and their African American trailblazing mothers. Hana invited Doc to "meet my mom, she's an emergency room doctor."[47] And Mason says in another segment "That's right Doc, my mum's a pilot." In both of these segments, Doc connects an episode to a real life African American woman. For instance she narrates "Remember when itty bitty Bess soared through the air as the toy version of Bessie Coleman, the first African American woman to hold a pilot's license, my friend Mason also knows someone who also flies above the clouds."[48] At the end of each featurette, a narrator asks the viewer "Will you become a doctor? Be inspired with Doc McStuffins."[49] It champions and spotlights Black women's excellence. It also contextualized Black History for young audiences and directly indicated why representation in science, particularly for Black women, mattered.

Messages for Tweens

For older children, tweens and teens, Disney also produced Black History Month featurettes that aired across many platforms, but particularly Disney XD and the Disney Channel. While some focused on historical moments and others on more contemporary events, the goal was to foster racial pride. Two featurettes that focused on historical moments were a trip by Disney actor Nate Potvin of the Disney XD's *Mech-X4* series to the Tomorrow's Aeronautical Museum in Compton, California. The other featured the late Disney star Cameron Boyce (*Descendants* and many Disney series for teens), who retold the story of his grandmother Jo Ann Boyce, one of the Clinton 12, who integrated the Tennessee town's high school. Again, both segments were hosted by well-known Disney stars, from popular series, who were Black/bi-racial, and who had stories personally connected to them.

Potvin's segment saw him alongside Black and brown children as they learned about the Tuskegee Airmen. The segment notes that Kimberly Anyadike, an African American girl, is a trailblazer just like Tuskegee Airman Charles "Chief" Anderson, who was the first African American to fly cross country. Anyadike tells the viewer "I was 15 years old when I set a world record by becoming the youngest African American female to pilot a plane from Compton, California to Newport News, Virginia." The segment connects one pioneering African American to a pioneering African American teen girl, who dares to defy expectations.

Cameron Boyce's featurette goes further than Potvin's in talking about the perseverance of African Americans. In fact, it directly speaks about the pain and hurt of racism in America. Boyce begins: "The Clinton 12 was the first group of Black students to integrate into an all white high school in Clinton, Tennessee, and my nana is one of the Clinton 12." Instantly, there is a personal connection between the host, Boyce, and the subject matter, his 'nana,' allowing fans of Boyce to empathize with the story he tells about his beloved grandmother. Boyce explains that his grandmother could not attend the high school near her home, and had to travel 20 miles to Knoxville for school.

Boyce allows audiences to empathize with what his grandmother faced when she was determined to attend the school: "It was against the law for them to go to this high school until it was integrated. . . . They don't know what they're going into. And then they walk down the hill and there are people lining the streets, throwing things, saying things, trying to break their spirit." The viewer sees white children lining the streets, taunting. Jo Ann Boyce directly addresses the racism of the time:

> Mostly, it has an important role in history and I like to call it our American history. It is part of something that needed to be done to correct some injustice, and the injustice was, we're living in a town, with a high school . . . we deserved to go to that school because it was our school, as well as the kids who were white. . . . No we were not going to be intimidated by walking down to the school, even though there were days when we were very fearful, we continued to walk.[50]

Boyce and his family accompany Jo Ann back to Clinton to see the statue depicting her and the Clinton 12. In underscoring the importance of commemoration, given recent debates about Confederate monuments, Cameron Boyce notes how important it is to have a statue erected to show future generations his 'nana's' "determination, incredible amount of courage."[51]

Lastly, Disney's Black History Month featurettes geared to tweens looked at contemporary figures and movements around Black Pride. One featurette titled "What Inspires You" asked viewers to sing like Ella Fitzgerald, Janelle Monáe, and Gary Clark Jr.; to "create epic tales" like Maya Angelou, Lee Daniels, and Shonda Rhimes. And also let viewers know that Harry Belafonte, Jessie Williams, and Viola Davis are not just actors, but "activists . . . too." The featurette tells viewers "You can be anyone you wanna be. Sing. Share, Lead."[52] Disney encouraged viewers to not just create, but to lead through activism.

Another featurette titled "History in the Making" featured young African American children, and mostly girls, doing unconventional things for their age and in unique fields from making eco-friendly clothes to inventing on a 3-D printer. The hosts of this segment were the stars of *Raven's Home*: Isaac Ryan Brown and Navia Robinson.[53] In another segment "Celebrating You" young African American tweens reflect on who inspires them and why Black History Month is important. Akin states that: "Black

History Month its important to me because I get to learn about Black people who did things to make our world a better place." The children name Bob Marley, Tracee Ellis Ross, and Michelle Obama as inspirations. Nathanial says that "Denzel Washington, he's been a trailblazer for actors of color for such a long time." They also talk about racial pride. Sena says that for Black History Month: "I look at what other people have done, confident Black women who have accomplished so much." And Bianca and Delsin follow up: "Black History Month means to be celebrating my color." A girl states in a voice-over that during Black History Month "I feel like it gives us a voice. A very, very beautiful color. Opportunity to teach people okay this is who we are."[54]

Disney Citizenship's Black History Month series for both younger children and teens coopts language of wokeness and Black pride. It speaks about injustices, and systemic oppression that provides opportunity for white children and not Black ones, and notes that this is an American story in the Boyce and Potvin segments. It calls for representation, either through statues of the Clinton 12, museums for the Tuskegee Airmen, or recognition of current role models from Shonda Rhimes to Janelle Monáe to Michelle Obama. It uses the language of wokeness, such as "gives us a voice," "celebrating my color" and "confident Black women." Message-wise, Disney aligned itself with current social consciousness within the Black community.

The Black History Month featurettes between 2015 and 2019 also demonstrated that Disney's content is authentically connected to communities of color. Disney demonstrated in the Black History Month segments that it understands its audience. The tone of the featurettes felt nothing like something out of a History Channel special on Black History. Instead, Disney did what it does best: entertain. To get a serious, and often politically correct message across, to not just children but families, Disney must first and foremost entertain. No matter how challenging the subject, or woke the language, the featurettes always felt upbeat. In this sense, Disney was able to connect its brand to diversity, in an authentic way, and position itself as socially conscious around issues of race, while holding its audience's attention.

RESPONSIBLE AND INSPIRING CAMPAIGNS AROUND GENDER

In 2016, Disney announced its "Dream Big Princess" campaign. Like its heritage month segments, "Dream Big Princess" shares a similar approach. It is featured on multiple platforms: Disney's channels, apps, and parks and it has its own designated website.[55] It features Disney stars or characters from Auli'i Cravalho (voice of Moana) to Sofia the First, and all of the Disney princesses, and live-action park versions of the princesses are featured in the campaign. It is entertaining, features a catchy anthem, is uplifting and inspiring, and holds attention for young audiences. Lastly, its language coopts that of women's empowerment discourse today. Where it expands from the cultural heritage month is that it connects to other Disney initiatives for girls. These have ranged from photography and film campaigns for young creative girls, another for young female athletes, to events at its theme parks.[56] The campaign also generated a hashtag #DreamBigPrincess and Disney donated $1 for every use of the hashtag during the campaign to raise funds for the United Nation Foundation's Girl Up initiative to advance girls in developing countries.[57]

These efforts attracted slightly older girls to participate in the "Dream Big Princess" campaign. However, for younger girls, the campaign aired featurettes across its platforms. We analyze how Disney exhibited "woke" branding around gender by examining the 14 Dream Big Princess Featurettes on the Disney NOW app.[58] Disney achieved this in two ways. Firstly, it provided lessons directly from the story lines of its princesses. Secondly, it showcased girls breaking norms and defying odds, while connecting real girls stories to the princesses.

Lessons from the Princesses

While all the "Dream Big Princess" featurettes included the Disney princesses, some specifically focused on particular princesses' stories, and connected them to a young girl with a dream. In "Ariel Side by Side" a young girl narrates that she wants to "explore the ocean" somewhat like a marine biologist and "that's why Ariel is someone I really relate to."[59] Many featurettes like these end with the slogan by an adult woman narrator "For every girl who dreams big. There's a princess to show her it's possible. Dream Big Princess."[60] In "I Dream: Belle" a girl walks with her book-bag and speaks about Belle's qualities. Belle urges the girl to see the goodness in everyone: "I dream of being the kind of girl that sees the good in others, no matter whether they are big, or small, human or candle stick."[61] Both Belle and the girl spin with a book in their hands. Another girl looks to the stars and in "I Dream: Tiana" she learns that for Tiana to get her own restaurant: "Dreams just don't happen when I sleep. Some dreams take work."[62]

In other featurettes, Sofia the First connects real life girls to live-action park princesses. Momoca meets her favorite princess Tiana and tells her she dreams to be the "best tennis player in the world." A live-action Tiana also shares her story about hard work.[63] Brooklyn wants to be a horseback rider, and Sofia shares with her in the "Rapunzel" featurette, how she too had a dream and it came true.[64] Sofia introduces Julia, who admires

Belle because she doesn't "judge a book by its cover." Julia wants to be a "great basketball player." We eventually see that one of her arms is either amputated or has a birth defect. Belle asks her what the phrase means and Julia states "don't look at the outside, look at the inside."[65]

The best known among the featurettes are the three that include the "Dream Big Princess" Anthem. One, the "Live Your Dream" music video matches the lyrics of the song to different Disney princesses and scenes from their movies that show them at empowered moments. The second, the "Dream It, Be It" also uses the anthem but girls rap/sing and appear alongside scenes of the princesses. The third one "Be A Champion" features girls in empowered roles that match the princesses.

In these featurettes, the Disney princesses are recast. In "Live Your Dream" a girl starts the anthem "Every Disney princess is different in their own way. They love taking chances and I like that."[66] In "Be A Champion" a racially diverse group of girls all demonstrate "breaking the mold" to the tune of the "Dream Big Princess" anthem. All of the activity is empowered. A father cheers his daughter on as she gets ready to swing in a softball game. Another girl yells a karate "kiai." Another girl works on an experiment in a science lab, while another one reads a book with her mother. Two girls sit on their father's heads at a rally. One holds a bullhorn and the other raises her fists as they hold a sign that reads "Peace on Earth."

A little girl runs for class office, making an impassioned speech in her auditorium, wearing a blazer with homemade sign saying: "Annabelle is on your side! Vote Annabelle." An African American girl poses in an as-

Figure 2.1. Disney's "Dream Big Princess: Be A Champion" Featurette scene.
Disney NOW, "Music Video: Be A Champion," Dream Big Princess Video, 1:00, accessed May 15, 2019, Disney NOW app. Screenshot.

tronaut outfit, another girl rides a horse. A girl with a prosthetic right foot does clog dancing. Another girl runs along the shore with her surfboard. A little girl skateboards at a skating park.[67]

Coupled with the imagery above, the lyrics of the anthem also reinforce Girl Power. The song begins with the empowered lyrics "You can be the greatest you can be the best"[68] as an African American young female gymnast on a uneven bars swings for the other bar as Rapunzel leaps with her hair. It is a nod to gymnasts like Gabby Douglas and Simone Biles who not only broke records as African American gymnasts, but who also bravely joined many other gymnasts in testifying against abuse by their team physician.

The song urges young girls to "Do it for your people, do it for your pride. Do it for your country. Do it for your name"[69] as a young Asian girl break dances, another girl swims in the ocean, and a bi-racial girl stands on a podium to receive a gold medal for sport. The song calls on girls to put their names into the "hall of fame" where the world will remember their names. The featurette spotlights overcoming obstacles as a little blind girl leads story time in her preschool, and a close up shows she is reading a book in braille. More young girls of all different ethnic backgrounds dare to set records and make their mark in the featurette as the song urges them to "Be students. Be teachers. Be politicians. Be preachers. Be believers. Be leaders. Be astronauts. Be champions."[70] Girls are shown as loving science, the arts, reading, sports, and even motorcross.[71]

More importantly, as the anthem's description shows, the visuals of the anthem featurettes reflect breaking gender norms. Girls skateboard, ride motocross, swing off trees, dive underwater, ride horses, do lab experiments, run for class office, and protest at a rally. The images of girls are racially diverse, ably diverse, and span a range of ages from very young girls to tweens and teens. Both in music and visuals, the anthem featurettes for "Dream Big Princess" inspire and entertain. Disney in essence has revived its princesses and recast them in a new light that reflects girlhood today. It allows Disney to keep its valuable princess franchise going, and to even become revisionist about characters like Snow White. The lesson is that there is a story to learn from each princess that can inspire girls to continue to dream today.

CONCLUSION

Disney has been strategic about positioning itself in response to social movements in the current times. This is outlined in its commitment statements about Disney Citizenship and reflected in the variety of campaigns it has either aligned itself with or has created in-house. This chapter showed that on issues of race and gender, Disney's in-house campaigns reflect wokeness and social consciousness. It is both explicit and implicit in its language that reflects the discourse of movements today.

More importantly, Disney has determined to create content around social consciousness that reflects its audience, aesthetic, and its desire to always entertain. Its campaigns reflect "Responsible and Inspiring" content creation that is marketed in ways that subtly connects its products to the communities and issues its audiences care about. Disney has so far stuck to "safer" discourses around racial and gender equality, health, and preserving the environment.

As Disney's report on its corporate social responsibility states, its citizenship initiatives are also good fiscally for the company. As the case studies in this chapter show, socially conscious branding and their campaigns can be profitable for companies, as it was in the Nike/Colin Kaepernick campaign. Likewise, Disney has developed its own model for family-friendly, socially "woke" and conscious branding that offends few, positions its company as modern and reflective of its global consumers, and that ultimately entertains.

NOTES

1. Quinetta M. Roberson, "Disentangling the Meanings of Diversity and Inclusion in Organizations, *Group & Organization Management* 31, no. 2 (2006): 212–236; J. E. McGrath, J. L. Berdahl, and H. Arrow, "Traits, Expectations, Culture and Clout: The Dynamics of Diversity in Work Groups," in *Diversity in Work Teams*, eds. S. E. Jackson & M. N. Ruderman (Washington, DC: American Psychological Association, 1995): 17–45; L.K. Larkey, "The Development and Validation of the Workforce Diversity Questionnaire," *Management Communication Quarterly* 9 (1996): 296–337; T. H. Cox, Jr., *Cultural Diversity in Organizations: Theory, Research and Practice* (San Francisco, CA: Berrett-Koehler, 1993).

2. Roberson, "Disentangling the Meanings of Diversity," 212–236; F. A. Miller, "Strategic Culture Change: The Door to Achieving High Performance and Inclusion," *Public Personnel Management* 27 (1998): 151–160; Mor M.E Mor-Barak and D. Cherin, "A Tool to Expand Organizational Understanding of Workforce Diversity," *Administration in Social Work* 22 (2008): 47–64.

3. Mandalit Del Barco, "Marvel Studios' Kevin Feige on the Future of Marvel Movies," *NPR*, April 26, 2018, https://www.npr.org/2018/04/26/605648453/marvel-studios-kevin-feige-on-the-future-of-marvel-movies.

4. Yohana Desta, "The Year Disney Started to Take Diversity Seriously," *Vanity Fair*, November 23, 2016, https://www.vanityfair.com/hollywood/2016/11/disney-films-inclusive.

5. Desta, "The Year Disney Started to Take Diversity Seriously."

6. Brent Lang, "'Star Wars:' Lucasfilm Chief Previews 'Rogue One' and Han Solo Spinoff," *Variety*, November 22, 2016, https://variety.com/2016/film/features/star-wars-rogue-one-lucasfilm-jj-abrams-kathleen-kennedy-1201923806/.

7. Rebecca Sun, "Lucasfilm's Force: Kathleen Kennedy Reveals an Executive Team More Than 50 Percent Female," December 7, 2016, *The Hollywood Reporter*, https://www.hollywoodreporter.com/news/lucasfilms-force-kathleen-kennedy-reveals-an-executive-team-more-50-percent-female-953156.

8. Amid Amidi, "Watch the First Public Appearance of Jennifer Lee, Disney Animation's New Chief Creative Officer," *Cartoon Brew*, July 10, 2018, https://www.cartoonbrew.com/disney/watch-the-first-public-appearance-of-jennifer-lee-disneys-new-chief-creative-officer-161796.html.

9. Archie B. Carroll, "The Pyramid of Corporate Social Responsibility: Toward the Moral Management of Organizational Stakeholders," *Business Horizons*, (July/August): 39–48; Keith Davis, "Can Business Afford to Ignore Social Responsibilities?" *California Management Review* 11, no. 3 (1960): 70–76.

10. Carroll, "The Pyramid of Corporate Social Responsibility," 39–48.

11. Alan Abitbol and Sun Lee Young, "Messages on CSR-Dedicated Facebook Pages: What Works and What Doesn't," *Public Relations Review* 43 (2017): 796–808.

12. Bahadir Birim, "Evaluation of Corporate Social Responsibility and Social Media as Key Source of Strategic Communication," *Social and Behavioral Sciences* 235 (2016): 70–75.

13. Birim, "Evaluation of Corporate Social Responsibility and Social Media," 70–75.

14. Oberseder, Schlegelmilch, and Murphy, "CSR Practices and Consumer Practices," *Journal of Business Research* 66, no. 10 (2013): 1839–1851; Commission of the European Communities. *Green Paper: Promoting a European Framework for Corporate Responsibility* (Brussels, Belgium: 2001).

15. Magdalena Oberseder, Bodo B. Schlegelmilch & Patrick E. Murphy, CSR Practices and Consumer Practices, *Journal of Business Research* 66, no. 10 (2013): 1839–1851.

16. "Her Story," *BlackLivesMatter.com*, accessed March 21, 2019, https://blacklivesmatter.com/about/herstory/Black Lives Matter.

17. "Her Story," *BlackLivesMatter.com*.

18. "History and Vision," *MeTooMovement.org*, accessed March 21, 2019, https://metoomvmt.org/about/#history.

19. Steve Wyche, "Colin Kaepernick Explains Why He Sat During the National Anthem," *NFL.com*, August 27, 2016, http://www.nfl.com/news/story/0ap3000000691077/article/colin-kaepernick-explains-why-he-sat-during-national-anthem.

20. Gina Martinez, "Despite Outrage, Nike's Sales Increased 31% After Kaepernick," *Time*, September 10, 2018, http://time.com/5390884/nike-sales-go-up-kaepernick-ad/.

21. Kate Gibson, "Colin Kaepernick is Nike's $6 Billion Man," *CBS News*, September 21, 2018, https://www.cbsnews.com/news/colin-kaepernick-nike-6-billion-man/.

22. Gibson, "Colin Kaepernick is Nike's $6 Billion Man"; Alex Abad-Santos, "Nike's Colin Kaepernick Ad Sparked a Boycott—and Earned $6 Billion for Nike," *Vox*, September 24, 2018, https://www.vox.com/2018/9/24/17895704/nike-colin-kaepernick-boycott-6-billion.

23. Gina Martinez, "Despite Outrage, Nike Sales Increased 31% After Kaepernick Ad."

24. Eben Novy-Williams, "Calls to #BoycottNike Don't Crack Top Five on the Outrage Meter," *Bloomberg*, September 5, 2018, https://www.bloomberg.com/news/articles/2018-09-05/calls-to-boycottnike-don-t-crack-top-five-on-the-outrage-meter.

25. Chloe Taylor, "Gillette Draws Fire for #MeToo Commercial That Challenges 'Toxic Masculinity,'" *CNBC*, January 15, 2019, https://www.cnbc.com/2019/01/15/gillette-draws-fire-for-metoo-commercial.html.

26. Taylor, "Gillette Draws Fire for #MeToo Commercial That Challenges 'Toxic Masculinity.'"

27. Ibid.

28. Nathaniel Meyersohn, "Gillette Says it's Satisfied With Sales After Controversial Ad," *CNN Business*, January 23, 2019, https://www.cnn.com/2019/01/23/business/gillette-ad-procter-and-gamble-stock/index.html.

29. Meyersohn, "Gillette Says it's Satisfied With Sales After Controversial Ad."

30. Daniel Victor, "Pepsi Pulls Ad Accused of Trivializing Black Lives Matter," *The New York Times*, April 5, 2017, https://www.nytimes.com/2017/04/05/business/kendall-jenner-pepsi-ad.html.

31. Victor, "Pepsi Pulls Ad Accused of Trivializing Black Lives Matter."

32. De Elizabeth, "Why People Are NOT Happy About Kendall Jenner's Pepsi Commercial," *Teen Vogue*, April 4, 2017, https://www.teenvogue.com/story/pepsi-commercial-kendall-jenner-reaction.

33. Alexander Smith, "Pepsi Pulls Controversial Kendall Jenner Ad After Outcry," *NBC News*. April 5, 2017, https://www.nbcnews.com/news/nbcblk/pepsi-ad-kendall-jenner-echoes-black-lives-matter-sparks-anger-n742811.

34. Smith, "Pepsi Pulls Controversial Kendall Jenner Ad After Outcry."

35. The Walt Disney Company, "Disney Citizenship 2014 Performance Summary," accessed May 15, 2019, https://ditm-twdc-us.storage.googleapis.com/FY14-Performance-Summary.pdf, 6.

36. The Walt Disney Company, "Disney Citizenship 2014 performance summary," 7.

37. Ibid., 7.

38. Ibid., 7.

39. Ibid., 7.

40. Disney on Broadway, "Disney on Broadway celebrates Asian American & Pacific Islander Heritage Month," YouTube video, 00:56, posted May 14, 2019, https://youtu.be/a_SqZx2qCQk.

41. Maribel Labindao, "Hispanic Heritage Sofia Carson," YouTube video, 1:00, posted September 16, 2018, https://youtu.be/qsRp32Zll5A.

42. Disney Channel, "Karan Brar, Asian Pacific American Heritage," YouTube video, 1:30, posted May 2, 2018, https://youtu.be/o2XNbMyxHeM.

43. Law Library of Congress, "Commemorative Observances," last modified June 6, 2019, https://www.loc.gov/law/help/commemorative-observations/index.php.

44. Disney Junior, "Doc McStuffins, Black History Month, Dr. Tucker," YouTube video, 1:00, posted April 9, 2015, https://youtu.be/MC6Rz4o-8OA.

45. Disney Junior, "Doc McStuffins, Black History Month, Dr. Backhus," YouTube video, 1:15, posted April 9, 2015, https://youtu.be/wZS8wOyObmU.

46. Disney Junior, "Doc McStuffins, Black History Month, Dr. Bradford," YouTube video, 1:00, posted April 10, 2015, https://youtu.be/c0U2Dw2QYk0.

47. Disney Junior, "Meet Dr. Myiesha, Black History Month," YouTube video, 0:45, posted February 17, 2017, https://youtu.be/VUcEUsxTbck.

48. Disney Junior, "Meet Captain Stephanie, Black History Month," YouTube video 0:45, posted February 16, 2017, https://youtu.be/w1iVsykGheA.

49. Disney Junior, "Meet Captain Stephanie, Black History Month."

50. Disney XD, "Cameron Boyce Honors the Clinton 12, Black History Month," YouTube video, 3:00, posted February 1, 2016, https://youtu.be/fgSKSeuTLAk.

51. Disney XD, "Cameron Boyce Honors the Clinton 12, Black History Month."

52. Disney Channel, "Black History Month, Be Inspired," YouTube video, 0:47, posted February 12, 2016, https://youtu.be/YilVX1GeZVc.

53. Disney Channel, "History in the Making, Black History Month, Be Inspired," YouTube video, 1:00, posted February 22, 2018, https://youtu.be/SRhjk59-F3U.

54. Disney Channel, "Celebrating You, Black History Month," YouTube video, 1:00, posted February 9, 2019, https://youtu.be/XxTCkPDpY4E.

55. Emily Southard, "'Dream Big, Princess' Launching New Global Photography Campaign," Disney Parks Blog, August 16, 2017, https://disneyparks.disney.go.com/blog/2017/08/dream-big-princess-launching-new-global-photography-campaign/.

56. Emily Southard, "'Dream Big, Princess' Launching New Global Photography Campaign."

57. Disney Lifestyle, "#DreamBigPrincess Photography Campaign Encourages Kids Around the Globe to Dream Big," Accessed May 15, 2019, https://partners.disney.com/dream-big-princess-photo-campaign.

58. Disney's 14 Dream Big Princess featurettes on the Disney Now app are: 1. "Music Video: Live Your Story," 2. "Music Video: Live Your Dream," 3. "Music Video: Ariel Side by Side," 4. "Music Video: Dream It, Be It," 5. "I Dream: Belle," 6. "I Dream: Ariel" 7. "Tiana," 8. "I Dream: Tiana," 9. "I Dream, Rapunzel," 10. "Rapunzel," 11. "Belle," 12. "Music Video: I Dream Anthem," 13. "Music Video: Be A Champion," 14. "Ariel."

59. Disney NOW, "Music Video: Ariel Side by Side," Dream Big Princess Video, 1:00, accessed May 15, 2019, Disney NOW app.

60. Disney NOW, "Music Video: Ariel Side by Side."

61. Disney NOW, "I Dream: Belle," Dream Big Princess Video, 1:00, accessed May 15, 2019, Disney NOW app.

62. Disney NOW, "I Dream: Tiana," Dream Big Princess Video, 1:00, accessed May 15, 2019, Disney NOW app.

63. Disney NOW, "Tiana," Dream Big Princess Video, 1:00, accessed May 15, 2019, Disney NOW app.

64. Disney NOW, "Rapunzel," Dream Big Princess Video, 1:00, accessed May 15, 2019, Disney NOW app.

65. Disney NOW, "Belle," Dream Big Princess Video, 1:00, accessed May 15, 2019, Disney NOW app.

66. Disney NOW, "Music Video: Live Your Dream," Dream Big Princess Video, 1:00, accessed May 15, 2019, Disney NOW app.

67. Disney NOW, "Music Video: Be A Champion."

68. Disney NOW, "Dream It, Be It."
69. Ibid.
70. Ibid.
71. Disney NOW, "Dream It, Be It," Dream Big Princess Video, 1:00, accessed May 15, 2019, Disney NOW app.

BIBLIOGRAPHY

Abad-Santos, Alex. "Nike's Colin Kaepernick Ad Sparked a Boycott—and Earned $6 Billion for Nike." *Vox*, September 24, 2018, https://www.vox.com/2018/9/24/17895704/nike-colin-kaepernick-boycott-6-billion.

Abitbol, Alan and Sun Young Lee. "Messages on CSR-Dedicated Facebook Pages: What Works and What Doesn't." *Public Relations Review* 43 (2017): 796–808.

Amidi, Amid. "Watch the First Public Appearance of Jennifer Lee, Disney Animation's New Chief Creative Officer." *Cartoon Brew*, July 10, 2018. https://www.cartoonbrew.com/disney/watch-the-first-public-appearance-of-jennifer-lee-disneys-new-chief-creative-officer-161796.html.

Ballew, Matthew, Allen Omoto, and Patricia Winter. "Using Web 2.0 and Social Media Technologies to Foster Proenvironmental Action." *Sustainability* 7, no. 8 (2015): 10620–10648.

Birim, Bahadir. "Evaluation of Corporate Social Responsibility and Social Media as Key Source of Strategic Communication," *Social and Behavioral Sciences* 235, (2016): 70–75.

Carroll, Archie B. "The Pyramid of Corporate Social Responsibility: Toward the Moral Management of Organizational Stakeholders." *Business Horizons*, (July/August): 39–48.

Commission of the European Communities. "Green Paper: Promoting a European Framework for Corporate Responsibility," Brussels, Belgium, 2001.

Cox, Taylor H., Jr. *Cultural Diversity in Organizations: Theory, Research and Practice.* San Francisco, CA: Berrett-Koehler, 1993.

Davis, Keith "Can Business Afford to Ignore Social Responsibilities?" *California Management Review* 11 no. 3, (1960): 70–76.

Del Barco, Mandalit. "Marvel Studios' Kevin Feige on the Future of Marvel Movies." *NPR*, April 26, 2018. https://www.npr.org/2018/04/26/605648453/marvel-studios-kevin-feige-on-the-future-of-marvel-movies.

Desta, Yohana. "The Year Disney Started to Take Diversity Seriously." *Vanity Fair*, November 23, 2016. https://www.vanityfair.com/hollywood/2016/11/disney-films-inclusive.

Disney Channel. "Karan Brar, Asian Pacific American Heritage," YouTube video, 1:30, Posted [May 2, 2018], https://youtu.be/o2XNbMyxHeM.

———. "Black History Month, Be Inspired." YouTube video, 0:47. Posted February 12, 2016, https://youtu.be/YilVX1GeZVc.

———. "History in the Making, Black History Month, Be Inspired." YouTube video, 1:00. Posted February 22, 2018. https://youtu.be/SRhjk59-F3U.

———. "Celebrating You, Black History Month." YouTube video, 1:00. Posted February 9, 2019, https://youtu.be/XxTCkPDpY4E.

Disney Junior. "Doc McStuffins, Black History Month, Dr. Tucker." YouTube video, 1:00. Posted April 9, 2015, https://youtu.be/MC6Rz4o-8OA.

———. "Doc McStuffins, Black History Month, Dr. Backhus." YouTube video, 1:15. Posted April 9, 2015, https://youtu.be/wZS8wOyObmU.

———. "Doc McStuffins, Black History Month, Dr. Bradford." YouTube video, 1:00. Posted April 10, 2015. https://youtu.be/c0U2Dw2QYk0.

———. "Meet Dr. Myiesha, Black History Month," YouTube video, 0:45, Posted February 17, 2017. https://youtu.be/VUcEUsxTbck.

———. "Meet Captain Stephanie, Black History Month." YouTube video 0:45. Posted February 16, 2017. https://youtu.be/w1iVsykGheA.

Disney Lifestyle. "#DreamBigPrincess Photography Campaign Encourages Kids Around the Globe to Dream Big." Accessed May 15, 2019. https://partners.disney.com/dream-big-princess-photo-campaign.

Disney NOW App. "Music Video: Ariel Side by Side," Dream Big Princess Video, 1:00. Accessed May 15, 2019. Disney NOW app.

———. "I Dream: Belle," Dream Big Princess Video, 1:00. Accessed May 15, 2019.

———. "I Dream: Tiana," Dream Big Princess Video, 1:00. Accessed May 15, 2019.

———. "Tiana," Dream Big Princess Video, 1:00. Accessed May 15, 2019.

———. "Rapunzel," Dream Big Princess Video, 1:00. Accessed May 15, 2019.

———. "Music Video: Live Your Story," Dream Big Princess Video, 3:00. Accessed May 15, 2019.

———. "Belle," Dream Big Princess Video, 1:00. Accessed May 15, 2019.

———. "Music Video: Live Your Dream," Dream Big Princess Video, 1:00. Accessed May 15, 2019.

———. "Music Video: Be A Champion," Dream Big Princess Video, 1:00. Accessed May 15, 2019.

———. "Dream It, Be It," Dream Big Princess Video, 1:00. Accessed May 15, 2019.

Disney XD. "True Heroes are Timeless, Black History Month." YouTube video, 3:00. Posted February 1 2017. https://youtu.be/zHpf80Bcl6g.

———. "Cameron Boyce Honors the Clinton 12, Black History Month." YouTube video, 3:00. Posted February 1, 2016. https://youtu.be/fgSKSeuTLAk.

Elizabeth, De. "Why People Are NOT Happy About Kendall Jenner's Pepsi Commercial." *Teen Vogue*, April 4, 2017. https://www.teenvogue.com/story/pepsi-commercial-kendall-jenner-reaction.

Gibson, Kate. "Colin Kaepernick is Nike's $6 Billion Man." *CBS News*, September 21, 2018, https://www.cbsnews.com/news/colin-kaepernick-nike-6-billion-man/.

"Her Story." Blacklivesmatter.com. Accessed March 21, 2019. https://blacklivesmatter.com/about/herstory/Black Lives Matter.

Kent, Michael L., and Maureen Taylor. "Building Dialogic Relationships through the World Wide Web." *Public Relations Review* 24, no. 3 (1998): 321–334.

Kiley, Rachel. "Disney Channel First: *Andi Mack* Character Says "I'm Gay."" *Pride.com*, Updated February 9, 2019. https://www.pride.com/tv/2019/2/09/disney-channel-first-andi-mack-character-says-im-gay.

Labindao, Maribel. "Hispanic Heritage Sofia Carson." YouTube video, 1:00, Posted September 16, 2018. https://youtu.be/qsRp32Zll5A.

Lang, Brent. "'Star Wars:' Lucasfilm Chief Previews 'Rogue One' and Han Solo Spinoff." *Variety*, November 22, 2016. https://variety.com/2016/film/features/star-wars-rogue-one-lucasfilm-jj-abrams-kathleen-kennedy-1201923806/.

Larkey, Linda Kathryn. "The Development and Validation of the Workforce Diversity Questionnaire." *Management Communication Quarterly 9*, (1996): 296–337.

Law Library of Congress, "Commemorative Observances," Updated June 6, 2019, https://www.loc.gov/law/help/commemorative-observations/index.php.

Martinez, Gina. "Despite Outrage, Nike's Sales Increased 31% After Kaepernick." *Time*, September 10, 2018. http://time.com/5390884/nike-sales-go-up-kaepernick-ad/.

McGrath, Joseph E., Jennifer Berdahl, and Holly Arrow. "Traits, Expectations, Culture and Clout: The Dynamics of Diversity in Work Groups." In *Diversity in Work Teams*, edited by Susan E. Jackson and Marian N. Ruderman, 17–45. Washington, DC: American Psychological Association, 1995.

Meyersohn, Nathaniel. "Gillette Says it's Satisfied With Sales After Controversial Ad." *CNN Business*, https://www.cnn.com/2019/01/23/business/gillette-ad-procter-and-gamble-stock/index.html.

Novy-Williams, Eben. "Calls to #BoycottNike Don't Crack Top Five on the Outrage Meter." *Bloomberg*, September 5, 2018. https://www.bloomberg.com/news/articles/2018-09-05/calls-to-boycottnike-don-t-crack-top-five-on-the-outrage-meter.

Oberseder, Magdalena, Bodo B. Schlegelmilch, and Patrick E. Murphy. "CSR Practices and Consumer Practices." *Journal of Business Research* 66, no. 10 (2013): 1839–1851.

Roberson, Quinetta M. "Disentangling the Meanings of Diversity and Inclusion in Organizations." *Group & Organization Management* 31, no. 2 (2006): 212–236.

Smith, Alexander. "Pepsi Pulls Controversial Kendall Jenner Ad After Outcry." *NBC News*, April 5, 2017. https://www.nbcnews.com/news/nbcblk/pepsi-ad-kendall-jenner-echoes-black-lives-matter-sparks-anger-n742811.

Southard, Emily. "'Dream Big, Princess' Launching New Global Photography Campaign." *Disney Parks Blog* August 16, 2017. https://disneyparks.disney.go.com/blog/2017/08/dream-big-princess-launching-new-global-photography-campaign/.

Taylor, Chloe. "Gillette Draws Fire for #MeToo Commercial That Challenges 'Toxic Masculinity.'" *CNBC*, January 15, 2019. https://www.cnbc.com/2019/01/15/gillette-draws-fire-for-metoo-commercial.html.

The Walt Disney Company. "Disney Citizenship 2014 Performance Summary." Accessed May 15, 2019. https://ditm-twdc-us.storage.googleapis.com/FY14-Performance-Summary.pdf.

Victor, Daniel. "Pepsi Pulls Ad Accused of Trivializing Black Lives Matter." *The New York Times*, April 5, 2017. https://www.nytimes.com/2017/04/05/business/kendall-jenner-pepsi-ad.html.

Wyche, Steve, "Colin Kaepernick Explains Why He Sat During the National Anthem." *NFL.com*. August 27, 2016. http://www.nfl.com/news/story/0ap3000000691077/article/colin-kaepernick-explains-why-he-sat-during-national-anthem.

3

✛

Sofia the First
A Princess Life Fit for a Preschool Audience

Sarah Maben

THE WORLD THROUGH THE EYES OF GIRLS

To a preschooler, Snow White, Cinderella, and Aurora are grown women, ready for marriage and their respective princes. While these iconic characters are likely teenagers, their experiences are beyond those of a younger audience—an audience with modern parents who want their children to aspire for more than a royal mate. Historically, Disney classics have often glossed over girlhood, and through platforms like the Disney channels, the studio's television arm is able to take a step back and reimagine all the possibilities that young girls can dream of, before they enter adolescence and womanhood.

Under Walt Disney Television, Disney Junior launched in 2011, markets to children under eight, and has expanded in both representation and narratives about the experiences and aspirations of young girls. Geared toward the preschool viewer, series like *Doc McStuffins* (2012), *Sheriff Callie's Wild West* (2013), *Vampirina* (2017), and *Fancy Nancy* (2018) create a world where young girls imagine themselves as doctors, law enforcers, the lead singer of a girls' "ghoul" band, or just a girl who loves the finer things about life. *Sofia the First* is unique among its sister programming because it connects preschoolers to Disney's classics. This chapter analyzes how Disney created a relatable princess for younger fans, updating and further extending its brand.

SOFIA THE FIRST

Sofia the First, a thirty-minute animated program for Disney, first aired in 2013. The pilot movie, *Once Upon a Princess*, aired in late 2012. The series chronicles Sofia, a commoner in the kingdom of Enchancia, who becomes an instant princess when her mother, Miranda, marries King Roland II. The namesake character is voiced by Ariel Winter, and her parents are voiced by Sara Ramirez and Travis Willingham.

In its news release announcing the series, Disney executives said the show was created for the two to seven age range and would "communicate positive messages and life lessons that are applicable to young children."[1] Disney positioned her as a "relatable peer-to-peer princess who is experiencing many of the same social situations as young viewers at home including learning how to fit in, making new friends and mastering new skills."[2]

Sofia lived in a village called Dunwiddie with her mother, a shoemaker. Her father was lost at sea, and her mother fell in love with the King after delivering a new pair of shoes to the palace. Sofia becomes a princess by her mother's marriage, and then moves into the palace and attends school at Royal Prep Academy. She also gains siblings, twins named Amber and James, whose own mother died when they were babies. Disney revisits stepfamily relations in a more positive light compared to the wicked stepsisters in *Cinderella*.

Sofia identifies with the ordinary girl, whose life is just fine, as a commoner. The possibility of exploring privilege as a princess for her is something that she wishes to write her own rules for. However, Sofia embarks on a journey to not follow the rules of privilege, but to rewrite the rules for the better of all of Enchancia. She is a contemporary take on how a young girl can harness the power of privilege for good.

WRESTLING WITH THE PRINCESS IMAGE

The concept of what it means to be a princess is woven throughout the series. Episode after episode challenges preconceived notions of what a princess wears, her interests, and how she behaves. Sofia is not a damsel or passive princess, nor is she looking for love.

In the episode "The Princess Test,"[3] Sofia's stepsister Amber (voiced by Darcy Rose Byrnes), and other neighboring princesses are put to a test—a princess test. Sofia stresses about whether her fan-fluttering skills, gown, or curtsy will pass muster. As the girls head to their test, each one passes a woman, Mrs. Higgins, asking for help. One by one the other princesses bypass Higgins, ignoring her requests for help because they are following the rule that a princess mustn't be late to her test. Reluctantly, Sofia decides to help Mrs. Higgins, who promises it won't take long. As the clock ticks away, Sofia begins to worry she will be late, and may not even make a portion of the test. She begins to regret helping the woman, but stays the course because she promised to help. She loses her fan. She falls in the mud, and her gown is now a mess, a sure-fire way to fail the princess test. It turns out that Mrs. Higgins was really one of her instructors in disguise and Sofia emerges as the only princess to demonstrate the most important trait of a princess—kindness. The fairies, their teachers, instruct the princesses that "A true princess always helps a person in need."

While the moral of the episode speaks to a modern princess' priorities, this lesson contrasts Sofia's actions with that of a one-dimensional princess. The rest of the princesses are consumed with a posture test, their gowns, handkerchiefs, and proper conversation. Would a preschooler see the moral or get caught up in the dainty preoccupations like curtsying? Recent research shows that preschool children are influenced positively by moral lessons on prosocial television.[4] This contradicts some older research that showed how children could not connect a moral lesson from Clifford, a dog, to their own lives,[5] and that morals needed to be literal and in line with the target age's development.

In the news release promoting the final episode, Disney defines a princess by her qualities: "Throughout her journey, she discovers that looking like a princess isn't all that difficult, but possessing the characteristics of a true princess—honesty, loyalty, compassion and grace—is what makes one truly royal."[6] In a 2017 study, Golden and Wallace Jacoby found that preschoolers displayed four princess themes: attention to beauty, focus on clothing and accessories, body movements, and excluding boys.[7] These themes are addressed throughout the series, as Sofia questions the traditions of the more entrenched royals. The show challenges notions of beauty by emphasizing inner beauty qualities and teaches children not to judge a book by its cover. One episode, called "Beauty Is the Beast,"[8] focuses on Princess Charlotte of Isleworth who turned into a beast. She refuses a goblin access to her royal party and was turned into a beast by the goblin's friend. She experiences ridicule for her looks, and learns her lesson about making assumptions about others, including goblins.

Sofia is an athletic princess. She likes to participate in derby and other outdoor endeavors. Other princesses are showcased twirling and curtsying, displaying a more traditional unspoken royal decree for poise and grace. Queen Miranda is seen with movements maybe unexpected from royalty, as she takes the helm of a ship.

As for excluding boys, a theme found in the 2017 Golden and Jacoby study, Sofia has friends of both genders, and animal characters are voiced by men and women.[9] The episodes tend to focus on Sofia and her female friends, but James (voiced by Zach Callison), her stepbrother, is a mainstay in the story lines.

Sofia challenges preconceived notions that a princess might be silly or frilly. When Chrysta (voiced by Jurnee Smollett-Bell) is charged with training Sofia as a Protector, she assumes Sofia is not tough enough. The two sing a duo laden with stereotypes of the privileged lifestyle. Chrysta sings, "A little royal, probably spoiled, such hard work must be something new."[10] Her perceptions are that Sofia or a royal would pay someone to do the work for them. Sofia responds with her own song explaining to Chrysta that her impressions are not reality, and are based on stereotypes. She sings, "But I am nothing of the kind. I am resourceful and strong." Time and again, throughout Sofia's journey, she seeks to reimagine the attributes of princess, from being less concerned with the superficial, but connected to the everyday person's realities.

FROM COMMONER TO ROYAL

Unlike many of the princesses in the Disney vault, Sofia is not born of royal blood. She becomes a princess by her mother's marriage. In this vein, almost anyone can be a princess. It opens the royal world and all of its allure, with a sense of hope, prospect, and opportunity.

Sofia's commoner roots are used to reveal themes of privilege, access, and excess. Bridging perceived differences between commoner and royal is another theme, one that may be promoted more than its debunked. In "Princess Jade,"[11] a student exchange occurs between the royal school and the school in the village Dunwiddie. In the school swap day, the curricula and dress are drastically different. The town students are in very plain garb compared to the ornate ball gowns and morning suits of the royal students. Amber leaves her posh school to learn architecture and science at the town school. She asked when they were going to have their lessons on posture or tea pouring. She was even asked to wear a toolbelt for a building exercise.

The episode's plot reflects public versus private school divides that demonstrate the realities of privilege and elite access to opportunities and resources. Other princesses learn to warm to Sofia's village friends Jade and Ruby. Initially, they are standoffish and snobbish. One episode, titled "Four's a Crowd,"[12] revolves around the two groups of friends, former friends from the village and new royal friends, learning to accept each other. By the end of the series, the town children and royal children work together to defeat a common foe and help Sofia.

The series also allows audiences to value domestic workers. Baileywick, the castle steward and trusted right hand of the king (voiced by Tim

Gunn), is a commoner who loyally serves the family. In "Baileywick's Day Off,"[13] the overly dependent children keep requesting help from Baileywick, despite knowing that he is trying to leave for a well-deserved break on his birthday. He patiently assists the children, and forfeits his day off. Even a typically thoughtful Sofia asked him to find butterflies. After a short chat with her mother, Sofia recognizes how unfair she and her siblings were. In the end, they plan a special party and honor Baileywick. "It's our turn to serve you," the king tells him. The entire episode smacks of privilege. Yet it leaves audiences with the moral of how to appreciate those who serve, not taking advantage of others, and to appreciate boundaries.

Throughout these experiences, Sofia struggles at first to find where she fits between the two worlds. In "Carol of the Arrow,"[14] Sofia hid her princess title and her tiara because the people around her believed that royals do not help. Carol, a Robin Hood–like character, said, "Someone's gotta help the folks of Enchancia. You don't see King Roland or the royal family out here." Sofia did not feel comfortable sharing her princess identity at first and pretended to be a girl from the village in order to join Carol and the Merry Band. She proved to Carol that royals can and do help by rescuing a member of the Merry Band and a baby raccoon. When Sofia's identity is exposed and she is upset, Queen Miranda delivered the moral, "you should always be proud of who you are no matter what anyone else thinks."

DIVERSIFYING THE WORLD AROUND THE PALACE

In *Sofia the First*, Disney seems to be cognizant of expanding its diversity of characters and moving the brand beyond a very white and homogenous fairy-tale world. In "Tri-Kingdom Picnic,"[15] the royal families from the surrounding kingdoms of Wei-Ling (based on China) and Khaldoun (based on Egypt) meet for a picnic where they try foods and traditions from other cultures. The children from the different lands interact at the Royal Prep Academy, showcasing a variety of skin tones. They wear traditional outfits from their lands. In one example, Sofia's friend Lani is from Hakolo, which resembles Polynesia. Sofia serves as her *akahuna*, or guide, in the Fire Pearl Ceremony, which is a rite of passage for a young person to prove her worth to join the circle of leadership. Sofia and Amber visit Tangu in "Two to Tangu,"[16] which is Middle Eastern in its appearance. Freezenburg, another location in the *Sofia* universe, is a Disney version of Scandinavia.

One misstatement from a Disney executive producer about Sofia being the first Latina princess lead to an outcry on social media prior to the series' release. She did not present as a classic Latina, according to some, or to others showed the diversity among Latinas. After generating numerous headlines of Disney's first Latina princess, social media erupted with opinions.[17] At the time, Disney officials would not confirm nor deny Sofia's heritage. News outlets ran this Disney statement: "the range of characters in Sofia the First and the actors who play them 'are a reflection of Disney's commitment to diverse, multicultural storytelling, and the wonderful early reaction to Sofia affirms that commitment.'"[18] Critics said Sofia represented a typical European royal, not a Latina princess. Disney officials later said Sofia was not intended to be Latina, but listened to its audiences and created *Elena of Avalor* (premiering in 2016), with a central Latina protagonist, as a spin-off.

The spin-off launched from the third season of Sofia with the three-episode crossover "Elena and the Secret of Avalor."[19] Elena, Sofia, and their friends unite the people of both kingdoms to defeat Shuriki. Elena, only sixteen, assumes the throne of Avalor and the kingdom rejoices, setting up the *Elena* series for adventures as the young Latina learns her new role as leader. Outside of the *Elena* crossover event, Sofia navigates diversity throughout a few episodes, typically acting as a bridge between people making judgments based on history, cultural misunderstandings, and outward appearance.

In "Her Royal Spyness,"[20] Amber and Sofia think they should protect their mother from the sealians—mythical creatures that a book says will lure boats out to a stormy triangle never to be found again. They meet up with Professor Zacharias Fleeber, the author of the book, who wants to be an expert on the half-seal, half-human creatures. His research about the sealians was based on stories from sailors. In a storm, sealians jump on the ship carrying Queen Miranda, Sofia, Amber, the captain, and Professor Fleeber. In a surfer-style drawl, one says: "How are we all doing? Don't be scared of us. We're very friendly." They asked the humans for help to get back home after the storm set in while they were surfing. The two groups help each other out of the storm and to their respective homes. "Fascinating, outrageously fascinating," the professor says as he observes the creatures. The episode highlights how one group views another, based on faulty information, and how indigenous peoples are viewed as something to be studied. For the younger viewer, a main takeaway is not to judge others, but for the older viewer, it is also a lesson in primary versus secondary sources. Once home, the sealians say: "These guys had some funny ideas about us, Dad." The professor asks if he may stay to better understand the group and tell their story accurately.

During season 1, the two-part "The Floating Palace"[21] highlights how humans and mermaids held preconceived notions about each other. The royal family sails to Merroway Cove for a summer vacation. "Mermaids are not real," the captain tells them. Soon after, Sofia and sidekick bunny Clover spot a mermaid tangled in a rope. When Sofia helps Oona out of the net, her amulet transforms her into a mermaid and she escorts an injured Oona home. The girls find similarities; both have magical accessories and how they can both talk to animals. The mermaids are worried about the humans in their waters. The mermaid queen announces: "A human vessel is in the cove." Her daughter, Oona, replies, "Oh, Mom. It's not like humans are dangerous or anything." The queen's advisor retorts, "Yes, they are." The queen tells of a time when the humans tried to catch mermaids and how many of their people were injured. She warns, "We could all be in grave danger." After Sofia helps the mermaids and saves the human ship, facilitating a happy ending, the royal family and mermaids officially meet. "I think it's about time we all became friends," Sofia says. Friendship is a mainstay theme of the series, particularly in understanding differences among diverse characters. Young audiences learn that in developing friendships with others who do not look like them or from different backgrounds, they will find common ground and meaningful relationships with other groups.

FAMILIAR FACES: PRESERVING THE ORIGINAL PRINCESSES

Sofia the First is an anchor to Disney's past because its episodes feature the older Disney princesses who pop in to guide the young princess-in-training. For the Disney brand, this creates cross-promotion and introductions to its line-up of princesses, movies, and merchandise. In season 3, Sofia finds a secret passage with a path leading to a boat that floats through a cave with artifacts from the other princesses on display for the avid fan to note in "The Secret Library."[22] Nothing is said, but viewers see the rose from *Beauty and the Beast*, Cinderella's pumpkin coach and slippers, Aladdin's lamp and flying carpet, Merida's bow and a target, Rapunzel's tower, hair and floating lanterns, swirling leaves from *Pocahontas* with a drum in the background and other homages to the official princess brand.

The older princesses arrive in Sofia's world in their original outfits, keeping with their own brands. Until recently (*Ralph Breaks the Internet*, 2018), the princesses in the princess brand did not interact with one another, in an effort to preserve their individual brands. The original princesses are trapped in their timelines and incorporating them into Sofia's world means focusing on themes that work in both. Jasmine sings a song to calm Sofia and Amber, and encourages them to tame their fears in "Two to Tangu."[23] Jasmine says, "I didn't rescue you . . . I helped you rescue yourselves." Belle appears in "The Amulet and the Anthem,"[24] where she sings with guidance for a young princess who was unkind to her friends. Sofia was proud and boastful earlier in the episode toward village friends Jade and Ruby, and was cursed with a croak. Belle sings, "to fix your mess, do more than confess . . . use all your might, to make it right" teaching her that actions speak louder than words. Belle floats around as she sings, in her full yellow ballgown and gloves.

Ariel appeared in the "The Floating Palace, pt. 2,"[25] teaching Sofia, via a song, about loving your family. Rounding out the first season's princess cameos was Aurora in "Holiday in Enchancia."[26] She is the first princess to forgo a song, and stands in one place. As see enters, you hear music from Sleeping Beauty softly introduce her. "Oh, Sofia, it's not my help you need . . . I could always count on my animal friends to help me through tough times, and so can you."

In season 2, Snow White, Mulan, Rapunzel, and Tiana appear to offer wisdom and encouragement. Like Aurora, Snow White does not sing but encourages Sofia to trust her intuition in "The Enchanted Feast."[27] Mulan sings "Stronger Than You Know" in an episode aptly titled "Princesses to the Rescue!"[28] King Roland, Sofia, James, and Amber are visiting friends in Wei-Ling. When the male counterparts are trapped, the princesses must tackle a series of gauntlets to rescue the emperor, king, and two princes. Mulan enters fiercely, with a sword and a warrior's helmet, and swings from vines as she sings. When the girls complain that their task is tough, Mulan simply responds, "You just have to be tougher." She sang, "it doesn't matter what they say, there's only one voice to obey, and it's that little voice inside, so let that be your guide, and then you can save the day."

Rapunzel sings "Dare to Risk It All" in "The Curse of Princess Ivy, pt. 2."[29] Her cameo is one of the most interactive. She lets down her hair to help Sofia and Amber out of a tough spot: "Here climb on up. We princesses have to stick together." Then, she rides a dragon with Amber and Sofia as she sings to Amber, who confesses to Rapunzel that her actions caused the current curse. Her song encourages Amber to do what is right and that she could change. In "Winter's Gift," Tiana helps Sofia solve a gift-giving problem central to the plot of the episode.[30] She sings that a gift should come from the heart. Animators gave her a long coat for the winter scene, but you can see her original outfit underneath. Merida, one of the more recent Disney princesses who was the first to break many of the traditional stereotypes, encourages Sofia to stand tall, believe in herself and then her "aim will always be true."[31]

Pocahontas was the only official princess at the time without a cameo. In a tweet, creator Craig Gerber said, "We tried to include her a few times but the stories never panned out."[32] Other theories are that she was the only character based on a real person, and she was not as popular as the other princesses. While not part of the princess brand at the time, Anna and Elsa were represented by Olaf, a snowman. Moana had not yet been added to the princess brand. Likely, *Sofia the First* served as a tool of redeeming more problematic princesses rather than the more recent ones who were already created as contemporary princesses.

Like *Ralph Breaks the Internet*, the *Sofia* series allowed the classic princesses to expand their own stories. In a small way, they can add an experience, and for some a new song, to their own stories. It modernizes the characters carefully, while preserving the original film. They empower Sofia to learn from their stories and exemplify some of their stronger characteristics.

Additionally, from the Disney vault, three fairies from *Sleeping Beauty*, Fauna, Flora, and Merryweather, are headmistresses of Royal Prep Academy, where Sofia and other royals attend school. The villains in *Sofia* are new, like Prisma, who is after the "wicked nine"—evil artifacts from the original villains, like Jafar's Snake Staff from *Aladdin*, Ursula's necklace from *The Little Mermaid*, and Lady Tremaine's Key from *Cinderella*. Even these small plotlines connect *Sofia* to the larger Disney princess brand.

CHALLENGING ORIGINAL "ROLES"

Challenging gender roles is another theme woven into *Sofia the First*. Prince Hugo really loves to ice dance, and secretly trains with partner Sofia for an exhibition. He bails on Sofia when the ice dancing event is at the same time of his ice hockey game, and he would be "found out." His father says "Men in our family don't ice dance" but comes around to the idea when his son turns out to be an excellent ice dancer.[33] In another episode titled "Just One of the Princes," Sofia races in the flying derby, which is usually reserved for the boy royals.[34]

Some research shows how even today, preschoolers exhibit gendered play patterns when given a box of princess outfits.[35] Moving away from the former gender standards set forth in early princess tales is a factor for media-savvy caregivers. Disney also capitalized on this, releasing a line of dolls of the original princesses dressed in ordinary gender-neutral outfits with the princesses wearing pants and casual attire from their appearance in *Ralph Breaks the Internet*.

The evil stepmother motif also gets a facelift. With blended families a reality for most, Disney cannot continue to make all stepmothers evil or villainous. Sofia's mother Miranda marries King Roland II, becoming Queen of Enchancia and the stepmother to James and Amber. Queen Miranda is more than just arm candy for the king, and is portrayed as more than a static character. She is adventurous and sometimes mysterious. In

"Her Royal Spyness," Miranda secretly learns to sail so she can surprise the king for his birthday.[36] She patches the sail (because she is a former shoemaker) in a pinch to save the ship during a storm.

Queen Miranda is kind and patient, and wants a relationship with each of her children. In "Mom's the Word," Miranda invites her stepchildren on the Mother's Day picnic tradition she and Sofia share each year.[37] When Sofia balks initially at the idea, Miranda says "I'm their mother, too." At the end of the episode, Sofia confesses that she tried to manipulate the trip so she could have time alone with her mother like it used to be. Miranda responded, "I have enough love for all three of you." There is a mother-daughter relationship on screen in *Sofia*. Before Merida in *Brave*, most mothers were deceased or the relationship was not highlighted because it was not central to the plot.

In Sofia, the central character has a stepfather, unlike Disney princesses before her. Sofia calls King Roland "Dad," but in "Dads and Daughters Day" she worries that she is the only one on the field trip who has a stepfather.[38] One princess suggests that Roland is not her "real" dad. They have a touching moment where he assures her that she is his "real" daughter. He says, "I'm your dad now and that makes me your real father." The blended family is more representative of today's families.

A FUTURE FOR THE DISNEY PRINCESS BRAND

Sofia fans lobbied online for a fifth season. But as of 2019, the online petition was closed, and more episodes seemed unlikely. With the success of *Sofia* and *Elena*, Disney Jr. will continue with the formula set by writers in *Sofia*. If not on the small screen, Disney sets up the evolution of the princess brand that can be continued in films, like *Ralph Breaks the Internet*, or through the Disney+ streaming service. In March 2019, the network ordered an animated series for the preschool crowd about a young detective named Mira, who is from Japur, a land inspired by India. Characterized as "brave and resourceful" Mira is a commoner appointed to royal detective.[39] It will feature voice actors of Indian descent.

The entry-level princess like Sofia, partnered with cameos from other Disney characters, expands the Disney brand to a younger audience while introducing or reconnecting them to the official princess brand. The co-branding solidifies the princess brand in the mind of the young viewer and reaches multi-generations in one show. Hine, Ivanovic, and England argued that a princess brand would be hard to kick.[40] Princesses represent an idyllic lifestyle with special treatment, privilege and prestige. *Sofia the First* sheds some of these dated characteristics and empowers girls in the show, as well as legions of young viewers.

The series is also an example of how to fuse an existing brand into a newer model, while preserving nostalgia for a multi-generational audience. Improvements on the Disney princess show that branding is a cocreative process between consumers and companies. The Disney princess brand was enhanced by one little princess named Sofia. She may not be invited to the official princess brand, but she is a steward for the positive and modern qualities parents desire. She is an active princess who drives her own stories, learning along the way. Sofia better reflects a princess for today's social movements of empowering young people, especially girls.

NOTES

1. "Disney Presents Its First Little Girl Princess in 'Sofia The First: Once Upon a Princess' Sunday, November 18 on Disney Channel." TV By The Numbers by Zap2it.com. September 20, 2012, accessed March 01, 2019. https://tvbythenumbers.zap2it.com/press-releases/disney-presents-its-first-little-girl-princess-in-sofia-the-first-once-upon-a-princess-sunday-november-18-on-disney-channel/.

2. Ibid.

3. *Sofia the First*, "The Princess Test," Season 1, Episode 8, directed by Jamie Mitchell, written by Laurie Israel and Rachel Ruderman, Disney Jr., April 12, 2013.

4. Drew P. Cingel and Marina Krcmar, "Prosocial Television, Preschool Children's Moral Judgments, and Moral Reasoning: The Role of Social Moral Intuitions and Perspective-Taking," *Communication Research* 46 no. 3 (2019): 355–74. doi:10.1177/0093650217733846.

5. Marie-Louise Mares and Emily Elizabeth Acosta, "Be Kind to Three-Legged Dogs: Children's Literal Interpretations of TV's Moral Lessons," *Media Psychology* 11 no. 3 (2008): 377–99. doi:10.1080/15213260802204355.

6. "'Sofia The First: Forever Royal' Premieres Saturday, September 8, on Disney Junior," Disney Junior Press, August 28, 2018, accessed March 21, 2019, https://www.wdtvpress.com/disneyjunior/pressrelease/sofia-the-first-forever-royal-premieres-saturday-september-8-on-disney-junior/.

7. Julia C. Golden and Jennifer Wallace Jacoby, "Playing Princess: Preschool Girls' Interpretations of Gender Stereotypes in Disney Princess Media," *Sex Roles* 79, no. 5–6 (2017): 299–313. doi:10.1007/s11199-017-0773-8.

8. *Sofia the First*, "Beauty Is the Beast," Season 3, Episode 23, directed by Jamie Mitchell and Larry Leichliter, written by Craig Gerber and Erica Rothschild, Disney Jr., August 12, 2016.

9. Golden and Wallace Jacoby, "Playing Princess: Preschool Girls' Interpretations of Gender Stereotypes in Disney Princess Media."

10. *Sofia the First*, "The Mystic Isles: The Princess and the Protector," Season 4, Episode 6, directed by Jamie Mitchell, written by Craig Carlisle and Craig Gerber. Disney Jr., June 30, 2017.

11. *Sofia the First*, "Princess Jade," Season 4, Episode 10, directed by Jamie Mitchell and Mircea Mantta, written by Craig Gerber and Matt Hoverman, Disney Jr., September 1, 2017.

12. *Sofia the First*, "Four's a Crowd," Season 1, Episode 24, directed by Jamie Mitchell and Larry Leichliter, written by Elizabeth Keyishian and Craig Gerber, Disney Jr., February 14, 2014.

13. *Sofia the First*, "Baileywick's Day Off," Season 1, Episode 24, directed by Jamie Mitchell and Larry Leichliter, written by Doug Cooney and Craig Gerber, Disney Jr., April 26, 2013.

14. *Sofia the First*, "Carol of the Arrow," Season 2, Episode 27, directed by Jamie Mitchell, written by Krista Tucker and Craig Gerber, Disney Jr., July 15, 2015.

15. *Sofia the First*, "Tri-Kingdom Picnic," Season 1, Episode 10, directed by Jamie Mitchell and Larry Leichliter, written by Laurie Israel, Rachel Ruderman, and Craig Gerber, Disney Jr., May 17, 2013.

16. *Sofia the First*, "Two to Tangu," Season 1, Episode 12, directed by Jamie Mitchell and Larry Leichliter, written by Erica Rothschild and Craig Gerber, Disney Jr., June 14, 2013.

17. Adrian Carrasquillo, "Disney's First Latina Princess: Mom Bloggers Respond," *NBC Latino*, October 19, 2012, accessed March 15, 2019. http://nbclatino.com/2012/10/19/disneys-first-latina-princess-mom-bloggers-respond/.

18. Carrasquillo, "Disney's First Latina Princess."

19. *Elena of Avalor*, "Elena and the Secret of Avalor," Season 1, Episode 11, directed by Jamie Mitchell and Mircea Mantta, written by Craig Gerber, Disney Jr., November 20, 2016.

20. *Sofia the First*, "Her Royal Spyness," Season 3, Episode 18, directed by Jamie Mitchell and Mircea Mantta, written by Laurie Israel and Craig Gerber, Disney Jr., April 8, 2016.

21. *Sofia the First*, "The Floating Palace," Season 1, Episode 22, directed by Jamie Mitchell and Larry Leichliter, written by Craig Gerber, Disney Jr., November 24, 2013.

22. *Sofia the First*, "The Secret Library," Season 3, Episode 6, directed by Jamie Mitchell and Mircea Mantta, written by Craig Gerber, Disney Jr., October 12, 2015.

23. *Sofia the First*, "Two to Tangu," Season 1, Episode 12, directed by Jamie Mitchell and Larry Leichliter, written by Erica Rothschild and Craig Gerber, Disney Jr., June 14, 2013.

24. *Sofia the First*, "The Amulet and the Anthem," Season 1, Episode 17, directed by Jamie Mitchell and Larry Leichliter, written by Matt Boren and Craig Gerber, Disney Jr., September 13, 2013.

25. *Sofia the First*, "The Floating Palace," Season 1, Episode 22, directed by Jamie Mitchell and Larry Leichliter, written by Craig Gerber, Disney Jr., November 24, 2013.

26. *Sofia the First*, "Holiday in Enchancia," Season 1, Episode 23, directed by Jamie Mitchell and Larry Leichliter, written by Craig Gerber, Disney Jr., December 1, 2013.

27. *Sofia the First*, "The Enchanted Feast," Season 2, Episode 2, directed by Jamie Mitchell and Mircea Mantta, written by Craig Gerber and Michael G. Stern, Disney Jr., April 4, 2014.

28. *Sofia the First*, "Princesses to the Rescue!" Season 2, Episode 12, directed by Jamie Mitchell and Mircea Mantta, written by Laurie Israel, Rachel Ruderman, and Craig Gerber, Disney Jr., August 15, 2014.

29. *Sofia the First*, "The Curse of Princess Ivy," Season 2, Episode 18, directed by Jamie Mitchell, written by Craig Gerber and Erica Rothschild, Disney Jr., November 23, 2014.

30. *Sofia the First*, "Winter's Gift," Season 2, Episode 19, directed by Jamie Mitchell and Mircea Mantta, written by Craig Gerber and Michael G. Stern, Disney Jr., December 12, 2014.

31. *Sofia the First*, "The Secret Library," Season 3, Episode 6, directed by Jamie Mitchell and Mircea Mantta, written by Craig Gerber, Disney Jr., October 12, 2015.

32. Craig Gerber, Twitter Post, August 22, 2018, 10:36 p.m., https://twitter.com/CraigGerber_/status/1032501764715556864.

33. *Sofia the First*, "Lord of the Rink," Season 3, Episode 13, directed by Jamie Mitchell, written by Craig Gerber, Laurie Israel, and Rachel Ruderman, Disney Jr., December 4, 2015.

34. *Sofia the First*, "Just One of the Princes," Season 1, Episode 1, directed by Jamie Mitchell, written by Craig Gerber, Disney Jr., January 11, 2013.

35. Golden and Wallace Jacoby, "Playing Princess."

36. *Sofia the First*, "Her Royal Spyness," Season 3, Episode 18, directed by Jamie Mitchell and Mircea Mantta, written by Laurie Israel and Craig Gerber, Disney Jr., April 8, 2016.

37. *Sofia the First*, "Mom's the Word," Season 2, Episode 4, directed by Jamie Mitchell and Larry Leichliter, written by Craig Gerber and Michael G. Stern, Disney Jr., April 25, 2014.

38. *Sofia the First*, "Dads and Daughters Day," Season 3, Episode 20, directed by Jamie Mitchell and Mircea Mantta, written by Laurie Israel, Craig Gerber, and Rachel Ruderman, Disney Jr., June 17, 2016.

39. Kimberly Nordyke, "Disney Junior Orders Animated Mystery Series Inspired by Indian Cultures and Customs," *The Hollywood Reporter*, March 28, 2019, accessed March 30, 2019. https://www.hollywoodreporter.com/live-feed/disney-junior-orders-mira-inspired-by-indian-cultures-customs-1164857.

40. Benjamin Hine, Katarina Ivanovic, and Dawn England, "From the Sleeping Princess to the World-Saving Daughter of the Chief," 161.

BIBLIOGRAPHY

Carrasquillo, Adrian. "Disney's First Latina Princess: Mom Bloggers Respond." October 19, 2012. Accessed March 15, 2019. http://nbclatino.com/2012/10/19/disneys-first-latina-princess-mom-bloggers-respond/.

Cingel, Drew P., and Marina Krcmar "Prosocial Television, Preschool Children's Moral Judgments, and Moral Reasoning: The Role of Social Moral Intuitions and Perspective-Taking." *Communication Research* 46, no. 3, (2019): 355–374. doi:10.1177/0093650217733846.

Elena of Avalor. "Elena and the Secret of Avalor." Season 1, Episode 11. Directed by Jamie Mitchell and Mircea Mantta. Written by Craig Gerber. Disney Jr., November 20, 2016.

Gerber, Craig. Twitter Post. August 22, 2018, 10:36 PM. https://twitter.com/CraigGerber_/status/1032501764715556864.

Golden, Julia C., and Jennifer Wallace Jacoby. "Playing Princess: Preschool Girls' Interpretations of Gender Stereotypes in Disney Princess Media." *Sex Roles* 79, no. 5–6 (2017): 299–313. doi:10.1007/s11199-017-0773-8.

Heinberg, Martin, Constantine S. Katsikeas, H. Erkan Ozkaya, and Markus Taube. "How Nostalgic Brand Positioning Shapes Brand Equity: Differences between Emerging and Developed Markets." *Journal of the Academy of Marketing Science* (2019). doi:10.1007/s11747.

Hine, Benjamin, Katarina Ivanovic, and Dawn England. "From the Sleeping Princess to the World-Saving Daughter of the Chief: Examining Young Children's Perceptions of 'Old' versus 'New' Disney Princess Characters." *Social Sciences* 7, no. 9 (2018): 161. doi:10.3390/socsci7090161.

La Gorce, Tammy. *#1000BlackGirlBooks Campaign Expands*. September 6, 2017. Accessed June 10, 2019. https://kristof.blogs.nytimes.com/2016/09/06/1000blackgirlbooks-campaign-expands/.

Laville, Sandra and Jonathan Watts. "Across the Globe, Millions Join Biggest Climate Protest Ever." *The Guardian,* September 20, 2019. https://amp.theguardian.com/environment/2019/sep/21/across-the-globe-millions-join-biggest-climate-protest-ever.

Mares, Marie-Louise, and Emily Elizabeth Acosta. "Be Kind to Three-Legged Dogs: Children's Literal Interpretations of TV's Moral Lessons." *Media Psychology* 11, no. 3 (2008): 377–399. doi:10.1080/15213260802204355.

Mason, Heather. *Meet Smart Girl Mari Copeny aka 'Little Miss Flint.'* August 22, 2017. Accessed June 10, 2019. https://amysmartgirls.com/meet-smart-girl-mari-copeny-aka-little-miss-flint-4131419a31bd.

McGrath, MaryEllen, and Morgan Winsor. *"'Wonder Girls': How Girl-led Activists are Changing the World.* October 6, 2017. Accessed June 10, 2019. https://abcnews.go.com/International/girls-girl-led-activists-changing-world/story?id=50186933.

McPherson, Susan. "Empowering Women and Girls, One Hashtag at a Time." May 29, 2014. Accessed March 21, 2019. https://www.forbes.com/sites/susanmcpherson/2014/05/27/empowering-women-and-girls-one-hashtag-at-a-time/#6843b2d658ac.

Nordyke, Kimberly. "Disney Channel Continues Overall Deal Push with 'Elena of Avalor' Creator (Exclusive)." November 27, 2018. Accessed March 20, 2019. Creator (Exclusive)." March 28, 2019. https://www.hollywoodreporter.com/live-feed/sofia-first-ep-craig-gerber-signs-deal-.

———. "Disney Junior Orders Animated Mystery Series Inspired by Indian Cultures and Customs." March 28, 2019. Accessed March 30, 2019. https://www.hollywoodreporter.com/live-feed/disney-junior-orders-mira-inspired-by-indian-cultures-customs-1164857.

Orenstein, Peggy. "What's Wrong with Cinderella?" December 24, 2006. Accessed March 21, 2019. https://www.nytimes.com/2006/12/24/magazine/24princess.t.html.

Santoro, Alessia. "Artist Shows What Follows 'Happily Ever After' with Her Drawings of Disney Princesses as Moms." POPSUGAR Family. August 11, 2017. Accessed June 27, 2019. https://www.popsugar.com/family/Disney-Princesses-New-Moms-41761602.

Shuler, Sherianne. "Raising (Razing?) Princess: Autoethnographic Reflections on Motherhood and The Princess Culture." *The Popular Culture Studies Journal* 3 (2015): 1–2.

Sofia the First. "Baileywick's Day Off." Season 1, Episode 24. Directed by Jamie Mitchell and Larry Leichliter. Written by Doug Cooney and Craig Gerber. Disney Jr., April 26, 2013.

———. "Beauty Is the Beast." Season 3, Episode 23. Directed by Jamie Mitchell and Larry Leichliter. Written by Craig Gerber and Erica Rothschild. Disney Jr., August 12, 2016.

———. "Bunny Swap." Season 3, Episode 17. Directed by Jamie Mitchell. Written by Erica Rothschild and Craig Gerber. Disney Jr., March 25, 2016.

———. "Buttercup Amber." Season 2, Episode 26. Directed by Jamie Mitchell and Larry Leichliter. Written by Craig Gerber and Michael G. Stern. Disney Jr., July 8, 2015.

———. "Carol of the Arrow." Season 2, Episode 27. Directed by Jamie Mitchell. Written by Krista Tucker and Craig Gerber. Disney Jr., July 15, 2015.

———. "Cool Hand Fluke." Season 3, Episode 1. Directed by Jamie Mitchell and Larry Leichliter. Written by Michael G. Stern and Craig Gerber. Disney Jr., August 5, 2015.

———. "Dads and Daughters Day." Season 3, Episode 20. Directed by Jamie Mitchell and Mircea Mantta. Written by Laurie Israel, Craig Gerber, and Rachel Ruderman. Disney Jr., June 17, 2016.

———. "Four's a Crowd." Season 1, Episode 24. Directed by Jamie Mitchell and Larry Leichliter. Written by Elizabeth Keyishian and Craig Gerber. Disney Jr., February 14, 2014.

———. "Her Royal Spyness." Season 3, Episode 18. Directed by Jamie Mitchell and Mircea Mantta. Written by Laurie Israel and Craig Gerber. Disney Jr., April 8, 2016.

———. "Holiday in Enchancia." Season 1, Episode 23. Directed by Jamie Mitchell and Larry Leichliter. Written by Craig Gerber. Disney Jr., December 1, 2013.

———. "Just One of the Princes." Season 1, Episode 1. Directed by Jamie Mitchell. Written by Craig Gerber. Disney Jr., January 11, 2013.

———. "Lord of the Rink." Season 3, Episode 13. Directed by Jamie Mitchell. Written by Craig Gerber, Laurie Israel, and Rachel Ruderman. Disney Jr., December 4, 2015.

———. "Minimus Is Missing." Season 3, Episode 2. Directed by Jamie Mitchell and Larry Leichliter. Written by Erica Rothschild and Craig Gerber. Disney Jr., August 12, 2015.

———. "Mom's the Word." Season 2, Episode 4. Directed by Jamie Mitchell and Larry Leichliter. Written by Craig Gerber and Michael G. Stern. Disney Jr., April 25, 2014.

———. "Princess Jade." Season 4, Episode 10. Directed by Jamie Mitchell and Mircea Mantta. Written by Craig Gerber and Matt Hoverman. Disney Jr., September 1, 2017.

———. "Princesses to the Rescue!" Season 2, Episode 12. Directed by Jamie Mitchell and Mircea Mantta. Written by Laurie Israel, Rachel Ruderman, and Craig Gerber. Disney Jr., August 15, 2014.

———. "The Amulet and the Anthem." Season 1, Episode 17. Directed by Jamie Mitchell and Larry Leichliter. Written by Matt Boren and Craig Gerber. Disney Jr., September 13, 2013.

———. "The Curse of Princess Ivy." Season 2, Episode 18. Directed by Jamie Mitchell. Written by Craig Gerber and Erica Rothschild. Disney Jr., November 23, 2014.

———. "The Enchanted Feast." Season 2, Episode 2. Directed by Jamie Mitchell and Mircea Mantta. Written by Craig Gerber and Michael G. Stern. Disney Jr., April 4, 2014.

———. "The Floating Palace." Season 1, Episode 22. Directed by Jamie Mitchell and Larry Leichliter. Written by Craig Gerber. Disney Jr., November 24, 2013.

———. "The Mystic Isles: The Princess and the Protector." Season 4, Episode 6. Directed by Jamie Mitchell. Written by Craig Carlisle and Craig Gerber. Disney Jr., June 30, 2017.

———. "The Princess Test." Season 1, Episode 8. Directed by Jamie Mitchell. Written by Laurie Israel and Rachel Ruderman. Disney Jr., April 12, 2013.

———. "The Secret Library." Season 3, Episode 6. Directed by Jamie Mitchell and Mircea Mantta. Written by Craig Gerber. Disney Jr., October 12, 2015.

———. "Tri-Kingdom Picnic." Season 1, Episode 10. Directed by Jamie Mitchell and Larry Leichliter. Written by Laurie Israel, Rachel Ruderman, and Craig Gerber. Disney Jr., May 17, 2013.

———. "Two to Tangu." Season 1, Episode 12. Directed by Jamie Mitchell and Larry Leichliter. Written by Erica Rothschild and Craig Gerber. Disney Jr., June 14, 2013.

———. "Winter's Gift." Season 2, Episode 19. Directed by Jamie Mitchell and Mircea Mantta. Written by Craig Gerber and Michael G. Stern. Disney Jr., December 12, 2014.

"'Sofia the First: Forever Royal' Premieres Saturday, September 8, on Disney Junior." August 28, 2018. Accessed March 21, 2019. https://www.wdtvpress.com/disneyjunior/pressrelease/sofia-the-first-forever-royal-premieres-saturday-september-8-on-disney-junior/.

The Second City. "Advice for Young Girls from The Little Mermaid." YouTube video, 1:17. Posted July 2010. https://www.youtube.com/watch?v=N8xCgC3w1zs.

4

From Princess to Heroine

Expanding Representations of Girls and Women

Jana Thomas and Holly Pate

Since 2009 when Disney acquired Marvel, and then in 2012 with its purchase of Lucasfilm, the cinematic Disney princess now includes powerful superhumans, galactic generals, technological engineers, and light-saber-wielding Jedi. At Disney Parks around the world little girls will now see the Dora Milaje and Rey, as much as they will meet Cinderella and Belle. Princesses on the big screen have evolved from damsels in distress, to fierce females who fight their own battles—and win. Disney has more recently positioned itself—with the release of films like *Star Wars: The Force Awakens* and *Captain Marvel*—to champion the empowerment of women by producing narratives with more complex and dynamic female lead roles.

Disney, with its multi-billion-dollar authority over Marvel Entertainment and Lucasfilm, has claimed economic and cultural dominance over princesses and heroines alike, commodifying the core tenets of postfeminist social justice movements through increased gender representation. This chapter will explore how Marvel and Lucasfilm's female characters, narratives, fandom, and economic dominance at the box office have shaped popular culture for a new generation of fans who are clearly ready for "girl power."

THE MARVEL CINEMATIC UNIVERSE

The Road to Superhero Representation

Spanning more than a decade and twenty-three movies as of 2019, the interconnected universe of films—known as the Marvel Cinematic Universe

(MCU)—has become the most successful studio endeavor in box office history. Collectively, MCU films by mid-2019 have earned $8.13 billion in domestic box office revenue and $21.408 billion worldwide,[1] beating out other top-grossing film franchises like *Star Wars* and *Harry Potter*.[2] Disney's $4-billion acquisition of Marvel Entertainment in 2009 has been credited with much of the MCU's multi-billion-dollar success, providing the financial stability it needed to take risks on new story lines and multi-superhero ventures like *The Avengers*, as well as the ability to brand and sell its 5,000+ characters across Disney's established media platforms and international markets.[3]

Until recently, Hollywood has largely gone without female superheroes in front of the camera. One reason, suggested by a Sony executive in 2015, was a question of profitability, citing female-led box office bombs *Elektra* (2005) and *Catwoman* (2004).[4] In short, critics argued that female superheroes don't sell tickets. At the time, the MCU had yet to introduce a female character on-screen with indelible superhuman abilities. And interestingly, the introduction of its first female character, deadly assassin Natasha Romanoff—aka Black Widow—had been characterized as that of a "sexy secretary,"[5] rather than a character with impressive fighting skills and resourcefulness, and as someone who would go on to become an indispensable member of the Avengers. Many Marvel executives most likely want to forget Agent Romanoff's first on-screen moments, immortalized with Pepper Potts' introduction of her[6] to Tony Stark in *Iron Man 2* as "a potentially very expensive sexual harassment lawsuit."[7]

The idea that female-led superhero films aren't profitable proves invalid when executives now look at the resounding success of DC Comics' 2017 release of *Wonder Woman*, grossing more than $821 million dollars worldwide[8] and receiving a 93 percent Tomatometer score[9]—the highest critic score at the time of any DC movie, including fan favorites *Batman v Superman: Dawn of Justice* and *The Dark Knight Rises*. Financial success at the box office has long been an indicator of a film's cultural and societal impact; clearly, representation of women is becoming a key ingredient for success in the superhero film genre. With women making up 51 percent of the movie-going audience in 2018,[10] it was time for Marvel to progress from featuring females in its movies as secondary characters and love interests, to superheroes leading the way in stand-alone films. Cue Air Force fighter pilot Carol Danvers and Marvel's 2019 release of *Captain Marvel*, the studio's first ever female-led and female-directed movie. Outperforming *Wonder Woman*'s success just two years earlier, *Captain Marvel*, who is arguably one of the MCU's most powerful heroes, went on to gross more than $1.128 billion at the box office worldwide.[11]

Girl Power in the MCU

MCU films introduced movie audiences to strong, intelligent, and courageous female characters, defying gender stereotypes: talented MI5 operative Agent Peggy Carter (*Captain America: The First Avenger*), brilliant astrophysicist Dr. Jane Foster (*Thor*), the ruthless and highly-skilled fighter Gamora (*Guardians of the Galaxy*), the powerful Scarlet Witch (*Avengers: Age of Ultron*), and all-around asskicker Janet van Dyne/Pym, aka The Wasp (*Ant Man and The Wasp*). Audiences have also seen female characters excel in traditionally male roles: Pepper Potts becomes chief executive Officer of Stark Industries (*Iron Man 2*), Shuri is a technological genius in the Kingdom of Wakanda, far surpassing the technological capabilities of Tony Stark and Bruce Banner (*Black Panther*), Valkyrie is an elite Asgardian warrior and ruler of New Asgard (*Thor: Ragnorak*), and General Okoye is the head of Wakanda's Dora Milaje, an elite group of female special forces (*Black Panther*). Yet in all these instances, as powerful as these female characters are, they remain in supporting roles to their male counterparts.

Marvel Studios' Executive Vice President of Production, Victoria Alonso—who helped produce record-breaking films *Black Panther* and *Captain Marvel*—said that while it took her fourteen years to achieve the number of female superheroes on screen today, women are indeed the future of Hollywood. Alonso promises even more MCU diversity and inclusion in the future. "I can tell you we are actively working on making our universe as diverse and inclusive as we can. Be patient with us. We have a lot coming in the future."[12]

Reviewing *Captain Marvel*

Despite box office success, there are challenges surrounding female superhero films, namely claims that Hollywood is cramming feminist agendas down movie-goers' throats and the on-going struggle to prove both relevance and worthiness in a male-dominated genre. The challenges seem particularly daunting in a time when user-generated content online can change the narrative with a few simple edits. One anonymous fan, for example, went to such lengths as to edit a pirated version of 2019's *Avengers: Endgame* to de-feminize the movie, including the complete removal of *Captain Marvel*'s Carol Danvers and scenes where women rescue male superheroes.[13]

Captain Marvel was widely hailed by critics as a spectacular feminist feat.[14] Noting at a 2018 'Women in Film' event that the majority of top box office movie reviews were written by "white dudes,"[15] Larson worked to increase access to diverse journalists—namely women—during *Captain Marvel*'s press tour leading up to the film's release.[16] This outspokenness was unfortunately perceived by anti-feminists as a proclamation that white men weren't welcome at the theater. Twitter user @iheartmindy, for example, tweeted:

> Instead of seeing Captain Marvel and it's man hating lead actress this weekend, see Alita: Battle Angel instead. It stars a strong female lead without all the SJW bullsh*t. #alitachallenge[17]

Hordes of online trolls—frustrated with what they perceived as Hollywood's attempts to push social justice movements—took to social media and review sites to profess their anger about *Captain Marvel*'s feminist propaganda. Reviewers lamented that Larson was too politically correct and forced diversity on audiences. Reviewers pointed out that she didn't smile enough, her character was overpowered, she was too arrogant, she was too cocky, and she was just plain boring.[18]

In response to the overwhelming negative reviews, review aggregator Rotten Tomatoes took steps in February 2019 to disable the comment function prior to a movie's release to keep trolls from "review bombing" films.[19] Three months after *Captain Marvel's* release, Rotten Tomatoes announced audience scores would also begin featuring "verified" ratings and reviews from users who had already purchased tickets to the movie.[20] YouTube, on the other hand, combatted critical video rants by changing its search algorithm in March 2019 to prioritize videos from more authoritative sources—such as news outlets—over non-constructive individual creator videos.[21]

Despite criticisms, the first female-led MCU film was still a groundbreaker. Carol Danvers doesn't require a love interest to propel her narrative forward; self-discovery and acts of heroism are masterfully undertaken without the assistance of a male character. Rather than featuring a romantic relationship for its lead, Marvel president Kevin Feige explained that *Captain Marvel* was instead "about Carol finding herself and growing and making mistakes and being bolstered up by her female mentors and female friends."[22] The film relishes strong female characters who truly believe in and support their heroine. Actress Lashana Lynch, who plays Danvers' best friend and fellow pilot Maria Rambeau, said "we've moved past that moment in the culture where one woman in every film represents female strength. We've come far enough to show women supporting each other."[23]

Branding Female Superheroes

Where Marvel succeeded on the big screen in its evolving representations of women, it failed to fully elevate female characters in other areas of its brand. Disney's acquisition of Marvel Entertainment in 2009 opened up a previously unavailable demographic—boys from their preteen years into young adulthood. Bringing in characters like Iron Man, Captain America, Thor, and The Hulk expanded Disney's consumer product audience, and that is where it chose to focus its attention. The introduction of Ant-Man to the MCU in 2015, for example, saw its first toy figurine released seven months prior to the movie opening in theaters. Conversely, it took two years after her on-screen introduction in 2010 for Black Widow to get an action figure. The release of *Avengers: Age of Ultron* in 2015 yielded similar results, where both Black Widow and Scarlet Witch were missing from action figure playsets.[24] And so ensued the fan-led social media hashtags #WheresNatasha, #WhereIsBlackWidow, and #IncludeTheGirls, giving voice to scores of disappointed women wondering when Disney would finally wake up and include female characters in its merchandising.[25] Fellow cast member Mark Ruffalo, who plays The Hulk, even tweeted "@Marvel we need more #BlackWidow merchandise for my daughters and nieces. Pretty please."[26]

Shortly after the release of *Guardians of the Galaxy* two years later, frustrated parents started a #WheresGamora hashtag.[27] The omission of Gamora from Guardians merchandise was particularly confounding since *Guardians of the Galaxy* movie-going audiences were 44 percent female—the largest share of female viewers for an MCU film at the time.[28] Like Gamora, Shuri and the many women of Wakanda were also omitted

Figure 4.1. Actor Mark Ruffalo tweets his support for female inclusivity in Avengers merchandising.

Mark Ruffalo, Twitter. April 29, 2015, 8:16 PM. Accessed June 25, 2019. https://twitter.com/MarkRuffalo, https://twitter.com/MarkRuffalo/status/593222325325209601.

as full-size dolls when *Black Panther* first released in 2018, prompting one creative fan to craft her own Shuri by modifying a Princess Tiana doll.[29]

With the release of *Captain Marvel* in 2018, Disney finally positioned itself to properly engage its forgotten female demographic. Three months prior to *Captain Marvel's* release, Hasbro launched a dedicated line of character toys featuring the mighty cosmic superhero so little girls could finally "imagine suiting up to protect the universe!"[30] The launch of *Captain Marvel* merchandise cleared up any misconception that girl toys and other female character merchandise do not sell.

LUCASFILM

For many years George Lucas, former owner and creator of Lucasfilm, had insisted that *Star Wars* was over as a film series.[31] But that all changed in October 2012, when Lucasfilm, the home of *Star Wars* and *Indiana Jones*, joined Marvel Entertainment, Pixar, and The Muppets under the Disney Corporation in a 4.05 billion-dollar deal.[32]

Disney aimed to broaden *Star Wars'* horizons, introducing strong female leads and a more diverse cast. In more recent years the iconic series has been criticized for its patriarchal ideologies and lack of character diversity.[33] The first installment in the *Star Wars* sequel trilogy featured its first female-led film, *The Force Awakens* directed by J.J. Abrams in 2015, and grossed over $2 billion in box office revenue worldwide.[34] In comparison, the first *Star Wars* film in the original trilogy, *A New Hope* (1977), earned $775 million worldwide.[35]

In addition to worldwide box office numbers, there are other contextual variables to consider. Abrams' film broke a number of other box office records. The movie became the first to cross the $100 million threshold of advanced ticket sales in one day boasting $120 million and beating the $91 million record previously set by the final Harry Potter movie. Furthermore, *The Force Awakens* topped the former, highest-grossing movie of all time in domestic revenue, 2009's *Avatar* ($760 million).[36] Those records spoke to both the anticipation and global interest in the reboot.

Looking broadly at the most recent series of films, Disney's sequel trilogy crushed George Lucas' original films at the box office. *The Last Jedi* (2017) and *Rogue One: A Star Wars Story* (2016) introduced brand new characters, including two lead females—Rey and Jyn Erso—and garnered over $1 billion in profits globally.

Disney's *Solo: A Star Wars Story* (2018) had one of the worst performances for any *Star Wars* movie, earning just $392 million worldwide. It's only triumph: outperforming the animated feature, *The Clone Wars* (2008).[37] Ironically, although racially diverse in characters, *Solo* is the only film post-Disney that did not include a major female lead. In fact, the one female character featured, Qi'ra (portrayed by actress Emilia Clarke), reverts back to the stereotypical gender role of a female love interest, supporting the development of Han Solo's character.

As of 2018, Disney's latest four *Star Wars* films have grossed more than $4.8 billion at the box office worldwide.[38] In comparison, the seven *Star Wars* films produced pre-Disney, grossed $4.4 billion at the box office worldwide.[39] This profitable *Star Wars* rebrand, featuring powerful female protagonists, has occurred under the leadership of a prominent Hollywood woman, Kathleen Kennedy.

Kennedy's Galactic Guidance

In 2012, eight-time Academy Award nominee for Best Picture as a producer, Kathleen Kennedy, expanded her seat as a long-time successful producer to succeed George Lucas as president of Lucasfilm. Later that year, Disney acquired Lucasfilm, and since then Kennedy has executive produced every project.[40]

Kennedy, who began her movie production career as Steven Spielberg's assistant, has now had her hand in more than sixty feature films totaling $11 billion in box-office receipts and earned more than one hundred Oscar nominations. In a 2013 *USA Today* interview, Kennedy noted: "The demographics within our business don't reflect society, and they certainly don't reflect the audience. . . . I will tell you that most of my meetings are in rooms with white males."[41]

Kennedy's vision for diversity and inclusion efforts were also criticized by some aspects of the *Star Wars'* fandom. For instance, on social media, critical online commentary exploded with anti–Kathleen Kennedy language, including the Twitter hashtag #FireKathleenKennedy. One tweet with this hashtag as a bookend shared an image that stated, "That is the problem with [the] 'Girl Power' thing, they want to take what men built. Can't they just build something?"[42] Another tweet by the same anti-fan stated: "#firekathleenkennedy her feminism is more important to her than a whole fictional universe that has been developed over years. . . . Her feminism has no place in *Star Wars!*"[43] The hashtag #BoycottStarWarsVII ignited in response to the release of *The Force Awakens* in 2015, fueled by an ugly dislike with the new stars' diversity in both gender and race.[44] Additionally, another hashtag #MakeStarWarsGreatAgain was propagated around *The Last Jedi*'s release, homologous to President Trump's controversial slogan, "Make America Great Again."

Notwithstanding the dark corners of the Internet, Kennedy's *Star Wars* empire has moved the needle on gender representations. In *Episode IV: A New Hope*, the original 1977 movie, women (including female robots and aliens) received just 15 percent of the film's screen time.[45] Women's screen time rose sluggishly under ownership of George Lucas, but capped at 23 percent in *Return of the Jedi* (1983). Conversely, in the latest Disney installments, women's screen time in *The Force Awakens* (2015) rose to 37 percent, stayed steady at 35 percent in *Rogue One* (2016), and peaked in *The Last Jedi* (2017), where women received 43 percent of film screen time. To put this further into perspective, an edited version dubbed "The Chauvinist Cut" removed every scene featuring female characters in a positive light within *The Last Jedi*, ultimately cutting the 152-minute film down to just 46 minutes.[46]

Additionally, *The Force Awakens* and *The Last Jedi* feature the franchise's first female protagonist, Rey, and its first non-white female lead, Rose (Kelly Marie Tran). In a modern take, an elderly Luke Skywalker now plans on leaving the Jedi order in the hands of Rey, a young woman. But, beyond ratios and story lines, most importantly, female characters both old (Princess Leia) and new (Rey and Rose) are expanding their gender roles in this sequel saga.

The Evolution of the Sexualized Princess Leia

Princess Leia Organa (portrayed by actress Carrie Fisher) has gained both figurative and literal layers since her iconic gold bikini scene, ranking proudly as General Leia in the last two Disney additions to the saga. However, when keyword searching "Princess Leia" in Google, after "costume" and "hair," still returns "gold bikini" and "slave costume." Princess Leia's bikini also merits its own Wikipedia page.[47]

In fact, in a 1978 review of contemporary media, Princess Leia, despite her spunkiness, was still considered the traditional damsel in distress.[48] Captured by Darth Vader in the beginning of *A New Hope*, Princess Leia provides the motivation for Ben Kenobi's return and Luke Skywalker's rescue mission. Although Leia takes a few shots from a laser gun, she is dependent on her male rescuers. The only action the Princess initiates during her rescue nearly gets them killed in a galactic garbage compactor. Despite being a powerful member of the Imperial Senate, and a spy for the Rebel Alliance, Leia's most memorable line comes as a billowing holographic image and cements her classic princess persona. Throughout the film, Princess Leia desperately pleads on repeat, "Help me, Obi-Wan Kenobi. You are my only hope."[49]

Under Kennedy's helm, as the Force was re-awakened, so has the princess' heroine potential. General Leia is now the leader of the Resistance in the new female-focused installment of the saga. Shortly before Carrie Fisher's death,[50] she completed the filming for her role in *The Last Jedi*, where she was depicted heroically leading the Resistance flagship, the

Raddus. When she and crew were expelled into space and attacked by the First Order, she used the Force to pull herself back to the ship in the nick of time. This time with impeccable aim and no garbage compactors present, General Leia shot and stunned Poe Dameron, who mutinied against her successor, Vice Admiral Holdo (portrayed by actress Laura Dern).

Rey: A New Hope

Seemingly, the obverse from royalty, Rey (portrayed by actress Daisy Ridley), the female main character in *The Force Awakens* and *The Last Jedi*, is a scavenger orphan. Rey's first introduction on-screen depicts her in ragged clothes, going through the motions of her labor-intensive foraging and pawning on the sandy and desolate planet, Jakku. Soon after the "routine" day begins, Rey bravely rescues the astromech droid BB-8. Then while being attacked by First Order troops, Rey saves runaway Stormtrooper Finn and valiantly steals and pilots the *Millennium Falcon* to escape. Later, she saves Finn again as dangerous space villains threaten the *Falcon*. Fittingly, Rey is described by screenwriter Michael Arndt as a "loner, hothead, gear-head, badass."[51] In true heroine form, Rey rescues a droid and a dude in distress—twice!

Yet, *Star Wars* anti-fandom have chosen fewer kind adjectives to describe Rey. Due to her powerful Force capabilities with limited training, Rey is labeled a "Mary Sue," a term that describes a character who is almost always female and who everybody loves for doing everything right. Most of this anti-fandom are online trolls offering their input primarily via social media, utilizing Twitter hashtags and private Star Wars Facebook groups to pose their discontent. In other words, anti-fandom diminishes Rey for being "too talented."[52] However, the concept of training or lack thereof was not questioned among the fandom when Luke blew up the Death Star in *A New Hope* prior to any formal Jedi teaching.

SOCIAL MEDIA STRIKES BACK

#WheresRey

With her role in the franchise, across social media platforms, fans responded to the noticeable lack of merchandise featuring Rey with the hashtag #WheresRey.[53] For example, one image that circulated on Twitter during the #WheresRey campaign was the Hasbro box set of six action figures featuring only the franchise's new male characters (Finn, Poe Dameron, and Kylo Ren) next to fan-favorite Chewbacca, and an anonymous stormtrooper and fighter pilot.

Richard Gottlieb, from Global Toy Experts, attributed this to the toy industry's belief that "a boy will not go to a 'girl' movie and that if you put a girl in a boy's toy, boys will not buy it."[54] This argument for the male-focused action figure is further diminished when learning Rey was yet again forgotten in Hasbro's monopoly set, a game trademarked as "fun for the entire family."[55] Players can now request a separate Rey piece through Hasbro's customer service free of charge.

One letter from eight-year-old fan Annie Rose from Illinois demanded answers from Hasbro and went viral on her mother's Twitter:

> Dear Hasbro, how could you leave out Rey!? She belongs in Star Wars Monopoly and all the other Star Wars games! Without her, THERE IS NO FORCE AWAKENS! It awakens in her and without her, the bad guys would have won! Besides, boys and girls need to see women can be as strong as men! Girls matter! Boy or girl who cares? We are equal, all of us! Sincerely, Annie Rose.[56]

Paul Southern, the head of Disney's *Star Wars* licensing, told Bloomberg that the companies involved with licensing the toys did not foresee how popular Rey would be, despite her position as the main protagonist.[57] And when Rey and other female characters such as Captain Phasma, Rose, and General Leia, were depicted in merchandise, they were found mostly in dress-up sets aimed largely at girls.[58] Even as female roles evolve on screen, their merchandising seem sealed in gendered toy boxes.

THE BOTTOM LINE

This chapter examined how expanded representation of female characters at the box office helped transform the traditional princess role model into galaxy-saving heroines. More importantly, this chapter exposed that such a shift is fueled by substantial financial opportunity. Two franchises—Marvel and Star Wars—proved to be even more profitable when women were at the helm both as executives and as leads. Disney's cultural dominance offered an unprecedented opportunity for film to align with demand for the empowerment of women and girls across its many studios and platforms.

Women-led films, despite earning more money in recent years,[59] continue to suffer from more intense scrutiny. The "Ishtar" effect, wherein a female director takes a bigger career hit for a box office flop than male directors,[60] has contributed to social and financial exclusion of female directors and increased the rates of women dropping out of the film industry.[61] Actress Anne Hathaway noted that "a male director can have a series of failures and still get hired."[62] The stakes are higher as studio executives and industry critics carefully watch box office financials and fan response for the slightest hint of audience dissent. While there is still a vocal segment of society that pushes back against film diversity and inclusion, it is clearly not as strong as the demand for cinematic stories that are well-written, smartly cast, and gender diverse.

NOTES

1. "Marvel Cinematic Universe," Box Office Mojo, accessed June 8, 2019. https://www.boxofficemojo.com/franchises/chart/?view=main&id=avengers.htm&p=.html.

2. "Highest Grossing Film Franchises and Series Worldwide 2019," Statista, March 28, 2019, accessed June 8, 2019, https://www.statista.com/statistics/317408/highest-grossing-film-franchises-series/.

3. David Goldman, "Disney to Buy Marvel for $4 Billion," *CNNMoney*, August 31, 2009, accessed June 9, 2019, https://money.cnn.com/2009/08/31/news/companies/disney_marvel/.

4. Eliana Dockterman, "Marvel CEO: Female Superhero Movies Have Been 'A Disaster,'" *Time*, May 05, 2015, accessed June 9, 2019, https://time.com/3847432/marvel-ceo-leaked-email/.

5. Brandon Zachary, "Black Widow's MCU Role Has Changed in Response to Fans," *CBR*, April 23, 2019, accessed June 12, 2019, https://www.cbr.com/black-widow-mcu-role-change-fan-response/.

6. Marvel Studios poster of Scarlett Johanssen as Black Widow in *Iron Man 2*, accessed June 8, 2019, https://i.pinimg.com/236x/b9/72/f5/b972f5752f52e141d40222cec2218a84.jpg.

7. Danette Chavez, "Iron Man 2 Made the MCU Look More Viable, Even as It Botched the Introduction of a Key Player," *AV Club*, April 07, 2019, accessed June 12, 2019, https://film.avclub.com/iron-man-2-made-the-mcu-look-more-viable-even-as-it bo 1833779498.

8. "Wonder Woman (2017)," Box Office Mojo, accessed June 13, 2019, https://www.boxofficemojo.com/movies/?id=wonderwoman.

9. "Wonder Woman," Rotten Tomatoes, accessed June 13, 2019, https://www.rottentomatoes.com/m/wonder_woman_2017.

10. "MPAA Report 2018: Women Represent 51% of Moviegoers, 47% of Ticket Buyers," April 10, 2019, accessed June 30, 2019, https://womenandhollywood.com/mpaa-report-2018-women-represent-51-of-moviegoers-47-of-ticket-buyers/.

11. "Marvel Cinematic Universe," Box Office Mojo, accessed June 30, 2019. https://www.boxofficemojo.com/franchises/chart/?view=main&id=avengers.htm&p=.html.

12. Cameron Bonomolo, "Marvel Studios Promises More Diversity and Inclusivity in Phase 4 and Beyond," Marvel. June 07, 2019, accessed June 21, 2019. https://comicbook.com/marvel/2019/06/05/marvel-studios-more-diversity-inclusivity-lgbtq-phase-4-beyond-victoria-alonso/.

13. Neda Ulaby, "'Avengers,' but Make It without Women, or Men Hugging, or Levity in General," *NPR*, June 18, 2019, accessed June 23, 2019, https://www.npr.org/2019/06/18/733479265/avengers-but-make-it-without-women-or-men-hugging-or-levity-in-general.

14. Dano Nissen, "'Captain Marvel' Reviews: What the Critics Are Saying." *Variety*, March 08, 2019, accessed July 13, 2019, https://variety.com/2019/film/news/captain-marvel-reviews-roundup-critics-1203155558/.

15. Hunter Harris, "Brie Larson Calls for More Inclusive Film Criticism," *Vulture*, June 14, 2018, accessed July 12, 2019, https://www.vulture.com/2018/06/brie-larson-calls-for-more-inclusive-film-criticism.html.

16. Keah Brown, "Brie Larson on Superheroes, Success and Her Hollywood Sisterhood," *Marie Claire*, February 07, 2019, accessed July 12, 2019, https://www.marieclaire.co.uk/entertainment/tv-and-film/brie-larson-641750.

17. Mindy Robinson, "Instead of Seeing Captain Marvel and It's Man Hating Lead Actress This Weekend, See Alita: Battle Angel Instead. It Stars a Strong Female without All the SJW Bullsh*t. #alitachallenge Https://t.co/hMRofc3R4H," Twitter, March 04, 2019, accessed July 13, 2019, https://twitter.com/iheartmindy/status/1102641283317678081.

18. "Captain Marvel–Movie Reviews," Rotten Tomatoes, accessed June 23, 2019, https://www.rottentomatoes.com/m/captain_marvel/reviews?type=user.

19. Ibid.

20. "We're Introducing Verified Ratings and Reviews to Help You Make Your Viewing Decisions," Rotten Tomatoes Movie and TV News Were Introducing Verified Ratings and Reviews to Help You Make Your Viewing Decisions Comments, May 23, 2019, accessed July 16, 2019, https://editorial.rottentomatoes.com/article/introducing-verified-audience-score/.

21. Julia Alexander, "YouTube's 'Brie Larson' Search Result Shift Shows How YouTube Could Fight Trolls," The Verge, March 08, 2019, accessed June 24, 2019. https://www.theverge.com/2019/3/8/18255265/brie-larson-youtube-captain-marvel-mcu-algorithm-review-bomb-trolls.

22. J.K. Schmidt, "Kevin Feige Explains Why 'Captain Marvel' Did Not Have a Love Interest," April 03, 2019, accessed July 12, 2019, https://comicbook.com/marvel/2019/03/25/kevin-feige-explains-why-captain-marvel-did-not-have-a-love-inte/.

23. Eliana Dockterman, "Captain Marvel Is More Than Her Gender, Brie Larson Says," *Time*, March 04, 2019, accessed July 13, 2019, https://time.com/5543360/captain-marvel-brie-larson/.

24. James Whitbrook, "Marvel Has a Serious Problem Merchandising Its Female Characters," Io9, December 16, 2015, accessed June 25, 2019, https://io9.gizmodo.com/marvel-has-a-serious-problem-merchandising-its-female-c-1682014327.

25. Victoria McNally, "Why Women Get Left Off of Superhero Merch—And How It's Changing for the Better," *MTV News*, May 04, 2015, accessed June 25, 2019, http://www.mtv.com/news/2146742/black-widow-merch.

26. Mark Ruffalo, Twitter. April 29, 2015, 8:16 PM. Accessed June 25, 2019. https://twitter.com/MarkRuffalo, https://twitter.com/MarkRuffalo/status/593222325325209601.

27. Emma Waverman, "It's Ridiculous That in 2015 We Need #IncludeThe-Girls," Today's Parent, March 29, 2017, accessed June 25, 2019, https://www.todaysparent.com/blogs/its-ridiculous-that-in-2015-we-need-includethegirls/.

28. "Guardians of the Galaxy Had Highest Percentage of Female Viewers of Any Marvel Studios Movie," Comicbook.com, September 01, 2016, accessed June 25, 2019, https://comicbook.com/blog/2014/08/04/guardians-of-the-galaxy-had-highest-percentage-of-female-viewers/.

29. Kendall Ashley, "A Mom Transformed a Barbie into an Amazing Shuri Doll, and #goals," Yahoo! March 16, 2018, accessed July 14, 2019. https://www.yahoo.com/lifestyle/mom-transformed-barbie-amazing-shuri-190025493.html.

30. Taimur Dar, "Hasbro's Captain Marvel Products Show That Women Can Sell Toys," The Beat, December 5, 2018, accessed June 26, 2019, https://www.comicsbeat.com/hasbros-captain-marvel-products-show-that-women-can-sell-toys/.

31. William Proctor, "Holy Crap, More Star Wars! More Star Wars? What If They're Crap?": Disney, Lucasfilm and Star Wars Online Fandom in the 21st Century,'" *Participations* 10, no. 1 (2013): 198–224.

32. Ben Quinn, "Disney to Buy Star Wars Production Company Lucasfilm for $4bn," *The Guardian*, October 31, 2012, accessed July 09, 2019, https://www.theguardian.com/film/2012/oct/30/disney-lucasfilm-star-wars-deal.

33. Kathleen Ellis, "New World, Old Habits: Patriarchal Ideology in Star Wars: A New Hope," *Australian Screen Education Online* 30 (2002): 135.

34. "Star Wars," Box Office Mojo, accessed June 28, 2019, https://www.boxofficemojo.com/franchises/chart/?id=starwars.htm.

35. "Star Wars (1977)," Box Office Mojo, accessed June 28, 2019, https://www.boxofficemojo.com/movies/?id=starwars4.htm.

36. Henry Barnes, "Star Wars: The Force Awakens Becomes Highest-Grossing Film of All Time in US," *The Guardian*, January 06, 2016, accessed June 19, 2019, https://www.theguardian.com/film/2016/jan/06/star-wars-the-force-awakens-becomes-highest-grossing-film-of-all-time-in-us.

37. Mat Elfring, "Every Star Wars Movie Ranked by Box Office Gross," GameSpot, June 20, 2018, accessed June 19, 2019, https://www.gamespot.com/gallery/every-star-wars-movie-ranked-by-box-office-gross/2900-1614/9/.

38. Sarah Whitten, "Disney Bought Lucasfilm Six Years Ago Today and Has Already Recouped Its $4 Billion Investment," *CNBC*, October 30, 2018, accessed June 19, 2019, https://www.cnbc.com/2018/10/30/six-years-after-buying-lucasfilm-disney-has-recouped-its-investment.html.

39. "Box Office History for Star Wars Movies," The Numbers–Where Data and Movies Meet, accessed July 09, 2019, https://www.the-numbers.com/movies/franchise/Star-Wars#tab=summary.

40. Matt Donnelly, "Kathleen Kennedy Extends Lucasfilm Deal through 2021," *Variety*, September 29, 2018, https://variety.com/2018/film/news/kathleen-kennedy-lucasfilm-deal-2021-1202961551/.

41. Marco R. Della Cava, "Lucasfilm's Kathleen Kennedy Has Produced Quite a Career," *USA Today*, June 06, 2013, accessed June 22, 2019, https://www.usatoday.com/story/life/movies/2013/06/05/kathleen-kennedy-innovators-and-icons-lucasfilm/2164285/.

42. Aidox, Twitter, December 29, 2018, 3:23 p.m. accessed July 10. 2019, https://twitter.com/aidoxik/status/1079125777071947777?s=20.

43. Aidox, Twitter, December 29, 2018, 2:54 p.m., accessed July 10. 2019, https://twitter.com/aidoxik/status/1079118419407134721?s=20.

44. Genevieve, Koski, "How 2 Racist Trolls Got a Ridiculous Star Wars Boycott Trending on Twitter," *Vox*, October 19, 2015, accessed June 20, 2019, https://www.vox.com/2015/10/19/9571309/star-wars-boycott.

45. "New Study Shows Just How Rarely Women Appear in Star Wars," *The Telegraph*, June 01, 2018, accessed June 13, 2019, https://www.telegraph.co.uk/films/2018/06/01/new-study-shows-just-rarely-women-appear-star-wars/.

46. "Star Wars Director and Cast Mock Fan Who Created 'De-feminized' Edit of The Last Jedi," *The Telegraph*, January 17, 2018, https://www.telegraph.co.uk/films/2018/01/17/star-wars-director-cast-mock-fan-created-de-feminized-edit-last/.

47. "Princess Leia's Bikini," Wikipedia, May 26, 2019, accessed June 15, 2019. https://en.wikipedia.org/wiki/Princess_Leia's_bikini.

48. Dan Rubey, "Star Wars Not So Long Ago, Not So Far Away," August 1978, accessed June 15, 2019, http://www.ejumpcut.org/archive/onlinessays/JC18folder/starWars.html.

49. *Star Wars IV: A New Hope*, directed by George Lucas, performed by Mark Hamill, Carrie Fisher, and Harrison Ford, Lucasfilm Ltd, May 25, 1977, film.

50. Andrew Blankenstein, "'Star Wars' Actress Carrie Fisher Has Died at 60," *NBCNews.com*, 2016, accessed July 10, 2019, https://www.nbcnews.com/news/us-news/star-wars-actress-carrie-fisher-dies-60-after-suffering-heart-n699641.

51. Phil Szostak, *The Art of Star Wars the Force Awakens* (New York: Harry N. Abrams Brooks, 2015).

52. Eric Kain, "No, Rey from 'Star Wars: The Last Jedi' Is Still Not a 'Mary Sue,'" *Forbes*, December 21, 2017, accessed June 28, 2019, https://www.forbes.com/sites/erikkain/2017/12/21/no-rey-from-star-wars-the-last-jedi-is-still-not-a-mary-sue/#4833ed594500.

53. Suzanne Scott, "#Wheresrey?: Toys, Spoilers, and the Gender Politics of Franchise Paratexts," *Critical Studies in Media Communication* 34, no. 2 (2017): 138–147.

54. Beatrice Verhoeven, "'Star Wars' Female Action Figures Are 'Flying Off Shelves' Despite #WheresRey Outrage, Retailers Say," December 11, 2015, accessed June 18, 2019, https://www.thewrap.com/star-wars-female-action-figures-are-flying-off-shelves-despite-wheresrey-outrage-retailers-say/.

55. Daniel Victor, "Where's Rey? Despite Uproar, Hasbro Makes Her Monopoly Game Piece Hard to Find," *The New York Times*, July 17, 2017, accessed June 28, 2019, https://www.nytimes.com/2017/07/17/business/star-wars-monopoly-rey.html.

56. Carrie Goldman, Twitter post, January 4, 2016, 2:40 p.m., https://twitter.com/CarrieMGoldman/status/684112303806111745.

57. Christopher Palmeri and Jeff Green, "'Star Wars' Toys Aren't Just for Boys Anymore as Rey Takes Over," Bloomberg.com, November 30, 2015, accessed June 18, 2019, https://www.bloomberg.com/news/articles/2015-11-30/-star-wars-toys-aren-t-just-for-boys-anymore-as-rey-takes-over.

58. Beatrice Verhoeven, "'Star Wars' Female Action Figures Are 'Flying Off Shelves' Despite #WheresRey Outrage, Retailers Say."

59. Cara Buckley, "Movies Starring Women Earn More Than Male-Led Films, Study Finds," *The New York Times*, The New York Times, 11 December 2018, www.nytimes.com/2018/12/11/movies/creative-artists-agency-study.html.

60. Rebecca Keegan, "'The 'Ishtar' Effect: When a Film Flops and Its Female Director Never Works Again," *Los Angeles Times*, November 06, 2015, accessed July 15, 2019, https://www.latimes.com/entertainment/movies/la-ca-mn-on-film-keegan-female-20151108-story.html.

61. Ibid.

62. Ibid.

BIBLIOGRAPHY

Aidox. Twitter. December 29, 2018 3:23 PM. Accessed July 10. 2019. https://twitter.com/aidoxik/status/1079125777071947777?s=20.

———. Twitter. December 29, 2018 2:54 PM. Accessed July 10. 2019. https://twitter.com/aidoxik/status/1079118419407134721?s=20.

Alexander, Julia. "YouTube's 'Brie Larson' Search Result Shift Shows How YouTube Could Fight Trolls." *The Verge*, March 08, 2019. Accessed June 24, 2019. https://www.theverge.com/2019/3/8/18255265/brie-larson-youtube-captain-marvel-mcu-algorithm-review-bomb-trolls.

Ashley, Kendall. "A Mom Transformed a Barbie into an Amazing Shuri Doll, and #goals." Yahoo!, March 16, 2018. Accessed July 14, 2019. https://www.yahoo.com/lifestyle/mom-transformed-barbie-amazing-shuri-190025493.html.

Barnes, Henry. "Star Wars: The Force Awakens Becomes Highest-Grossing Film of All Time in US." *The Guardian*, January 06, 2016. Accessed June 19, 2019. https://www.theguardian.com/film/2016/jan/06/star-wars-the-force-awakens-becomes-highest-grossing-film-of-all-time-in-us.

Blankenstein, Andrew. "'Star Wars' Actress Carrie Fisher Has Died at 60." NBC News.com, 2016. Accessed July 10, 2019. https://www.nbcnews.com/news/us-news/star-wars-actress-carrie-fisher-dies-60-after-suffering-heart-n699841.

Bonomolo, Cameron. "Marvel Studios Promises More Diversity and Inclusivity in Phase 4 and Beyond." Marvel, June 07, 2019. Accessed June 21, 2019. https://comicbook.com/marvel/2019/06/05/marvel-studios-more-diversity-inclusivity-lgbtq-phase-4-beyond-victoria-alonso/.

"Box Office History for Star Wars Movies." The Numbers–Where Data and Movies Meet. Accessed July 09, 2019. https://www.the-numbers.com/movies/franchise/Star-Wars#tab=summary.

Brown, Keah. "Brie Larson on Superheroes, Success and Her Hollywood Sisterhood." *Marie Claire*, February 07, 2019. Accessed July 12, 2019. https://www.marieclaire.co.uk/entertainment/tv-and-film/brie-larson-641750.

Buckley, Cara. "Movies Starring Women Earn More Than Male-Led Films, Study Finds." *The New York Times*, 11 December 2018. www.nytimes.com/2018/12/11/movies/creative-artists-agency-study.html.

"Captain Marvel–Movie Reviews." Rotten Tomatoes. Accessed June 23, 2019. https://www.rottentomatoes.com/m/captain_marvel/reviews?type=user.

Cava, Marco R. Della. "Lucasfilm's Kathleen Kennedy Has Produced Quite a Career." *USA Today*, June 06, 2013. Accessed June 22, 2019. https://www.usatoday.com/story/life/movies/2013/06/05/kathleen-kennedy-innovators-and-icons-lucasfilm/2164285/.

Chavez, Danette. "Iron Man 2 Made the MCU Look More Viable, Even as It Botched the Introduction of a Key Player." AV Club, April 07, 2019. Accessed June 12, 2019. https://film.avclub.com/iron-man-2-made-the-mcu-look-more-viable-even-as-it-bo-1833779498.

Dar, Taimur. "Hasbro's Captain Marvel Products Show That Women Can Sell Toys." The Beat, December 5, 2018. Accessed June 26, 2019. https://www.comicsbeat.com/hasbros-captain-marvel-products-show-that-women-can-sell-toys/.

Dockterman, Eliana. "Captain Marvel Is More Than Her Gender, Brie Larson Says." *Time*, March 04, 2019. Accessed July 13, 2019. https://time.com/5543360/captain-marvel-brie-larson/.

———. "Marvel CEO: Female Superhero Movies Have Been 'A Disaster.'" *Time*, May 5, 2015. Accessed June 9, 2019.https://time.com/3847432/marvel-ceo-leaked-email/.

Donnelly, Matt. "Kathleen Kennedy Extends Lucasfilm Deal through 2021." *Variety*, September 29, 2018. https://variety.com/2018/film/news/kathleen-kennedy-lucasfilm-deal-2021-1202961551/.

Elfring, Mat. "Every Star Wars Movie Ranked by Box Office Gross." GameSpot, June 20, 2018. Accessed June 19, 2019. https://www.gamespot.com/gallery/every-star-wars-movie-ranked-by-box-office-gross/2900-1614/9/.

Ellis, Kathleen. "New World, Old Habits: Patriarchal Ideology in Star Wars: A New Hope." *Australian Screen Education Online* 30 (2002): 135.

Goldman, Carrie. Twitter post, January 4, 2016, 2:40 p.m. https://twitter.com/CarrieMGoldman/status/684112303806111745.

Goldman, David. "Disney to Buy Marvel for $4 Billion." *CNNMoney*, August 31, 2009. Accessed June 9, 2019. https://money.cnn.com/2009/08/31/news/companies/disney_marvel/.

"Guardians of the Galaxy Had Highest Percentage of Female Viewers of Any Marvel Studios Movie." Comicbook.com, September 01, 2016. Accessed June 25, 2019. https://comicbook.com/blog/2014/08/04/guardians-of-the-galaxy-had-highest-percentage-of-female-viewers/.

Hailey, Caroline. "The Incredible Career, Fame and Fortune of Carrie Fisher." GOBankingRates, December 08, 2017. Accessed June 18, 2019. https://www.gobankingrates.com/net-worth/celebrities/carrie-fisher-net-worth/.

Harris, Hunter. "Brie Larson Calls for More Inclusive Film Criticism." *Vulture*, June 14, 2018. Accessed July 12, 2019. https://www.vulture.com/2018/06/brie-larson-calls-for-more-inclusive-film-criticism.html.

Hayek, Salma. Instagram. July 20, 2019. Accessed July 22, 2019. https://www.instagram.com/salmahayek/.

Hernandez, Patricia. "Marvel Gets First Woman of Color Director for The Eternals." The Verge, September 21, 2018. Accessed July 22, 2019. https://www.theverge.com/2018/9/21/17888042/the-eternals-director-marvel-chloe-zhao.

"Highest Grossing Film Franchises and Series Worldwide 2019 | Statistic." Statista, March 28, 2019. Accessed June 8, 2019. https://www.statista.com/statistics/317408/highest-grossing-film-franchises-series/.

Holmes, Adam. "Salma Hayek Reacts to Joining Marvel's Eternals in Gender-Swapped Role." Cinemablend, July 22, 2019. Accessed July 23, 2019. https://www.cinemablend.com/news/2476923/salma-hayek-reacts-to-joining-marvels-eternals-in-gender-swapped-role.

Kain, Erik. "No, Rey from 'Star Wars: The Last Jedi' Is Still Not a 'Mary Sue.'" *Forbes*, December 21, 2017. Accessed June 28, 2019. https://www.forbes.com/sites/erikkain/2017/12/21/no-rey-from-star-wars-the-last-jedi-is-still-not-a-mary-sue/#4833ed594500.

Keegan, Rebecca. "The 'Ishtar' Effect: When a Film Flops and Its Female Director Never Works Again." *Los Angeles Times*, November 06, 2015. Accessed July 15, 2019. https://www.latimes.com/entertainment/movies/la-ca-mn-on-film-keegan-female-20151108-story.html.

Knight, Rosie. "'Avengers: Endgame' Failed Scarlett Johansson's Black Widow." *Esquire*, April 26, 2019. Accessed July 15, 2019. https://www.esquire.com/entertainment/movies/a27274694/avengers-endgame-black-widow-death-marvel-failure/.

Koski, Genevieve. "How 2 Racist Trolls Got a Ridiculous Star Wars Boycott Trending on Twitter." *Vox*. October 19, 2015. Accessed June 20, 2019. https://www.vox.com/2015/10/19/9571309/star-wars-boycott.

Lincoln, Ross A. "J.J. Abrams Explains His 'Star Wars' 'Boys Thing' Comment." Deadline, December 07, 2015. Accessed June 18, 2019. http://deadline.com/2015/12/jj-abrams-explains-boys-thing-star-wars-commentmisunderstood-1201653533/.

Liptak, Andrew. "Future Marvel Projects Will Include the X-Men, Fantastic Four, and Captain Marvel 2." The Verge, July 20, 2019. Accessed July 22, 2019. https://www.theverge.com/2019/7/20/20702391/marvel-cinematic-universe-phase-5-x-men-mutants-fantastic-four-captain-marvel-2-black-panther.

Mandell, Andrea. "Early Reviews Cheer on 'Captain Marvel': 'It's Retro & Trippy, Mysterious & Dorky.'" *USA Today*, February 20, 2019. Accessed July 13, 2019. https://www.usatoday.com/story/life/movies/2019/02/20/captain-marvel-early-reviews-praise-brie-larson-superhero-movie/2924230002/.

"Marvel Cinematic Universe." Box Office Mojo. Accessed June 8, 2019. https://www.boxofficemojo.com/franchises/chart/?view=main&id=avengers.htm&p=.html.

"Marvel Studios Wants a Female-Led Superhero Film." ComingSoon.net, August 13, 2014. Accessed June 20, 2019. https://www.comingsoon.net/movies/news/108585-marvel-studios-wants-a-female-led-superhero-film.

McClintock, Pamela. "Box Office: 'Captain Marvel' Flies to Historic $153M in U.S., $455M Globally." *The Hollywood Reporter*, July 03, 2019. Accessed July 12, 2019. https://www.hollywoodreporter.com/heat-vision/box-office-captain-marvel-opens-historic-153m-us-455m-globally-1193585.

McNally, Victoria. "Why Women Get Left Off of Superhero Merch—And How It's Changing for the Better." *MTV News*, May 04, 2015. Accessed June 25, 2019. http://www.mtv.com/news/2146742/black-widow-merch.

Menta, Anna. "'Star Wars: The Last Jedi' Owes Its Box-Office Success to Women." *Newsweek*, March 05, 2018. Accessed June 22, 2019. https://www.newsweek.com/star-wars-last-jedi-female-fans-747611.

"MPAA Report 2018: Women Represent 51% of Moviegoers, 47% of Ticket Buyers." Women and Hollywood, April 10, 2019. Accessed June 30, 2019. https://womenandhollywood.com/mpaa-report-2018-women-represent-51-of-moviegoers-47-of-ticket-buyers/.

Nissen, Dano. "Brie Larson on Diversity in the Marvel Cinematic Universe: 'We Gotta Move Faster.'" *Variety*, April 26, 2019. Accessed July 13, 2019. https://variety.com/2019/film/news/brie-larson-marvel-diversity-representation-1203198196/.

———. "'Captain Marvel' Reviews: What the Critics Are Saying." *Variety*, March 08, 2019. Accessed July 13, 2019. https://variety.com/2019/film/news/captain-marvel-reviews-roundup-critics-1203155558/.

Palmeri, Christopher, and Jeff Green. "'Star Wars' Toys Aren't Just for Boys Anymore as Rey Takes Over." Bloomberg.com, November 30, 2015. Accessed June 18, 2019. https://www.bloomberg.com/news/articles/2015-11-30/-star-wars-toys-aren-t-just-for-boys-anymore-as-rey-takes-over.

"Phase Four." Marvel Cinematic Universe Wiki. Accessed July 21, 2019. https://marvelcinematicuniverse.fandom.com/wiki/Phase_Four.

Pollitt, Katha. "Hers; The Smurfette Principle." *The New York Times*, April 07, 1991. Accessed June 28, 2019. https://www.nytimes.com/1991/04/07/magazine/hers-the-smurfette-principle.html.

"Princess Leia's Bikini." Wikipedia, May 26, 2019. Accessed June 15, 2019. https://en.wikipedia.org/wiki/Princess_Leia's_bikini.

Proctor, William. "'"Holy crap, More Star Wars! More Star Wars? What If They're Crap?": Disney, Lucasfilm and Star Wars Online Fandom in the 21st Century.'" *Participations* 10, no. 1 (2013): 198–224.

Quinn, Ben. "Disney to Buy Star Wars Production Company Lucasfilm for $4bn." *The Guardian*, October 31, 2012. Accessed July 09, 2019. https://www.theguardian.com/film/2012/oct/30/disney-lucasfilm-star-wars-deal.

Robinson, Mindy. "Instead of Seeing Captain Marvel and It's Man Hating Lead Actress This Weekend, See Alita: Battle Angel Instead. It Stars a Strong Female without All the SJW Bullsh*t. #alitachallenge https://t.co/hMRofc3R4H." Twitter. March 04, 2019. Accessed July 13, 2019. https://twitter.com/iheartmindy/status/1102641283317678081.

Rubey, Dan. "Star Wars Not So Long Ago, Not So Far Away." August 1978. Accessed June 15, 2019. http://www.ejumpcut.org/archive/onlinessays/JC18folder/starWars.html.

Ruffalo, Mark. Twitter. April 29, 2015, 8:16 PM. Accessed June 25, 2019. https://twitter.com/MarkRuffalo.

Ryzik, Melena. "Ava DuVernay's Fiercely Feminine Vision for 'A Wrinkle in Time.'" *The New York Times*, March 1, 2018. www.nytimes.com/2018/03/01/movies/a-wrinkle-in-time-ava-duvernay-disney.html.

Sakoui, Anousha. "Trolls Targeted 'Captain Marvel,' but Disney Was Ready for Them." Bloomberg.com, March 6, 2019. Accessed June 23, 2019. https://www

.bloomberg.com/news/features/2019-03-06/-captain-marvel-hit-by-online-trolls-but-disney-was-ready.

Schmidt, J.K. "Kevin Feige Explains Why 'Captain Marvel' Did Not Have a Love Interest." April 03, 2019. Accessed July 12, 2019. https://comicbook.com/marvel/2019/03/25/kevin-feige-explains-why-captain-marvel-did-not-have-a-love-inte/.

Scott, Suzanne. "#Wheresrey?: Toys, Spoilers, and the Gender Politics of Franchise Paratexts." *Critical Studies in Media Communication* 34, no. 2 (2017): 138–147.

Smith, Neil. "Marvel Phase 4: A New Era For Diversity in Hollywood." *BBC News*, July 22, 2019. Accessed July 23, 2019. https://www.bbc.com/news/entertainment-arts-49070232.

Star Wars IV: A New Hope. Directed by George Lucas. Performed by Mark Hamill, Carrie Fisher, and Harrison Ford. Lucasfilm Ltd, May 25, 1977. Film.

"Star Wars." Box Office Mojo. Accessed June 28, 2019. https://www.boxofficemojo.com/franchises/chart/?id=starwars.htm.

"Star Wars (1977)." Box Office Mojo. Accessed June 28, 2019. https://www.boxofficemojo.com/movies/?id=starwars4.htm.

Star Wars. "Star Wars: The Rise of Skywalker—Teaser." YouTube. April 12, 2019. Accessed July 10, 2019. https://www.youtube.com/watch?v=adzYW5DZoWs.

Stedman, Alex. "'Star Wars: The Force Awakens' Merchandise to Hit Stores Sept. 4." *Variety*, May 03, 2015. Accessed July 01, 2019. https://variety.com/2015/film/news/star-wars-the-force-awakens-merchandise-release-sept-4-1201486363/.

Szostak, Phil. *The Art of Star Wars the Force Awakens*. New York: Harry N. Abrams Books, 2015.

Telegraph Reporters. "New Study Shows Just How Rarely Women Appear in Star Wars." *The Telegraph*, June 01, 2018. Accessed June 13, 2019. https://www.telegraph.co.uk/films/2018/06/01/new-study-shows-just-rarely-women-appear-star-wars/.

———. "Star Wars Director and Cast Mock Fan Who Created 'De-feminized' Edit of The Last Jedi." *The Telegraph*, January 17, 2018. https://www.telegraph.co.uk/films/2018/01/17/star-wars-director-cast-mock-fan-created-de-feminized-edit-last/.

"The Bechdel Test, About." Bechdel Test. Accessed July 10, 2019. http://bechdeltestfest.com/about/.

"The Superhero Diversity Problem." *Harvard Political Review* The Superhero Diversity Problem Comments. October 24, 2014. Accessed June 12, 2019. http://harvardpolitics.com/books-arts/superhero-diversity-problem/.

"Transcript: Donald Trump's Taped Comments about Women." *The New York Times*, October 08, 2016. Accessed June 20, 2019. https://www.nytimes.com/2016/10/08/us/donald-trump-tape-transcript.html.

Ulaby, Neda. "'Avengers,' but Make It Without Women, or Men Hugging, or Levity in General." NPR, June 18, 2019. Accessed June 23, 2019. https://www.npr.org/2019/06/18/733479265/avengers-but-make-it-without-women-or-men-hugging-or-levity-in-general.

Verhoeven, Beatrice. "'Star Wars' Female Action Figures Are 'Flying Off Shelves' Despite #WheresRey Outrage, Retailers Say." TheWrap, December 11, 2015.

Accessed June 22, 2019. https://www.thewrap.com/star-wars-female-action-figures-are-flying-off-shelves-despite-wheresrey-outrage-retailers-say/.

Victor, Daniel. "Where's Rey? Despite Uproar, Hasbro Makes Her Monopoly Game Piece Hard to Find." *The New York Times*, July 17, 2017. Accessed June 28, 2019. https://www.nytimes.com/2017/07/17/business/star-wars-monopoly-rey.html.

Waverman, Emma. "It's Ridiculous That in 2015 We Need #IncludeTheGirls." Today's Parent, March 29, 2017. Accessed June 25, 2019. https://www.todaysparent.com/blogs/its-ridiculous-that-in-2015-we-need-includethegirls/.

"We're Introducing Verified Ratings and Reviews to Help You Make Your Viewing Decisions." Rotten Tomatoes Movie and TV News Were Introducing Verified Ratings and Reviews to Help You Make Your Viewing Decisions Comments. May 23, 2019. Accessed July 16, 2019. https://editorial.rottentomatoes.com/article/introducing-verified-audience-score/.

Whitbrook, James. "Marvel Has a Serious Problem Merchandising Its Female Characters." Io9, December 16, 2015. Accessed June 25, 2019. https://io9.gizmodo.com/marvel-has-a-serious-problem-merchandising-its-female-c-1682014327.

Whitten, Sarah. "Disney Bought Lucasfilm Six Years Ago Today and Has Already Recouped Its $4 Billion Investment." *CNBC*, October 30, 2018. Accessed June 19, 2019. https://www.cnbc.com/2018/10/30/six-years-after-buying-lucasfilm-disney-has-recouped-its-investment.html.

———. "Disneyland Scores Permits to Build Microbrewery, Retail Shop and Meet-and-Greet Area at Marvel Park Expansion." *CNBC*, June 13, 2019. Accessed June 24, 2019. https://www.cnbc.com/2019/06/12/disneyland-scores-permits-to-build-marvel-inspired-theme-park-land.html.

"Wonder Woman (2017)." Box Office Mojo. Accessed June 13, 2019. https://www.boxofficemojo.com/movies/?id=wonderwoman.

"Wonder Woman." Rotten Tomatoes. Accessed June 13, 2019. https://www.rottentomatoes.com/m/wonder_woman_2017.

Zachary, Brandon. "Black Widow's MCU Role Has Changed in Response to Fans." CBR, April 23, 2019. Accessed June 12, 2019. https://www.cbr.com/black-widow-mcu-role-change-fan-response/.

5

✛

Pop, Hip-Hop, and the "Hamiltonization" of the Disney Soundtrack

Daron Roberts and Turon Nicholas

THE HAMILTONIZATION OF THE DISNEY SOUND

Acclaimed musical theater from *Pirates of Penzance, Phantom of the Opera* to *My Fair Lady*, to name a few,[1] were all scored in such a way that it called for a particular overall sound—in instrumentation and vocal technique that also impacted choreography. Many of the most celebrated works on Broadway and the West End set the standard for musicals in the modern era. They are considered canons.[2] These original works broadly stayed close to their musical predecessors: the opera and the operettas of historical periods.[3] With the exception of some popular musical influences in works like *West Side Story, Porgy and Bess*,[4] and *Oklahoma!*[5] few musicals placed genres like jazz, swing and even gospel as being central styles in their compositions. While musicals like *Jesus Christ Super Star*[6] included rock, hip-hop, gospel, and pop, rapping altogether, remained secondary and even marginalized.

Musicals had been dominated by mostly white, male composers, and their preferred genres were reflected in the style of music used for songwriting and scoring. Likewise, the preferred actors cast to perform such works were not always diverse, were classically trained vocalists, the choreographers were trained in either classical or contemporary dance, and the orchestras comprised of performers trained on classical instruments.[7]

Enter Lin-Manuel Miranda.[8] Before *Hamilton*, there was *In the Heights*, described as a hip-hop version of *Rent*[9] which featured a diverse cast, and a diverse subject matter. It allowed Miranda, who at the time was most known to wider audiences for rapping on *Sesame Street* and *The Electric Company*, to fully expand as a composer, actor, lyricist, playwright, and television producer.[10] *Hamilton* took Miranda's unique approach to musicals even further.[11] It has been credited for influencing a number of cultural milestones, as Miranda sought to weave American history, modern hip-hop culture, and politics surrounding race, into one unique experience.[12] What Miranda did with this work, theater critics and scholars noted was risky all while being groundbreaking.[13] Traditionally, musicals would be typically set in the classical genre. What is even more interesting is that the musical is about one of America's founding fathers—Alexander Hamilton,[14] a historical piece as it were, yet this musical is sung and rapped throughout.

Lin-Manuel Miranda's *Hamilton* is iconic as it shattered those defining markers of what is deemed acceptable genres and performances for musical theater. For the most part, the scoring of *Hamilton* is delivered by rapping. For example, in the eponymous song that introduces Alexander Hamilton in the musical; the entire dialogue is delivered by rapping, interludes of spoken word, with harmonic choral verses that vary from R&B to gospel and nineties hip-hop. In "My Shot" the performers vary the style of rapping with lyrical flow of many easily recognizable East and West Coast rappers. "'The Schuyler Sisters'" gives the feel of musical theater of old on some trio sections; however, Miranda adds hip-hop beats to the accompaniment, and the phrasing of some of the trio's bars seem out of a Destiny's Child or En Vogue nineties album. Likewise, to fully punctuate the delivery required for such performance techniques, both in singing, rapping, and also choreography, Hamilton's cast primarily consisted of non-white performers.

The record-breaking success of *Hamilton* catapulted Miranda's career, earning him Grammys, a Pulitzer Prize, an Emmy, a MacArthur Genius award, several Tony awards and an Oscar nomination.[15] However, what made Miranda mainstream was the fact that he touched something that seemed untouchable: U.S. founding history, something revered as a white, male's domain, but told it in the voices, style, and lens of the art forms of people of color. He therefore was able to appeal to all audiences, those curious about American history, and those who love hip-hop, and bring them to sit side by side, at the theater.

Miranda created *Hamilton* while working on songs for *Moana*.[16] Therefore, Disney had already tapped into Miranda's creativity long before *Hamilton* was in production. Given this timeline, Disney added Miranda to their composer pool for works that extended to future projects like *Mary Poppins Returns* and *The Little Mermaid* live-action. In these works, we see some of the influence of *Hamilton* coming through. Miranda shared in an interview with *Vulture* on connections between the three works:

Actually, musically, the three could not be more different but it's interesting because *Hamilton* and *Moana* do share some DNA. I got the job writing for *Moana* about seven and a half months before we started rehearsals off Broadway for *Hamilton*, so there was a period where I was sort of writing both at the same time. They're siblings. I do see them in a relationship to each other.[17]

Miranda has expanded his work with Disney taking on the voice of Gizmoduck for Disney XD channel's *DuckTales*. As a child, he was inspired by Disney citing *The Little Mermaid* as one of his all-time favorite movies and even *DuckTales* for shaping his lyrical flow as a rapper. At the 2019 San Diego Comic Con he revealed how the *Darkwing Duck* theme song alerted his attention to a triple internal rhyme.

> The Darkwing Duck theme song is so important to my development as a man, as an artist and as a songwriter, it's my first awareness of a triple internal rhyme was 'when there's trouble, you call DW,' which I went on to use in my Tony-winning musical "In the Heights," when Nina sings 'just me and the GWB, asking gee Nina, What'll you be?' You can trace a direct line from *Darkwing Duck* to my first show.[18]

As a child Disney shaped Miranda's life, now as an adult, he has now risen among Disney's musical ranks to influence the sound of the studio's content for his children and future generations of children. Like *Hamilton* marks several shifts for musical theater, in this chapter, we outline how Disney's sound in the last decade also mirrors a similar musical paradigm shift. We describe this shift as a "Hamiltonization,"[19] borrowing from Miranda's recent connections to changes in both musical spheres. We identify that "Hamiltonization" takes a traditional performance genre, once considered "canon" or standard, and recreates it with artforms that were originally excluded. In essence "Hamiltonization" is counter-hegemonic. By taking musical artforms of African Americans and global peoples of color, and applying them to works that were primarily performed by white talent and consumed by white and elite audiences, "Hamiltonization" elevates marginal artforms as being equal to canons.

SHIFTS IN DISNEY'S ORIGINAL SCORES

In looking at Disney's scoring choices in the last decade, we map how this area of musicals has been impacted by shifts in popular musical entertainment. In *The Princess and the Frog*, this 2009 release managed to capture the essence of African American music, particularly New Orleans jazz, whilst still incorporating some of the fundamental Western classical instrumentation frequently heard by Disney in the earlier years. Academy Award–winning composer Randy Newman composed, arranged, and conducted all but one work on this animated film where he traced the historical roots of jazz. R&B recording artist Ne-Yo wrote the track "Never Knew I Needed."[20] Genres such as rhythm & blues (R&B), swing, the blues, zydeco, and gospel were all evidently present and manipulated throughout this film. These genres created by African Americans embody their journey of struggle, ambition, love, perseverance, and innovation. The *Princess and the Frog* tells the story of a main character known as Tiana, who has her dreams to open a restaurant in New Orleans. Composer Randy Newman captures the vibrant music scene of New Orleans through his orchestration and authentic instrumentation by musicians from the city and region.

In one of the film's original songs "Gonna Take You There,"[21] zydeco music is heavily represented by the use of the accordion, the washboard, the triangle, and additional drums and rhythm guitars.[22] Despite the compact instrumentation, the counterpoint within the composition creates an exciting and energetic display of emotions. Contrasting from a thin texture of sound to a thick texture of full big band and rhythm section, the song "When We're Human"[23] allows the composer to experiment with elements of "Benny Goodman-esque" clarinet scoring within the jazz band setting. Throughout the arrangement there is a constant interaction between brass and woodwinds, with a two-beat swing pattern played by the drums, complimented by upright bass and rhythm guitar. The call and response between the lead vocalist and trumpet is heard throughout the song, creating this sort of improvised and spontaneous conversation.

Randy Newman's strong grasp on the elements of African American music is further acknowledged in the song "Dig a Little Deeper."[24] With this composition, he utilizes the power of the Pinnacle Gospel Choir, providing the background harmonies for Mama Odie (Jenifer Lewis) and Tiana (Anika Noni Rose). This arrangement takes the listener straight to church from the use of the organ, to the intricate harmonic movement, to the rich and robust choral accompaniment, and lastly to the empowering message behind the lyrics.

As the diversity of Disney soundtracks expands to include global sounds, the original scores of *Moana* (2016) shed a new light on what can be achieved. The concept of a purely South Pacific musical setting with hints of Broadway is what allowed for this film to hit the charts and open doors to a wider listening palette of the die-hard Disney fan. The collaborative efforts of Miranda, Mark Mancina, and Opetaia Foa'i resulted in a masterpiece that not only respected Polynesian culture, but made the public more aware of it. Although a huge majority of this film uses Broadway and pop performance approaches, the composers were still able to elicit the right atmosphere through orchestration, dynamics, and rhythmic punctuation.

For example, "We Know The Way"[25] is one of the songs that truly highlight the Polynesian culture. Driven by lots of native percussion, the introduction opens up for a combination of male war chant and full Pacific choir accompaniment, sitting on a bed of strings and guitars that show Foa'i's ability to score Western classical instruments while still creating a culturally appropriate experience. "You're Welcome"[26] featuring Dwayne Johnson is another song that shows the brilliance and understanding of characteristic qualities of various instruments by the composers. The use of percussion to give the authentic feel, along with the plucked strings, both compliment the *Sprechgesang* vocal technique where Dwayne Johnson alternates between speaking and singing. The first part of this song politely acknowledges the culture being represented, which then evolves into a full Broadway experience with accented horns, electric bass, drumset, and keyboard. Despite the extensive use of classical instruments and American styles of music, the full score contained Polynesian vocals and percussion, along with woodwinds made up of bamboo from the South Pacific. The idea of traditional music played a pivotal role in the success of *Moana,* and the writers and musicians were able to raise awareness of an old culture, though new for many Western audiences, through subtle musical elements.

Marvel Studios' *Black Panther* was praised as a cultural moment expressing Black excellence and resilience. The film's Swedish born composer/producer Ludwig Göransson, a hip-hop producer and collaborator for artists like Childish Gambino and Kendrick Lamar, created a score so deeply rooted in Africa and African American tradition that every note played was effectively executed. Consisting of a 132-piece Western classical orchestra, African percussionists, and a 40-person choir,[27] Göransson was able to capture the sounds that transcended each character of the film. These elements can be seen in the African talking drum being used to introduce T'Challa, or with the hip-hop infused sound effects to introduce Killmonger. "Wakanda"[28] is one of the songs that features Senegalese singer and guitarist Baaba Maal, mixed with sparse drums and legato strings behind the chant, making way for the triumphant horns playing a unison line that is used throughout the film to represent the stronghold that is Wakanda.

Another unique orchestration is on the song "Killmonger"[29] that begins with a plucked instrument coupled with the fula flute, which is then accompanied by the full string section of the orchestra. Additionally, Göransson uses the popular trap style of music to show the modernism/Americanism of the character. This aggressive nature and timbre of arrangement clearly describes the type of character that Killmonger was.

Despite the huge number of Western classical instruments used in the orchestra, the composer ensured each song on the track list had its own identity and purpose with strong roots in African culture.

These three films stand out because of how far-reaching their scoring were influenced by either indigenous or urban musical forms. However, elsewhere, across recent Disney works, signs of these scoring shifts are visible. Movies such as *Descendants* (2015), *Mary Poppins Returns* (2018), *Aladdin* (2019), and *The Lion King* (2019) have all contributed something refreshing to the Disney sound with amalgamations of hip-hop, rap, trap, spoken word, and Arabic sensibilities. This shift in Disney scores have been positively received by audiences, have impacted the overall state of film scoring for musicals, and most importantly have elevated overlooked cultures. The significance of these shifts should be noted, given that music in its films is something that Disney has taken seriously and nurtured over decades. It also means that more musicians of color are being elevated among the ranks of long-time Disney composers and songwriters, like Pharrell Williams teaming up with Hans Zimmer for *The Lion King* and Miranda and Foa'i with Mencina in *Moana*. The additions of new song-writing teams like husband-wife team Robert Lopez and Kristen Anderson-Lopez (*Frozen, Frozen II,* and *Coco*), and Benj Pasek and Justin Paul of Pasek and Paul (*Aladdin* and a live-action *Snow White and the Seven Dwarfs*), these latest composers and song-writers bring Disney original songs into the modern era with heavy influences of pop music today.

SHIFTS IN DISNEY'S ORIGINAL SONGS

Although the basic elements of musicianship have remained in terms of choral harmonies, dynamics, form, and melodic progressions, we see a shift for the new Disney movies in terms of tone color, rhythm, and texture, as they venture into the hip-hop and contemporary styles that reflects a new age of viewing audiences.

In 2019's *Aladdin,* the introduction of "Prince Ali"[30] begins with a classical S-A-T-B form of orchestration as a processional entrance sung with a reserved flair. A slow rhythmical "marche militaire" shapes the singing. But the accompaniment combines horns with syncopated Middle Eastern rhythms fused with a slight cross-over to Bollywood, with the music performed in binary style. Mostly monophonic in texture and joined eventually by a rich choral sound of male and female voices, with modulations on two occasions, the music combines some hip-hop. With Will Smith as lead vocals on this song, his hip-hop background fuses with musical theater across the number. Smith's opening bars have him singing in show-style, but as he proceeds to the chorus with background vocals, Smith deviates by filling the off-beat with hip-hop hype with "aha, aha" and "everybody help me out."[31] Hip-hop has an audience participatory, sometimes call and response, like the popular: "when I say hey, you say—ho," that the arrangers splice in to give Smith authenticity in the delivery of this remake. Smith brings "Big Willie Style" personality to the chorus work and invites audiences to proverbially "get up on their feet and dance." Then as the bridge slows, both accompaniment and singing supports Middle Eastern tempo and folk dance choreography that blends the classical arrangement of singing with regional interpretations.

However, it is in "Friend Like Me"[32] that the composers fully tap into Smith's background. He starts off this number with the call: "Let me show you what I'm working with."[33] The performance is a showstopper with some magnificent color painting in Smith's vocals with his ability to maintain his pitches while experimenting with syncopated beats and "scat" singing, while exploring the jazz idiom. This can be felt when he sings the bars "Mister, hey what's your name, what will your pleasure be" and "Life is your restaurant and I'm your maître D.'"[34] Smith has the ability to be very improvisational in his approach to marrying the lyrics to the beat, even when they were just spoken. Smith's former rap experience aids this musical presentation of the song. The pitching and tone-coloring work well because of his rap experience. His delivery of "Friend Like Me"[35] is monophonic in texture but progresses to polyphonic in sound since so many of the musical lines were performed simultaneously inclusive of chorus line. Similarly, in Black performance tradition, rap, mixes with harmony, and polyphonic texture that provide complicated harmonic arrangements that can be heard in any Black church. Then during the coda, Smith beatboxes, as he raps: "Can your friends do this" and raps "I'm the Genie of the lamp, I can sing, rap, dance, if you give me a chance."[36] Naturally the choreography includes a range from B-boy break dancing to crumping to match the vocal delivery.

Lin-Manuel Miranda also mixes musical theater and hip-hop in two Disney musicals. *Moana*'s "You're Welcome"[37] sung by Dwayne Johnson, uses the playful nature of the role of Maui to mix styles to bring out the cheeky sarcasm of the number. Further, Miranda infused rap into this selection, a style that married very nicely with Johnson's vocal abilities. It is rhythmically effective as one gets that "ad libitum" (at the performer's pleasure) feel throughout as he paces out of pocket with the accompaniment with "I see what's happening here"[38] that is synonymous with World Music. This selection which is presented in a ternary form (A-B-A; three sections) displays both homophonic and polyphonic texture as it embodies all the vocal features necessary to create intrigue. There is the call and response segment between him and Moana that aids in adding color and life to the musical offering. When Johnson delivers the bridge his rapping pace, word flow, rhyming pattern is distinctly Miranda. Miranda's intellectual lyrics and word placement shows up when Johnson raps: "What's a lesson, what is the take away. Don't mess with Maui when he's on the break away."[39]

Miranda is allowed to demonstrate his own rapping abilities when he plays the role of Jack, a cockney lamplighter in *Mary Poppins Returns* in his delivery in "A Cover Is Not the Book."[40] Lin-Manuel Miranda raps the entire second section of the song, further showing *Hamilton*'s reach. It clearly shows both Miranda's theater background mixed with his hip-hop background. In fact, in "Trip a Little Light Fantastic" the song's lyrics makes reference to a line made popular by known hip-hop artist 50 Cent—"take it to the shop, like a lollipop."[41]

For ballads, Disney musicals tug on viewer emotion and connection with lead characters, often song by princesses, as the story plot meets a turning point. In the current era, we can see how the singing style of these iconic Disney ballads are influenced by the vocal training of more diversely cast singers. In *Moana*, Miranda pens "How Far I'll Go"[42] for teen Hawaiian singer Auliʻi Cravalho, a blend of soul and pop"; that create a space for her to utilize vocal theatrics to some extent and in this case, which created a dramatic crescendo to reflect the song's emotion and intent. In *Aladdin*, Naomi Scott's musical influences have been steeped in Christian contemporary pop as she started her performing in her family's church. "Speechless"[43] is heavily influenced with contemporary adult pop style, a distinct song-writing trait of *The Greatest Showman*'s songwriters Pasek and Paul,[44] who mix pop with soul and contemporary soft rock. These styles are delivered by Scott with a glissando when she sings: "But I won't cry and I won't start to crumble. Whenever they try to shut me or cut me down," and "I won't be silent, you can't keep me quiet."[45]

While Beyoncé is known for a range of R&B, hip-hop, soul, and pop, she goes back to her church roots, where she started singing, and where most African American pop acts first performed. Her ballad "Spirit"[46] is resounding gospel backed by African choral harmonies. She shows the versatility, range, and tone color of many gospel singers who in the same bars can grovel as a raspy contralto and hit a full-voice octave belt. As she builds with the refrain "Rise up," the chorus line "Spirit, watch the heaven's open"[47] mirrors a traditional gospel chord progression from major to minor mode that elicits soulful harmony, with African American traditional church piano accompaniment. One of Beyoncé's strongest deliveries of the gospel genre can be heard in the phrasing and melodic delivery of the end of the bridge: "So go into that far out land, and be one with the great I am."[48] But what makes this song distinct is that it is a blend of an authentic African American vocal style with the unmistakable sound of African voices, which allows it to have a global Black diaspora feel, which fits a song for a film that features the continent.

Even for remixes of classical songs, Disney Channel's *Descendants* took the classic song "Be Our Guest" made popular from *The Beauty and the Beast*, and creates a hip pop remix. The song is delivered a capella, with the rhythmic harmonies coming together forming the backdrop for the hip-hop melodic line carried by lead actor Mitchell Hope. The background line also carries a "beat box" rhythm; that is vocal percussion, which is synonymous with the hip-hop genre as well. Hope and his castmates were required to show their versatility in vocal delivery by rapping "make it sing, sing, sing, make it dance, dance, dance," showing that even classically trained actors will need to perform across genres.

IMPACT ON MUSICALS GOING FORWARD

The evolution of the Disney sound, specifically, within the last decade, has ripple effects for the music industry going forward. Firstly, this shift benefits performers of color. Just as *Hamilton* featured a majority nonwhite cast, in *Aladdin* (2019), the casting was considered to be one of the most diverse in the studio's film history.[49] Similar casting choices were made for *Moana* and *The Lion King* (2019). When looking at both *Moana* and *The Lion King*, the musical sound brought Western performers of color together with well-acclaimed and popular artists from the regions native to those sounds. In fact, Beyoncé's collaboration with several Nigerian, Cameroon, and South African music stars on her *Lion King*–inspired album *The Lion King: The Gift* received global attention on social media.[50] Her song "Brown Skin Girl" that was a collaboration that featured Beyoncé, her daughter Blue Ivy, and Nigerian rapper Wizkid spawned viral videos of children on the African continent and around the world, embracing their Black beauty.[51] And although it was not the official soundtrack of the film, its connection to a successful Disney musical links that trans-Atlantic collaboration to the studio. Even though many of the African musicians were well known in their respective countries, through their work directly on these soundtrack albums, or affiliated soundtrack albums, they now gain global recognition.

Secondly, it means more lead roles for actors of color, and puts creatives of color in charge of these musicals. One of Disney's most daring choices was to cast a Black Little Mermaid. Halle Bailey, part of the R&B duo Chloe x Halle was cast more for the quality of her voice, than the color of her skin. In 2019, Will Smith is a Black rapping Genie, while the late Robin Williams was the first choice for Genie in 1992. Renowned opera singer Audra McDonald was cast as the wardrobe Madame Garderobe in 2017's

Beauty and the Beast and leads off singing "Tale as Old as Time." And a Puerto Rican American, Lin-Manuel Miranda, appears across the Atlantic in London as co-lead to Emily Blunt in *Mary Poppins Returns*. Disney executives make such daring choices, betting that consumers won't blink an eye, because it wants actors who can embody the styles its new songs require. More importantly, those Disney executives assigned to remake musicals or greenlight new ones, are increasingly diverse. For instance *Aladdin*'s executive producer was Taiwanese American Dan Lin, and the film hired African American Jamal Sims, who has also choreographed and acted in *The Descendants* films, to bring hip-hop moves to these recent works. Therefore, both in front and behind the camera, Disney has shown that in order to successfully pull off these shifts, it must put more diverse talents in positions of power.

Thirdly, the shelf life of Disney musicals doesn't end after the release of a feature film. Each musical spawns additional revenue streams for the company. For instance, a single musical feature film will then be turned into a Broadway production, like "Lion King the Musical" and "Aladdin the Musical." There are also traveling shows for smaller audiences under Disney on Ice, for example. Each musical can be adapted for community, college, and high school theater shows that carry royalties. At Disney Parks, there are parades and live performances that feature songs and arrangements from the original or Broadway shows. Lastly, the music itself can be partitioned off and sold as albums, or used in other films. For instance, in *The Lion King* (2019), Timon breaks into a rendition of "Be Our Guest" which is an original song from a sister Disney musical *Beauty and the Beast*. Disney can also incorporate its musicals or their songs into a Disney channel series or Disney+ content that can result in more voice actors being cast, and more songwriters and composers being hired to expand the collection of music beyond the original work. Therefore, diversifying the original work multiplies when you consider how Disney monetizes one film into a continuous stream of extended content, as described above. More diverse performers, songwriters, musicians, producers, and directors can be tapped beyond the original film.

Lastly, the broadening of the Disney soundtrack gives validity to chosen fields of study within the music fraternity. Courses specific to contemporary styles: rap, hip-hop, R&B, and even jazz, now can receive greater appreciation, acknowledgment, and even economic support. Traditionally, benefactors of the arts have supported opera houses and community theaters, but rarely do contemporary arts associations, particularly for younger performers, receive equal levels of investment. Now spoken word clubs, steel orchestras, jazz institutes, hip-hop workshops and the like which have been outlets for children and communities of color, can fight for more funding and support among the arts. In colleges and conservatories, research has shown that for the flexibility demanded across the contemporary commercial music styles, cross training is a healthy vocal approach, which supports an easy transition.[52] Students who seek to become professionals in film and on stage will perceive classes on hip-hop and World Music as being beneficial to their careers. Many musical theater teachers have little or no training in vocal pedagogy in styles that veer away from the classical technique. But professionals who teach these artforms can become more valuable for employment alongside classical teachers. Children around the world who enjoy the arts and who may not have seen themselves on stage now can imagine that rapping, gospel, and hip-hop have a place in a Hollywood musical. This allows the arts to become more inclusive at a young age, in schools, and in communities, to reflect all artforms, alongside classical tradition.

While this representation is important for future generations of artists, history has shown that the appropriation of marginalized cultures by mainstream economic entities has not always benefited those groups.[53] The use of African music in the first *Lion King* did not fully make many African artists become household names around the world. Whenever a native or marginalized group's cultural artforms are used in mainstream ways, it also opens those traditions up for performance and consumption by communities who may not understand or appreciate the roots of heritage or struggle attached to performance. The tension remains going forward on how to ensure that commercialization of marginalized music and culture reaps benefits for those artists and communities that these sounds come out from, and not only for the powerful companies who wish to capitalize from them.

NOTES

1. Leo N. Miletich, *Broadway's Prize-Winning Musicals: An Annotated Guide for Libraries and Audio Collectors* (Binghamton, NY: The Haworth Press, 1993).

2. Geoffrey Block, "The Broadway Canon from Show Boat to West Side Story and the European Operatic Ideal," *The Journal of Musicology* 11, no. 4 (1993): 525–544.

3. Larry Stempel, *Showtime: A History of the Broadway Musical Theater* (New York: W.W. Norton, 2010).

4. Eric Salzman, "Whither American Music Theater?" *The Musical Quarterly* 75, no. 4 (1991): 235–247.

5. Tim Carter, *Oklahoma!: The Making of An American Musical* (New Haven: Yale University Press, 2008.)

6. Ellis Nassour and Richard Broderick, *Rock Opera: The Creation of Jesus Christ Superstar, from Record Album to Broadway Show and Motion Picture* (New York: Hawthorn Books, 1973).

7. Elizabeth Titrington Craft, "'Is This What It Takes Just to Make It to Broadway?!': Marketing *In the Heights* in the Twenty-First Century," *Studies in Musical Theatre* 5, no. 1 (2011): 49–69.

8. Brian Eugenio Herrera, "Miranda's Manifesto," *Theater* 47, no. 2 (2017): 23–33.

9. Michael Gioia, "Lin-Manuel Miranda and Leslie Odom, Jr. Reveal How *Rent* Shaped History and *Hamilton*," *Playbill*, February 11, 2015, http://www.playbill.com/article/lin-manuel-miranda-and-leslie-odom-jr-reveal-how-rent-shaped-history-and-hamilton-com-341546.

10. Kristen Rajczak Nelson, *Lin-Manuel Miranda: From Broadway to the Big Screen* (Farmington Hills, MI: Greenhaven Publishing LLC, 2018).

11. Brian Eugenio Herrera, "Miranda's Manifesto."

12. Eric Piepenburg, "Why Hamilton Has Heat," *The New York Times*, August 12, 2015, https://www.nytimes.com/interactive/2015/08/06/theater/20150806-hamilton-broadway.html.

13. William Hogeland, Joanne B. Freeman, Lyra D. Monteiro, Leslie M. Harris, Catherine Allgor, Michael O'Malley, and David Waldstreicher, *Historians on Hamilton: How a Blockbuster Musical Is Restaging America's Past* (New Brunswick: Rutgers University Press, 2018); Marvin McAllister, "Toward a More Perfect Hamilton," *Journal of the Early Republic* 37, no. 2 (2017): 279–288; Lyra D. Monteiro, "Race-Conscious Casting and the Erasure of the Black Past in Lin-Manuel Miranda's Hamilton," *The Public Historian* 38, no. 1 (2016): 89–98.

14. Catherine E. Kelly, "Introduction: Lin-Manuel Miranda's Hamilton: An American Musical and the Early American Republic," *Journal of the Early Republic* 37, no. 2 (2017): 251–253.

15. Lin-Manuel Miranda Awards, Internet Movie Database, https://www.imdb.com/name/nm0592135/awards.

16. Kyle Buchanan and John Horn, "Lin-Manuel Miranda: 'Chase What Inspires You, and Finish It,'" *Vulture*, February 11, 2017, https://www.vulture.com/2017/02/lin-manuel-miranda-on-what-moana-shares-with-hamilton.html.

17. Kyle Buchanan and John Horn, "Lin-Manuel Miranda: 'Chase What Inspires You, and Finish It.'"

18. Entertainment Weekly, "'DuckTales Stars Lin-Manuel Miranda, Ben Schwatz & Cast, SDCC 2019," YouTube video, 8:54, posted July 22, 2019, https://youtu.be/Rmm6PFCdrZA.

19. In conceptualizing this chapter, the authors acknowledge the volume editor Shearon Roberts for coining and framing the term "Hamiltonization."

20. Walt Disney Records, "Never Knew I Needed," written and performed by Ne-Yo, *The Princess and the Frog Soundtrack*, 2009, 3.38.

21. Walt Disney Records, "Gonna Take You There," written by Randy Newman, performed by Jim Cummings featuring Terrance Simien on accordion, *The Princess and the Frog Soundtrack* 2009, 1:46.

22. For instance scholars emphasize African and African American culture in the development of zydeco music: Marcia G. Gaudet and James C. McDonald, eds. *Mardi Gras, Gumbo, and Zydeco: Readings in Louisiana Culture* (Jackson: University Press of Mississippi, 2011); Robert Kuhlken and Rocky Sexton, "The Geography of Zydeco Music," *Journal of Cultural Geography* 12, no. 1 (1991): 27–38; Sara Le

Menestrel, "The Color of Music: Social Boundaries and Stereotypes in Southwest Louisiana French Music," *Southern Cultures* 13, no. 3 (2007): 87–105; Mark Mattern, "Let the Good Times Unroll: Music and Race Relations in Southwest Louisiana," *Black Music Research Journal* (1997): 159–168; Jared Snyder, "Leadbelly and His Windjammer: Examining the African American Button Accordion Tradition," *American Music* 12, no. 2 (1994): 148–167.

23. Walt Disney Records, "When We're Human," written by Randy Newman, performed by Michael Leon Wooley, Bruno Campos, and Anika Noni Rose, featuring Terence Blanchard, *The Princess and the Frog Soundtrack*, 2009, 2:22.

24. Walt Disney Records, "Dig a Little Deeper," written by Randy Newman, performed by Jenifer Lewis featuring the Pinnacle Gospel Choir and Anika Noni Rose, *The Princess and the Frog Soundtrack*, 2009, 2:48.

25. Walt Disney Records, "We Know the Way," written by Opetaia Foa'i and Lin-Manuel Miranda, music by Opetaia Foa'i, performed by Opetaia Foa'i and Lin-Manuel Miranda, *Moana Soundtrack*, 2016, 2:21.

26. Walt Disney Records, "You're Welcome," written and produced by Lin-Manuel Miranda, performed by Dwayne Johnson, *Moana Soundtrack*, 2016, 2:43.

27. Sean Gerber, "'Black Panther' Original Score Available Digitally on February 16," February 13, 2018, *Marvel Studio News*, https://marvelstudiosnews.com/2018/02/13/black-panther-original-score-available-digitally-february-16/.

28. Hollywood Records (Disney Music Group), "Wakanda," composed by Ludwig Göransson, featuring Baaba Maal, *Black Panther Original Score*, 2018, 2:20.

29. Hollywood Records (Disney Music Group), "Killmonger," composed by Ludwig Göransson, *Black Panther Original Score*, 2018, 2:55.

30. Walt Disney Records, "Prince Ali," composed by Alan Menken, lyrics by Howard Ashman, performed by Will Smith, *Aladdin Soundtrack*, 2019, 3:29.

31. Walt Disney Records, "Prince Ali."

32. Walt Disney Records, "Friend Like Me," composed by Alan Menken, lyrics by Howard Ashman, performed by Will Smith, *Aladdin Soundtrack*, 2019, 2:35.

33. Walt Disney Records, "Friend Like Me."

34. Ibid.

35. Ibid.

36. Ibid.

37. Walt Disney Records, "You're Welcome."

38. Ibid.

39. Ibid.

40. Walt Disney Records, "A Cover Is Not the Book," music by Marc Shaiman, written by Shaiman and Scott Wittman, performed by Emily Blunt, Lin-Manuel Miranda and chorus, *Mary Poppins Returns Soundtrack*, 2018, 4:25.

41. Walt Disney Records, "Trip a Little Light Fantastic," music by Marc Shaiman, written by Shaiman and Scott Wittman, performed by Emily Blunt, Lin-Manuel Miranda, Tarik Freepong, Pixie Davies, Joel Dawson, Nathanael Saleh and Leeries (lamplighters chorus), *Mary Poppins Returns Soundtrack*, 2018, 7:02.

42. Walt Disney Records, "How Far I'll Go," written and produced by Lin-Manuel Miranda, performed by Auli'i Cravalho, *Moana Soundtrack*, 2016, 2:43.

43. Walt Disney Records, "Speechless," music by Alan Menken, written by Benj Pasek and Justin Paul, performed by Naomi Scott, *Aladdin soundtrack*, 2019, 3:28.

44. Ruthie Fierberg, "The Pasek & Paul Song That Got Them Hired for The Greatest Showman," Playbill, December 19, 2017, http://www.playbill.com/article/the-pasek-paul-song-that-got-them-hired-for-greatest-showman.
45. Walt Disney Records, "Speechless."
46. Walt Disney Records, "Spirit," music by Hans Zimmer, written by Elton John, Emma Rolfe, Tim Rice, Ilya Salmanzadeh, Labrinth, and Beyoncé, performed by Beyoncé, The Lion King soundtrack, 2019, 4:33.
47. Walt Disney Records, "Spirit."
48. Ibid.
49. Sara Aridi, "Disney's Aladdin: Mena Massoud on His Big Break and the Film's Big Issues," *The New York Times*, May 26, 2019, https://www.nytimes.com/2019/05/26/movies/aladdin-mena-massoud.html.
50. Princess Irede Abumere, "Beyoncé Champions African Music Stars with Lion King Soundtrack," *BBC Africa*, July 29, 2019, https://www.bbc.com/news/world-africa-49077673.
51. Dream Catchers Dance, "Brown Skin Girls (Dance Video) by The Happy African Kids (Dream Catchers) ft. Wizkid," YouTube video, 4:18, posted July 20, 2019, https://youtu.be/yk_snRm99J8.
52. Andrey Guy, "Music Theatre Vocal Pedagogy: Considering 'Cross-Training' for Practice," *Australian Voice* 18 (2017): 23–29.
53. Janice Brace-Govan and Hélène de Burgh-Woodman, "Sneakers and Street Culture: A Postcolonial Analysis of Marginalized Cultural Consumption," *Consumption, Markets and Culture* 11, no. 2 (2008): 93–112; Erich Hatala Matthes, "Cultural Appropriation without Cultural Essentialism?" *Social Theory and Practice* 42, no. 2 (2016): 343–366; Carol M. Motley and Geraldine Rosa Henderson, "The Global Hip-Hop Diaspora: Understanding the Culture," *Journal of Business Research* 61, no. 3 (2008): 243–253; Richard Rogers, "From Cultural Exchange to Transculturation: A Review and Reconceptualization of Cultural Appropriation," *Communication Theory* 16, no. 4 (2006): 474–503; Bruce Ziff and Pratima V. Rao, eds. *Borrowed Power: Essays on Cultural Appropriation* (New Brunswick: Rutgers University Press, 1997).

BIBLIOGRAPHY

Abumere, Princess Irede. "Beyoncé Champions African Music Stars with Lion King Soundtrack." *BBC Africa*, July 29, 2019. https://www.bbc.com/news/world-africa-49077673.
Aridi, Sara. "Disney's Aladdin: Mena Massoud on His Big Break and the Film's Big Issues," *The New York Times*, May 26, 2019. https://www.nytimes.com/2019/05/26/movies/aladdin-mena-massoud.html.
Block, Geoffrey. "The Broadway Canon from Show Boat to West Side Story and the European Operatic Ideal." *The Journal of Musicology* 11, no. 4 (1993): 525–544.
Brace-Govan, Janice, and Hélène de Burgh-Woodman. "Sneakers and Street Culture: A Postcolonial Analysis of Marginalized Cultural Consumption." *Consumption, Markets and Culture* 11, no. 2 (2008): 93–112.

Buchanan, Kyle, and John Horn. "Lin-Manuel Miranda: 'Chase What Inspires You, and Finish It.'" *Vulture*, Feb. 11, 2017. https://www.vulture.com/2017/02/lin-manuel-miranda-on-what-moana-shares-with-hamilton.html.

Carter, Tim. *Oklahoma!: The Making of an American Musical*. New Haven: Yale University Press, 2008.

Craft, Elizabeth Titrington. "'Is This What It Takes Just to Make It to Broadway?!': Marketing In the Heights in the Twenty-First Century." *Studies in Musical Theatre* 5, no. 1 (2011): 49–69.

Dream Catchers Dance. "Brown Skin Girls (Dance Video) by The Happy African Kids (Dream Catchers) ft. Wizkid." YouTube video, 4:18. Posted July 20, 2019. https://youtu.be/yk_snRm99J8.

Entertainment Weekly, "'DuckTales' Stars Lin-Manuel Miranda, Ben Schwatz & Cast, SDCC 2019." YouTube video, 8:54, posted July 22, 2019. https://youtu.be/Rmm6PFCdrZA.

Fierberg, Ruthie. "The Pasek & Paul Song That Got Them Hired for The Greatest Showman." *Playbill*, December 19, 2017. http://www.playbill.com/article/the-pasek-paul-song-that-got-them-hired-for-greatest-showman.

Gaudet, Marcia G., and James C. McDonald, eds. *Mardi Gras, Gumbo, and Zydeco: Readings in Louisiana Culture*. Jackson: University Press of Mississippi, 2011.

Gerber, Sean. "'Black Panther' Original Score Available Digitally on February 16." February 13, 2018, *Marvel Studio News*. https://marvelstudiosnews.com/2018/02/13/black-panther-original-score-available-digitally-february-16/.

Gioia, Michael. "Lin-Manuel Miranda and Leslie Odom, Jr. Reveal How *Rent* Shaped History and *Hamilton*." *Playbill*, February 11, 2015. http://www.playbill.com/article/lin-manuel-miranda-and-leslie-odom-jr-reveal-how-rent-shaped-history-and-hamilton-com-341546.

Guy, Andrew. "Music Theatre Vocal Pedagogy: Considering 'Cross-Training' for Practice." *Australian Voice*, 18 (2017): 23–29.

Henderson, Errol A. "Black Nationalism and Rap Music." *Journal of Black Studies* 26, no. 3 (1996): 308–339.

Herrera, Brian Eugenio. "Miranda's Manifesto." *Theater* 47, no. 2 (2017): 23–33.

Hogeland, William, Joanne B. Freeman, Lyra D. Monteiro, Leslie M. Harris, Catherine Allgor, Michael O'Malley, and David Waldstreicher. *Historians on Hamilton: How a Blockbuster Musical Is Restaging America's Past*. New Brunswick: Rutgers University Press, 2018.

Hollywood Records (Disney Music Group). "Wakanda." Composed by Ludwig Göransson, featuring Baaba Maal. *Black Panther Original Score*, 2018, 2:20.

———. "Killmonger." composed by Ludwig Göransson, *Black Panther Original Score*, 2018, 2:55.

Kelly, Catherine E. "Introduction: Lin-Manuel Miranda's Hamilton: An American Musical and the Early American Republic." *Journal of the Early Republic* 37, no. 2 (2017): 251–253.

Kuhlken, Robert, and Rocky Sexton. "The Geography of Zydeco Music." *Journal of Cultural Geography* 12, no. 1 (1991): 27–38.

Le Menestrel, Sara. "The Color of Music: Social Boundaries and Stereotypes in Southwest Louisiana French Music." *Southern Cultures* 13, no. 3 (2007): 87–105.

Lin-Manuel Miranda Awards, Internet Movie Database. https://www.imdb.com/name/nm0592135/awards.

Mattern, Mark. "Let the Good Times Unroll: Music and Race Relations in Southwest Louisiana." *Black Music Research Journal* (1997): 159–168.

Matthes, Erich Hatala. "Cultural Appropriation without Cultural Essentialism?" *Social Theory and Practice* 42, no. 2 (2016): 343–366.

McAllister, Marvin. "Toward a More Perfect Hamilton." *Journal of the Early Republic* 37, no. 2 (2017): 279–288.

Miletich, Leo N. *Broadway's Prize-Winning Musicals: An Annotated Guide for Libraries and Audio Collectors.* Binghampton, NY: The Haworth Press, 1993.

Monteiro, Lyra D. "Race-Conscious Casting and the Erasure of the Black Past in Lin-Manuel Miranda's Hamilton." *The Public Historian* 38, no. 1 (2016): 89–98.

Motley, Carol M., and Geraldine Rosa Henderson. "The Global Hip-Hop Diaspora: Understanding the Culture. *Journal of Business Research* 61, no. 3 (2008): 243–253.

Nassour, Ellis, and Richard Broderick. *Rock Opera: The Creation of Jesus Christ Superstar, from Record Album to Broadway Show and Motion Picture.* New York: Hawthorn Books, 1973.

Nelson, Kristen Rajczak. *Lin-Manuel Miranda: From Broadway to the Big Screen.* Farmington, Hills, MI: Greenhaven Publishing LLC, 2018.

Piepenburg, Eric. "Why Hamilton Has Heat." *The New York Times*, August 12, 2015, https://www.nytimes.com/interactive/2015/08/06/theater/20150806-hamilton-broadway.html.

Rogers, Richard A. "From Cultural Exchange to Transculturation: A Review and Reconceptualization of Cultural Appropriation." *Communication Theory* 16, no. 4 (2006): 474–503.

Salzman, Eric. "Whither American Music Theater?" *The Musical Quarterly* 75, no. 4 (1991): 235–247.

Snyder, Jared. "Leadbelly and His Windjammer: Examining the African American Button Accordion Tradition." *American Music* 12, no. 2 (1994): 148–167.

Stempel, Larry. *Showtime: A History of the Broadway Musical Theater.* New York: W.W. Norton, 2010.

Walt Disney Records. "Dig a Little Deeper." Written by Randy Newman, performed by Jenifer Lewis featuring the Pinnacle Gospel Choir and Anika Noni Rose. *The Princess and the Frog Soundtrack*, 2009, 2:48.

———."Gonna Take You There." Written by Randy Newman, performed by Jim Cummings featuring Terrance Simien on accordion. *The Princess and the Frog*, 2009, 1:46.

———."Never Knew I Needed." Written and performed by Ne-Yo. *The Princess and the Frog Soundtrack*, 2009, 3.38.

———. "When We're Human." Written by Randy Newman, performed by Michael Leon Wooley, Bruno Campos, and Anika Noni Rose, featuring Terence Blanchard. *The Princess and the Frog Soundtrack*, 2009, 2:22.

———. "How Far I'll Go." Written and produced by Lin-Manuel Miranda, performed by Auli'i Cravalho. *Moana Soundtrack*, 2016, 2:43.

———. "We Know the Way." Written by Opetaia Foa'i and Lin-Manuel Miranda, music by Opetaia Foa'i, performed by Opetaia Foa'i and Lin-Manuel Miranda. *Moana Soundtrack*, 2016, 2:21.

———. "You're Welcome." Written and produced by Lin-Manuel Miranda, performed by Dwayne Johnson. *Moana Soundtrack*, 2016, 2:43.

———. "A Cover Is Not the Book." Music by Marc Shaiman, written by Shaiman and Scott Wittman performed by Emily Blunt, Lin-Manuel Miranda, and chorus. *Mary Poppins Returns Soundtrack*, 2018, 4:25.

———. "Trip a Little Light Fantastic." Music by Marc Shaiman, written by Shaiman and Scott Wittman, performed by Emily Blunt, Lin-Manuel Miranda, Tarik Freepong, Pixie Davies, Joel Dawson, Nathanael Saleh, and Leeries (lamplighters chorus). *Mary Poppins Returns Soundtrack*, 2018, 7:02.

———. "Friend Like Me." Composed by Alan Menken, lyrics by Howard Ashman, performed by Will Smith. *Aladdin Soundtrack*, 2019, 2:35.

———. "Prince Ali." Composed by Alan Menken, lyrics by Howard Ashman, performed by Will Smith. *Aladdin Soundtrack*, 2019, 3:29.

———."Speechless." Music by Alan Menken, written by Benj Pasek and Justin Paul, performed by Naomi Scott. *Aladdin Soundtrack*, 2019, 3:28.

———. "Spirit." Music by Hans Zimmer, written by Elton John, Emma Rolfe, Tim Rice, Ilya Salmanzadeh, Labrinth, and Beyoncé, performed by Beyoncé, *The Lion King Soundtrack*, 2019, 4:33.

Ziff, Bruce H., and Pratima V. Rao, eds. *Borrowed Power: Essays on Cultural Appropriation*. New Brunswick: Rutgers University Press, 1997.

II

DIVERSIFYING THE DISNEY PRINCESS

6

✛

Elena of Avalor and Mama Coco

Latina Sheroes and Knowledge Keepers

Alberto Rodriguez and Veronica Nohemi Duran

Elena of Avalor made her debut on the Disney Channel in 2016 as a sixteen-year-old princess that lost both her parents. *Elena of Avalor* documents the role of a strong Latina that not only has to be a caretaker of her younger sister Isabel but also her kingdom. What sets Elena apart from other works on Latina sheroes is that in every episode she links her history to the indigenous past. Elena is aware of her long history to the Native Peoples of Latin America and in turn introduces jaguars, Xolo dogs, chocolate, pyramids, native language, indigenous folk stories, and music from her ancestors.

Likewise Disney's 2017 animated film *Coco* depicts the central role that women play in Mexican and Latino families as memory keepers and matriarchs. Central in this film is Mama Coco as the memory keeper of her family's past. Abuelita Elena, Mama Imelda, and other women in the film all hold important roles as matriarchs and keepers of family history. Although the history of strong Latinas has been at the center of many Spanish-speaking peoples as documented in classic works, few films and series geared for younger audiences have set Latina sheroes and Knowledge Keepers as the major narrative. This chapter explores Latinas as strong, central characters within their families and as leaders in their communities in recent Disney programming.

BRINGING VISIBILITY TO LATINO HISTORY AND CULTURE

For centuries Latinos have been negatively represented through biased stereotypes like the sleeping Mexican, as the hypersexualized Latino woman, as domestic, trade, or agricultural workers, and as violent criminals.[1] In media and popular culture these prevailing racial ideologies have continued to render Latino visibility as nonexistent or forced Latino actors to take on minimal roles as stereotypical representations of domestic workers, gangsters, or farmers. Even when Latinos are given leading roles in movies, such as *Maid in Manhattan, Stand and Deliver,* and *Chasing Papi,* there are traces of bias and racial stereotyping in the way the script is written or in the formation of their characters, rendering them once more into the roles of domestic workers, underachieving Mexicans, and the hypersexualized Latina.[2]

While xenophobia toward Latino immigration to the U.S. is at the root of much of the recent discourse surrounding Latino visibility and representation, assimilation, integration, it also comes amidst a surge of Latino pride and celebration of Latino people and culture. While generations of Latino immigrant families marginalized speaking in Spanish and other cultural traditions to assimilate, current generations of Latinos have sought to reconnect to their native, and in many cases, indigenous roots. Disney has capitalized on this search for identity and strengthening of community with its expansion into new characters and stories geared toward both Latino markets in the U.S. and in Latin America through *Elena of Avalor* and *Coco.*

ELENA OF AVALOR: BUILDING THE PAN-LATINO WORLD

The Environment of Avalor

Elena is part of a complex series of characters that link Latin America to Asia, India, Africa, Europe, and Mesoamerica. At the center of the series are its well-informed creators Craig Gerber and Silvia Cardenas Olivas. The Kingdom of Avalor is based somewhere in Latin America and influenced by Aztec, Inca, and Maya homelands. Choosing not to give preference to a specific country the creators of the series state that Avalor can be any Latin American country. As a result, it is Elena's vision to build bridges and not walls between kingdoms as seen in season 1, episode 6 when the Avalor and Cordoba Kingdoms survey sites for a new Bienvenido Bridge that would allow trade and peace between both kingdoms. In the process of deciding on a site, they are confronted by Yacalli, a Mayan wooden giant and protector of owls.[3] By linking both indigenous and

Spanish histories of the Americas, Elena sets the stage for the complex spaces that she and the surrounding kingdoms share.

The indigenous culture is ever present in *Elena of Avalor* and can be seen in the constant artworks of the First Peoples. For example, her royal wizard Mateo's sorcerers' room is adorned with a golden eagle dressed in Mexico's colors (white/green/red), has Mayan drawings on the walls, and the books he reads are also in an indigenous language. When Elena decides that she will enter a highly competitive fencing tournament she trains on an Aztec pyramid. In both seasons 1 and 2, playing Olaball is an Avalor pastime for the visitors that come to meet with Elena. Olaball is a type of soccer game played with one's hips and scoring is done by having a rubber ball pass across a ring on a high wall. This game was known as Ulama by Mesoamericans and played both by Mayans and Aztecs.

Mesoamerican culture once again take center stage when Princess Valentina Montañez Torres from the Kingdom of Paraíso (A Southern Kingdom) visits Avalor and a competitive debate takes place on which kingdom makes the best chocolate.[4] In the middle of season 2, Avalor's rubber is set to be one of the best inventions of the kingdom.[5] Both chocolate and rubber were highly valuable in Mesoamerica and often used in trade and peace offerings.

The environment continues to be part of *Elena of Avalor* when volcanoes and Sirenas (mythical sea creatures) became part of both season 1 and 2. Charoca and Charica are volcanoes that have a tense relationship with villagers from the Kingdoms of Avalor and Cordoba. Elena takes on the task of bringing peace between earth and its inhabitants, negotiating on both behalfs and resulting in both living as one.[6] The ocean is the livelihood for most of the kingdoms neighboring Avalor and as a result the myth of the Sirenas is also taken on by Elena. In season 2, the myth of the Sirenas as villains and killers of sea people is challenged when Elena befriends them. The Sirenas and their seahorse, Cuco, give Elena a special plant to cover her chest that allows her to breathe underwater and forever linking the relationship between land and sea.

The Creatures of Avalor

The role that animals take in *Elena of Avalor* demonstrates that writers of the series are in tune with the histories of the Americas. Jaquins are magical flying creatures that are part jaguar and macaw and are the guardians of the Kingdom of Avalor. Panthera onca or the jaguar was part of "almost every ancient Mesoamerican civilization [who] revered the jaguar in some way" and was seen as a divine animal.[7] For example, "the Olmec {circa 1200–400 B.C.} heavily featured jaguars in their art and religion. Sculptures of cats were popular, as were depictions of deities who appear to be half human, half jaguar."[8] The jaguar is native to the southwestern part of the United States, Mexico, Central and South America and is still seen as a powerful symbol of military and political dominance there.

The other part of the Jaquin is the macaw, a colorful bird that is native to Mexico, the Caribbean, Central and South America. Recently scientists and archaeologists have discovered that "for more than two millennia, indigenous peoples in Mesoamerica have traded macaws and included their feathers in rituals. The birds held immense symbolic value and represented sun gods in both Maya and Aztec culture."[9] By using both the jaguar and the macaw *Elena of Avalor* links the indigenous culture of the American Southwest, Mexico, Caribbean, Central and South America but more importantly the series is documenting the linking of First Peoples.

Four other animals are links to the history of Latin America: Noblins, Xolo dogs, flying sunbirds, and coyotes. Noblins are small magical creatures that live deep in the forest, turn things into gold, and transform into Xolo dogs (Mexican hairless dogs). Jiku, the leader of the Noblins, and his followers are imprisoned by the evil sorceress Shuriki over a period of forty-one years and forced to make gold for her kingdom. Noblins have a close resemblance to the Latin American myth of Los Duendes, gnome-like creatures that live deep in the forest, close to water or rivers, have a close relationship with young children, and shape shift. Xolo dogs come to life in the second season when Princess Valentina Montañez Torres, a rival from the southern Kingdom of Paraìso visits Elena and a spell is released bringing a giant Twin Xolo dog statue to life causing chaos in the Kingdom of Avalor. The Xolos is a 3,000-year-old breed that is the "ancient Aztec dog of the gods" and often appeared in paintings of Diego Rivera and Frida Kahlo.[10]

Keeping with Mesoamerica, *Elena of Avalor* introduces four flying sunbirds, Quita Moz, Lama, Hool, and Qapa that are serpent like. The resemblance to Quetzalcoatl, the Feathered Serpent of Olmec, Aztec and Mayan mythology, is quite striking. The Aztecs held the Feathered Serpent god in such high regards that they built the Temple of Quetzalcoatl in Teotihuacan to honor the powerful god. Finally, the addition of Troyo, the evil magical coyote, allows the series to once again link all the Americas to one of the most hated animals in history that is often associated with a negative image. Coyote are often affiliated with deviant behavior, whether it be Wile E. Coyote from *The Road Runner Show* or the person who smuggles undocumented migrants into the United States.

As Elena learns to govern her kingdom, she is guided by her spirit animal Zuzo, who is a fox and native to most Latin American countries. Cacahuate, a sloth that is native to Central and South America, is Mateo's spirit animal and guides him as he follows in his grandfather's footsteps as a royal wizard for the Avalor Kingdom. A collection of animals makes cameos such as Bobo, a spider monkey with poor judgment that is kicked out of Spirit Guide school, raccoons, squirrels, and owls are also part of the spirit animal world. In turn, the series of *Elena of Avalor* uses animals much as it has used the environment to tell the stories and histories of the old world and the Americas. The same can be seen when Elena and her cast of characters use song and dance to articulate the links between peoples of the world, both old and new.

The Sound of Avalor

Music and singing have always been part of Latina/o culture from the Toña la Negra to Vicente Fernández.[11] The tradition of Latin music is a large part of the *Elena of Avalor* series from episode one, when Elena and grandfather Francisco sing a corrido titled "Ready to Rule."[12] Elena and her sister Isabel sing a salsa song titled "Sister Time" documenting the link between Isa and her older sister Elena.[13] A Mariachi song played by Isabel and Francisco titled "Avalor Birthday Song" sung to cousin Esteban for his birthday showcases Isa's invention of a new instrument which is part guitar and accordion.[14] A Rumba beat titled "Cast a Spell with Me" sung by the wizard Mateo takes the music over to the Caribbean and its Cuban roots.[15] Argentine Tango with artwork and dress take center stage in "Feel Free to Have Fun" sung by Elena and Prince Alonso, linking the Kingdoms of Avalor and Cordoba.[16] Rap songs are also part of the series and sung by Zuzo, Elena's spirit animal, Captain Chiloya, the Jamaican leader of a 400-year-old sea crew, and Victor and Carla, a team of father and daughter whose mission is to overtake the Kingdom of Avalor. Rap songs are also sung by Elena and her cousin Esteban.[17] Merengue music is sung by Orizaba, a villain moth fairy who hopes to destroy earth; Princess Valentina Montañez Torres and Elena, all engage the Haitian and Dominican beats.[18] Flamenco Dance and music is sung by King Verago leader of the Jaquins linking the roots of the Romany peoples of Latin America.[19] Finally Banda music is sung by Elena and Naomi paying tribute to Northern Mexico, especially the state of Durango.[20] Much like the environments, animals, song and dance *Elena of Avalor* will also engage food as a way to honor the past.

The Taste of Avalor

The cast of *Elena of Avalor* uses food to build bridges and links with other kingdoms and visitors throughout the series. One of the most common foods that appear in both season 1 and 2 are Dona Luisa's (Elena's Grandmother) tamales that are the best in the kingdom according to Don Francisco. In season 2 the art of making tamales is passed on to Elena who teaches her sister Isa, cousin Esteban, and best friend Naomi Turner. In the episode celebrating Christmas Eve, tamales, ponche navideño, and dulces are part of the foods, treats, and drinks showcased as guest arrived to celebrate Nochebuena.[21] Other drinks that are mentioned in the series are Horchata, Té de Manzanilla, and Té de Limon.[22] Latin American pastries such as Tres Leches cake is baked for cousin Esteban's birthday party during season 1, sweet empanadas and Pan de Muerto are also part of the showcasing of Latina/o foods.[23] Sopa de Fideo con Pollo is made by Mateo's mother as a comfort food for the young wizard who had a rough day in his sorcerers' office. Queso Gutierrez, the finest in the world, becomes a point of contention when Armando, the chief of the castle, is forced to face his over-competitive brother Santos who attends Elena's All Kingdoms Fair, selling their family's prized queso.[24] Food is part of the story-telling of *Elena of Avalor* that allows viewers to understand the importance of the cultures and traditions of Latin America and the Caribbean.

THE NUMBER FORTY-ONE AND FORTY-ONE YEARS

One of the most interesting plotlines of the *Elena of Avalor* series that connects to real events is the usage of the number forty-one for the number of years Elena is trapped in the amulet by the evil sorceress Shuriki. The night of November 17, 1901, remains a moment of great debate within Mexican myth and history. On that night, forty-two men were discovered in what newspapers called El Baile de Los Cuarenta y Uno where half of the men dressed as women and the other half as males. Local authorities became alarmed by neighbors who noted that the women had broad shoulders, wigs, and mustaches. When police arrived, they found some of the most prominent people of Mexico City, one of them was Ignacio de la Torre y Mier, son-in-law to Porfirio Díaz. Torre y Mier was married to Díaz's favorite daughter, Amada Díaz Quiñones, and was considered the first son-in-law of Mexico. In order to save his daughter's honor and not bring shame to the Díaz name, it has been documented that Porfirio Díaz had his son-in-law removed from the arrested group leaving the number apprehended at forty-one.[25] Ignacio de la Torre y Mier, who was saved from public, economic, and social embarrassment by his father-in-law later takes a liking to Emiliano Zapata, an action that is noted by his wife Amada Díaz Quiñones.

The events of the night of November 17, 1901, and El Baile de Los Cuarenta y Uno has also made the number forty-one a taboo. According to Francisco L. Urquizo, Mexican soldier, revolutionary general, writer, and historian:

En México el número 41 no tiene ninguna validez y es ofensivo para los mexicanos [. . .] La influencia de esa tradición es tal que hasta en lo oficial se pasa por alto el número 41. No hay en el ejército División, Regimiento o Batallón que lleve el número 41. Llegan hasta el 40 y de ahí se salta al 42. No hay nómina que tenga renglón 41. No hay en las nomenclaturas municipales casas que ostenten el número 41. Si acaso y no hay remedio, el 40 bis. No hay cuarto de hotel o de Sanatorio que tenga el número 41. Nadie cumple 41 años, de los 40 se salta hasta los 42. No hay automóvil que lleve placa 41, ni policía o agente que acepte ese guarismo.[26]

In Mexico, the number 41 has no validity and is offensive. . . . The influence of this tradition is so strong that even officialdom ignores the number 41. No division, regiment, or battalion of the army is given the number 41. From 40 they progress directly to 42. No payroll has a number 41. Municipal records show no houses with the number 41; if this cannot be avoided, 40 is used. No hotel or hospital has a room 41. Nobody celebrates their 41st birthday, going straight from 40 to 42. No vehicle is assigned a number plate with 41, and no police officer will accept a badge with that number.

The negative image of the number forty-one has been part of both film and news stories in recent years. In 1994 a telenovela on *Televisa* by the name El Vuelo del Aguila showcased in 140 episodes the history of the Mexican Revolution.[27] It is within the recasting of Los Cuarenta y Unos and the LGBTQ community[28] that *Elena of Avalor* uses the number as the years she is trapped in the amulet. The number forty-one has a long history within Mexican society and just as the environment, animals, songs, foods that the series details are extremely well researched, honoring all aspects of Latina/o culture.

"REMEMBER ME": WOMEN, MEMORY, AND CULTURE THROUGH DISNEY-PIXAR'S *COCO*

Coco, released in 2017 by Walt Disney and Pixar Animation Studios, represents traditional Mexican culture, values, and people.[29] It is a film about a young boy's journey, but is titled after his great-grandmother. Miguel's journey connects to Mama Coco's story, as rich cultural details weave into every aspect of this film, depicting the role that women play within their communities as matriarchs and memory keepers. The Rivera women are strong business owners, storytellers, skilled workers, and talented artisans that demonstrate their strength within their homes and communities. They represent Latina women who throughout centuries have worked, raised families, and become integral parts of their communities.

"We are your family, Mijo": Women in Mexican Culture

Women and storytelling are a central part of the narrative presented in *Coco*. Mama Imelda, Mama Coco, and Abuelita Elena all hold key roles in the Rivera family and history. It is largely through these female characters that the family's narrative is revealed to the audience and as the story unravels the audience can clearly gauge that most family decisions are made by them or require their approval. The film begins with Miguel narrating how Mama Imelda was forced to make drastic alterations to her life when she finds herself alone and with a child to raise; she learns how to make shoes and passes this trade on to her family. She originates the family's business success. Since Mama Imelda believed her husband left the family in his pursuit of a music career, she made the decision to forbid music within the Rivera household. This is a decision that stood for many years and that was upheld by her family even after her passing. The respect for Mama Imelda's decision and the dislike for the walk-away musician that abandoned her is seen through Abuelita Elena's adamant refusal to allow Miguel to play his guitar or be a part of the music talent show in Mariachi Plaza.[30]

Miguel's retelling of Mama Imelda's experience, Abuelita's refusal to allow music in the household and the family's support of her decision to not allow Miguel to play in the music competition all exemplify how Mama Imelda's story has dictated the family's trajectory and attitude toward music and musicians and the role that women play within the family. Her disdain for music is less about music itself, but the desire to pass down notions of survival, one she has had to endure herself. This family dynamic, in which women are the decision makers, storytellers, and business leaders, goes against the machista system associated with Mexican culture which argues that Mexican women have been subjected to Mexican men's oppressive attitudes and kept at a social disadvantage.[31] Mama Imelda and Abuelita Elena exemplify the strong, central status that Mexican women have played in families and communities, contrary to popular depictions that contends men are the dominant force within the home.

"*Recuerdame*": Memory and Storytelling in Mexican Culture

Memory plays an important part in *Coco*. The premise of the movie centers on memory and storytelling. On one side there is the memory that is constructed around the absence of Mama Coco's father, which causes Mama Imelda to reconstruct herself as a strong, rigid woman that outlawed music in the Rivera household. This memory is passed down to Miguel's grandmother, Elena, who continues to abhor the memory of the man who abandoned his family and maintains the ban on music in her home. On the other hand, there is the real story that Miguel unravels along his journey in the Land of the Dead, where he discovers that Hector Rivera is his great great-grandfather, who was murdered by Ernesto De La Cruz when he tried to return home to his family in Santa Cecilia. De La Cruz poisoned Hector because he feared that without Hector's songs his career would be over. After De La Cruz murders Hector, he, too, creates a different memory for his audience, based on the lies that he constructs to claim Hector's songs as his own, build his musical career, and recreate his image as the greatest musician of all time. Yet there is another memory that is held by Mama Coco, she is the keeper of Hector's true history. Although she does not know about his murder, she knows about her father's talent and holds on to his picture, letters, and poems. It is through this evidence that Hector's true story is revealed to the Rivera family and to the people of the Land of the Living.[32] Mama Coco holds the piece of memory that ties this story together, the evidence that proves Hector's existence, musical talent, and association to the Rivera family. The piece of the photograph that she stored amongst her possessions, and which she hid from Mama Imelda as a young girl, quite literally completes her family picture, saves Hector from being forgotten and brings the Rivera family together with their ancestors.

As with family relationships, women play a key role in the keeping of memory. At the beginning of the movie Miguel sets up the premise of his family history by detailing how Mama Imelda was abandoned by her musician husband with a child to raise and how this led to the family's distaste for music. However, this premise is based on the story that Mama Imelda constructed and that was passed down to Elena, Miguel's grandmother. As the movie continues, it is Abuelita Elena who explains to Miguel the importance of having an altar for Dia de Los Muertos and the significance of placing your family's photographs on the altar so that their spirit can cross into the Land of the Living on this special day. She, however, makes it clear that a photo of Imelda's husband will never be placed in the *ofrenda* because, as she understood it, he chose his pursuit of music over his family. Additionally, in a passing scene, Miguel's mother is seen explaining to two young children the proper way to spread the *flor de cempasúchil* petals, creating a path to guide their ancestors spirit home. This again demonstrates how memory and storytelling is passed down from one generation to the next.[33]

Like *Coco*, Mexican and Mexican American scholars, along with other Latina/o writers, have explored female roles in the family, memory keeping, and storytelling through autobiographies, children books, and *cuentos*. Works like *Bless Me, Ultima* by Rudolfo Anaya, *Y No Se Lo Trago La Tierra* by Tomás Rivera, *Burro Genius: A Memoir* by Victor Villaseñor, *Tomás and the Library Lady* by Pat Mora, *Hoyt St: An Autobiography* by Mary Helen

Ponce, *Barefoot Heart: Stories of a Migrant Child* by Elva Trevino Hart, *Woman Hollering Creek and Other Stories* and *The House on Mango Street* by Sandra Cisneros exemplify the ways in which authors have used literature to analyze female space, memory, and the importance of storytelling within the family.

"*El Camino a Casa*": Immigration as Seen through *Coco*

Immigration features greatly in *Coco* as Miguel travels from the Land of the Living to the Land of the Dead. There can be many parallels made between the immigration story in *Coco* and the real immigration story of Latinos traveling into the United States. After the argument with his family in their home in which Abuelita Elena destroys Miguel's guitar, Miguel runs away and heads toward Mariachi Plaza, later ending up at Cementerio Santa Cecilia, where De La Cruz is buried. Here *Coco* touches up on the immigration narrative of many Latinos when Miguel first visits Ernesto De La Cruz' tomb. When examined closer, the *cempasúchil* flower petals are guiding Miguel's path to the cemetery, they disappear when he is at the plaza because that is not where the petals, which represent his ancestors, want him to go. When Miguel enters De La Cruz' tomb, the cempasuchil petals begin shimmering, a sign that Miguel is meant to go there. When he touches the guitar, which the audience later finds out is really Hector's guitar, the petals again shimmer. Miguel then plays the guitar and is immediately transported into the Land of the Dead. As he struggles to understand what is going on with his body, viewers see that both his living and dead family are present in the cemetery. This symbolizes how Miguel is caught between two worlds, the living and the dead. However, it is not until he falls into an open tomb, which symbolizes his crossing over into the Land of the Dead, that he then meets his ancestors. Interestingly, it is a woman, dressed as a *catrina* that pulls him out of the open tomb. The *catrina* symbolizes Death literally pulling him into the Land of the Dead and is a direct tie to Mexico's relationship with La Santa Muerte and their ideology on death and the afterworld.[34]

Miguel's journey into the Land of the Dead can be paralleled to the pattern of Latino immigration into the United States; where immigrants follow chain migration, continuing immigration patterns started by family or other relations who have traveled earlier and relocating to cities where relatives or their own ethnic groups live. These patterns can be observed in American cities with a history of high Latino immigration like Los Angeles.[35] More recently, however, studies have focused on other cities and regions, like the Midwest, where there has been a rise in Latino immigration. In states like Nebraska, where many immigrants have been employed in meatpacking or other "Latino industrial niches," communities have relied on kinship networks to supplement modest incomes. For immigrant Latino families, as with other groups, women represent a large part of these networks. The central status of women as the conductors of support systems for their families and communities is reminiscent of the leadership role that the women portrayed in *Coco* take within the family's economic and family structure.[36]

Like in *Coco*, where the two worlds are connected through a bridge, Mexico is connected to the American southwest through bridges, rivers, oceans, and a desert. Through these man-made crossing points and natural boundaries, border-crossers from both countries travel north and south, from one country to the other. In Southern states, like California, and other border points, the economy, culture, and politics are closely tied to border dynamics; both countries rely on each other for progress. People in these border areas are influenced by socioeconomic factors on both sides of the border.[37] The communities of these border regions contend with the "symbol and the reality" of the border daily and maneuver with the unique experience of what it means to live between two worlds.[38]

Miguel's discussion on the significance of the *ofrenda* with both his living family and his ancestors parallels the way in which U.S.-born Latinos keep the culture of their immigrant parents and family alive. Family rituals, especially those relating to family unity, religion, and work ethic, along with the constant influx of new immigrants, is essential to keeping Latin American culture alive in the United States through generations.[39]

Lastly, a similar way that immigration is referenced in *Coco* is by the *cempasúchil* petal and the family photos on the *ofrendas* that serve as a passport that allows for travel between the Land of the Living and the Land of the Dead. When Mama Imelda adds conditions to her blessing, Miguel goes on a quest to find De La Cruz, whom he believes to be his great grandfather, and get his blessing so that he can go back to the Land of the Living to pursue music. As the film develops further, he then changes his objective and wants his family's blessing so that he can put Hector's *foto* on the family's ofrendas. In all this, his family's blessing must be given so that the *cempasúchil*, which acts as a passport between worlds, will be able to transport him back to Santa Cecilia. This mirrors the story of many immigrants who travel to the United States with a passport, and sometimes without it, in hopes of a better life and with the intention to fulfill their family's dreams.[40]

"The Mighty Xolo dog": *Alebrijes* and Other Spirit Guides

Likewise, *alebrijes*, *ofrendas*, and Dia de Los Muertos are a large part of Mexican culture, *Coco* brings these pieces of Mexican folklore to movie audiences throughout the film in wonderfully artistic and accurate ways.

Dante, Miguel's dog whom he named after Ernesto de la Cruz' horse, starts off in this story as a street dog that Miguel befriends. However, from the beginning of the film, Dante plays an integral, yet subtle, role in the development of Miguel's journey. With close attention audiences can see that it is Dante who continuously leads Miguel toward the truth of his ancestry. Dante is the character who breaks the photo in the altar, leading Miguel to believe that Ernesto de la Cruz is his great-great grandfather. When Miguel first crosses into the Land of the Dead, Dante is the only one from the Land of the Living that can still see Miguel and he then leads Miguel to his ancestors. When Miguel's ancestors decided that they need to find Mama Imelda in the Land of the Dead in order to send Miguel back to the Land of the Living, Dante easily crosses into the Land of the Dead with them. Furthermore, when the family is crossing into the Land of the Dead, they must undergo an inspection, like immigration inspections in the United States, where Dante is identified by the agent as an *alebrije*. Later Frida Kahlo's character will also identify Dante as an *alebrije*. Ultimately, it is Dante who constantly steers Miguel toward Hector, first at the inspection station and then later after the music competition, and who helps him discover the truth of his ancestry. Yet it is not until Miguel declares him to be a "good spirit guide" that Dante transforms into an *alebrije*.[41]

Dante, like Dia de Los Muertos, acts as a link between the two worlds, a connection between ancestors and their living family. *Alebrijes*, or spirit animals, have a long history in Mexico. Authors and artists have used animals to express a link between different worlds, convey spiritual ideologies or as companions to their artistic subjects. *Coco* references one such artist, Frida Kahlo; many of her paintings include animals and a link between two selves. Authors, such as Rudolfo Anaya in *Bless Me, Ultima* have also used animals to convey a link between people and a spiritual world.

CONCLUSION

While both *Elena of Avalor* and *Coco* take a first and significant step toward bringing recognition to Latino culture and toward giving young Latino audiences characters with whom they can identify, there are limitations to what these two examples alone can achieve. One such limitation is the singling out of Latino groups and culture that, while working to bring Latino culture to mainstream audiences, by consequence leaves out other groups. In this matter *Elena of Avalor* and *Coco* differ, as one approaches Latino culture from an ethnically ambiguous lens while the other very distinctly centers on Mexican culture. By taking this approach, Disney and Pixar are either meshing all Latino culture and peoples into one, with little regard to the differences that make each group historically, culturally, and socially unique or they are projecting their understanding of Latino culture as it applies solely to Mexican culture. Neither of these approaches adequately gives credit to the intricacies and uniqueness of different Latino groups.

Additionally, *Elena of Avalor* and *Coco* only work part of the way in showcasing true diversity amongst Latino groups. As significant as their contributions are to Latino visibility, there is still work to be done to create space for dark skinned mestizos, indigenous peoples, and Afro-Latinos amongst Latino groups. While recent works like *Rogue One*, *Roma*, *Ant-Man*, *Overboard*, and *Game of Thrones* have paved some ground toward creating this visibility for more diverse Latino casting choices, there is still a long way to go before these instances are the norm and not a rare occurrence. Lastly, there is still much work to be done when it comes to analyzing the complex stories of Latinos that do not center on the narrative of immigration or colonization. There are rich, contemporary Latino stories around feminism, family, leadership, and determination that have yet to be told. Among these current movements that call for visibility of all Latinos or all backgrounds, and not just those in the U.S. but across the Americas, these stories are begging to be told.

NOTES

1. Clara E. Rodriguez, *Latin Looks: Images of Latinas and Latinos in the US Media* (New York, NY, Routledge, 2018).
2. Ibid.
3. *Elena of Avalor*, Season 1, Episode 6, "Prince Too Charming," directed by Nathan Chew and written by Mercedes Valle, aired September 16, 2016, Disney Junior, https://www.disneyabcpress.com/disneychannel/shows/11836.
4. *Elena of Avalor*, Season 2, Episode 2, "Royal Rivalry," directed by Nathan Chew and written by Tom Rogers, aired October 28, 2017, Disney Junior, https://www.disneyabcpress.com/disneychannel/shows/11836.
5. *Elena of Avalor*, Season 2, Episode 12, "Class Act," directed by Nathan Chew and written by Kerri Grant, aired July 28, 2018, Disney Junior, https://www.disneyabcpress.com/disneychannel/shows/11836.
6. *Elena of Avalor*, Season 2, Episode 15, "Song of the Sirenas," directed by Elliot M. Bour and written by Silvia Olivas and Rachel Ruderman, aired September 21, 2018, Disney Junior, https://www.disneyabcpress.com/disneychannel/shows/11836.
7. Isabel Bueno, "Jaguars Were the Divine Felines of the Ancient Americas," *National Geographic*, October 16, 2018, accessed 15 March 2019, https://www.nationalgeographic.com/archaeology-and-history/magazine/2018/07-08/jaguar-natural-history-mesoamerica.
8. Ibid.

9. Michael Greshko, "Early Native Americans Imported Exotic Parrots, DNA Reveals," *National Geographic*, August 13, 2018, accessed 15 March 2019, https://www.nationalgeographic.com/science/2018/08/news-ancient-dna-chaco-canyon-pueblo-macaws-archaeology.

10. American Kennel Club, "American Kennel Club," Xoloitzcuintli, March 18, 2018, accessed 15 March 2019, https://www.akc.org/dog-breeds/xoloitzcuintli.

11. Manuel Peña, *Música Tejana: The Cultural Economy of Artistic Transformation* (College Station, Texas: Texas A&M University Press, 1999); Guadelupe San Miguel Jr., *Tejano Proud: Tex-Mex Music in the Twentieth Century* (College Station, Texas: Texas A&M University Press, 2002); and Catherine Ragland, *Musica Nortena: Mexican Migrants Creating a Nation Between Nations* (Philadelphia, Pennsylvania: Temple University Press, 2009).

12. *Elena of Avalor*, Season 1, Episode 1, "First Day of Rule," directed by Jamie Mitchell and written by Craig Gerber, aired June 20, 2016, Disney Junior, https://www.disneyabcpress.com/disneychannel/shows/11836.

13. *Elena of Avalor*, Season 1, Episode 2, "Model Sister," directed by Elliot M. Bour and written by Becca Topol, aired July 22, 2016, Disney Junior, https://www.disneyabcpress.com/disneychannel/shows/11836; *Elena of Avalor*, Season 1, Episode 9, "A Day to Remember," directed by Elliot M. Bour and written by Silvia Olivas, aired October 16, 2016, Disney Junior, https://www.disneyabcpress.com/disneychannel/shows/11836, *Elena of Avalor*, Season 1 Episode 10, "The Scepter of Light," directed by Robb Pratt and written by Mercedes Valle, aired November 4, 2016, Disney Junior, https://www.disneyabcpress.com/disneychannel/shows/11836, and *Elena of Avalor*, Season 2 Episode 2, "Royal Rivalry," directed by Nathan Chew and written by Tom Rogers, aired October 28, 2017, Disney Junior, https://www.disneyabcpress.com/disneychannel/shows/11836.

14. *Elena of Avalor*, Season 1, Episode 4, "Island of Youth," directed by Nathan Chew and written by Tom Rogers, aired August 12, 2016, Disney Junior, https://www.disneyabcpress.com/disneychannel/shows/11836.

15. *Elena of Avalor*, Season 2, Episode 7, "Rise of the Sorceress," directed by Robb Pratt and written by Don Perez, aired March 3, 2018, Disney Junior, https://www.disneyabcpress.com/disneychannel/shows/11836. *Elena of Avalor*, Season 1, Episode 5, "Rise of the Sorceress," directed by Robb Pratt and written by Don Perez, aired August 26, 2016, Disney Junior, https://www.disneyabcpress.com/disneychannel/shows/11836.

16. *Elena of Avalor*, Season 1, Episode 6, "Prince Too Charming," directed by Nathan Chew and Written by Mercedes Valle, aired September 16, 2016, Disney Junior, https://www.disneyabcpress.com/disneychannel/shows/11836; *Elena of Avalor*, Season 2 Episode 15, "Song of the Sirenas," directed by Elliot M. Bour and written by Silvia Olivas and Rachel Ruderman, aired September 21, 2018, Disney Junior, https://www.disneyabcpress.com/disneychannel/shows/11836, and *Elena of Avalor*, Season 1, Episode 24, "Blockheads," directed by Robb Pratt and written by Tom Rogers, aired September 16, 2017, Disney Junior, https://www.disneyabcpress.com/disneychannel/shows/11836.

17. *Elena of Avalor*, Season 1 Episode 24, "A Spy in the Palace," directed by Robb Pratt and written by Rachel Ruderman, aired November 25, 2017, Disney Junior, https://www.disneyabcpress.com/disneychannel/shows/11836; *Elena of Avalor*,

Season 2, Episode 8, "Shapeshifters," directed by Nathan Chew and written by Laurie Israel, aired March 10, 2018, Disney Junior, https://www.disneyabcpress.com/disneychannel/shows/11836, and *Elena of Avalor*, Season 1, Episode 23, "Party of a Lifetime," directed by Robb Pratt and written by Mercedes Valle, aired August 25, 2017, Disney Junior, https://www.disneyabcpress.com/disneychannel/shows/11836.

18. *Elena of Avalor*, Season 1, Episode 10, "The Scepter of Light," directed by Robb Pratt and written by Tom Rogers, aired November 4, 2016, Disney Junior, https://www.disneyabcpress.com/disneychannel/shows/11836, *Elena of Avalor*, Season 2, Episode 2, "Royal Rivalry," directed by Nathan Chew and written by Tom Rogers, aired October 28, 2017, Disney Junior, https://www.disneyabcpress.com/disneychannel/shows/11836, and *Elena of Avalor*, Season 1, Episode 10, "Snow Place Like Home," directed by Robb Pratt and written by Tom Rogers, aired November 24, 2018, Disney Junior, https://www.disneyabcpress.com/disneychannel/shows/11836.

19. *Elena of Avalor*, Season 1, Episode 21, "Realm of the Jaquins," directed by Elliot M. Bour and written by Silvia Olivas and Craig Gerber, aired August 12, 2017, Disney Junior, https://www.disneyabcpress.com/disneychannel/shows/11836.

20. *Elena of Avalor*, Season 2, Episode 13, "All Kingdoms Fair," directed by Robb Pratt and written by Tom Rogers, aired August 4, 2018, Disney Junior, https://www.disneyabcpress.com/disneychannel/shows/11836.

21. *Elena of Avalor*, Season 1, Episode 10, "Snow Place Like Home," directed by Robb Pratt and written by Tom Rogers, aired November 24, 2018, Disney Junior, https://www.disneyabcpress.com/disneychannel/shows/11836.

22. *Elena of Avalor*, Season 1 Episode 2, "Model Sister," directed by Elliot M. Bour and written by Becca Topol, aired July 22, 2016, Disney Junior, https://www.disneyabcpress.com/disneychannel/shows/11836; and *Elena of Avalor*, Season 2, Episode 2, "Royal Rivalry," directed by Nathan Chew and written by Tom Rogers, aired October 28, 2017, Disney Junior, https://www.disneyabcpress.com/disneychannel/shows/11836.

23. *Elena of Avalor*, Season 1, Episode 4, "Island of Youth," directed by Nathan Chew and written by Tom Rogers, aired August 12, 2016, Disney Junior, https://www.disneyabcpress.com/disneychannel/shows/11836.

24. *Elena of Avalor*, Season 21, Episode 21, "Movin' On Up," directed by Nathan Chew and written by Jeffrey M. Howard, aired February 16, 2019, Disney Junior, https://www.disneyabcpress.com/disneychannel/shows/11836; *Elena of Avalor*, Season 1, Episode 5, "Rise of the Sorceress," directed by Robb Pratt and written by Don Perez, aired August 26, 2016, Disney Junior, https://www.disneyabcpress.com/disneychannel/shows/11836; and *Elena of Avalor*, Season 2, Episode 13, "All Kingdoms Fair," directed by Robb Pratt and written by Tom Rogers, aired August 4, 2018, Disney Junior, https://www.disneyabcpress.com/disneychannel/shows/11836.

25. Eduardo Castrejon, *Cuarenta Y Uno: Novela Critico Social* (Mexico D.F.: Universidad Nacional Autónoma de México, 2012).

26. Miguel Hernandez Cabrera, *"Los "Cuarenta y Uno," Cien Años Después'."* Los "Cuarenta y Uno," Cien Años Después, January 1, 2002, accessed 15 March 2019, https://web.archive.org/web/20071130032556/http:/www.islaternura

.com/APLAYA/HOMOenHISTORIA/HomoHistoria2005/Los%2041%20en%20 mexico/En%20el%20centenario%20de%20los%2041%20Diciembre2005.htm.

27. Televisa S.A. de C.V., "*El Vuelo del Aguila,*" IMDb, July 4, 1994, accessed 15 March 2019, https://www.imdb.com/title/tt0159930/fullcredits.

28. Alberto Najar, "*BBC Mundo Ciudad de México.*" ¿Por Qué en México el Número 41 se Asocia Con la Homosexualidad y Sólo Ahora se Conocen Detalles Secretos de su Origen? January 11, 2017, accessed 15 March 2019, https://www.bbc.com/mundo/noticias-america-latina-38563731.

29. "Coco (2017)," IMDb, accessed June 20, 2019, https://www.imdb.com/title/tt2380307/.

30. *Coco*, directed by Lee Unkrich and Adrian Molina (2017; Emeryville and Burbank, California, Pixar and Walt Disney Pictures, 2017), DVD.

31. Martha P. Cotera, *Diosa y Hembra: The History and Heritage of Chicanas in the U.S.* (Austin: Statehouse Printing, 1976), 154.

32. *Coco*, DVD.

33. *Coco*, DVD.

34. *Coco*, DVD.

35. Joan Moore and James Diego Vigil, "Barrios in Transition" in *In the Barrios: Latinos and the Underclass Debate*, edited by Joan Moore and Raquel Pinderhughes (New York: Russell Sage Foundation, 1993), 26–30, 31.

36. Lourdes Gouveia and Rogelio Saenz, "Global Forces and Latino Population Growth in the Midwest: A Regional and Subregional Analysis," *Great Plains Research* 10, no. 2 (Fall 2000): 307–309, 312, 320, accessed July 19, 2019, https://www.jstor.org/stable/23778286.

37. Katrina Burgess and Abraham F. Lowenthal, "Challenges from the South: Enhancing California's Mexico Connection" in *The California-Mexico Connection* edited by Abraham F. Lowenthal and Katrina Burgess (Standord: Stanford University Press, 1993), 254–259.

38. Mario T. Garcia, "*La Frontera*: The Border as a Symbol and a Reality in Mexican-American Thought" in *Between Two World: Mexican Immigrants in the United States* edited by David G. Gutierrez (Wilmington: A Scholarly Resources Inc., 1996), 89–90.

39. Leo R. Chavez and Rebecca G. Martinez, "Mexican Immigration in the 1980s and Beyond: Implications for Chicanas/os" in *Chicanas/os at the Crossroads: Social, Economic, and Political Change*, edited by David R. Maciel and Isidro D. Ortiz, (Tucson: The University of Arizona Press, 1996), 33.

40. *Coco*, DVD.

41. *Coco*, DVD.

BIBLIOGRAPHY

American Kennel Club. "American Kennel Club: Xoloitzcuintli." Last Modified March 18, 2018. Accessed 15 March 2019. https://www.akc.org/dog-breeds/xoloitzcuintli.

Bueno, Isabel. "Jaguars Were the Divine Felines of the Ancient Americas." *National Geographic*, Last Modified October 16, 2018. Accessed March 15, 2019.

https://www.nationalgeographic.com/archaeology-and- history/magazine/2018/07-08/jaguar-natural-history-mesoamerica.

Burgess, Katrina and Lowenthal, Abraham F. "Challenges from the South: Enhancing California's Mexico Connection." In *The California-Mexico Connection*, edited by Abraham F. Lowenthal and Katrina Burgess, 254–278. Stanford: Stanford University Press, 1993.

Carter, Dorinda J., Flores, Stella M., Reddick, Richard J. ed. *Legacies of Brown: Multiracial Equity in American Education*. Cambridge: Harvard Educational Review, 2004.

Castrejon, Eduardo. *Cuarenta Y Uno: Novela Critico Social*. Mexico D.F.: Universidad Nacional Autónoma de México, 2012.

Chavez, Leo R. and Martinez, Rebecca G. "Mexican Immigration in the 1980s and Beyond: Implications for Chicanas/os." In *Chicanas/os at the Crossroads: Social, Economic, and Political Change*, edited by David R. Maciel and Isidro D. Ortiz, 25–51.Tucson: The University of Arizona Press, 1996.

Donato, Ruben. *Mexicans and Hispanos in Colorado Schools and Communities, 1920–1960*. Albany: State University of New York Press, 2007.

Elena of Avalor. "A Day to Remember." Directed by Elliot M. Bour. 2016, Los Angles: Disney Junior.

———. "Island of Youth." Directed by Nathan Chew. 2016, Los Angles: Disney Junior.

———. "Model Sister." Directed by Elliot M. Bour. 2016, Los Angles: Disney Junior.

———. "Prince Too Charming." Directed by Nathan Chew. 2016. Los Angles: Disney Junior.

———. "The Scepter of Light." Directed by Robb Pratt. 2016, Los Angles: Disney Junior.

———. "A Spy in the Palace." Directed by Robb Pratt. 2017, Los Angles: Disney Junior.

———. "Blockheads." Directed by Robb Pratt. 2017, Los Angeles: Disney Junior.

———. "Party of a Lifetime." Directed by Robb Pratt. 2017, Los Angles: Disney Junior.

———. "Realm of the Jaquins." Directed by Elliot M. Bour. 2017, Los Angles: Disney Junior.

———. "Rise of the Sorceress." Directed by Robb Pratt. 2018, Los Angles: Disney Junior.

———. "Royal Rivalry." Directed by Nathan Chew. 2017. Los Angles: Disney Junior.

———. "First Day of Rule." Directed by Jamie Mitchell. 2016, Los Angles: Disney Junior.

———. "All Kingdoms Fair." Directed by Robb. 2018, Los Angles: Disney Junior.

———. "Class Act." Directed by Nathan Chew. 2018, Los Angles: Disney Junior.

———. "Shapeshifters." Directed by Nathan Chew. 2018, Los Angles: Disney Junior.

———. "Snow Place Like Home." Directed by Robb Pratt. 2018, Los Angles: Disney Junior.

———. "Song of the Sirenas." Directed by Elliot M. Bour. 2018, Los Angles: Disney Junior.

———. "Movin' On Up." Directed by Nathan Chew. 2019, Los Angles: Disney Junior.

Garcia, Mario T. "*La Frontera*: The Border as a Symbol and a Reality in Mexican-American Thought." In *Between Two World: Mexican Immigrants in the United States* edited by David G. Gutierrez, 89–117. Wilmington: A Scholarly Resources Inc., 1996.

Gouveia, Lourdes and Rogelio Saenz. "Global Forces and Latino Population Growth in the Midwest: A Regional and Subregional Analysis." *Great Plains Research* Vol. 10, No. 2 (Fall 2000): 307–309, 312, 320. Accessed July 19, 2019. https://www.jstor.org/stable/23778286.

Greshko, Michael. "Early Native Americans Imported Exotic Parrots, DNA Reveals." *National Geographic*, Last Modified August 13, 2018. Accessed March 15, 2019. https://www.nationalgeographic.com/science/2018/08/news-ancient-dna-chaco-canyon-pueblo-macaws- archaeology.

Hernandez Cabrera, Miguel. "Los "Cuarenta y Uno," Cien Años Después." La Jornada Semanal. Last Modified January 1, 2002. Accessed 15 March 2019. https://www.jornada.com.mx/2001/12/09/sem-hernandez.html.

Martha P. Cotera, *Diosa Y Hembra: The History and Heritage of Chicanas in the U.S.* Austin: Statehouse Printing, 1976.

Moore, Joan Moore and Vigil, James Diego. "Barrios in Transition." In *In The Barrios: Latinos and the Underclass Debate*, edited by Joan Moore and Raquel Pinderhughes, 27–50. New York: Russell Sage Foundation, 1993.

Najar, Alberto. "¿Por Qué en México el Número 41 se Asocia Con la Homosexualidad y Sólo Ahora se Conocen Detalles Secretos de su Origen?" BBC Mundo Ciudad de México. Last Modified January 11, 2017. Accessed 15 March 2019. https://www.bbc.com/mundo/noticias-america-latina-38563731.

Peña, Manuel. *Música Tejana: The Cultural Economy of Artistic Transformation*. College Station, Texas: Texas A&M University Press, 1999.

Ragland, Catherine. *Musica Nortena: Mexican Migrants Creating a Nation Between Nations*. Philadelphia, Pennsylvania: Temple University Press, 2009.

San Miguel Jr., Guadalupe. *Tejano Proud: Tex-Mex Music in the Twentieth Century*. College Station, Texas: Texas A&M University Press, 2002.

Televisa S.A. de C.V. "'El Vuelo del Aguila." IMDb. Last Modified July 4, 1994. Accessed 15 March 2019. https://www.imdb.com/title/tt0159930/fullcredits.

Unkrich, Lee and Molina, Adrian. *Coco*. DVD. Directed by Lee Unkrich and Adrian Molina. Emeryville and Burbank, California, Pixar Animation Studios and Walt Disney Animation Studios, 2017.

7

✢

#NolaBorn

Tiana and the Road Home for New Orleans Residents

Sheryl Kennedy Haydel

A PRINCESS EMERGES AFTER A STORM

The familiar rhythm of the city had vanished. The carefree spirit that once possessed the storied corners and creases of the French Quarters was overrun with national journalists desperate to piece together how New Orleans would pull herself back together again after a devastating levee breach. This emptiness was palpable throughout the city from Uptown to Downtown, from Gentilly to Holly Grove, and from New Orleans East to the Garden District. In neighborhoods that served as home base for generations of families, once boasted enviable property values and beamed with cultural pride as well as novelty, were now shifting through waterlogged homes to find their footing in the malaise of FEMA[1] applications, the benevolence of Christian organizations offering a hand up, and the rediscovery of what it means to start over—yet again. New Orleanians have danced with hurricanes before, but Katrina was different. Her aftermath was unprecedented and revealed gaping cracks in the city's aging infrastructure and bureaucratic political tapestry making it: Hurricane Katrina, more than a weather event. It was an assault on the city's legacy and African American identity—firmly rooted in cuisine, social aid, pleasure clubs, and high school bragging rights. So from the streetcars grinding along the St. Charles Avenue tracks to the expansive rolling greens of City Park, New Orleans had lost her compass and in many ways so did her people—more specifically her children who were displaced, judged, and abandoned for almost ten years.

A generation who are now millennials remember the feelings of displacement as their families, in some cases, ran for refuge to states like Texas, Georgia, or even California, lured by the promise of a better education, safer neighborhoods, and economic prosperity. And while many families relocated because they were unable for a myriad of reasons to hit the reset button on their lives in New Orleans, they weathered an assortment of emotions and realities that ran counter to prior generations. The loss of space, community, schools, and neighborhoods, without hesitation, transformed the youngest residents of this city, many of whom were now looking for something to tether their identity to. Known as Katrina Babies—the storm left in its wake a generation of children who were New Orleans born, elsewhere raised, or even raised in a city that's an unrecognizable shell of itself.[2]

Media images and reports full of anguish, uncertainty, and bleak pronouncements lasted for months. As theorist George Gerbner[3] posited in his work around the power of television, everyone was being cultivated to believe the constant narrative that New Orleans would never be the same, and it was deflating. Undergirded by accusations that African Americans were being deliberately pushed out of the city to make room for a whiter majority, residents were unhinged by even the suggestion of this notion. In the midst of what seemed like endless despair, Walt Disney Animation Studios announced it "will continue its fairy tale legacy in animation by taking moviegoers on an all-new 'once upon a time' musical adventure with its 2009 release of *The Frog Princess*." The backdrop for this next installment would be "the legendary birthplace of jazz—New Orleans"[4] and the latest princess would be a young African American girl named Maddy (early name choice for Tiana). This Black princess would be

> living amid the charming elegance and grandeur of the fabled French Quarter. From the heart of Louisiana's mystical bayous and the banks of the mighty Mississippi comes an unforgettable tale of love, enchantment and discovery with a soulful singing crocodile, voodoo spells and Cajun charm at every turn.[5]

This character was therefore a young Black girl, attached to a place, a distinctively recognizable space. The reaction to the news of an African American princess ranged from joy to skepticism primarily because of Disney's history of mining in racialized tropes, particularly in depicting Black people.[6] The collective wisdom did not want to see Blackness associated with a frog, and other nagging stereotypes. Additionally, New Orleanians were cautious not to aggravate the plight of Black residents with a nostalgic take on the city, given the realities of breached levees, trailer living, displaced families, and a ravaged city. The juxtaposition of a fairy-tale New Orleans full of charm, beauty, and unblemished aesthetics may have alienated if not angered residents, at first. Disney even brought in Oprah Winfrey to sell it (a Black princess) to the Black community and also heightened the authenticity of the character by weaving the identity of Princess Tiana to that of legendary restauranteur Leah Chase. It was an intentional decision to gain favor with a community of people who felt disenfranchised from their home and in some cases their country. Being represented on the big screen and linking it to a local shero made this movie even more endearing to the rebuilding of the city's emotional fortitude.

Ten years later, at the 2019 Essence Festival, an event rooted in music and gender enpowerment, the organizers held a special screening of *The Princess and the Frog*. Since 2009, many scholars have since deconstructed the portrayal of Disney's first Black princess.[7] Therefore, this chapter reflects on one often overlooked context of Tiana's portrayal—less that she was a Black princess who may have been problematic, but that she represented a connection to place and space for New Orleans residents who had lost their home, city, community, culture, and heritage.

TIANA: A VERY REAL PRINCESS AND THE LEGACY OF LEAH CHASE

She was never short on words. Forever honest yet anchored in knowing who she was and whose she was. Surrounded by pots with stained black bottoms, well-worn recipes, and a community she adored and that mirrored her affection, Leah Chase personified the culture of New Orleans with her natural wit, easy charm, and dedication to communal uplift and liberation. She embodied resiliency, might, and compassion from her perch on the corner of North Miro Street and Orleans Avenue. The Dooky Chase Restaurant had seen its share of dignitaries, an influx of business and at other times, a slower stream of patrons, but the sentiment that it was an integral New Orleans institution was undeniable. Everyone from American presidents to community organizers to far-flung suburbanites to neighborhood families found their way to the restaurant. The fried chicken, po'boys, or greens was one of two reasons to leave the familiar New Orleans haunts nestled in downtown corridors—the other reason: Momma Chase. Her affinity for New Orleans was poured into the preparation of her famous gumbo, it also was present when she fussed over guests and gave interviews to the legions of reporters who sat at her knee to hear a serving of wisdom. Leah Chase, known as the Creole Queen, was a legend. She was certainly someone who used her love for cooking as a muse to champion racial equality and fortify the Civil Rights

Movement as well as a global means to honor her city. It is through her cooking legacy that many men and women found their inspiration to create a path for themselves to make a difference. Leah Chase embodied New Orleans.

For a silver-haired woman to embody womanhood is not a revealing fact. What is most striking is how she remained humbled, but forever impactful. Zella Palmer, whose work as the director and endowed chair of the Ray Charles Program in African American Material Culture at Dillard University summed up how important Chase was to the fiber of the city:

> The world knew Leah Chase from Beyoncé's iconic "Lemonade" video and the majestic cameo shots of Beyoncé softly brushing her hair evoking the beauty of black womanhood. Children knew a version of her story from the character Tiana portrayed in Disney's *Princess and the Frog*. Chefs and historians knew her as the chef and co-proprietor of Dooky Chase Restaurant, the most important restaurant in the country. Civil Rights activists, HBCU presidents, and Essence knew that her and her husband Edgar 'Dooky' Chase Jr., since 1941, created the safest space to meet and dine for Black folks in the South. New Orleans knew her as their queen; 'tell it like it is' elder; gatekeeper of New Orleans Creole cuisine and culture; ambassador; Oracle; leader; friend and an incredible cook. Her family knew her as their beloved mother and grandmother. I knew her from the time I was a teenager.[8]

What New Orleanians appreciate most is authenticity. Someone who comes without the trappings of pretense. Someone who embraces candor over hesitation. And someone who never forgets that New Orleans is more than a playground for tourists but a place of substance, will and fortitude. All of these attributes made her a role model to every little Black girl. Whether it was direct or indirect, her contributions were pervasive to how women thought and behaved. When news began to spread about her death in June 2019, social media exploded with love under the hashtag #LeahChase. New Orleans Mayor LaToya Cantrell led tributes to Chase:

> Leah Chase served presidents and celebrities, she served generations of locals and visitors, and she served her community. She was a culture-bearer in the truest sense. We are poorer for her loss, and richer for having known and having loved her. She will be badly missed.[9]

Her death set off a petition to rename Lee Circle, named after Confederate General Robert E. Lee, gathering over 13,000 signatures.[10] The National Food and Beverage Foundation offered to cover the costs of a statue dedicated to Chase in the circle, the site where the city took down one of four Confederate monuments in May 2017 in a drawn-out contentious civic fight. Statue or not, on June 10, Chase was serenaded home in a New Orleans second line as Troy "Trombone Shorty" Andrews and Terence

Blanchard (who performed on the film's soundtrack), led a procession of the hymn "I'll Fly Away," out of St. Peter Claver Catholic Church. Zulu Social Aid and Pleasure Club led the community in a second line through Tremé to celebrate her life.[11]

In her restaurant with walls beautifully adorned by artwork full of color as well as slices of history, there is a framed picture from the movie *The Princess and the Frog* that captures long gazes. It reads: "Thank you so very much Ms. Chase for all your inspiration! You are the REAL PRINCESS of New Orleans.!!" And these simple yet powerful words are symbolic of what Leah Chase has meant to New Orleans. Her legacy is one that will not only live through Disney's movie, but in the lives of young girls and women everywhere who are finding their voice, shattering stereotypes and standing tall in a never-ending movement to change the world. Residents paid tribute to her legacy during her homecoming:

> Thank you for inspiring, teaching, and loving on us all. Dooky now has his Queen. Rest in delicious peace Ms. Chase. Her memory will ALWAYS be a blessing. #LeahChase #WithOurAncestors.[12]

TIANA AND IDENTITY

Just like Leah Chase belongs to New Orleans, for better or worse, so does Tiana. There is only one African American princess among Disney's franchise and she is Tiana. It allowed young African American girls to own a cultural moment for themselves, or a doll that looked like them with her tiara on her head. Young Black girls were able to host birthday parties with a Black princess. And for children from New Orleans scattered and displaced in other cities, they were able to hold their head high knowing that Tiana reflected to the world the best of the place they were born in. The Road Home program[13] became a policy to support New Orleans' families in their bid to return to their native city. But for many families, this mechanism was not a reality, because of job security in other cities after Katrina. However, Tiana provided a mediated Road Home for families who longed to return to the Crescent City.

When Disney announced it had cast an African American actress to play Ariel in the live-action remake of *The Little Mermaid*, Tiana began trending on social media with the controversy over the Little Mermaid casting. Fans celebrated having a second Black princess, after Tiana. As critics used the hashtag #NotMyAriel, they argued that if Disney could cast Ariel as Black, then supporters of the casting change should accept that in a live-action remake of *Princess and the Frog*, Tiana could be cast white. One Twitter user posted in response to the casting decision for Ariel: "I look forward to a

Chinese, Indian or White actress playing Tiana. Let's see if this 'the best qualified actress' argument works then. #NotMyAriel."[14]

However Disney fans pointed out that to make Tiana white, was to whitewash the Black experience in New Orleans.

> Fun Fact: Tiana was actually based off of a woman named Leah Chase, a well-known chef in New Orleans and [John] Lasseter specifically wanted to make a story around the black experience there. So before you make the argument, no it's not the same as making Tiana white. #NotMyAriel[15]

Other fans clarified that the specific cultural context of the story line of Tiana speaks to the Black experience in New Orleans, referencing a line in the film where Tiana is told that a woman of her background was not suitable to own her restaurant. They argued that Leah Chase's story inspired the development of Tiana, because she developed Dooky Chase at a time when African Americans faced discrimination and segregation. Fans pointed out that Tiana's story line cannot be separated from this fact.

> To all y'all #NotMyAriel people saying "wHy cAn'T TiAnA bE wHiTe tHeN", she cant be cuz she's BASED OFF OF A REAL PERSON. Leah Chase served as inspiration for the creation of Tiana. She was a chef in New Orleans & owner of Dooky Chase- her own restaurant. Ariel is a fishlady.[16]

> 5./ If you do not understand importance of race when it comes to [Tiana] & the Princess and the frog, I sincerely recommend you pick up a history book. It still plays a huge role, even when it's not talked about. Don't compare a mermaid to a real human being. PERIOD.[17]

In 2009, *Times Picayune* reporter Mike Scott wrote an article with the headline "'The Princess and the Frog' reflects Disney's determination to nail New Orleans Details."[18] This headline embodies the spirit of New Orleans—eclectic, distinctive, and demanding. Her people are detailed and expect the same of those who tell stories about life in their crescent shaped home along the Mississippi River. Her people require a commitment anchored in respect, admiration, and deference from those who tell her story. Get the accent wrong or call the neutral ground a medium and you have lost their confidence and deemed unfit to speak about their city. And even though she welcomes thousands of visitors to feast on her world-famous dishes as well as indulge in her music and culture, there is an unwavering expectation that access equates to tenderness and an investment that equals if not surpasses that of a native. At first glance, it may appear that New Orleans has no floor or ceiling—unrestrained and unashamed—with arms open and no expectations of loyalty, but that reality is false. The city keeps long hours and her people do the same between a bevy of weekend festivals and the parades that bounce between Mardi Gras, Easter, and Mother's Day, but what is intrinsic to this narrative is finding the balance. Nestled among the revelers are real people with joys and misgivings. So for all of these reasons, the movie caught the attention of critics and the Disney faithful and primarily New Orleanians who may appear easy until you disappoint or deceive them. The film had this sentiment as its compass. Scott's reporting captured this fact about New Orleans. Details and the people around them. The fact that the filmmakers embraced this striking characteristic was vital to not only the movie, but for the city's people to adopt *The Princess and The Frog* as their own. Scott continued:

> The film is steeped in such New Orleans details. The name of the newspaper read by the characters is correct: *The Times-Picayune*. The look of the buildings is spot-on. The music—written by Randy Newman, who spent much of his childhood here, and performed by several New Orleans artists—is pitch-perfect, running the gamut of local musical styles, from jazz to gospel to zydeco.[19]

Scott also shares how the filmmakers spent a great deal of time consulting with famed New Orleanians such as Leah Chase and storyteller Coleen Salley showing their deference to the city and all of her attributes by spending time with two legends. He shares that filmmakers combed through every detail to make sure phrasing reflected the city's signature dialect.

However the film did produce some "Big Easy oopsies" as Scott's article noted. Early screenings by residents pointed out the use of y'all for singular references, when it is used in the plural. A Mardi Gras parade processed through the French Quarter (not the real route) and a Mardi Gras krewe king serves this role for five consecutive years—also not the case in real life traditions. A final image of the city shows the Mississippi River visible from a skyline view of the city. Musker notes that "We cheated geography a bit."[20]

The Princess and the Frog became a galvanizing point for a city reeling from the wrath of Mother Nature and frailty of a manmade levee. Before and after the movie was released even the New Orleans Tourism and Marketing Corporation (NOTMC) referenced the film as a way for visitors to connect to New Orleans. During the summer of 2014, NOTMC launched a tourism campaign that allowed budding visitors to experience New Orleans through the lens of the movie and its characters. The campaign encouraged visitors to "followhermagic.com" for a real life, spatial experience that were all landmarks in the movie by entering a sweepstakes for an all-expense paid trip. The goal of the campaign was to not only attract people to New Orleans, but to position the city more commonly known for adult entertainment as a place for families—a place that is warm, safe, and magical.

The 'Follow Your NOLA' custom content from Disney's *The Princess and the Frog* retraces the magic of New Orleans from this beloved story line. NOTMC has added Princess Tiana as one of its many celebrities that visitors can connect with on their website.[21]

By all accounts the movie was a defining moment for a city left breathless in the midst of a what felt like a never-ending nightmare. Residents' attachment to the movie was not by chance. It was cultivated much like scholar George Gerbner asserts in his theoretical framework providing emotional cues for audiences that packaged symbols and nostalgia as salient entertainment. The filmmakers made sure that their messages were situated in the correct frame that New Orleanians would treasure and celebrate. This intentionality by the filmmakers is what made this movie vibrant at the time it was made and released. It echoed similar attempts at filmmaking in and about New Orleans, as was evident in the production and reception of the HBO series *Treme*.[22] It was this approach to marry authenticity with the magical wonder of Disney that made the movie a classic. From the research that was poured into it to the connection to the city's matriarch, *The Princess and the Frog* is enduring.

To separate Leah Chase and the experiences of African Americans to the story of Tiana is an erasure of Blackness in mainstream discourse. When Chase met her husband Dooky in 1944 when his family owned a sandwich shop, she recalled: "I just made it grow. Did what I like to do. Stumbled a lot. But that's what life is all about. You just stumble and keep going."[23] The story of stumbles and recovery, triumph and community, the making of culture and heritage, are what make New Orleans an irreplaceable American space. It was through Tiana that many of us, young and old alike, were able to find a small piece of the road home, when adversity threatened to uproot and displace us in 2005. And for those of us still settled in other cities, we had a small cultural moment of nostalgia to celebrate New Orleans.

NOTES

1. FEMA stands for Federal Emergency Management Agency.
2. Edward Buckles, *Katrina Babies*, 2015, documentary film.
3. George Gerbner, and Larry Gross, "Living with Television: The Violence Profile," *Journal of Communication* 26, no. 2 (1976): 172–199.
4. "Disney Announces the Frog Princess for 2009," Coming Soon, March 8, 2017, accessed July 1, 2019, https://www.comingsoon.net/movies/news/19250-disney-announces-the-frog-princess-for-2009.

5. "Disney Announces the Frog Princess for 2009," Coming Soon.

6. Richard M Breaux, "After 75 Years of Magic: Disney Answers Its Critics, Rewrites African American History, and Cashes in on Its Racist Past," *Journal of African American Studies* 14, no. 4 (2010): 398–416; Kheli R. Willetts, "Cannibals and Coons: Blackness in the Early Days of Walt Disney," in *Diversity in Disney Films: Critical Essays on Race, Ethnicity, Gender, Sexuality, and Disability*, edited by Johnson Cheu (Jefferson, NC: McFarland, 2013).

7. Lauren Dundes and Madeline Streiff, "Reel Royal Diversity? The Glass Ceiling in Disney's *Mulan* and *Princess and the Frog*," *Societies* 6, no. 4 (2016): 35; Scott Foundas, "Disney's *Princess and the Frog* Can't Escape the Ghetto," *Village Voice* 24 (2009): 2009–1; Sarita McCoy Gregory, "Disney's Second Line: New Orleans, Racial Masquerade, and the Reproduction of Whiteness in *The Princess and the Frog*," *Journal of African American Studies* 14, no. 4 (2010): 432–449; Kimberly R. Moffitt and Heather E. Harris, "Of Negation, Princesses, Beauty, and Work: Black Mothers Reflect on Disney's *The Princess and the Frog*," *Howard Journal of Communications* 25, no. 1 (2014): 56–76; Neal A. Lester, "Disney's *The Princess and the Frog*: The Pride, the Pressure, and the Politics of Being a First," *The Journal of American Culture* 33, no. 4 (2010): 294; Fabio Parasecoli, "A Taste of Louisiana: Mainstreaming Blackness through Food in the Princess and the Frog," *Journal of African American Studies* 14, no. 4 (2010): 450–468; Jena Stephens, "Disney's Darlings: An Analysis of *The Princess and the Frog, Tangled, Brave* and the Changing Characterization of the Princess Archetype," *Interdisciplinary Humanities* 31, no. 3 (2014): 95–107.

8. Zella Palmer, "A Love Letter to Leah Chase, the Queen of New Orleans," *Essence*, June 4, 2019, https://www.essence.com/feature/a-love-letter-to-leah-chase-the-queen-of-new-orleans/. Dillard Today, "Tribute to Leah Chase," accessed July 1, 2019, http://www.dillard.edu/dillard-newsroom/campus-news/leah-chase-tribute.php.

9. Mayor LaToya Cantrell, @mayorcantrell, Twitter Post, June 1, 2019, 9:57 p.m., https://twitter.com/mayorcantrell/status/1135047774339293184.

10. "Make It Leah's Circle," Change.org, accessed July 1, 2019, https://www.change.org/p/new-orleans-city-council-make-it-leah-s-circle-494f28f4-30d6-4032-9141-6871945b5f7f?fbclid=IwAR03mlNwAALzKzvwci6nohIPqSTCW6JDT1K3MhguiwmGDnjtYX3WbOl5gos.

11. Doug MacCash, "Remembering Leah Chase's Second-Line Parade in New Orleans," *Nola.com, Times-Picayune*, June 13, 2019, https://www.nola.com/entertainment_life/article_3557f318-bf8d-57ef-8b55-11f5fdf9ce8e.html.

12. DngerousBeauty1908 (@dngerousb), Twitter post, June 2, 2019, https://twitter.com/DngerousB/status/1135098683249299456.

13. The Road Home, accessed July 1, 2019, https://www.road2la.org/HAP/Default.aspx.

14. ElmTree, @ElmTree11347006, Twitter Post, August 15, 2019, https://twitter.com/ElmTree11347006/status/1162062416039075840.

15. Not Leah, @NotteLeah, Twitter post, July 10, 2019, 3:12 p.m. https://twitter.com/NotteLeah/status/1149048766499971072.

16. Nicholas Ndreca @Ndreca_Official, Twitter post, July 25, 2019, 4:40 p.m. https://twitter.com/Ndreca_Official/status/1154536925405089792.

17. Nicholas Ndreca @Ndreca_Official, Twitter post, July 31, 2019, 11:07 a.m. https://twitter.com/Ndreca_Official/status/1156627366380277760.

18. Mike Scott, "'The Princess and the Frog' Reflects Disney's Determination to Nail New Orleans Details," *The Times Picayune*, December 9, 2009, https://www.nola.com/entertainment_life/movies_tv/article_fcf78d96-bf45-5b29-956e-b2413ea00cf9.html.

19. Ibid.

20. Ibid.

21. Travel Pulse, "New Orleans Tourism Lets You See Nola Like Princess Tiana," June 25, 2014, accessed June 1, 2019, https://www.travelpulse.com/news/destinations/new-orleans-tourism-lets-you-see-nola-like-princess-tiana.html.

22. Dominique, Gendrin, Catherine Dessinges, and Shearon Roberts (Eds.), *HBO's* Treme *and Post-Katrina Catharsis: The Mediated Rebirth of New Orleans* (Lanham, MD: Lexington Books: 2017).

23. Quote from Oprah.com article on Leah Chase tweeted by Nicholas Ndreca @Ndreca_Official, Twitter post, July 25, 2019, 4:40 p.m. https://twitter.com/Ndreca_Official/status/1154536925405089792.

BIBLIOGRAPHY

Breaux, Richard M. "After 75 Years of Magic: Disney Answers Its Critics, Rewrites African American History, and Cashes in on Its Racist Past." *Journal of African American Studies* 14, no. 4 (2010): 398–416.

Buckles, Edward. *Katrina Babies*. 2015. Documentary Film.

Change.org. "Make It Leah's Circle." Accessed July 1, 2019. https://www.change.org/p/new-orleans-city-council-make-it-leah-s-circle-494f28f4-30d6-4032-9141-6871945b5f7f?fbclid=IwAR03mlNwAALzKzvwci6nohIPqSTCW6JDT1K3MhguiwmGDnjtYX3WbOl5gos.

Coming Soon. "Disney Announces the Frog Princess for 2009." March 8, 2017. Accessed July 1, 2019. https://www.comingsoon.net/movies/news/19250-disney-announces-the-frog-princess-for-2009.

DngerousBeauty1908 (@dngerousb), Twitter post, June 2, 2019, https://twitter.com/DngerousB/status/1135098683249299456.

Dundes, Lauren, and Madeline Streiff. "Reel Royal Diversity? The Glass Ceiling in Disney's *Mulan* and *Princess and the Frog*." *Societies* 6, no. 4 (2016): 35.

ElmTree, @ElmTree11347006. Twitter Post. August 15, 2019. https://twitter.com/ElmTree11347006/status/1162062416039075840.

Foundas, Scott. "Disney's *Princess and the Frog* Can't Escape the Ghetto." *Village Voice* 24 (2009).

Gendrin, Dominique, Catherine Dessinges, and Shearon Roberts (Eds.) *HBO's* Treme *and Post-Katrina Catharsis: The Mediated Rebirth of New Orleans*. Lanham, MD: Lexington Books: 2017.

Gerbner, George, and Larry Gross. "Living with Television: The Violence Profile." *Journal of Communication* 26, no. 2 (1976): 172–199.

Gregory, Sarita McCoy. "Disney's Second Line: New Orleans, Racial Masquerade, and the Reproduction of Whiteness in *The Princess and the Frog*." *Journal of African American Studies* 14, no. 4 (2010): 432–449.

Lester, Neal A. "Disney's *The Princess and the Frog*: The Pride, the Pressure, and the Politics of Being a First." *The Journal of American Culture* 33, no. 4 (2010): 294.

MacCash, Doug. "Remembering Leah Chase's Second-Line Parade in New Orleans." *Nola.com, Times-Picayune*, June 13, 2019. https://www.nola.com/entertainment_life/article_3557f318-bf8d-57ef-8b55-11f5fdf9ce8e.html.

Mayor LaToya Cantrell. @mayorcantrell, Twitter post. June 1, 2019, 9:57 p.m. https://twitter.com/mayorcantrell/status/1135047774339293184.

Moffitt, Kimberly R., and Heather E. Harris. "Of Negation, Princesses, Beauty, and Work: Black Mothers Reflect on Disney's *The Princess and the Frog*." *Howard Journal of Communications* 25, no. 1 (2014): 56–76.

Not Leah, @NotteLeah, Twitter post, July 10, 2019, 3:12 p.m. https://twitter.com/NotteLeah/status/1149048766499971072.

Nicholas Ndreca @Ndreca_Official, Twitter post, July 25, 2019, 4:40 p.m. https://twitter.com/Ndreca_Official/status/1154536925405089792.

———. @Ndreca_Official, Twitter post, July 31, 2019, 11:07 a.m. https://twitter.com/Ndreca_Official/status/1156627366380277760.

Palmer, Zella. "A Love Letter to Leah Chase, the Queen of New Orleans," *Essence*, June 4, 2019, https://www.essence.com/feature/a-love-letter-to-leah-chase-the-queen-of-new-orleans/.

Parasecoli, Fabio. "A Taste of Louisiana: Mainstreaming Blackness through Food in the Princess and the Frog." *Journal of African American Studies* 14, no. 4 (2010): 450–468.

Scott, Mike. "'The Princess and the Frog' Reflects Disney's Determination to Nail New Orleans Details." *The Times Picayune*, December 9, 2009. https://www.nola.com/entertainment_life/movies_tv/article_fcf78d96-bf45-5b29-956e-b2413ea00cf9.html.

Stephens, Jena. "Disney's Darlings: An Analysis of *The Princess and the Frog, Tangled, Brave* and the Changing Characterization of the Princess Archetype." *Interdisciplinary Humanities* 31, no. 3 (2014): 95–107.

Travel Pulse. "New Orleans Tourism Lets You See Nola Like Princess Tiana." June 25, 2014. Accessed June 1, 2019. https://www.travelpulse.com/news/destinations/new-orleans-tourism-lets-you-see-nola-like-princess-tiana.html.

Willetts, Kheli R. "Cannibals and Coons: Blackness in the Early Days of Walt Disney," in *Diversity in Disney Films: Critical Essays on Race, Ethnicity, Gender, Sexuality, and Disability*. Edited by Johnson Cheu. Jefferson, NC: McFarland, 2013.

8

Moana

Daughter of the Chief and Polynesian (in)Visibility

Jenny Banh

Moana, which means "ocean" is Disney's 2016 "princess of color."[1] Certainly, until now, there has not been a lot of Pacific Islander representation in mainstream media, so upon first glance Disney's *Moana* has given much needed visibility to Polynesian stories, actors, culture, and environment. Upon further examination, the entirety of the film including commercial marketing, plot, and history, share problematic elements that cannot be seen. These invisibilities of neglected histories span Anglo and Asian settler colonialism, the erasure of indigenous Hawaiian people, and the cultural appropriation of Pacific Islander culture. As much as the film brought the rich culture to young audiences, *Moana* also perpetuates a fine line of exoticizing and "othering" Polynesian culture.

This chapter examines both the visibilities and invisibilities of producing a work like *Moana* that focuses on a culture rarely featured in mainstream media. Firstly, I examine how *Moana* boasts Pacific Islander visibility while simultaneously rending some Pacific Islander histories invisible. Secondly, I examine how the film illuminates environmentalism and Pacific Island life, in contexts that depoliticizes it. Thirdly, I examine the portrayal of Moana as "The Daughter of the Village Chief," and lastly, I look at how in selling Moana, Disney continues a legacy of costuming brownness and cultural appropriation.

VISIBILITY: THE MAKING OF
PACIFIC ISLANDER MOANA

Moana received strong and positive audience reception particularly for the film's attempts to be culturally accurate.[2] Disney amassed a team of cultural experts that it termed the Oceanic Story Trust. Research and development for Moana began in 2011 when the film's creative team made a three-week trip to the Pacific, spending time in Fiji, Samoa, and French Polynesia.[3] The Oceanic Story Trust was comprised of an eclectic group of artists, cultural practitioners, academics, and community leaders, all of whom possessed expertise in various parts of Pacific Islander culture, history, and language.[4] The Oceanic Trust was "critical for revealing the complex and negotiable process of exchange that transpired between Pacific cultural consultants and Disney film executives during the making of *Moana*."[5]

The experts of the Oceanic Trust communicated through video chat, email, and in-person visits with the corporation in Los Angeles. Disney and the Trust would view all the different steps of the film for further comments throughout the movie process. Disney wanted to avoid the cultural criticism they received over past Disney ventures such as Hong Kong Disney and Euro Disneyland.[6] Earlier in the company's history, Disney's portrayal of Pacific Islander culture mined in racialized tropes in works like the 1937 short film *Hawaiian Holiday* and in the 1989 comedic farce *The Parent Trap: Hawaiian Honeymoon*. With *Moana,* the company's use of a story trust allowed the filmmakers access to voices that could provide a more considered and sensitive approach in telling stories.[7]

The film constitutes a bricolage of ancestral narratives borrowed from across the Pacific, specifically Polynesia.[8] Generations of Pacific Islanders have been altering their stories for creative inspiration or to address political issues. One can view *Moana* as not exactly identical to the Polynesian stories but rather "as part of a legacy of storytelling that is flexible, creative . . . and to a large extent, negotiable."[9] In creating a story line inspired by a range of folk narratives from the region, Disney could take creative license, while at the same time not alienating the peoples it wished to represent by leaving any one group out, or by mischaracterizing a well-known story.

Yet despite the film's use of a trust, the majority of the important players of a film's creative team were creatives who were not from the region or of the culture. The film's producers, directors, and screenwriters were all long-time, well-known Disney classic names. Ron Clements and John Musker returned to direct *Moana*—the duo having co-directed a slate of Disney classics: *The Little Mermaid, Aladdin, Hercules,* and *The Princess and the Frog*. Identical twins Aaron and Jordan Kandell, both born and raised in Hawaii, were added to the writing team to connect many of the missing emotional and cultural elements.[10] However, Jared Bush is credited as the final screenwriter. Therefore the film's development was not primarily driven by people from the region, they were consulted.

While Pacific Islanders had limited visibility among those with creative decision-making over the film, Disney put them front and center in other areas. The film's music was praised for using Pacific Islander voices. For example, the film's soundtrack featured the choral group Pasifika Voices, based at the University of the South Pacific, Fiji, and led by celebrated choir director Igelese Ete.[11] The chart-topping soundtrack, with its unmistakable Pasifika beats, was co-written (along with Broadway's Hamilton impresario Lin-Manuel Miranda and veteran Disney composer Mark Mancina) by Tokelauan/Tuvaluan musician Opetaia Foa'i of the proclaimed pan-Pacific group Te Vaka.[12] Yet despite Polynesian talent, Robin Armstrong argued that the music suffered from Western ethnocentrisms. He explained that although the film is culturally accurate in its use of Polynesian musical traits, they frame the sounds that are unfamiliar within those that are familiar by wrapping them with Western musical characteristics.[13] Nevertheless Moana does make more visible Pacific Islander music despite its hybridization with Disney music.

The films voice cast, however, was made up almost entirely of full or part Pacific Islander descended people.[14] In looking at voice casting in Disney films during the Disney Renaissance, the majority of the speaking and also singing roles went to white actors for films featuring diverse cultures. *Moana* follows *Princess and the Frog* in Disney's current Second Revival in having voice and singing casts that reflect the shades and backgrounds seen on the screen.

INVISIBILITY: CONCEPTUAL, SPATIAL, RACIAL, AND POLITICAL

On one hand *Moana* is a significant step forward for Pacific Islander visibility in the Disney brand and in popular culture. Yet, this visibility is not a deep dive. In the film's story line, something valuable has been taken from Te Fiti that turns her into a destructive force. Likewise, the real histories of many of the islands involves colonial taking that have been destructive to the peoples and the lands of the region. For it is not generally known that on January 17, 1893, Hawaii's monarchy was overthrown when a group of businessmen and sugar planters forced the Hawaiian Queen Liliuokalani to abdicate.[15] Five years later in 1898, the U.S. annexed Hawaii and it became a U.S. territory. These businessmen then started importing foreign populations of Asian and Portuguese sugar cane workers which displaced indigenous Hawaiians. In 1959 it became the fiftieth state.

Settler colonialism which displaces the local indigenous community with colonializers is also part of the histories of the region that the film avoids. This is currently the real experience of Pacific Islanders. Lisa Hall points out the many ways that Hawaiians, in particular, have been erased: "conceptually, spatially, racially and politically."[16] The "conceptual erasure" of Hawaiians and Hawaii history as a colonized group and landmass is also whitewashed in the U.S. curriculum. Hall asserts that the U.S.-colonial takeover of Hawaii is invisible or as she pithily posits it: "U.S. colonialism is off the intellectual map."[17] While African slavery, Native American "removals," and the war with Mexico are glossed over and whitewashed in public school history in the U.S., there is a conceptual erasure of the fact that the U.S. is an Empire that holds many lands, including Puerto Rico, the Philippines, the U.S. Virgin Islands, Guam, and American Samoa. Few Americans know the story of how Alaska was attained as a state. The mere thought that Hawaii was violently taken over by a colonizing entity like the United States is also never mentioned, far less taught to students.

"Spatial erasure" also contributes to invisibility in that most U.S. maps do not present the other U.S. "controlled" landmasses of Guam, American Samoa, and Puerto Rico. Hall in her studies noted having to consult the online CIA World Fact Book to find out what U.S. land was put under U.S. control and the date it happened.

"Racial erasure" of indigenous Hawaiians and other Pacific Islanders occurs as most racial "othering" has often been in the shadows of a Black/White binary around racial discourse. Like Asians, Latinos, and Native Americans, Pacific Islanders are less often individually examined for their specific oppressive histories.[18] Additionally other people of color, such as Asian Americans in Hawaii, do not realize that they are also part of a settler colonization project that exploited the Hawaiian people.[19]

The question remains in the region: Who can call themselves Pacific Islander? If one had never traveled to Hawaii and had only watched the film *Moana*; one would have the impression that the Pacific Islands are dominated by native indigenous peoples. In fact, the opposite is true in Hawaii as the indigenous are a statistical population minority of 10 percent. According to the Census Bureau, the population of Hawaii is composed of Asian: 38.02 percent, White: 25.13 percent, two or more races: 23.81 percent, Native Hawaiian or Pacific Islander: 10.03 percent, Black or African American: 1.82 percent, Other race: 0.99 percent and Native American: 0.19 percent.[20] Lindstrom outlines how race and identity are conflated:

> ... in Hawai'i (the most ethnically complex Pacific archipelago) and New Zealand, where individuals must define themselves in terms of powerful ethnic categories of Māori, (other) Pacific Islander, or pākehā (European) (see

King 1991). And in contemporary Hawai'i, a second system of group identity that contrasts "local" with "nonlocal"—relying on behavioral attributes such as residence, language, and dress—overlaps with the understanding of ethnic identity as based on essential features of race or ancestry . . . People's use of ethnicity gets constructed beyond the Pacific.[21]

Lastly, "political erasure" is very intertwined by present-day Asian Americans and Anglo-White Americans that currently dominate Hawaii politically and economically.[22] Settler colonialism occurred historically when an invading body slowly took over indigenous people's lands. Colonization perpetrated by Anglo settlers in Hawaii introduced diseases such as measles, syphilis, and others that killed a significant number of Hawaiians.[23] Today, the unfortunate legacy continues that Hawaiians have a higher rate of disease than other ethnic groups because of this.

Nomenclature also becomes politically murky with Asian Americans who self-identify as Hawaiians. Asian Americans are not native to Hawaii but were brought over in the 1800s to farm various plantations. They were certainly exploited and have lived in Hawaii for several generations, but that does not make them native Hawaiians. They are also part of the settler colonization project. Hawaiians are classified as "Native Americans" along with American Indian and Alaskans but rarely addressed in Native American courses.[24] Hall asserts that the acronym API (Asian Pacific Islander) is an inappropriate term in that it erases Pacific Islander histories: Polynesian, Melanesian, and Micronesian.

Disney safely created a film about Polynesia that spans a time period before the impacts of settler colonization. And it makes economic sense. It also renders the realities of the Pacific today as pristine and exotic, devoid of the complexities of these spaces after enduring the impacts of Anglo colonization. However, it also amounts to erasure and invisibility. We are allowed to be lured by the histories we find entertaining, but not the histories we find inconvenient. Since Disney's works on native peoples become global tropes, as was the case for Pocahontas, such cinematic choices and interpretations continue to have audiences perceive indigenous spaces as corporate entities wish they were, rather than how they actually are now. This matters economically because after *Moana*, Disney opened an $800 million resort on O'ahu, Hawaii. To open the resort, Disney's head Robert Iger appeared in a Hawaiian shirt and flip-flops welcoming tourists and noting that Disney "committed ourselves to ensuring that Aulani [the resort] is respectful and appreciative of the unique Hawaiian culture and traditions."[25] However, journalists noted the juxtaposition that the new resort was located on the doorsteps of indigenous Hawaiian communities that carried the lowest economic indicators in the state.[26] This underscores how much cinematic works can often be political and in their framing of narratives often push economic interests that further marginalizes the peoples these works claim to empower in the first place.

ENVIRONMENTALISM AND PACIFIC ISLAND LIFE

One of the key modern themes of Moana is environmentalism and Pacific Island life. Climate change has re-emerged as a part of our social discourse today and this progressive theme is subtly woven into *Moana*'s story line. In various scenes, the characters discuss how humans have impacted the environment. It contrasts with depictions of traditional Pacific Islander life, which demonstrated how humans lived in harmony with the environment. Today, a story about Pacific Island lifestyles is most appropriate for this type of theme because their land shows the effects of global warming.

While environmental activism is not new (in the '50s, '60s, and '70s, it focused on pollution's impact on the ozone and global warming), it has taken on a new form in the 2000s, particularly due to globalization. The shift in focus on language from global warming to climate change particularly is rooted in extreme weather events.[27] Scientists conclude that such extreme weather phenomenon are human-induced,[28] increasing global activism around climate change and prompting global political action like the 2016 Paris Agreement.

Humans started to affect the climate in the 1950s when the world population increased by over 60 percent.[29] The amount of carbon dioxide in the atmosphere has increased by more than 20 percent. There are many examples of climate change and global warming in Hawaii that prove detrimental to an economy that relies so much on tourism to survive. One example in the Hawaiian Pacific is chronic erosion that threatens coastal development and will lead to further beach loss if beaches are not allowed to recede naturally where the coastal plain is composed of sand. Beach erosion will become an increasing problem in Hawaii in coming decades should the rate of sea level rise accelerate as predicted."[30] The shoreline will erode and there will be rising sea levels.[31] Moana certainly shows all of these effects on the fictitious island of Motunui.

Visibility: *Moana*'s Climate Change and Global Warming Metaphors

In Moana, the environmental vegetation turns dark and dies which is a metaphor for how global warming lays waste to once thriving environments.[32] The first Disney film to address environmental themes is *Bambi* (1942). Hunters invade and kill Bambi's mother which starts the destruction of the forest.[33] Another film carrying environmental and sustainability themes is *WALL-E* (2008).[34] The film depicts a society that has come to rely exclusively on technology (or technocentrism). In *WALL-E* it takes the discovery of a plant—fresh organic life that reminds society about its lost humanity. In *Pocahontas* (1995), British settlers arrive in the "New World," and their ambitions will eventually, in real life, be disastrous for Native peoples and their way of life.[35]

More recently, as a corporate strategy Disney has embarked on environmental initiatives, among them, going green at its parks and resorts.[36] There are many examples of climate change and global warming throughout Moana; it is central to the movie. Moana's journey and character development is driven by the threat to her homeland and people by a mysterious "darkness" that destroys the islands, vegetation, and fish. This darkness has taken many forms when looking at modern developments in the Pacific region. Firstly, the "darkness" could be a metaphor for environmental degradation, climate change and global warming, and additionally human being's role in it, since Maui's greed for power prompted him to steal the heart of Te Fiti. In the past, the major environmental pollutants came from manufacturing and natural resource industries, such as pesticides, mining, logging, and the oil industry.[37] Secondly, the "darkness" of the twentieth century can also be from tourism. Eventually, while pollution can be reduced, another notable increase that is more problematic to address is the impacts of tourism. Providing tours and services to tourists and the combined actions of those who provide tourist services are causing increased environmental destruction.[38] This darkness or tourism can be seen "consuming" the island, people and its wildlife. Finally, the "darkness" could be modernization and advancement. Native Hawaiians in 2019, with the support of *Moana* star Dwayne "The Rock" Johnson, protested the construction of the billion-dollar Thirty Meter Telescope project that is a joint venture of universities and institutions from the U.S., Canada, India, and Japan.[39] Like activism against the Dakota Access Pipeline by Native Americans, Native Hawaiians are against further degradation of sacred lands, in this case, several sacred sites on the mountain Mauna O Wakea, that includes an indigenous burial site. Native Hawaiians raised concerns about the project since 2009. Protesters stand at odds against modern scientific aims and its economic interests in preserving traditional beliefs about the land.[40]

In all these instances above, this "darkness" signals Native peoples beliefs in the consequences of man's (or in this case a half-man/demi-god) actions to the environment. The main catalyst for change in the environment is the taking of something valuable from a god, because of greed. Maui was also not interested in restoring the heart to Te Fiti. There are several scenes that hint at or more overtly show how such powerful human actions lead to environmental destruction. The coconuts become inedible and viewers see much of the vegetation turn black. Also, the nets are catching fewer and fewer fish. This can be seen in present day climate change in that fish populations have seen reduced catches all over the world. One reason for this is global warming and the over-fishing of the sea.

Te Fiti had the power to create life and shared it with the world but her heart was stolen from her. This is the reason the Polynesian village Motunui is dying. Thus, Moana has to return the heart of Te Fiti in order to save her village and people. Moana's father is against her leaving the island and forbids her to go beyond the reef. Moana is against the status quo, which she refers to as "old ways." She says that they're obsolete for the current problems. She argues that there is fish beyond the reef. And in her journey to save her island, she learns that her ancestors also knew to keep voyaging. One metaphorical way to look at this is that we must change our deleterious environmental "old ways" and seek out new solutions. And in Moana teaching her people how to voyage again, as a people, they rediscover how man can co-exist with their environment and its finite resources. In *Moana,* Disney brings visibility to environmental themes. However it subverts it in the narrative, amplifying accessible aspects around notions of saving an island, and ignoring more complex aspects around environmental debates taking place today.

MOANA: THE DAUGHTER OF THE VILLAGE CHIEF

Moana is different from Disney traditional princesses who have come before her. Certainly, she is different from Snow White and Cinderella but also different from Elsa and Anna. When Maui tells Moana she is a princess, she tells him that she is not. Using logic, Maui says she is technically a princess because she is the daughter of a village chief who is a sort of king. In the song, "I Am Moana (Song of the Ancestors)" performed by Rachel House and Auli'i Cravalho, Moana sings: "I am the daughter of the village chief." Even in the film *Wreck-It Ralph 2* when all the princesses gather and describe the traits of the princess to a arcade game "princess" Vanellope von Schweetz, Moana does not fit many of those tropes.[41]

The princesses give Vanellope the list of princess characteristics, which include: magical hair/hands, curses, being poisoned, kidnapped/enslaved, saved by true love's kiss, has "daddy issues," has no mother, or has made a deal with an underwater witch. The last on the list is that your problems are solved by a strong man. Moana, Tiana, and Mulan do not have many of these princess prerequisites.

Moana fights for herself and her village without any curses or magical hands. Mulan cross-dresses as a man throughout the movie, while

Tiana is a frog for a majority of her film. Including Moana, the three "princesses" are not given the same treatment as others even if they have positive traits that do not render them hopeless but strong and independent, however each is helped, in some measure, to reach their goal by a male character.[42] Even her home is not glamorous with a large castle and Moana is not clothed in elegant attire.[43] It is traditional and functional. Some scholars have even argued that Mulan and Tiana face a "glass ceiling" in that they are not entitled to a life of leisure and privilege that white Disney princesses enjoy.[44]

These so-called princesses who are also "princesses of color" are not often perceived as Disney princesses because they do not follow the usual princess script.[45] They do not actively desire to marry princes, consider themselves princesses, and exhibit far more agency than princesses before them. In surveys, global audiences do not view them as princesses.[46] Moana is the daughter of a village chief who dreams of the ocean, but her father forbids her from ever going past the reef. Her attitude throughout the movie is seen as courageous, and transgressive of her society's norms, a quality that not all the early Disney princesses exhibited. At the end of the film she moves from her technical "princess" title to become the chief (or King).

This visibility of agency is what makes Moana in line with recent "princesses" like her from Tiana to Merida and Elsa (with an assist from Anna). What is also important is that girls of color can see themselves represented in that agency. And while such representation is celebrated, the commodification of a brown heroine is the invisible downside of the Disney machine.

SELLING MOANA: #IAMNOTYOURCOSTUME

Disney's diversification of its princess franchise may now include Pacific Islander representation, but Disney has an (in)visible problem in its merchandising of cultures which expands beyond the film. When the film's creators generated the Oceanic Trust expert team, Disney was very careful to not create any cultural backlash, but somehow Disney mishandled the *Moana* Halloween Disney costume merchandising. Pacific Island culture is consumed all over the world and the Disney film *Moana* made it much more visible, but further problematic commodification of deemed "exotic" cultures and peoples. Hawaiian culture, for instance, has been consumed around the world and engaged in ways that are offensive to the local indigenous Pacific Islanders. Even white supremacist protesters who marched in Charlottesville, Virginia, in 2017 at a Unite the Right rally, used tiki torches[47] they can pick up at any crafts store for a backyard luau. That tiki torches can now be used at a hate rally is a sad example of how far Polynesian culture has now become everyday consumer behavior, stripped of its cultural origins. And while the film is very beloved in the community, there were Polynesians who objected to Western forms of the commodification of the culture, specifically in the form of Halloween costumes.[48] Some called the costumes cultural appropriation and perpetuating Polynesian stereotypes.

Polynesian Culture: Stereotype and Commodification

If there were elaborate, nuanced, and many depictions of Polynesians in mainstream media, then the debate about how Polynesians are depicted would not be as intense. Additionally, Polynesian culture has had a long history of commodification in the West. Specifically, Elvis Presley films in the 1960s like *Blue Hawaii, Elvis: Paradise Hawaii Style*, and *Girls, Girls, Girls*, exoticized Hawaii for Western audiences. There are several stereotypes of Pacific Islanders, men and women, that are detrimental: ". . . the touristic commodification of culture and land in Hawai'i proceeds most notably (and profitably) through the marketing of a feminized and eroticized image of the islands as a hula girl."[49] Hawaiian women are also depicted as invisible in stories as a backdrop to the main Anglo-white male character.

"Polynesian men are either completely erased from the picture, relegated to the background as musicians for the female dancers, or similarly sexualized as the surfer, beach boy."[50] An example is the fire-knife dancer and surfer David Kawena's character in *Lilo and Stitch* (2002) who is depicted as unsophisticated and lacking any sense. Other Hawaiian male depictions in popular culture are depicted as criminal, violent, lazy, non-intellectual, and unable to adapt to modernity.[51] Hawaiian men are often depicted as "happy go lucky," non-adult males, and "offered white women and men a bronzed well-muscled promise of social, sexual, physical and moral freedom."[52]

Maui in Moana is shown as a dull buffoon; he is unconcerned about the future even though he was the one who stole the heart of Te Fiti, which caused so much havoc. He is depicted as an over-sized jokester. He is on the largest spectrum in body types, which was very controversial because some see him as obese. In fact, the Oceanic Trust objected to one sketch of Maui without hair that prompted the film's creative team to give him a full mane of hair.[53] Other critics also objected to Maui's larger than life frame, although it is depicted in the film as being muscular, they did not want the stereotyped depiction of an overweight Polynesian.[54] These persistent images of Pacific Island men and women also dominate present-day tourist postcards that are sold in every store in Hawaii.

Brownface: Moana Maui Halloween Costume #IAmNotYourCostume

It is one thing to exoticize Pacific Islanders through the tourist gaze, another is to play dress up as another culture. This form of appropriation—costuming, strips cultures of their dignity, tradition, and renders them stock entertainment. Disney sold a Maui and Moana costume which were brown-colored body suits with tribal tattoos which cost around $44–$50.[55] You could also complete the costume with "Polynesian hair" which was a long dark curly wig. The marketing language used in costuming an indigenous culture also permits consumers to participate, ridding it of offence. One product description of the *Moana* costume read,

> Get Your Ideal Celebration Costume Now. For any occasions like Halloween Party, Christmas, New Year, Birthday or stage show, you do want special clothes to catch everybody's eyes and be the star—This Is the One, either for yourself or as a gift! Life-Like Tattoos Guaranteed with high quality 3D printing in the suit, your body will look like it is really tattooed! Along with our comfy material they will suit perfectly on your body, adding the real effects of tattoo, and also showing your shape, like a real tattooed body show![56]

While there were some Polynesians who were not offended by the outfit, there was a very vocal Twitter response from others who were upset with the *Moana* tattoo costumes. They called it *brownface* and *cultural appropriation*, on social media. Brownface is when an Anglo or another culture dresses up as that ethnic group. Cultural appropriation is when you take the traditional aspect of a culture and you reduce it to that small part which becomes a harmful stereotype.

"As a Poly I support our folk involved in #MOANA. But this? NO. Our Brown Skin/Ink's NOT a costume," one user tweeted.[57] "Many people are rightfully upset about this new piece of #Moana merch. Cultures are NOT costumes," tweeted another. "Hey heads up, I've seen that Moana costume, and I seriously don't want to see it again. It sickens me, please don't ask me to talk about it," tweeted a third. "This might be the creepiest thing Disney has ever done. 'Wear another culture's skin!'" yet another person tweeted.[58] People accused Disney of selling a costume that let people "Play Hawaiian." Disney eventually came under fire for the Moana Halloween costumes and eventually pulled the costume off the shelves and apologized.[59]

While Moana allowed a Polynesian girl to be seen around the world, Disney's extended economic activity: the merchandizing and franchising of its films, rendered her new found visibility, invisible, when her culture was reduced to a costume. As Disney diversifies its cinematic works, with the global reach of this media company, it is important to underscore that such good will can be spent when cultures the company seeks to bring to the screen, become caricature in other areas.

CONCLUSION

This chapter examined both invisibility and visibility within and beyond *Moana*, Disney's attempt at spotlighting Polynesian/Pacific Island culture. While the film made visible a wide range of cultural values from the region, it avoided current conceptual, spatial, racial, and economic erasure of the Pacific Islands via settler colonization. It demonstrates how easily entertainment can cherry-pick parts of histories it wishes to profit from, leaving other histories as inconvenient truths. No one wants to vacation at a *Moana*-themed resort, while having to think about exploitation, settler colonization, and the desecration of indigenous lands. Neither do they want to consider environmental impacts that can threaten to raise sea levels that can wipe out beach resorts or many islands themselves. Therefore, in presenting environmental themes in *Moana*, Disney simplifies how we can save an island, with one girl's actions, but stays away from more complicated discourse around man's actions that create climate change in the first place. It fits Disney's good corporate citizenship around environmentalism, allowing the company to go green at its parks, but still build resorts on beachfronts.

Moana also provides visibility to young girls of color outside of Black, Latino, and Asian groups. Not only is the Polynesian Moana diverse, she defies what is expected of a girl. *Moana* is the first story line of the Disney princess franchise where there is no love interest, not even hinted at, or refused, as was the case in *Brave*. However, as much as Moana's diversity among Disney representations is applaudable, other economic ventures in franchise-making create invisible effects. The selling of *Moana* Halloween outfits continued a practice of cultural appropriation and brownface of Pacific Island/Polynesian culture. As Disney aims to expand who can be its "princess" the company must aim to become culturally competent in all its economic activities, not just in its filmmaking process alone.

Disney's Moana did many things right but there are some ways the company can improve their cultural competence for future films. Scholars of the racialization of Pacific Island culture note that instead of prescribing "one proper set of decolonial practices, but rather create spaces in which decolonialization can be deeply considered and experimented with in the specific contexts of different places."[60] In addition: Stephanie Teves and Maile Arvin recommend that Disney and anyone who deals with Pacific Islander history "1) Acknowledge that the land is indigenous 2) Stop using terms like API (Asian Pacific American) or Asian Pacific

Women 3) Recognize that Hula is a distinguished art form and not your Halloween costume or cardio exercise class 4) Others must learn about Pacific Islander culture and history and not just invite Pacific Islanders to dance 5) Reconsider your use of the term "Hapa" and 5) Expand the native Hawaiian and Pacific Islander curricula."[61] If Disney is to truly not just co-opt diversity for economics, it would have to go further than simply changing the color of its princesses, otherwise it is participating in a mediated form of settler colonization.

NOTES

1. Walt Disney Animation Studios, *Moana*, directed by Ron Clements and John Musker, written by Jared Bush, 2016.
2. Robin Armstrong, "Time to Face the Music: Musical Colonization and Appropriation in Disney's Moana," *Social Science* 7, no. 7 (2018): 113.
3. A. Mārata Ketekiri Tamaira and Dionne Fonoti, "Beyond Paradise? Retelling Pacific Stories in Disney's Moana," *The Contemporary Pacific* 30, no. 2 (2018): 311.
4. Ibid., 312.
5. Ibid., 298.
6. Kimberley Choi, "Disneyfication and Localization: The Cultural Globalization Process of Hong Kong Disneyland," *Urban Studies* 49, no. 2 (2012): 383–397, http://www.jstor.org/stable/26150847; Andrew Lainsbury, *Once Upon an American Dream: The Story of Euro Disneyland* (Lawrence: University Press of Kansas, 2000).
7. A. Mārata Ketekiri Tamaira and Dionne Fonoti, "Beyond Paradise? Retelling Pacific Stories in Disney's Moana," 309–310.
8. Ibid., 305–306.
9. Ibid., 306.
10. Billy V, "Hawaii Brothers Write for Disney's 'Moana," *Hawaii News Now*, last modified July 2, 2019, November 18, 2016, https://www.hawaiinewsnow.com/story/33746886/interview-aaron-and-jordan-kandell-hawaii-boys-in-hollywood.
11. A. Mārata Ketekiri Tamaira and Dionne Fonoti, "Beyond Paradise? Retelling Pacific Stories in Disney's Moana," 311.
12. Ibid., 310.
13. Robin Armstrong, "Time to Face the Music: Musical Colonization and Appropriation in Disney's Moana," 113.
14. "*Moana* Cast," IMDb, accessed July 2, 2019, https://www.imdb.com/title/tt3521164/fullcredits?ref_=tt_ov_dr#directors/.
15. Learning Network, "Hawaiian Monarchy Overthrown by America-Backed Businessmen," The Learning Network, January 17, 2012, accessed July 2, 2019, https://learning.blogs.nytimes.com/2012/01/17/jan-17-1893-hawaiian-monarchy-overthrown-by-america-backed-businessmen/.
16. Lisa Kahaleole Hall, "Strategies of Erasure: U.S. Colonialism and Native Hawaiian Feminism," *American Quarterly* 60, no. 2 (2008): 275, http://www.jstor.org/stable/40068535.

17. Lisa Kahaleole Hall, "Strategies of Erasure."
18. Ibid., 273–280.
19. Candace Fujikane and Jonathan Y. Okaruma (editors), *Asian Settler Colonialism* (Honolulu: University of Hawaii Press, 2008).
20. World Population Review, "Hawaii," accessed on July 15, 2019, http://worldpopulationreview.com/states/hawaii-population/.
21. Lamont Lindstrom, "Social Relations," in *The Pacific Islands: Environment and Society, Revised Edition,* edited by Rapaport Moshe, 172–181 (Honolulu: University of Hawaii Press, 2013).
22. Ronald Takaki, *Strangers from a Different Shore,* (New York: Little Brown, 1998).
23. Erin Blakemore, "How Measles Helped Destroy the Hawaiian Monarchy," History, February 5, 2019, accessed July 15, 2019, https://www.history.com/news/hawaii-monarchy-downfall-measles-outbreak.
24. Lisa Kahaleole Hall, "Strategies of Erasure," 276.
25. Tina Grandinetti, "Moana Might be Great for Representation but It's Not All Heartwarming for Hawaii," *The Guardian,* January 12, 2017, accessed at https://www.theguardian.com/film/2017/jan/13/moana-might-be-great-for-representation-but-its-not-all-heartwarming-for-hawaii.
26. Hall, "Strategies of Erasure," 276.
27. Anne K. Armstrong, Marianne E. Krasny, and Jonathon P. Schuldt, "Climate Change Science: The Facts," in *Communicating Climate Change: A Guide for Educators,* 7–20 (Ithaca; London: Cornell University Press, 2018).
28. Dim Coumou and Stefan Rahmstorf, "A Decade of Weather Extremes," *Nature Climate Change,* no. 2 (2012): 491–496.
29. Veerabhadran Ramanathan, "Global Warming," *Bulletin of the American Academy of Arts and Sciences* 59, no. 3 (2006): 1.
30. Bradley M. Romine and Charles H. Fletcher, "A Summary of Historical Shoreline Changes on Beaches of Kauai, Oahu, and Maui, Hawaii," *Journal of Coastal Research* 29, no. 3 (2013): 605–614.
31. Andrew P. Sturman and Hamish A. McGowan. "Climate," in *The Pacific Islands: Environment and Society, Revised Edition,* edited by Rapaport Moshe, 9 (Honolulu: University of Hawaii Press, 2013).
32. Walt Disney Animation Studios, *Moana,* 2016.
33. Walt Disney Productions, *Bambi,* directed by David Hand, 1942.
34. Pixar Animation Studios-Walt Disney Pictures, *WALL-E,* directed by Andrew Stanton, 2008.
35. Walt Disney Pictures, *Pocahontas,* directed by Mike Gabriel, 1995.
36. Walt Disney Parks, "Championing Environmental Stewardship, Environmental Fact Sheet," accessed July 12, 2019, https://aboutwaltdisneyworldresort.com/releases/environmental-fact-sheet/
37. Ruth H. Allen, Michelle Gottlieb, Eve Clute, Montira J. Pongsiri, Janette Sherman, and G. Iris Obrams, "Breast Cancer and Pesticides in Hawaii: The Need for Further Study," *Environmental Health Perspectives* 105 (1997): 679–683, doi:10.2307/3433389.
38. David S. May, "Tourism and the Environment," *Natural Resources & Environment* 14, no. 1 (1999): 57–61. http://www.jstor.org/stable/40924705.

39. Megan Murry, "Why Are Native Hawaiians Protesting Against a Telescope?" *New York Times*, July 22, 2019, https://www.nytimes.com/2019/07/22/us/hawaii-telescope-protest.html

40. David S. May, "Tourism and the Environment."

41. Walt Disney Animation Studios, *Ralph Breaks the Internet*, directed by Rich Moore and Phil Johnston, starring John C. Reilly, Sarah Silverman, Jane Lynch, Alan Tudyk, Mindy Kaling, Ed O'Neill, Jack McBrayer, 2018, Digital copy.

42. Lauren Dundes and Madeline Streiff, "Reel Royal Diversity? The Glass Ceiling in Disney's Mulan and Princess and the Frog," *Societies* 6, no. 4 (2016): 2.

43. Lauren Dundes and Madeline Streiff, "Reel Royal Diversity?" 2.

44. Ibid.

45. Ibid.

46. Charu Uppal, "Over Time and Beyond Disney—Visualizing Princesses through a Comparative Study in India, Fiji, and Sweden," Social Science 8, no. 4 (2019): 105.

47. Paul P. Murphy, "White Nationalists Use Tiki Torches to Light Up Charlottesville March," *CNN*, last modified August 14, 2017, https://www.cnn.com/2017/08/12/us/white-nationalists-tiki-torch-march-trnd/index.html.

48. Tongantarian, "Polynesian Responds to SJW's on Moana Costumes," YouTube video, 17:41, posted October 27, 2017, https://www.youtube.com/watch?v=72qzINJYcbA; Lily Kim-Dela Cruz, "Hawaiian Girl's Thoughts on Moana Costume," YouTube Video, 5:01. posted October 26, 2017, https://www.youtube.com/watch?v=QPvL5WdUHao; Travis Andrews, "Brown Skin Is Not a Costume': Disney Takes Heat for 'Moana' Halloween Costume," *The Washington Post*, September 20, 2016, accessed July 16, 2019, https://www.washingtonpost.com/news/morning-mix/wp/2016/09/20/brown-skin-is-not-a-costume-disney-takes-heat-for-moana-halloween-costume/?utm_term=.a3401d7e9150; Doug Herman, "How the Story of 'Moana' and Maui Holds Up Against Cultural Truths," Smithsonian.com, December 2, 2016, accessed on July 16, 2019, https://www.smithsonianmag.com/smithsonian-institution/how-story-moana-and-maui-holds-against-cultural-truths-180961258/.

49. Ty P Kāwika Tengan, *Native Men Remade: Gender and Nation in Contemporary Hawaii* (Durham, NC: Duke University Press, 2009), 8.

50. Ibid., 8.

51. Ibid., 8 and 44–45.

52. Ibid., 8 and 44–45.

53. Walt Disney Animation Studios, "Voices of the Island."

54. Nick Perry, "Moana a Disney Hit but Portrayal Irks Some in the Pacific," *The Associated Press*, November 29, 2016, accessed July 26, 2019, https://www.apnews.com/cb755ae10e164c3aaca8c445b9e3708b.

55. WEEOH, "Maui Costume," accessed July 16, 2019, https://www.amazon.com/FEEAA-Tattoo-Halloween-Cosplay-Costume/dp/B07F1Z57HB/ref=sr_1_1?keywords=FEEAA&qid=1563235859&s=gateway&sr=8-1.

56. "Maui Costume Product Description," accessed on July 15, 2019, https://www.amazon.com/FEEAA-Tattoo-Halloween-Cosplay-Costume/dp/B07F1Z57HB/ref=sr_1_1?keywords=FEEAA&qid=1563235859&s=gateway&sr=8-1=.

57. E News! Facebook repost, accessed July 16, 2019, https://www.facebook.com/enews/posts/10153724889865736?comment_id=10153725051150736&reply_comment_id=10153725409325736&comment_tracking=%7B%22tn%22%3A%22R%22%7D.
58. Travis Andrews, "'Brown Skin Is Not a Costume.'"
59. Michelle Van Dyke. "Disney Pulls Costume after People Angered over Brownface," *Buzzfeed*, September 18, 2016, accessed 26, 2019, https://www.buzzfeed.com/mbvd/people-say-disney-moana-maui-costume-is-brownface.
60. Judy Rohrer, "Staking Claim: Settler Colonialism and Racialization in Hawaii, 184.
61. Stephanie Teves and Maile Arvin, "Decolonalizing API: Centering Indigenous Pacific Islander Feminism." In *Asian American Feminisms and Women of Color Politics*, edited by Lynn Fujiwara and Shireen Roshanravan (Seattle: University of Washington Press, 2018).

BIBLIOGRAPHY

Allen, Ruth H., Michelle Gottlieb, Eve Clute, Montira J. Pongsiri, Janette Sherman, and G. Iris Obrams, "Breast Cancer and Pesticides in Hawaii: The Need for Further Study," *Environmental Health Perspectives* 105 (1997): 679–83, doi:10.2307/3433389.

Andrews, Travis. "Brown Skin Is Not a Costume': Disney Takes Heat for 'Moana' Halloween Costume," *The Washington Post*, September 20, 2016, accessed July 16, 2019, https://www.washingtonpost.com/news/morning-mix/wp/2016/09/20/brown-skin-is-not-a-costume-disney-takes-heat-for-moana-halloween-costume/?utm_term=.a3401d7e9150.

Armstrong, Anne K., Marianne E. Krasny, and Jonathon P. Schuldt. "Climate Change Science: The Facts." In *Communicating Climate Change: A Guide for Educators*, 7–20. Ithaca; London: Cornell University Press, 2018.

Armstrong, Robin. "Time to Face the Music: Musical Colonization and Appropriation in Disney's Moana." *Social Science* 7, no. 7 (2018): 113.

Billy, V. "Hawaii Brothers Write for Disney's 'Moana." *Hawaii News Now*, Last modified July 2, 2019, November 18, 2016. https://www.hawaiinewsnow.com/story/33746886/interview-aaron-and-jordan-kandell-hawaii-boys-in-hollywood.

Blakemore, Erin. "How Measles Helped Destroy the Hawaiian Monarchy." History, February 5, 2019. Accessed July 15, 2019, https://www.history.com/news/hawaii-monarchy-downfall-measles-outbreak.

Choi, Kimberley. "Disneyfication and Localization: The Cultural Globalization Process of Hong Kong Disneyland." *Urban Studies* 49, no. 2 (2012): 383–397.

Coumou, Dim and Stefan Rahmstorf. "A Decade of Weather Extremes." *Nature Climate Change*, 2 (2012): 491–496.

Dundes, Lauren, and Madeline Streiff. "Reel Royal Diversity? The Glass Ceiling in Disney's Mulan and Princess and the Frog," *Societies* 6, no. 4 (2016): 2.

Fujikane, Candace, and Jonathan Y. Okaruma (editors), *Asian Settler Colonialism*. Honolulu: University of Hawaii Press, 2008.

Grandinetti, Tina. "Moana Might Be Great for Representation But It's Not All Heartwarming for Hawaii." *The Guardian*, January 12, 2017, accessed at https://www.theguardian.com/film/2017/jan/13/moana-might-be-great-for-representation-but-its-not-all-heartwarming-for-hawaii.

Herman, Doug, "How the Story of 'Moana' and Maui Holds Up Against Cultural Truths," Smithsonian.com, December 2, 2016. Accessed on July 16, 2019, https://www.smithsonianmag.com/smithsonian-institution/how-story-moana-and-maui-holds-against-cultural-truths-180961258/.

Kahaleole Hall, Lisa. "Strategies of Erasure: U.S. Colonialism and Native Hawaiian Feminism." *American Quarterly* 60, no. 2 (2008): 273–280.

Kim-Dela Cruz, Lily. "Hawaiian Girl's Thoughts on Moana Costume," YouTube Video, 5:01. posted October 26, 2017, https://www.youtube.com/watch?v=QPvL5WdUHao;

Lainsbury, Andrew. *Once Upon an American Dream: The Story of Euro Disneyland*. Lawrence: University Press of Kansas, 2000.

Learning Network. "Hawaiian Monarchy Overthrown by America-Backed Businessmen." The Learning Network, January 17, 2012. Accessed July 2, 2019, https://learning.blogs.nytimes.com/2012/01/17/jan-17-1893-hawaiian-monarchy-overthrown-by-america-backed-businessmen/.

Lindstrom, Lamont. "Social Relations." In *The Pacific Islands: Environment and Society, Revised Edition*, edited by Rapaport Moshe, 172–181. Honolulu: University of Hawaii Press, 2013.

May, David S. "Tourism and the Environment," *Natural Resources & Environment* 14, no. 1 (1999): 57–61.

"*Moana* Cast." IMDb. Accessed July 2, 2019. https://www.imdb.com/title/tt3521164/fullcredits?ref_=tt_ov_dr#directors/.

Moana Costume Product Description. Accessed on July 15, 2019, https://www.amazon.com/FEEAA-Tattoo-Halloween-Cosplay-Costume/dp/B07F1Z57HB/ref=sr_1_1?keywords=FEEAA&qid=1563235859&s=gateway&sr=8-1=.

Murphy, Paul P. "White Nationalists Use Tiki Torches to Light Up Charlottesville March." *CNN*, Last modified August 14, 2017, https://www.cnn.com/2017/08/12/us/white-nationalists-tiki-torch-march-trnd/index.html.

Murry, Megan. "Why Are Native Hawaiians Protesting Against a Telescope?" *New York Times*, July 22, 2019, https://www.nytimes.com/2019/07/22/us/hawaii-telescope-protest.html.

Ramanathan, Veerabhadran "Global Warming," *Bulletin of the American Academy of Arts and Sciences* 59, no. 3 (2006): 1.

Romine, Bradley M., and Charles H. Fletcher. "A Summary of Historical Shoreline Changes on Beaches of Kauai, Oahu, and Maui, Hawaii." *Journal of Coastal Research* 29, no. 3 (2013): 605–614.

Sturman, Andrew P. and Hamish A. McGowan. "Climate." In *The Pacific Islands: Environment and Society, Revised Edition*, edited by Rapaport Moshe, 9. Honolulu: University of Hawaii Press, 2013.

Takaki, Ronald. *Strangers from a Different Shore*. New York: Little Brown, 1998.

Tamaira, A. Mārata Ketekiri, and Dionne Fonoti. "Beyond Paradise? Retelling Pacific Stories in Disney's Moana," *The Contemporary Pacific* 30, no. 2 (2018): 311.

Tengan, Ty P Kāwika, *Native Men Remade: Gender and Nation in Contemporary Hawaii*. Durham, NC: Duke University Press, 2009.

Teves, Stephanie, and Maile Arvin. "Decolonalizing API: Centering Indigenous Pacific Islander Feminism." In *Asian American Feminisms and Women of Color Politics*, edited by Lynn Fujiwara and Shireen Roshanravan. Seattle: University of Washington Press, 2018.

Tongantarian, "Polynesian Responds to SJW's on Moana Costumes," YouTube video, 17:41, Posted October 27, 2017, https://www.youtube.com/watch?v=72qzINJYcbA.

Uppal, Charu. "Over Time and Beyond Disney—Visualizing Princesses through a Comparative Study in India, Fiji, and Sweden," *Social Science* 8, no. 4 (2019): 105.

Van Dyke, Michelle. "Disney Pulls Costume after People Angered over Brownface," *Buzzfeed*, September 18, 2016, accessed 26, 2019, https://www.buzzfeed.com/mbvd/people-say-disney-moana-maui-costume-is-brownface.

Walt Disney Productions, *Bambi*, directed by David Hand, 1942.

Pixar Animation Studios-Walt Disney Pictures, *WALL-E*, directed by Andrew Stanton, 2008.

Walt Disney Pictures, *Pocahontas*, directed by Mike Gabriel, 1995.

Walt Disney Parks, "Championing Environmental Stewardship, Environmental Fact Sheet," accessed July 12, 2019, https://aboutwaltdisneyworldresort.com/releases/environmental-fact-sheet/.

Walt Disney Animation Studios. *Moana*. Directed by Ron Clements and John Musker. Written by Jared Bush, 2016.

Walt Disney Animation Studios, *Ralph Breaks the Internet*, directed by Rich Moore and Phil Johnston, starring John C. Reilly, Sarah Silverman, Jane Lynch, Alan Tudyk, Mindy Kaling, Ed O'Neill, Jack McBrayer, 2018, Digital copy.

Walt Disney Animation Studios, "Voices of the Island," Moana, Digital Bonus Features, 2017, Digital copy.

WEEOH. "Maui Costume." Accessed July 16, 2019, https://www.amazon.com/FEEAA-Tattoo-Halloween-Cosplay-Costume/dp/B07F1Z57HB/ref=sr_1_1?keywords=FEEAA&qid=1563235859&s=gateway&sr=8-1.

World Population Review. "Hawaii." Accessed on July 15, 2019, http://worldpopulationreview.com/states/hawaii-population/.

9

✢

#MakeMulanRight

Retracing the Genealogy of Mulan from Ancient Chinese Tale to Disney Classic

Jenny Banh

The 1998 Disney cartoon character Mulan sings about how she is forced into many roles and it does not reflect who she really is inside.[1] The Mulan story has been retold many times but its meaning, characters, and morals have changed relative to the context and the country of its delivery.[2] For example, in 2016 a script for Disney's live-action remake leaked, revealing a "white male savior" character who would save Mulan and all of China.[3] This caused a Twitter outrage in which #MakeMulanRight quickly trended to show displeasure over the casting and plot. Mulan is a well-known Chinese story about filial piety and patriotism. There are no white Anglo American saviors in the story nor is there a male love interest.

The original story is unlike the 1998 *Mulan* Disney animated film that appropriates a well-known Chinese folktale to transform it into a Disney formulaic princess film.[4] Mulan is set to a musical, with a sidekick, where she sings: "Look at me . . . I will never pass for a perfect bride. . . . Can it be, I'm not meant to play this part? . . .When will my reflection show who I am inside?"[5] In 2020, Disney ditched Mulan's sidekick dragon, Mushu, and put action in front of singing as the company hoped its live-action would be more faithful to the original telling of this narrative. However, it is important to revisit the original telling of the story of Mulan to understand why Hollywood portrayals of her have been fraught, contentious, and underperformed in Asian markets.

In this chapter, I first reintroduce the many renditions of Mulan: from the original *Ballad of Mulan* to the most recent Disney live-action script that revealed a "white male savior" narrative. I then revisit what brought *Mulan* to Disney's attention, which is Maxine Hong Kingston's *The Woman*

Warrior (1976) book which retells the Mulan story intertwined with her own narrative. Second, I analyze the cinematic attempts such as the 1998's *Mulan* in which Mike Pence called "liberal propaganda" for women in the military. I contrast the 1998 animation with China's 2009 live-action version *Mulan: Rise of a Warrior* to show how it is a more faithful rendition of the Mulan tale. I critique Hollywood practices such as whitewashing native narratives or casting an Anglo actor to play an Asian role. I outline the practice of yellowface, where white actors assume roles, as well as White savior tropes where an Anglo-American actor saves an Asian country or Asian people. Finally, I will discuss the debacle of the 2016 leaked live-action *Mulan* Disney script, which carried problematic examples of the White savior motif.

MANY RENDITIONS OF MULAN

The Ballad of Mulan first appeared in China between the fourth and sixth century and became popular in the West after the 1989 Disney film *Mulan*.[6] Mulan is a legendary heroine, the only record of whom is a 360-word poem written in the Northern Wei Dynasty (386–534 AD) by an anonymous poet. The poem has many different renditions but the stories share a similar plot point. In the poem, Mulan's elderly father is drafted for the war but he cannot physically fight because of his age and physical condition. Since he does not have a son who can take his place, Mulan buys a horse and decides to serve in her father's place. Hua Mulan cross-dresses as a man and fights valiantly as a male soldier for years without anyone detecting her true gender. In *The Ballad of Mulan*, the tale suggests that Hua Mulan kills many of her foes on the battlefield. She is intelligent, strong, and quickly gets promoted because of her aptitude on the battlefield. For twelve years, she leads her men heroically and then returns home. She dresses in her female clothes, applies her powder make-up, and adjusts her hair to reveal her original gender to her amazed soldiers.

木 兰 诗 *The Ballad of Mulan* (386–534 AD)

唧唧复唧唧，木兰当户织。不闻机杼声，唯闻女叹息。
问女何所思？问女何所忆？"女亦无所思，女亦无所忆。
昨夜见军帖，可汗大点兵。军书十二卷，卷卷有爷名。
阿爷无大儿，木兰无长兄。愿为市鞍马，从此替爷征。"
东市买骏马，西市买鞍鞯，南市买辔头，北市买长鞭。
朝辞爷娘去，暮宿黄河边。不闻爷娘唤女声，但闻黄河流水鸣溅溅。
旦辞黄河去，暮至黑山头。不闻爷娘唤女声，但闻燕山胡骑声啾啾。

万里赴戎机，关山度若飞。朔气传金柝，寒光照铁衣。将军百战死，壮士十年归。
归来见天子，天子坐明堂。策勋十二转，赏赐百千强。
可汗问所欲，"木兰不用尚书郎，愿借明驼千里足，送儿还故乡。"
爷娘闻女来，出郭相扶将；阿姊闻妹来，当户理红妆；
小弟闻姊来，磨刀霍霍向猪羊。开我东阁门，坐我西阁床；
脱我战时袍，着我旧时裳；当窗理云鬓，对镜帖花黄。
出门看火伴，火伴皆惊惶。"同行十二年，不知木兰是女郎。"
雄兔脚扑朔，雌兔眼迷离。双兔傍地走，安能辩我是雄雌？[7]

Battle of Mulan

Tsiek tsiek and again tsiek tsiek,[8]
Mu-lan weaves, facing the door.
You don't hear the shuttle's sound,
You only hear Daughter's sighs.
They ask Daughter who's in her heart,
They ask Daughter who's on her mind.

"No one is on Daughter's heart,
No one is on Daughter's mind.
Last night I saw the draft posters,
The Khan is calling many troops,
The army list is in twelve scrolls,
On every scroll there's Father's name.
Father has no grown-up son,
Mu-lan has no elder brother.
I want to buy a saddle and horse,
And serve in the army in Father's place."

In the East Market she buys a spirited horse,
In the West Market she buys a saddle,
In the South Market she buys a bridle,
In the North Market she buys a long whip.
At dawn she takes leave of Father and Mother,
In the evening camps on the Yellow River's bank.
She doesn't hear the sound of Father and Mother calling,
She only hears the Yellow River's flowing water cry tsien tsien.

At dawn she takes leave of the Yellow River,
In the evening she arrives at Black Mountain.
She doesn't hear the sound of Father and Mother calling,
She only hears Mount Yen's nomad horses cry tsiu tsiu.
She goes ten thousand miles on the business of war,
She crosses passes and mountains like flying.
Northern gusts carry the rattle of army pots,
Chilly light shines on iron armor.

> Generals die in a hundred battles,
> Stout soldiers return after ten years.
> On her return she sees the Son of Heaven,
> The Son of Heaven sits in the Splendid Hall.
> He gives out promotions in twelve ranks
> And prizes of a hundred thousand and more.
> The Khan asks her what she desires.
> "Mu-lan has no use for a minister's post.
> I wish to ride a swift mount
> To take me back to my home."
>
> When Father and Mother hear Daughter is coming
> They go outside the wall to meet her, leaning on each other.
> When Elder Sister hears Younger Sister is coming
> She fixes her rouge, facing the door.
> When Little Brother hears Elder Sister is coming
> He whets the knife, quick quick, for pig and sheep.
> "I open the door to my east chamber,
> I sit on my couch in the west room,
> I take off my wartime gown
> And put on my old-time clothes."
>
> Facing the window she fixes her cloudlike hair,
> Hanging up a mirror she dabs on yellow flower powder
> She goes out the door and sees her comrades.
> Her comrades are all amazed and perplexed.
> Traveling together for twelve years
> They didn't know Mu-lan was a girl.
> "The he-hare's feet go hop and skip,
> The she-hare's eyes are muddled and fuddled.
> Two hares running side by side close to the ground,
> How can they tell if I am he or she?"[9]

This tale above about a woman who takes the place of her father in combat is about filial piety and nationalism. Filial piety (孝 pinyin: xiào) is about respecting one's parents, elders, ancestors, and country.[10] This Confucian concept is central to Chinese culture as dedicating yourself to your parents is a fundamental way of Chinese social and familial ordering of society. The young must take care of the old and carry on their family name in an honorable manner. This extends outside of the house in that youth must protect their country and king. For example, Confucius said a woman must follow her father in youth, husband in adulthood, and son in old age.[11] Despite China's diversity with over 1.3 billion citizens of many ethnic and linguistic groups, filial piety remains a common social contract that everyone follows.[12]

MAXINE HONG KINGSTON'S WOMAN WARRIOR

But how was this ancient and revered Chinese poem brought to Disney's attention? Distinguished Chinese American author Maxine Hong Kingston's award winning, *The Woman Warrior: Memoirs of a Girlhood among Ghosts* (1976) is a genre-defining book because it mixes ancient Chinese tales with her personal hidden family stories.[13] It was well received and also became a best seller and was widely read in United States' college classes. To date, Maxine Hong Kingston is one of the most widely read authors that is living today inspiring people such as President Barack Obama in writing his memoir.[14] Disney most likely became aware of the Mulan story through her famous book as discussed next.

Kingston's *Woman Warrior* chapter two titled "White Tigers" is about her mother's childhood stories of Fa Mu Lan who became a national leader of China. In this version, Maxine Kingston puts herself into the story of *Fa Mu Lan*. Magically Kingston is transported to China as an adolescent and trains in martial arts for many years. She trains to be a warrior by an elderly couple. She has a husband and son in this version and she battles giants. Then this intersects with her life in America and her abusive boss who she dares to speak out against. She depicts her struggles as a Chinese American woman to Mulan in some respects in that both have to go against stereotypes.

Later in 1994 Kingston commissioned a nearly three-hour, three-act play based on *The Woman Warrior* and her other memoir, *China Men*.[15] Disney representatives contacted Kingston when her play was being run at the Zellerbach Playhouse on the University of California's Berkeley campus and she was concerned that Disney would plagiarize her story.[16] Disney also contacted Kingston about their version of the epic poem and the author was ready to sue them if they took her story plot without permission. Disney assured her that their version had a talking dragon and was not the same. This is important to note that Disney probably found out about *The Ballad of Mulan* from Kingston's book, but it was not a copy of her work. It is important to distinguish the two as Kingston's rendition of the Mulan tale was not the same as the traditional Mulan tale from China.

DISNEY'S 1998 *MULAN*: THE HOLLYWOOD TREATMENT

Eventually Disney adapted the *Mulan* tale into one of their Disney princess animated films. This film did quite well at the box office in the United States and was rated one of the most successful films of that year.[17] The domestic box office was $120,620,254 and the foreign box office was

$183,700,00.[18] Interestingly, this film was not a hit in China and even received criticism. Yin contends that the Disney film appropriated the classic Chinese tale and "simultaneously reinforced the existing racial and gender ideologies through deprecating Chinese culture as Oriental despotisms and dissolving feminism into cultural/racial hierarchy."[19]

First, the film has a comedic story line and does not illustrate true filial piety. In the animation, Li argues in many ways Mulan is like a classic American teenager who is looking for adventure.[20] She is also not shown as competent or commanding the respect of all of her troops.

The *Mulan* film from Disney did poorly in China for several reasons. The Chinese are very aware of their culture and their history and the scholars note that the Disney film did not respect their well-known Confucius-tinged tale.[21] For example, in the animation there is a cartoon dragon called Mushu as well as a Lucky Cricket. Most of the animals were cast for comedic effect—a choice that goes against the ancient and patriotic tone of *The Ballad of Mulan*.

Also, the Disney tale refers to a Han Chinese character. This is very significant as the original poem was most likely from an ethnic minority group in China so they may not have believed in Confucianism. The People's Republic of China now recognizes over fifty-five ethnic groups, with ethnic Han Chinese being the most numerous. Throughout history these groups have been fighting for control and many non-Han women were very hearty and trained to fight if need be.

> The rulers of the northern dynasties were from non-Han ethnic groups, most of them from Turkic peoples such as the Toba (Tuoba, also known as Xianbei), whose Northern Wei dynasty ruled most of northern China from 386–534. This background explains why the character Mulan refers to the Son of Heaven as "Khan"—the title given to rulers among the pastoral nomadic people of the north, including the Xianbei—one of the many reasons why the images conveyed in the movie "Mulan" of a stereotypically Confucian Chinese civilization fighting against the barbaric "Huns" to the north are inaccurate.[22]

In contrast to the poor Chinese reception, Disney's *Mulan* was a huge hit in the United States and it also defied a lot of stereotypes of who a Disney princess is supposed to be. Many lauded the film for being a new wave of Disney princess feminism as it was one of the first Disney princesses that showed agency and self-determination. One test that measures female representation in literature and cinema is the Bechdel test.[23] The Bechdel test was developed by famous graphic novel memoirist Alison Bechdel—known for her comic strip *Dykes to Watch Out For*. The test asks three simple questions: Are there two female characters? Do they have names? And do the female characters talk about something other than a man? The

Mulan film passes the Bechdel test. She has many conversations with her mother, the matchmaker, and her grandmother on topics such as her life and honor. Mulan also sings with her family and other female characters "Honor to Us All" (1998) written by Matthew Wilder and David Zippel.

While some saw the movie as lauding female empowerment, others felt it was left wing indoctrination. In 1999, a news report broke the story that then talk show host (now vice president) Mike Pence wrote an op-ed declaring that Disney's 1998 *Mulan* was "Liberal Propaganda."[24]

Pence took his grandchildren to see the movie claiming that there was a secret agenda that advocated for including women in the army with men. Pence said that the movie's example of a military woman falling in love with her superior was evidence that women should not be allowed to serve in the military or they would fraternize with their male counterparts. He wrote, "I suspect that some mischievous liberal at Disney assumes that *Mulan*'s story will cause a quiet change in the next generation's attitude about women in combat and they just might be right."[25] He continued to write:

> Obviously, this is Walt Disney's attempt to add childhood expectation to the cultural debate over the role of women in the military. . . . Many young women find many young men to be attractive sexually. Put them together, in close quarters, for long periods of time, and things will get interesting. Just like they eventually did for young Mulan. Moral of story: women in military, bad idea.[26]

Therefore, 1998's *Mulan* was socially problematic both in the West and in China where its story originated. For Chinese audiences, it appropriated a tale without truly living up to the essence of the original *Ballad*. In the West, it was lauded as progressive for some audiences, but pushing an agenda for conservative audiences.

CHINA'S 2009 LIVE-ACTION VERSION OF MULAN

In 2009, China came out with its own live-action version of the Mulan tale and it was well received in China. There are significant differences between the Chinese version of Mulan versus Disney's *Mulan*. Jinhua Li describes the significant differences between the two films. Li argued that this live-action Chinese film *Hua Mulan* 花木兰 directed by Jingle Ma 马楚成 "demands a transnational interpretation because of Disney's globally popular Mulan (1998) franchise." Li argued that the Disney 1998 animation homogenizes the Chinese heroine to fit into the Disney princess gallery of showing personal growth, individualism, and an independent spirit.[27] On the other hand, the Chinese *Hua Mulan* (2009) live-action film is a transnational discourse that expresses Chinese national patriotism in a post-feminist cinematic way which is depicted in many modern Chinese films.

Here, Chinese post-feminism is defined as having female lead characters portrayed in a definitive feminine way versus Eurocentric feminism. Jin Yin's "Toward a Confucian Feminism: A Critique of Eurocentric Feminist Discourse" defines Confucian feminism as based on the principle of *ren* (humanness), the notion of rights as *fen* (share), and duty-based ethics.[28] Yin also argues that Chinese feminism is based on relationalism, filial piety, and loyalty which is the "Chinese preference for the collective."[29] On the other hand, Eurocentric feminism is based on "universalism, individualism, and right-based ethics."[30] These two different scripts of female behavior are not fully compatible.[31] Yin notes that the *Hua Mulan* (2009) exhibits post-feminism. The Mainland Chinese version of the Mulan film is shown in a stereotypical feminine role acting very girlish. For example, she is not seen as very aggressive and instead as very demure. The Mainland Chinese director of *Hua Mulan*, Jingle Ma, had made public announcements that the film was about Chinese nationalism, filial piety, and self-sacrifice.[32] Li contends that *Mulan* (1998) depoliticizes the Chinese tale while the *Hua Mulan* (2009) represents the original patriotic intent of the Chinese legend.

WHITEWASHING, YELLOWFACE, AND WHITE SAVIORS

As audiences demand better representation of the media content they consume, Hollywood has come under even more scrutiny for its casting and characterization of Asian narratives. Whitewashing of Asian films occurs when a European or Anglo-American plays the role of a defined Asian character set in Asia or a majority-Asian populated area.[33] *The Last Airbender* series (2005–2008) on the Nickelodeon channel had definitive Asian characters in a seemingly Asiatic world. Yet, director M. Night Shyamalan made a live-action (2010) version that replaced all the Asian characters with other ethnic groups. Scarlet Johansson plays a Japanese character based on a Japanese Manga in the film *Ghost in the Shell* (2017). Director Cameron Crowe's *Aloha* (2015) cast Emma Stone in the role of Allison Ng who was supposed to be of mixed Chinese, Anglo, and Hawaiian descent. *Dragonball: Evolution* (2009) was based on a Japanese animation of Japanese characters and instead they cast Canadian-Anglo Justin Chatwin to play the main Japanese role, Goku. In the Disneyverse, Tilda Swinton was cast as the Ancient One in *Doctor Strange*, who originally in the comics was the negative Asian stereotype. One of the most racist portrayals of a Japanese American character is by famous Scottish American actor Mickey Rooney in *Breakfast at Tiffany's* (1961) who plays

Mr. Yunoshi. Rooney wears fake buckteeth, tapes his eyes to create slits, and screams in a heavy faux Asian accent at the female protagonist.[34]

Another trope that has been popular in Hollywood films is the white savior trope.[35] This is when an Anglo-European character saves a non-white person or entire minority population. In *The White Savior Film: Content, Critics, and Consumption*, Matthew Hughey wrote that a white savior "features messianic characters in unfamiliar or hostile settings discovering something about themselves and their culture in the process of saving members of other races from terrible fates."[36] The white character is often portrayed as a conflicted teacher, lawyer, coach, or warrior that is pushed against all odds to save the uneducated, non-logical, or "non-modern" minority population. A notable example of this was Tom Cruise in *The Last Samurai* (2003) who is the white savior that supposedly upholds the Japanese Samurai tradition. In *Gran Torino* (2008), Clint Eastwood plays a Polish American Walt Kowalski, a Korean war veteran who lets himself get intentionally murdered by a group of Hmong gang members to free a Hmong boy. In the film *The Great Wall* (2016), Matt Damon was accused of both whitewashing and also playing the white savior of China.[37] This is because the plot involves that he and another European male is battling supernatural beasts to save China. In the film he eventually does survive to save China where most of the main Asian cast were murdered.

Robert Lee argues there is a huge negative impact on these whitewashing narratives and white savior films. Lee says that Asians and especially Asian Americans are then seen as the forever foreigner who is exotic and encased in an amber of tradition.[38] In turn they are subject to anti-Asian legislature such as the 1882 Chinese Exclusion Act which banned all Chinese and later all Asians. Asians are objectified and racistly cast as "the Pollutant, Coolie, Deviant, Yellow Peril, Model Minority, or Gook."[39]

Asian Canadian and Asian American actors, such as Sandra Oh called out the issue of Emma Stone's whitewashing in the film *Aloha* (2015) during Golden Globes awards ceremony. Stone promptly screamed back, "I'm sorry!" Things are slowly changing. There are recent television and film examples such as *Fresh Off the Boat* (Renewed for a 6th season), *Crazy Rich Asians* (2018), and *Searching* (2018). Netflix has had very popular Asian American written and casted films such as *To All the Boys I Loved Before* (2018) and *Always Be My Maybe* (2019). *Crazy Rich Asians* and *To All the Boys I Loved Before* were so popular that there was the celebratory hashtag #AsianAugust.

There are also other hashtags on Twitter that call for an Asian American leading men and women in Hollywood. Korean American social media mastermind William Yu started the viral hashtags #StarringJohnCho and #SeeAsAmStar which is about Asian American leading Hollywood blockbusters. Yu superimposes John Cho's body and face on Hollywood film posters.

#MAKEMULANRIGHT: WHITE-
WASHING AND WHITE SAVIOR

In October 2016, #MakeMulanRight trended as the *Angry Asian Man* blog leaked a live-action script for Mulan that had a white hero as the main character.[40] There was an anonymous Open Letter posted on the *Angry Asian Man* blog to Disney that objected to the contents of the script.[41] The script centered on an older thirty-something European trader who fights for the Chinese Imperial army because he falls for a very young Mulan. This story line can be interpreted as an example of Yellow Fever. The term refers to when a person has a fetishistic love for solely Asian women because of their perceived docility.[42] These racist assumptions fuel the attraction to a mail order Asian bride. Critics noted the leaked script can be read in this context of having Yellow Fever perpetuating a middle-aged man's intimate interest in a teenage Mulan.

This leaked script prompted many activists and concerned citizens alike to question this interpretation. They saw it as continuing in the long line of cinematic whitewashing and white savior tropes. According to the *Angry Asian Man* blog, there was not one Asian American or Chinese writer for the script.[43] Over nineteen thousand people signed a petition to object to this script.[44] Writer Jessica Yang released "#MakeMulanRight: A Reading List" to provide academic sources for the tale.[45]

None of the elements of the original *Ballad of Mulan*—filial piety, sacrifice or patriotism—were honored in these story lines the Open Letter recounts. That this script would make Mulan a side character and object to some erotic Anglo male fantasy was insulting to Asian Americans. Disney seemed to get the message as *Vanity Fair* reported, "Don't Worry: *Mulan* Will Not Feature a White Male Lead" which reported that this script would not be used.[46] They reported they would use an all Asian cast but audiences would have to wait until 2020, after Disney pushed back the release of the live-action remake. The Twitter campaign is evidence that people will no longer easily accept white saviors, whitewashing or yellow fever Asian stories.

CONCLUSION

In this chapter, I showed the genealogy of many of the renditions of Mulan. The original *Ballad of Mulan* was a sixth-century poem that was intended to show filial piety, patriotism, and humility likely written by a non-Han Chinese ethnic group of Turkic descent.[47] The 1998 Disney *Mulan* film was unsuccessful in China because it was perceived as a watered-down, trivialized rendition of a beloved national story. The Disney version transformed the Mulan ballad to make it a standard princess story line neglecting its cultural and ethnic specifications.

The Mainland Chinese (2009) *Hua Mulan* live-action film was a more faithful cultural rendition as it was from the country of origin where the original ballad was written. There are deep transcultural implications in the story of Mulan as it travels from China to the U.S., back to China and again to the U.S. It is originally a well-known Chinese poem from the sixth century that had specific aims of showing filial piety. Curiously, Disney transformed the tale to be a regular Disney princess tale. The Disney film corporation has had a history of whitewashing, and using white savior plots.[48]

Disney is one of the largest transnational multi-media corporations in the world. The global human population is 60 percent Asian with people of Chinese ethnic descent numbering 18–23 percent of the world population.[49] There are many types of Asian and specifically Chinese stories that Hollywood can greenlight which should be Asian written, produced, and casted. Instead of bending stories such as *Mulan* to fit typical Disney princess tropes or fit their stable of princesses of color, Disney should instead explore the infinite positive Asian female stories for young global audiences to learn from.

NOTES

1. *Mulan*, 1998, directed by Tony Bancroft and Barry Cook. USA, 1998.

2. Lan Dong, *Mulan's Legacy and Legacy in China and the United States* (Philadelphia: Temple University Press, 2010).

3. ConcernedForMulan (Anonymous), "An Open Letter to the Creators of Disney's Live Action Mulan," October 11, 2016, accessed March 15, 2019, https:// thenerdsofcolor.org/2016/10/11/an-open-letter-to-the-creators-of-disneys-live-action-mulan/.

4. Jinhua Li, "Mulan (1998) and *Hua Mulan* (2009) National Myth and Trans-Cultural Intertextuality," in *Heroism and Gender in War Films*, edited by Ritzenhoff, Karen and Jakub Kazecki (New York: Palgrave Macmillan. 2004): 187–208.

5. Matthew Wilder and David Zippel, "Reflections," Track 2 on *Mulan: An Original Walt Disney Records Soundtrack*: RCA, 1998, compact disc.

6. Lan Dong, *Mulan's Legacy and Legacy in China and the United States*, 1.

7. "The Ballad of Mulan," accessed March 1, 2019, http://people.wku.edu/haiwang.yuan/China/tales/mulan.htm.

8. "The Ballad of Mulan translation," accessed July 30, 2019, https://en.m.wikisource.org/wiki/Translation:Ballad_of_Mulan.

9. Translated by Han H. Frankel, *The Flowering Plum and the Palace Lady: Interpretations of Chinese Poetry*.

10. Roger T. Ames and Henry Rosemont, Jr., *The Chinese Classic of Family Reverence: A Philosophical Translation of the Xiaojing* (Honolulu: University of Hawaii Press, 2008); Asia for Educators, Columbia University, The Ballad of Mulan (Ode of Mulan), accessed March 1, 2019, http://afe.easia.columbia.edu/ps/china/mulan.pdf; and see Confucius and Annping Chin (Ed./Translator), *The Analects* (New York: Penguin Classics, 2014).

11. Xiongya Gao, "Women Existing for Men: Confucianism and Social Injustice Against Women in China," *Race, Gender & Class*, 10, no. 3 (2003): 114–125.

12. Guang Xing, "The Teaching and Practice of Filial Piety in Buddhism," *Journal of Law and Religion*, 31, no. 2 (2016), 212–226. doi:10.1017/jlr.2016.20.

13. Maxine Hong Kingston, *The Woman Warrior: Memoirs of a Girlhood among Ghosts* (New York: Vintage, 1989).

14. Julia H. Lee, *Understanding Maxine Hong Kingston* (Columbia, South Carolina: University of South Carolina Press, 2018).

15. Aljean Hametz, "Theater: It's Tough to Get Ghosts to Be Human on Stage," *New York Times*, June 5, 1994, https://www.nytimes.com/1994/06/05/theater/theater-it-s-tough-to-get-ghosts-to-be-human-on-stage.html.

16. Maxine Hong Kingston, "Annual Undergraduate Conference on Multiethnic Literatures of the Americas," Keynote Speaker, March 15, 2019. California State University, Fresno.

17. Box Office Mojo, *Mulan*, accessed April 22, 2019. https://www.boxofficemojo.com/movies/?id=mulan.htm.

18. Box Office Mojo, *Mulan*.

19. Jing Yin, "Toward a Confucian Feminism: A Critique of Eurocentric Feminist Discourse," *China Media Research*, 2, no. 3. (2006), accessed April 21, 2019. http://www.chinamediaresearch.net/index.php/back-issues?id=39; Jing Yin, "Popular Culture and Public Imaginary: Disney vs. Chinese Stories of Mulan," *Javnost–The Public*, 18 no. 1 (2011), 53–74, doi: 10.1080/13183222.2011.11009051.

20. Jinhua Li, "*Mulan* (1998) and *Hua Mulan* (2009) National Myth and Trans-Cultural Intertextuality."

21. Ibid.

22. Asia for Educators, Columbia University, The Ballad of Mulan (Ode of Mulan).

23. "Bechdel Test," accessed April 21, 2019, https://bechdeltest.com/.

24. Andrew Kaczynski, "Mike Pence Argued in an Op-Ed That Disney's 'Mulan' Was Liberal Propaganda," *BuzzFeed News*, July 17, 2016, https://www.buzzfeednews.com/article/andrewkaczynski/mister-ill-make-a-man-out-of-you.

25. Andrew Kaczynski, "Mike Pence Argued in an Op-Ed That Disney's 'Mulan' Was Liberal Propaganda."

26. Ibid.

27. Jinhua Li, "*Mulan* (1998) and *Hua Mulan* (2009) National Myth and Trans-Cultural Intertextuality."

28. Jing Yin, "Toward a Confucian Feminism: A Critique of Eurocentric Feminist Discourse"; Jing Yin, "Popular Culture and Public Imaginary: Disney vs. Chinese Stories of Mulan."

29. Ibid.

30. Ibid.

31. Confucian Weekly Bulletin, "Confucian Feminism: The (In)Compatibility of Confucianism and Feminist Ethics- 儒家思想与女性主义伦理的（无）兼容性, accessed April 21, 2019, https://confucianweeklybulletin.wordpress.com/tag/Confucian-feminism/.

32. *Hua Mulan, Mulan: Rise of a Warrior*, directed by Jingle Ma, China, 2009, Film.

33. There are many recent film examples of whitewashing: *The Last Airbender, Aloha, Ghost in the Shell, Death Note,* and *Dragonball: Evolution.*

34. For a deeper look into this see Robert Lee, *Orientals: Asian Americans in Popular Culture* (Philadelphia: Temple University Press, 1999).

35. Matthew Hughey, *The White Savior Film: Content, Critics, and Consumption* (Philadelphia: Temple University Press, 2014).

36. Matthew Hughey, *The White Savior Film: Content, Critics, and Consumption,* 1–18.

37. Livia Truffaut-Wong, "'The Great Wall' Has a White Savior Problem, but the Film's Asian Cast Still Marks a Step in the Right Direction," *Bustle,* February 16 2017, https://www.bustle.com/p/the-great-wall-has-a-white-savior-problem-but-the-films-asian-cast-still-marks-a-step-in-the-right-direction-38641.

38. Robert Lee, *Orientals: Asian Americans in Popular Culture.*

39. Ibid.

40. Jake Pitre, "Mulan Leak Shows Disney Wasn't Prepared to Bring the '90s Back in Live Action," *Polygon,* October 27, 2016, https://www.polygon.com/2016/10/27/13438526/disney-live-action-mulan-aladdin-controversy.

41. ConcernedForMulan (Anonymous), "An Open Letter to the Creators of Disney's Live Action Mulan."

42. Ibid.

43. See *Angry Asian Man* Blog, accessed April 21, 2019, http://blog.angryasianman.com/.

44. 18 Million Rising, "Petition to Activating Asian America. Disney: #MakeMulanRight" Petition, 2016, http://action.18mr.org/makemulanright/?source=direct_link&.

45. Jessica Yang, "#MakeMulanRight: A Reading List," October 12, 2016. https://bookriot.com/2016/10/12/makemulanright-a-reading-list/.

46. Yohana Desta, "Don't Worry: *Mulan* Will Not Feature a White Male Lead," *Vanity Fair,* October 10, 2016, https://www.vanityfair.com/hollywood/2016/10/mulan-white-male-lead-disney.

47. Asia for Educators, Columbia University, The Ballad of Mulan (Ode of Mulan).

48. See recent Marvel films such as *Dr. Strange* (2016) and other Marvel blockbuster which have that character such as *Avengers: Infinity War* (2018). Also see Disney *Pocahontas* (1995) story.

49. Lynn Pan, *The Encyclopedia of Chinese Overseas* (Cambridge: Harvard University Press, 1998), 228–233; Allen Chun. "Fuck Chineseness: On the Ambiguities of Ethnicity as Culture as Identity," *Boundary 2* 23, no. 2 (1996): 111–138. doi:10.2307/303809.

BIBLIOGRAPHY

18 Million Rising. "Petition to Activating Asian America. Disney: #MakeMulan Right." Petition, 2016. http://action.18mr.org/makemulanright/?source=direct_link&.

Ames, Roger T., and Henry Rosemont, Jr. *The Chinese Classic of Family Reverence: A Philosophical Translation of the Xiaojing*. Honolulu: University of Hawaii Press, 2008.

Angry Asian Man Blog. Accessed April 21, 2019, http://blog.angryasianman.com/.

"Bechdel Test." Accessed April 21, 2019, https://bechdeltest.com/.

Box Office Mojo. *Mulan*. Accessed April 22, 2019. https://www.boxofficemojo.com/movies/?id=mulan.htm.

Chun, Allen. "Fuck Chineseness: On the Ambiguities of Ethnicity as Culture as Identity." *Boundary 2* 23, no. 2 (1996): 111–38. doi:10.2307/303809.

Columbia University. "The Ballad of Mulan (Ode of Mulan)," Asia for Educators. Accessed March 1, 2019. http://afe.easia.columbia.edu/ps/china/mulan.pdf.

ConcernedForMulan (Anonymous). "An Open Letter to the Creators of Disney's Live Action Mulan." October 11, 2016. Accessed March 15, 2019. https://thenerdsofcolor.org/2016/10/11/an-open-letter-to-the-creators-of-disneys-live-action-mulan/.

Confucian Weekly Bulletin. "Confucian Feminism: The (In)Compatibility of Confucianism and Feminist Ethics- 儒家思想与女性主义伦理的（无）兼容性." Accessed April 21, 2019, https://confucianweeklybulletin.wordpress.com/tag/Confucian-feminism/.

Confucius and Annping Chin (Ed./Translator). *The Analects*. New York: Penguin Classics, 2014.

Desta, Yohana. "Don't Worry: *Mulan* Will Not Feature a White Male Lead." *Vanity Fair*, October 10, 2016, https://www.vanityfair.com/hollywood/2016/10/mulan-white-male-lead-disney.

Dong, Lan. *Mulan's Legacy and Legacy in China and the United States*. Philadelphia: Temple University Press, 2010.

Frankel, Han H. (translator). *The Flowering Plum and the Palace Lady: Interpretations of Chinese Poetry*. New Haven: Yale University Press, 1976.

Gao, Xiongya. "Women Existing for Men: Confucianism and Social Injustice Against Women in China." *Race, Gender & Class*, 10, no. 3 (2003): 114–125.

Hametz, Aljean. "Theater: It's Tough to Get Ghosts to Be Human on Stage," *New York Times*, June 5, 1994, https://www.nytimes.com/1994/06/05/theater/theater-it-s-tough-to-get-ghosts-to-be-human-on-stage.html.

Hua Mulan. *Mulan: Rise of a Warrior*. Directed by Jingle Ma. China, 2009. Film.

Hughey, Matthew. *The White Savior Film: Content, Critics, and Consumption*. Philadelphia: Temple University Press, 2014.

Kaczynski, Andrew. "Mike Pence Argued in an Op-Ed That Disney's 'Mulan' Was Liberal Propaganda," *BuzzFeed News*, July 17, 2016, https://www.buzzfeednews.com/article/andrewkaczynski/mister-ill-make-a-man-out-of-you.

Kingston, Maxine Hong. *The Woman Warrior: Memoirs of a Girlhood among Ghosts*, New York: Vintage, 1989.

———. "Annual Undergraduate Conference on Multiethnic Literatures of the Americas," Keynote Speaker, March 15, 2019. California State University, Fresno.

Lee, Julia A. *Understanding Maxine Hong Kingston*. Columbia, South Carolina: University of South Carolina Press, 2018.

Lee, Robert. *Orientals: Asian Americans in Popular Culture*. Philadelphia: Temple University Press, 1999.

Li, Jinhua. *"Mulan* (1998) and *Hua Mulan* (2009) National Myth and Trans-Cultural Intertextuality." In *Heroism and Gender in War Films*, edited by Ritzenhoff, Karen and Jakub Kazecki, 187–208. New York: Palgrave Macmillan. 2004.

Mulan. Walt Disney Pictures. Directed by Tony Bancroft and Barry Cook. USA, 1998.

Pan, Lynn. *The Encyclopedia of Chinese Overseas*. Cambridge: Harvard University Press, 1998.

Pitre, Jack. "Mulan Leak Shows Disney Wasn't Prepared to Bring the '90s Back in Live Action." *Polygon*, October 27, 2016, https://www.polygon.com/2016/10/27/13438526/disney-live-action-mulan-aladdin-controversy.

Truffaut-Wong, Livia. "'The Great Wall' Has a White Savior Problem, but the Film's Asian Cast Still Marks a Step in the Right Direction," *Bustle*, February 16 2017, https://www.bustle.com/p/the-great-wall-has-a-white-savior-problem-but-the-films-asian-cast-still-marks-a-step-in-the-right-direction-38641.

Xing, Guang. "The Teaching and Practice of Filial Piety in Buddhism," *Journal of Law and Religion*, 31, no. 2 (2016), 212–226. doi:10.1017/jlr.2016.20.

Yang, Jessica. "#MakeMulanRight: A Reading List." October 12, 2016. https://bookriot.com/2016/10/12/makemulanright-a-reading-list/.

Yin, Jing. "Toward a Confucian Feminism: A Critique of Eurocentric Feminist Discourse," *China Media Research*, 2, no. 3. (2006), Accessed April 21, 2019. http://www.chinamediaresearch.net/index.php/back-issues?id=39.

———. "Popular Culture and Public Imaginary: Disney vs. Chinese Stories of Mulan," *Javnost–The Public*, 18 no. 1 (2011), 53–74, doi: 10.1080/13183222.2011.11009051.

Yuan, Haiwang. "Mulan Story Retold." 2003-2005. Accessed March 1, 2019. http://people.wku.edu/haiwang.yuan/China/tales/mulan.htm.

10

✢

Pocahontas

Digital Coloniality, Coercive Fiction, and "Renewing" Western Hegemonic Power

Leece Lee-Oliver

Disney's animated film *Pocahontas* (1995) is set in the early 1600s, during the life and death struggle of the Powhatan peoples and their epistemologies in the early stages of colonial expansion and annexation on the eastern seaboard. Visually stimulating and evocative, the film focuses on the establishment of Jamestown colony, its political and economic systems, and the overturn of the confederacy of the Powhatan. Its thematic tension is built on the trope of "first contact" and casts Native Americans as primitives in the midst of an ostensibly more advanced and white European civilization. One figure, the "Indian Princess squaw," stands out as the protagonist. Called "Pocahontas," her characterization entangles the girl with the youthful exuberance of primitive innocence, English sensibilities, and an audacity of European individualism. The Princess squaw's mischievous antics liken "Pocahontas" to a young feminist. A female lead who thwarts convention may be perceived by American audiences as a model of empowerment. However, such renderings, when set in the racialized minds of U.S. audiences, erase the complexities of Native American phenomenology and the vulgar grips of colonialism. It conflates notions of white European racial and patriarchal superiority with anti-Indianism and racist misogyny.

Numerous examples of the actual Pocahontas and other Native American women leaders reside in the annals of history, and can be found in everything from academic scholarship to social media today. Plenty of Native American experts advised on the film.[1] Yet still, the writing and illustrations in *Pocahontas* enable the characters and the story itself to serve up tropes that impart deep discriminatory elements into the social imaginary and perpetuate the states of dehumanization that affect Native Americans today. For these reasons, for Disney to remake *Pocahontas* today remains extremely problematic, in light of the opaqueness of movements among Native Americans, many led by women, that challenge long lasting effects of colonization. This chapter examines the life of Pocahontas and the Powhatan confederacy accounted for in the sacred Mattaponi oral history, and questions the utility of tropic visions in Disney's *Pocahontas*. I also offer a critical race and feminist critique of Disney's *Pocahontas*, including its live show, to reveal how the fictional work enacts a didactic effect, rouses audiences into states of "Indianophobia,"[2] and exceptionalizes colonial and U.S. nation-formation. I conclude with an exploration of the works of contemporary Native Americans whose works undertake the problems of anti-Indianism today. I begin with an examination of the Mattaponi oral history of Pocahontas's life and the Peoples reclamation of their ancestor and beloved young leader.

SPEAKING TRUTH TO POWER

Mattaponi Oral Tradition, Pocahontas, and the Powhatans

The Mattaponi sacred oral history is the foundational archive of the Powhatan confederacy.[3] The history of Pocahontas, the Powhatan, and the settlement of Jamestown is offered in detail within the scope of the Powhatan history,[4] at that crucial time in world history. Pocahontas's history, what she experienced and witnessed during the decade or so of English colonial settlement, has been preserved for literally four centuries in the oral history, and its recollections stand in stark contrast to Disney's *Pocahontas*. The critical arc in the Mattaponi oral history points to the geo-political foundation of Jamestown as an effort to develop the Powhatan territory as a major player in the global tobacco industry, and shows how agents of British colonial annexation used threats, violence, cajolery, and the abduction and rape of Native American girls, women, men and boys to overthrow the Powhatan confederacy and seize control over the territories.[5] Likewise, colonial agents used intimacy as an entry point to yielding cultural knowledge to gain access to indigenous rights.[6] Pocahontas's story in the movie is set as if she was under the occupation of the British. *Pocahontas*, rather than telling the actual history, overcast her legacy and integrity with inferences of disloyalty, contamination, and adulteration. At a fundamental level, the Powhatan oral history reflects such seismic philosophical and historical differences as well between the Powhatan ethos and colonial aims:

The Powhatan and English had different agendas. The English did not understand the very civil and political structure of the Powhatan nation. They did not want to understand it. They wanted to look at the Powhatan people as savages. Because the English considered the Powhatan people savages, they considered it to be okay to kill them and take their land.[7]

The metanarrative of *Pocahontas* tempers the impacts of colonization and minimizes the political and cultural soundness of the Powhatan. The overtones of primitivity simultaneously support representatives of colonization and colonizers with benevolence and civility—Captain John Smith is a hero. Yet, in reality, even for Smith and the other colonists, the Powhatan government structures and institutional systems were apparent. They found themselves among government officials who were well aware of world affairs, and the mark left by Spanish colonizers on Indigenous peoples in the Americas.[8]

When Chief Wahunsenaca contemplated what options he would afford the newcomer, the oral history suggests that he considered Powhatan principles of community before he decided to appease the subject with an opportunity to coexist, stating, "the Spanish threat influenced Wahunsenaca to both build alliances, and to make friends with the English when they arrived in 1607."[9] In an effort to appease the newcomers and grow alliances with them, the oral history explains that Chief Wahunsenaca and his leadership offered to recognize John Smith as a "werowance" of the English colonists, aiming to make in Smith a leader of the English within the Powhatan nation. The record also holds that Chief Wahunsenca told Smith that the English could settle in a more habitable place than Jamestown Island. The alternative site "had freshwater, plenteous seafood, and was adequately navigable for their ships. Wahunsenaca was letting the whole English settlement come in to be a part of Powhatan society. . . . Establishing an English settlement east of Werowocomoco would provide a protective barrier from the Spanish for the Powhatan secular capital."[10] A ceremony ensued, and Smith rose to his position. Smith gave his word, which amounted to a legal agreement, and the leaders accepted Smith's oath and commitment to steward the colony and to "protect the Powhatan people from the Spanish."[11]

How U.S. audiences learned that Pocahontas fit into this initial point of contact is only through fiction. She is presented as sitting in the political arena, and always defending Smith. The sacred record holds that she did not, and could not, usher in any colonist, nor did she give him safe passage, or defend him against anyone including the Powhatan leadership. "Pocahontas," as she is imagined in the Disney script, is granted political agency unknown to Powhatan peoples. For example, both the oral history and the film affirm that after Smith returned to England, he wrote that

Pocahontas saved his life during the ceremony. The oral history questions whether Smith imagined his vulnerability or simply added an "embellishment to dramatize his narrative."[12] In the first years of Smith's life in the colony, Pocahontas would have been a minor and under ten years of age. The record is unequivocal that children of any status were not permitted in such ceremonies.

That Pocahontas was a favorite daughter of Chief Wahunsenaca is not a myth. Pocahontas was born into the Powhatan leadership family around 1558 to Pocahontas and Wahunsenaca. The two married for love and the sacred oral history shares that Pocahontas, the mother, was not a political wife, nor an affiliate of a village or the Chief, though marriages of political alliance were common at that time. She died giving birth to their daughter Mataoka, who Wahunsenaca called Pocahontas after her mother is said to have adored his wife and endured a deep mourning after her death. Pocahontas was known to be a beloved and honored child, not only by her father, but by her people and leaders. The oral history recalls that Pocahontas was approximately eight to ten years old when Captain John Smith and his crew landed in what was determined to be Jamestown in 1607. She came of age between the ages of twelve to fourteen years, and participated in the girls' ceremony to mark her transition and elevate to her new level of familial and community political responsibility. She was a high-ranking member of a "royal" family, tutored in the principles, philosophy, sacred values, education, and methods of diplomacy and self-defense. It was not that Pocahontas possessed a particularly elevated altruism but, the sacred oral history shows that she exhibited the Powhatan ethic of autonomous community commitment and was well educated in it.

As the oral history illuminates, Pocahontas would not have been left alone, nor would she have the ability to depart from her village and wander the forest, lakes, and rivers by herself as she does throughout the film. Noted in the oral history, "Being a member of the Powhatan paramount chief family, Pocahontas was always chaperoned by warriors and/or quiakros." For example, in the film "Pocahontas" commandeers a canoe and travels down river and more, to contemplate how to get out of marriage. The fictional depiction is more than a simple redirection. It dissuades audiences from understanding her actual political agency and leadership role among her people. "Pocahontas" is not imagined as a young leader, but as a love-struck escapist and young feminist who literally and figuratively runs away from her peoples. Physically, whether child or adult, one individual could not have commandeered a canoe made in the style she had ridden in. The weight of such a vessel, "made out of trees, could easily weigh 400 pounds" which meant that "Pocahontas, a ten-year-old girl, would not have been able to handle such a canoe, all by herself for such a long journey."[13] It would have been impossible, for all of these reasons, and also because her positionality and ethos would have prevented her from considering such an option.

The meaning of her clothing, now one of the favored Halloween costumes in the U.S., is important too for the messages it delivers about "Pocahontas's" agency. Pocahontas's ceremonial arrival into young adulthood was accompanied by a change in clothing to denote her age, family, and status. From the beginning of the film, "Pocahontas" is portrayed in the clothing of a young woman. When she meets John Smith, she is wearing an off-shoulder, fringed dress, which would have been antithetical to Powhatan cultural customs and norms. Pocahontas's "re-dressing," as it were, sublimates "Pocahontas" to fit the arc of John Smith's story and the colonial imaginary. It serves colonial historicity to have "Pocahontas" vacillate between the unfamiliar, infantilized, naïve primitive child, who is simultaneously a remarkably mature, sexually interested, and available adolescent.[14] For the characterization of John Smith as a representative of the good side of white colonial masculinity, it required that Pocahontas's primitivity and sexual availability lead her to be the romantic aggressor.[15] To do so effectively, she could not be portrayed as a young child. Rather, her image sat easily in the multitude of Hollywood "maidens" as a stereotypical wonton Native squaw. The epistemological stretches and reversals in Disney's portrayal enables "Pocahontas" to model all sorts of tropes that fit into narratives that support things like western individualism, nationalism, and misogyny. Colonial women, who had long-since been denounced as adults, and mired in the codex as property, would find "women" like Pocahontas an example of women's liberation. Yet, her portrayal in the film represents her as culturally and epistemologically bankrupt and a threat to the overall wellness of the Powhatan nation. Such racialization of Native Americans like Pocahontas have been critical as instruments in Native American deracination efforts.[16]

The sacred oral history explains too that after Pocahontas came of age, she married Kokoum and had a son. The two lived as a married couple among the Powhatan, but because of the quiakros intelligence gathering, they moved the couple to another village to protect Pocahontas and her family. The quiakros had learned that a British Captain by the name of Samuel Argall had come to the Jamestown colony in 1612, "looking for Pocahontas."[17] It was gathered that he had planned to abduct Pocahontas and manipulate Chief Wahunsenaca to hand over ransom in the form of food, land holdings, and knowledge about agriculture. Eventually Captain Argall succeeded and held the young mother captive for over a year. He also sent in a few of his men to ambush and kill Pocahontas's husband, Kokoum. Their son survived. It was not the first time the English had leveled unabashed violence on the Powhatan. The oral history states:

The English colonists would train the Powhatan children to be their servants, claiming that they would civilize these poor children and teach them the Christian doctrine to save their souls. . . . Powhatan women were sexually assaulted and raped. The English men even sought to rape the Powhatan children. . . . Due to their own atrocious acts, the English colonists were in constant fear of Wahunsenaca retaliating, for the balance of power still lay with the Powhatan people.[18]

Pocahontas and her father suffered great bouts of depression due to her abduction and captivity. The sacred record indicates that the Chief continued to negotiate for her release, but instead received a message requesting that he send someone to care for Pocahontas. He sent Pocahontas's sister, Mattachanna, and her husband, Uttamattamakin, a well-respected spiritual leader. The ship's Captain Argall accepted the assistance and set sail to England with the intention of using Pocahontas to demonstrate the colony's success.[19] The strategy of parading the "Indian Princess" Pocahontas as the Crown's subject was successful. The Virginia Company "assessed the profitability of tobacco in the new colony"[20] making the likelihood of refinancing the colony probable for some time to come.

During the voyage, Pocahontas confided in her sister that she had been raped multiple times while in captivity. At some point, the two realized that Pocahontas was impregnated by one of her rapists. The oral history states that "Sir Thomas Dale, Reverend Alexander Whitaker and John Rolfe worked tirelessly to convert Pocahontas and to teach her English ways" in order that a colonist could marry her.[21] Once she submitted to Christianity, Rolfe submitted a letter to Dale requesting to marry "the creature" Pocahontas. The oral history notes that Pocahontas bore a second son, Thomas, out of wedlock—oddly not named after his father, who also omitted the child from the colony census. In typical colonial practice, for Rolfe the marriage yielded him "an extensive tract of land" from Sir Thomas Dale and substantial access to Powhatan agricultural knowledge from the quiakros, who schooled him in growing and curing tobacco crops for sale.[22]

While in England, the oral history says that Pocahontas sought out John Smith and accused him of betraying the Powhatan peoples. This piqued Argall's nerve and he feared that because "there were people in England who did not approve of the Native people having been mistreated [there] was a possibility that support, including financial, moral, and support from royal charters, might have been withdrawn if it were known how the leaders of the colony were actually treating the Powhatan people."[23] According to Mattachanna's account, Pocahontas "had recognized what her presence in England really meant." On the eve of their return to the colony, Pocahontas and John Rolfe were required to dine with the Captain. Pocahontas returned to her room complaining of a stomach ache. She told her sister that she believed she had been poisoned. Pocahontas became violently ill and as she began to convulse, "Mattachanna went to get Rolfe. When they returned, Pocahontas had died." She was buried in Gravesend, England. Rolfe "abandoned little Thomas in England in the care of relatives while he returned to Virginia to proceed with his tobacco business and help fulfill England's plans to destroy the Powhatan nation." The oral history of the Mattaponi state: "Pocahontas had been murdered in England."[24] The quiakros believe that Argall premeditated the murder to ensure that Pocahontas did not return to the colonial world where her revelations would have emboldened the Powhatan to overthrow the colony.

DIDACTICISM AS PRAXIS AND RE-FLEXING THE COLONIAL GAZE

To many Native American scholars and communities, it seems obvious that Disney's *Pocahontas* situates and insinuates Indigenous peoples in simplified modalities as "Indians" and that its depictions of the Powhatans engenders racism and comfort with it. A critical intervention in which a false narrative enables white supremacy, *Pocahontas* is a tool of white reflexology. There is power in scripting a "savage" girl with desires for the colonial elite and feminist preoccupations. There are also deeper connotations for audiences who see "Pocahontas's" ability to enmesh herself in the colonial efforts to submit the Powhatan leadership to the Crown.

For many Native Americans, *Pocahontas* naturalizes "Indian primitivity" and reifies biological determinism. "Pocahontas" is an "Indian" in the film whose role is to demonstrate futurism in the waxing and waning of her epistemological adaptation to modernity—represented by heteronormative marriage and mercantilism. "Pocahontas's" characterization and that of the Powhatan confederacy, speak to the remnants and products of colonial racism, "orientalism,"[25] and "Indianophobia."[26] Michel-Rolph Trouillot captures the sentiment and sentimentality in the contradictions herein:

> Some Europeans and their colonized students saw in this alleged absence of rules the infantile freedom that they came to associate with savagery, while others saw in it one more proof of the inferiority of non-whites.[27]

Probably the most critical interlocutions of the fictional "Pocahontas" are found in what her abduction and death tell about colonial intentions, Jamestown history, and the Disney writers. "Pocahontas" is often revered as being "like Europeans" with a pension for British social capital. "Pocahontas" is a "good Indian" who knows that she should move away from Powhatan traditions and toward her own independence, which can only be realized through her colonization. Numerous in their form, M. Elise Marubbio's *Killing the Indian Maiden*[28] shows how "Indian Princesses" and "squaws" in U.S. film productions illustrate tropes about "Indian savagery" where Native American women and girls are portrayed as open, and permeable, for the colonizing forces. Racializing Pocahontas as an exoticized "squaw" helps audiences be attracted to but retain distance from her.

"Pocahontas" re-presented as a remarkably adult-like beautiful child, who is coquettish in nature, enables a sense of her independence that makes her different but relatable.[29] "Pocahontas" becomes the guide who allows viewers to enter into a safe sphere as witnesses to vast cultural differences, and find an ally in "Pocahontas." She is a lone traveler even when among her peoples, who is seeking a new diaspora, and finds her way into American hearts as a young émigré looking for solid ground in a new and better colonial society. Audiences are inspired, if not coerced, to follow in her footsteps, root against Indigenous villains, and empathize with colonial expansionists. They are also encouraged to find comfort in her epistemological turns, because she is turning toward the roots of settler colonialism. They are affirmed by her choice to abandon the Powhatan, and by the renderings of colonialism as benevolent; in the script, "Pocahontas's" desire to partner with Smith is referred to as choosing the "way of love."[30] Yet, the constant reminders of her "Indianness" also help to seal the differences between whiteness and Indianness as "Pocahontas'" remains in a constant state of liminality as the exotic "Other."[31]

PLAYING WITH POCAHONTAS: SPATIAL RELATIONSHIPS AND INTERACTIVE EXHIBITS

With all of the critiques of the film and Disney for perpetuating anti-Indianism, it is curious that Disney moved forward with a live show, where audiences can watch excerpts from the movie and then interact with "Pocahontas."[32] "Pocahontas's" image, diction, dress, and character are the same as in the movie, but the 2008 live show brings audiences together with the individual and her cohort of animal and vegetative friends. [33] Like in the film, "Pocahontas" evokes a spiritual turn toward colonial expansionism and her own struggle to find permission to move away from the Powhatan. As she enters the stage, performs the episode from the film when she retreats from a discussion with her father about marriage and considers the possibility of departing from Powhatan life. She seeks the wisdom and guidance of her grandmother, a tree. As "Pocahontas" gazes out over the audience, viewers are induced to empathize with the heroine and reflect inward, revisit their own epistemological centers, the cosmos, and their place in it. The positioning of the characters and props in the live show provides "the impression of an exchange of gazes between equals." Such depictions "did not often acknowledge [Native American artists in depictions] to be part of the same modern world as the non-Native artists, but continued to idealize them as part of a preindustrial ideal doomed by modernity."[34] "Pocahontas's" message is always the same—move away from primitivity and the Tribe. Her phenomenological transformation, from a "savage" to a child of England, comes to fruition as she sings and reminds audiences that we all carry in ourselves a revolutionary ethic and the ability to demand changes among our peoples. There is a breath of exceptionalism in her epistemological turn and she makes visible what Thomas Jefferson proposed, that the coming together of Euro-American settlers and Native Americans could reveal something better. The ways that "Indianness" provides grounds for asserting Euro-American white exceptionalism is impressive. The obsession is often underpinned by deeper economic interests, but the metanarrative reflects ethical goals instead. In real life, the "Pocahontas exception" in Virginia's 1924 Racial Purity law asserts that families who could claim descendancy from Pocahontas could be counted as "white," despite one-drop rules, enabled some families to claim indigenous rights and material privileges.[35]

In the film and in the live show, the story and imagery generate feelings about the life choices of "Pocahontas" and creates pathways for audiences to travel and experience new languages, materials objects, the natural world and, importantly, to find permission to occupy spaces as settler families. Likewise, costuming as "Pocahontas" during Halloween is a pathway each year for American families to occupy this space. In 2017, the Urban Native Era collective advanced the hashtag #IAmNotACostume to have Native American voices express how such costuming demeans their identity and reduces them to caricature.[36] It is a story and practice that is widely defended in popular culture, but that defense has perplexed many Decolonial critics. Considering the precarity of truth in postcolonial European historicities, Haitian scholar Michel-Rolph Trouillot shares his puzzlement about revisionism as praxis and wonders why mainstream audiences play along.[37] Recollecting data from expansionist journals, diaries, maps, and archives, it becomes clear that "there were too many signs here for history to remain official."[38] Despite the truth presented to them, Disney's rendering of Pocahontas is a thoughtful engagement in didactic practice to carry forward the storytelling of colonial Europe about itself.[39] In part and in total, the narrative arc explores how "Pocahontas" advocates tolerance of colonial violence for some greater good.

Elizabeth Hutchinson's research on the strange phenomenon of "Indian exoticization" examines how the:

> generic appropriation of 'Indianness' was part of a larger European-American passion for "playing Indian".... At the beginning of the twentieth century, "playing Indian" became annexed to antimodernism. Woodcraft Indians and Campfire Girls (early rivals to the Boy and Girl Scouts), hunting and camping enthusiasts, and amateur craftspeople all played Indian to express an alliance with what they saw as traditional "American" values threatened by modern life.[40]

Important to take note of is that "playing Indian" is to perform in the fight between European-Americans, not as a form of solidarity or connectedness with Native Americans. The costumes and performances, as it were, provide props to emphasize one's ideological standing.[41] Suffice it to say that the film follows a long tradition in Europe and the U.S. scholarly traditions to distinguish whiteness as exceptional among the earth's peoples and capitalize on "Indianophobia."[42] The term, coined by Robert Williams, notes that:

> Indianophobia as generated by the language of Indian savagery in American history, is an important part of who we are as a people in America. It's one of the original, founding forms of racism and racial hostility cultivated by Europeans in the New World, and it constitutes a primal, driving force in defining how we became who we are as a people today. An overtly racist, hostile, and violent language of Indian savagery can be found in the first official U.S. legal document promulgated by the Founding Fathers, the Declaration of Independence.[43]

Pocahontas reminds audiences of the lofty refrain that European expansion was necessary and vanquishing the "Indians" was preferable to leaving the colonies open to the dangers posed when primitivity is tolerated or left uncontested. The story mitigates an otherwise brutal and egregious history of colonial expansion, and places the onus of guilt on the ostensible patriarchs of the tribe, portrayed as the wily and primitive men of North America's First Peoples. They serve as the formidable foes whom the colonialist surmount and survive.[44]

MASTERING THE NARRATIVE: AUTHENTICITY AND AUTHORIAL POWER

A review of a 2015 celebration of the movie's twentieth anniversary may help expose the culture of white protectionism around the film that aims to silence naysayers. *Pocahontas* and its fictionalization is deemed necessary, ethical, and unproblematically feminist in "Revisiting *Pocahontas* at 20."[45] Writer Sophie Gilbert uses the event to explore alternative ways to look at the problematics that haunt one of Disney's highest grossing animated films.[46] Gilbert acknowledges that "the movie might have fudged some facts to allow for a compelling romantic story" but offers that the writers "had a progressive attitude when it came to interpreting history, depicting the English settlers as plunderers searching for non-existent gold who were intent upon murdering the 'savages' they encountered in the process."[47]

Gilbert's appropriation of the feminist prototype, and silencing of critiques is not new. Sally Roesch Wagner's "Is Equality Indigenous?"[48] exposes the exploitation and then silencing of Haudenosaunee women's influence on suffragists, leaving a legacy for U.S. feminists to build on.[49] Wagner claims that she too "had been haunted by a question to the past, a mystery of feminist history: How did the radical suffragist come to their vision, a vision not of Band-Aid reform but of a reconstituted world completely transformed?"[50] Wagner notes all of the evidence that she had seen herself, but "realized I had been skimming over the source of their inspiration without noticing it. My own unconscious white supremacy had kept me from recognizing what these prototypical feminists kept insisting in their writings: They caught a glimpse of the possibility of freedom because they knew women who lived liberated lives, women who had always possessed rights beyond their wildest imagination—Iroquois women. The more evidence I uncovered of this indelible Native American influence on the vision of early United States feminists, the more certain I became that this story must be told."[51] Connecting the ideological lineages between Haudenosaunee Clan mothers and the ethos of Iroquois peoples to U.S. suffragists and feminists changes the arc of feminist history dramatically. Wagner's willingness to engage in auto-ethnographic self-reflection and retell the foundations behind U.S. women's efforts to achieve full political enfranchisement, helps make visible the work that needs to be done. Thinkers like Gilbert may likewise need time. It is challenging to face one's privilege, articulate it, live with it, and hand over authority granted by it. To wait, however, on the privileged to assuage themselves is costly to the underrepresented, and for those who face anti-Indian racism every day.

One of the deep undercurrents in the messaging of Disney's *Pocahontas* is how thinly it portrays the capacity of Indigenous survivance and how the film engenders the old racist ideology of merit-based achievement. Ignorance and the lack of understanding racialized tropes today, typically unpacked in works on implicit bias, tend to placate and create comfort for those living within the spectrum of privilege. Native Americans face anti-Indian sentiments and actions today and according to esteemed Native

American scholars, stem from the perpetuation of what Robert Williams calls "language of Indian savagery"[52] and, I would add, the logic that arises in the scripts and imagery of imaginary "Indians." The language of savagery itself is used to fuel rebuffs by those who cling to anti-Indian racism as a defense. Holding on to racist sports mascots, like the Redskins, Braves, and Indians, the monikers are defended as honors to Native American peoples. The subtly of other forms of implicit bias, like recasting Pocahontas and Sacagawea as feminist archetypes for a feminism that did not include women of color is another example.

Similar defenses aim to render critiques about *Pocahontas*, and its power to perpetuate racism and misogyny, moot. There is power in the ways that didacticism enables and stabilizes existing systems of power. Resistance to the scholars and activists working today to reverse the current of anti-Indianism express notable investment in exposing and ameliorating the material effects of anti-Indianism, is palpable in defenses that perpetrate the "master narrative."[53]

WHERE DO WE GO FROM HERE?

Native American women role models exist historically and today, including Pocahontas. Her service to her people never ended. Even in death, she sent one last message—that she and the Powhatan had been betrayed. Pocahontas was a fierce and brave protector, a wonderful role model that Disney could have capitalized on if that is the role Disney insists on playing. Pocahontas is also not the only Native American woman who retains their cultural epistemologies, protects Indigenous sovereignty, and succeeds in U.S. history. Osage and Scottish American ballerina Maria Tallchief remains the first Prima Ballerina in U.S. history and the performer who put the New York Ballet Company on the map. Her story seems perfect for Disney's typically heteronormative preferences—a ballerina who changes the landscape of dance and puts the United States on the map as a competitor in a European classic form of dance.[54] There was also the work of Piute scholar, educator, and activist Sarah Winnemucca Hopkins, the first Native American woman to be published in the United States. In *Life among the Piutes: Their Wrongs and Claims*[55] Winnemucca Hopkins serves up a scathing rebuke of white civility, white masculinity, and the ill-fitted ethos of the Piute peoples to comprehend or address such egregiousness. After its publishing, Winnemucca Hopkins traveled the U.S. performing plays and reading her works to audiences in an effort to pique their empathy and democratic oath, to little avail.[56] These two represent important historical figures whose lives and successes provide story lines that also exemplify Native Americans who remained epistemologically grounded, yet adaptive to social change.[57]

Today, there are numerous Native American women scholars, activists, bloggers, videographers, and filmmakers whose works disentangle Native American peoples from the grips of racism, misogyny, and heteronormativity. Winona LaDuke and the late Wilma Mankiller are highly public figures who expound on the necessity of eradicating racism from America's popular cultures and laws in their fights to sustain the treaty rights of Native Americans. LaDuke's book, *All Our Relations: Native Struggles for Life and Land*[58] became a major text that articulates the fundamental ways that treaties connect the protections of Native American peoples, cultural practices, lands and waters, and the ways that they are breached for corporate interests.

Indigenous communities are doing the work of activism and advocacy today. However the work of shifting popular culture around Native peoples extends broadly across many institutions. Disney and the media in general could engage in critical thinking. Teachers could advance new curriculum, instead of revisionist pedagogies. Legislators could embrace their onus. There are possibilities for change and the change has to grow from within those institutions and individuals powerful enough to have a choice in the matter.

NOTES

1. Religion News Service, "Pocahontas Legend Hides Unromantic Realities: Cultures: Disney Tale Reflects Current Values More Than Historical Truths, Experts Say," *The Los Angeles Times*, June 24, 1995, accessed July 19, 2019, https://www.latimes.com/archives/la-xpm-1995-06-24-me-16637-story.html; Helen Roundtree, "Pocahontas: The Hostage Who Became Famous," In *Sifters: Native American Women's Lives*, edited by Theda Perdue, 14–28 (New York: Oxford University Press, 2001).

2. Robert A. Williams, Jr., *Like a Loaded Weapon: The Rehnquist Court, Indian Rights, and the Legal History of Racism in America* (Minneapolis: University of Minnesota Press, 2005).

3. Linwood "Little Bear" Custalow and Angela L. "Silver Star" Daniel, *The True Story of Pocahontas: The Other Side of History*.

4. Linwood "Little Bear" Custalow and Angela L. "Silver Star" Daniel, *The True Story of Pocahontas: The Other Side of History, from the Sacred History of the Mattaponi Reservation People*, 2007: xxiii.

5. Ibid.

6. Rayna Green, "The Pocahontas Perplex: the Image of Indian Women in American Culture," in *Unequal Sisters: A Multicultural Reader in U.S. Women's History*, Ellen Carol Dubois and Vicki Ruiz, 15–21 (New York: Routledge 1975/1990);

Laura Ann Stoler, *Carnal Knowledge and Imperial Power: Race and the Intimate in Colonial Rule* (Berkeley: University of California Press, 2002); Leece Lee-Oliver, "Contemporary Modernity and 'Death Ethics': Antecedents and Impacts of Western Expansion as War in the Northern Plains, 1820–1880" (PhD dissertation, University of California, Berkeley, 2013).

7. Linwood "Little Bear" Custalow and Angela L. "Silver Star" Daniel, *The True Story of Pocahontas: The Other Side of History, From the Sacred History of the Mattaponi Reservation People*, 36.

8. Ibid., 15.
9. Ibid., 17.
10. Ibid., 19.
11. Ibid., 20.
12. Ibid., 19.
13. Ibid., 25–26.

14. Rayna Green, "The Pocahontas Perplex: The Image of Indian Women in American Culture"; M. Annette Jaimes and Theresa Halsey, "American Indian Women: At the Center of Indigenous Resistance in North America," in *The State of Native America: Genocide, Colonization and Resistance*, edited by M. Annette Jaimes, 311–344 (Boston: South End Press, 1992); Kate Flint, *The Transatlantic Indian, 1776-1930* (New Jersey: Princeton University Press, 2009); Patricia Penn Hilden and Leece M. Lee, "Indigenous Feminism: The Project," in *Indigenous Women and Feminism: Politics, Activism, Culture*, edited by Cheryl Suzak, Shari M. Huhndorf, Jeanne Perreault, and Jean Barman, 56–78 (Vancouver, BC: UBC Press, 2010).

15. Rudo Kemper, "Writing Maroon Culture into Nature: On the Agency of Colonial Representations of Black and Green in Suriname," PhD diss. (The University of North Carolina at Chapel Hill, 2014); Leece Lee-Oliver, "Contemporary Modernity and 'Death Ethics': Antecedents and Impacts of Western Expansion as War in the Northern Plains, 1820–1880."

16. Donna Barbie, "Sacagawea: The Making of a Myth," *Sifters: Native American Women's Lives* (2001): 60–76; Kate Flint, *The Transatlantic Indian, 1776-1930*; Linwood "Little Bear" Custalow and Angela L. "Silver Star" Daniel, *The True Story of Pocahontas: The Other Side of History*; Rudo Kemper, "Writing Maroon Culture into Nature: On the Agency of Colonial Representations of Black and Green in Suriname"; Leece Lee-Oliver, "Imagining New Worlds: Anti-Indianism and the Roots of United States Exceptionalism," in *Global Raciality: Empire, Postcoloniality, Decoloniality*, edited by Paolo Bachetta, Sunaina Maira, and Howard Winant (New York: Routledge, 2018).

17. Linwood "Little Bear" Custalow and Angela L. "Silver Star" Daniel, *The True Story of Pocahontas: The Other Side of History*, 2007, 47.

18. Ibid., 37.
19. Ibid., 75.
20. Ibid., 75.
21. Ibid., 57.

22. Laura Ann Stoler, *Carnal Knowledge and Imperial Power: Race and the Intimate in Colonial Rule*; Linwood "Little Bear" Custalow and Angela L. "Silver Star" Daniel, *The True Story of Pocahontas: The Other Side of History*, 73.

23. Linwood "Little Bear" Custalow and Angela L. "Silver Star" Daniel, *The True Story of Pocahontas: The Other Side of History*, 79–80.
24. Ibid., 83.
25. Edward Said, *Orientalism* (London: Penguin Books, 1978).
26. Robert A. Williams, Jr., *Like a Loaded Weapon: The Rehnquist Court, Indian Rights, and the Legal History of Racism in America*," 39.
27. Michel-Rolph Trouillot, *Silencing the Past: Power and the Production of History* (Boston: Beacon Press 1994), 7.
28. M. Elise Marubbio, *Killing the Indian Maiden: Images of Native American Women in Film* (Lexington: University Press of Kentucky, 2006).
29. Gayatri Chakravorty Spivak, "Can the SubAltern Speak?" in *Maxism and the Interpretation of Culture*, edited by Cary Nelson and Lawrence Grossberg, 24–28 (London: MacMillan, 1988); Spivak, Gayatri, "History." In *A Critique of Postcolonial Reason: Toward a History of the Vanishing Present*, 198–311 (Cambridge: Harvard University Press, 1999).
30. *Pocahontas*, Walt Disney Pictures, directed by Mike Gabriel and Eric Goldberg, staring Irene Bedard and Mel Gibson, 1995, 81 minutes.
31. Edward Said, *Orientalism*; Gayatri Spivak, "History."
32. Disney Parks Moms Panel, "Is There a Pocahontas's Show at Animal Kingdom? We Just Loved It," March 8, 2017, accessed July 15, 2019, https://disneyparksmomspanel.disney.go.com/question/pocahontass-show-animal-kingdom-loved-333080/.
33. "Pocahontas Spectacular," The Disney Fandom Wiki, accessed July 15, 2019, https://disney.fandom.com/wiki/Pocahontas_Spectacular; "The Spirit of Pocahontas," Yesterland, updated February 6, 2009, accessed July 15, 2019, https://www.yesterland.com/spirit.html.
34. Elizabeth Hutchinson, *The Indian Craze: Primitivism, Modernism, and Transculturation in American Art, 1890–1915* (Durham: Duke University Press, 2009), 138–149.
35. Leece Lee-Oliver, "Mapping Colonial Resistance: Colonialism, Anti-'Indianism,' and Contested Nationalisms in the Americas," in *Critical Terms in Caribbean and Latin American Thought*, edited by Yolanda Martínez-San Miguel, Ben. Sifuentes-Jáuregui, and Marisa Belausteguigoitia (New York: Palgrave MacMillan, 2016); Kevin Noble Maillard, "The Pocahontas Exception: The Exemption of American Indian Ancestry from Racial Purity Law," *Michigan Journal of Race and Law*, 12, no. 107 (2007), http://dx.doi.org/10.2139/ssrn.871096.
36. Tino Granados, "#IAmNotACostume," October 5, 2017, accessed July 19, 2019, https://www.urbannativeera.com/2017/10/05/1/.
37. Michel-Rolph Trouillot, *Silencing the Past: Power and the Production of History*.
38. Ibid., 106–107.
39. Edward Said, *Orientalism*.
40. Elizabeth Hutchinson, *The Indian Craze: Primitivism, Modernism, and Transculturation in American Art, 1890–1915*, 104.
41. Ibid.
42. Robert A. Williams, Jr., *Like a Loaded Weapon: The Rehnquist Court, Indian Rights, and the Legal History of Racism in America*."

43. Ibid., 39.

44. Jodi A. Byrd, *The Transit of Empire: Indigenous Critiques of Colonialism* (Minneapolis: University of Minnesota Press, 2011); Rudo Kemper, "Writing Maroon Culture into Nature: On the Agency of Colonial Representations of Black and Green in Suriname."

45. Sophie Gilbert, "Revisiting *Pocahontas* at 20," *The Atlantic*, June 23, 2015, accessed June 20, 2019, https://www.theatlantic.com/entertainment/archive/2015/06/revisiting-pocahontas/396626/.

46. Sophie Gilbert, "Revisiting *Pocahontas* at 20."

47. Ibid.

48. Sally Roesch Wagner, *Sisters in Spirit: Haudenosaunee (Iroquois) Influence on Early American Feminists* (Summertown, TN: Native Voices Book Publishing Company, 2001).

49. Sally Roesch Wagner, *Sisters in Spirit: Haudenosaunee (Iroquois) Influence on Early American Feminists*.

50. Ibid., 21.

51. Ibid.

52. Robert A. Williams, Jr., *Like a Loaded Weapon: The Rehnquist Court, Indian Rights, and the Legal History of Racism in America*."

53. Ronald Takaki, *A Different Mirror: A History of Multicultural America* (New York; Back Bay Books, 2008).

54. Sandy Osawa, *Maria Tallchief*, Upstream Productions, 2007, 57 minutes, documentary film.

55. Sarah Winnemucca Hopkins, *Life among the Piutes: Their Wrongs and Claims*, (Boston: G.P. Putnam's Sons, 1883, reprint Los Angeles: Enhanced Media, 2017).

56. Sarah Winnemucca Hopkins, *Life among the Piutes: Their Wrongs and Claims*.

57. Sarah Winnemucca Hopkins, *Life among the Piutes: Their Wrongs and Claims*; Patricia Penn Hilden and Leece M. Lee, "Indigenous Feminism: The Project," *Indigenous Women and Feminism: Politics, Activism, Culture* (2010): 56–78.

58. Winona LaDuke, *All Our Relations, Native Struggles for Land and Life* (Cambridge, MA: South End Press, 1999).

BIBLIOGRAPHY

Barbie, Donna. "Sacagawea: The Making of a Myth." *Sifters: Native American Women's Lives* (2001): 60–76.

Byrd, Jodi A. *The Transit of Empire: Indigenous Critiques of Colonialism*. Minneapolis: University of Minnesota Press, 2011.

Custalow, Linwood "Little Bear," and Angela L. "Silver Star" Daniel. *The True Story of Pocahontas: The Other Side of History, from the Sacred History of the Mattaponi Reservation People*. Golden, Colorado: Fulcrum Publishing, 2007.

Disney Parks Moms Panel. "Is There a Pocahontas's Show at Animal Kingdom? We Just Loved It." March 8, 2017. Accessed July 15, 2019. https://disneyparks momspanel.disney.go.com/question/pocahontass-show-animal-kingdom-loved-333080/.

Flint, Kate. *The Transatlantic Indian, 1776-1930*. New Jersey: Princeton University Press, 2009.
Gilbert, Sophie. "Revisiting *Pocahontas* at 20." *The Atlantic*, June 23, 2015. Accessed June 20, 2019. https://www.theatlantic.com/entertainment/archive/2015/06/revisiting-pocahontas/396626/.
Granados, Tino. "#IAmNotACostume." October 5, 2017. Accessed July 19, 2019. https://www.urbannativeera.com/2017/10/05/1/.
Green, Rayna. "The Pocahontas Perplex: The Image of Indian Women in American Culture," in *Unequal Sisters: A Multicultural Reader in U.S. Women's History*, Ellen Carol Dubois and Vicki Ruiz, 15–21. New York: Routledge 1975/1990.
Hilden, Patricia Penn, and Leece M. Lee, "Indigenous Feminism: The Project," in *Indigenous Women and Feminism: Politics, Activism, Culture*, edited by Cheryl Suzak, Shari M. Huhndorf, Jeanne Perreault, and Jean Barman, 56–78. Vancouver, BC: UBC Press, 2010.
Hopkins, Sarah Winnemucca. *Life among the Piutes: Their Wrongs and Claims*. Boston: G.P. Putnam's Sons, 1883, reprint Los Angeles: Enhanced Media, 2017.
Hutchinson, Elizabeth. *The Indian Craze: Primitivism, Modernism, and Transculturation in American Art, 1890–1915*. Durham: Duke University Press, 2009.
Jaimes, Annette, M. and Theresa Halsey. "American Indian Women: At the Center of Indigenous Resistance in North America." In *The State of Native America: Genocide, Colonization and Resistance*, edited by M. Annette Jaimes, 311–344. Boston: South End Press, 1992.
Kemper, Rudo. "Writing Maroon Culture into Nature: On the Agency of Colonial Representations of Black and Green in Suriname." PhD diss., The University of North Carolina at Chapel Hill, 2014.
LaDuke, Winona. *All Our Relations, Native Struggles for Land and Life*. Cambridge, MA: South End Press, 1999.
Lee-Oliver, Leece. "Contemporary Modernity and 'Death Ethics': Antecedents and Impacts of Western Expansion as War in the Northern Plains, 1820–1880." PhD diss., University of California, Berkeley, 2013.
———. Mapping Colonial Resistance: Colonialism, Anti-'Indianism,' and Contested Nationalisms in the Americas, in *Critical Terms in Caribbean and Latin American Thought*, edited by Yolanda Martínez-San Miguel, Ben. Sifuentes-Jáuregui, and Marisa Belausteguigoitia. New York: Palgrave MacMillan, 2016.
———. "Imagining New Worlds: Anti-Indianism and the Roots of United States Exceptionalism." In *Global Raciality: Empire, Postcoloniality, Decoloniality*, edited by Paolo Bachetta, Sunaina Maira, and Howard Winant. New York: Routledge, 2018.
Maillard, Kevin Noble. "The Pocahontas Exception: The Exemption of American Indian Ancestry from Racial Purity Law." *Michigan Journal of Race and Law*, 12, no. 107 (2007). http://dx.doi.org/10.2139/ssrn.871096.
Marubbio, M. Elise. *Killing the Indian Maiden: Images of Native American Women in Film*. Lexington: University Press of Kentucky, 2006.
"Pocahontas Spectacular." The Disney Fandom Wiki. Accessed July 15, 2019. https://disney.fandom.com/wiki/Pocahontas_Spectacular; "The Spirit of Pocahontas," Yesterland, updated February 6, 2009, accessed July 15, 2019, https://www.yesterland.com/spirit.html.

Religion News Service. "Pocahontas Legend Hides Unromantic Realities: Cultures: Disney Tale Reflects Current Values More Than Historical Truths, Experts Say." *The Los Angeles Times*, June 24, 1995. Accessed July 19, 2019. https://www.latimes.com/archives/la-xpm-1995-06-24-me-16637-story.html.

Said, Edward. *Orientalism*. London: Penguin Books, 1978.

Spivak, Gayatri. "Can the SubAltern Speak?" In *Maxism and the Interpretation of Culture*, edited by Cary Nelson and Lawrence Grossberg, 24–28. London: MacMillan, 1988.

———. "History." In *A Critique of Postcolonial Reason: Toward a History of the Vanishing Present*, 198–311. Cambridge: Harvard University Press, 1999.

Stoler, Laura Ann. *Carnal Knowledge and Imperial Power: Race and the Intimate in Colonial Rule*. Berkeley: University of California Press, 2002.

Takaki, Ronald. *A Different Mirror: A History of Multicultural America*. New York; Back Bay Books, 2008.

Trouillot, Michel-Rolph. *Silencing the Past: Power and the Production of History*. Boston: Beacon Press 1994.

Wagner, Sally Roesch. *Sisters in Spirit: Haudenosaunee (Iroquois) Influence on Early American Feminists*. Summertown, TN: Native Voices Book Publishing Company, 2001.

Walt Disney Pictures. *Pocahontas*. Directed by Mike Gabriel and Eric Goldberg, staring Irene Bedard and Mel Gibson, 1995. 81 minutes. Film.

Williams, Jr., Robert A. *Like a Loaded Weapon: The Rehnquist Court, Indian Rights, and the Legal History of Racism in America*." Minneapolis: University of Minnesota Press, 2005.

11

✣

A Whole New Worldview

Gender Norms, Islamophobia, and Orientalism

Krystal Ghisyawan

SOUTH-ASIAN MEDIATED STEREOTYPES AND SOCIAL MOVEMENTS

On Valentine's Day 2019 in Brampton, Ontario, Riya Rajkumar celebrated her eleventh birthday with her father, Roopesh. He had been sending threatening messages to her mother, Priya Ramdin, indicating his intention to harm himself and his daughter. Priya alerted the police, who found Riya's body in her father's home. He was later held in Orillia, Ontario, and after several days succumbed to a self-inflicted gunshot wound. Lotus, a grassroots organization in Toronto, Canada, which focuses on building social connections, educational initiatives, and empowering the lives of Indo-Caribbean women, released a statement on Riya's death.[1] They lamented the legacy of violence and intergenerational trauma that plague Indo-Guyanese communities in the diaspora. They noted "We can also point to all the intersecting structural problems of toxic masculinity, patriarchal systems, gender ideologies, and lack of mental health support that got played out in this case."[2] They also noted that healing as a community meant locating these men within histories that indoctrinate them into a normalized use of violence against women and girls. Their statement sparked some hostility by mentioning that racialized groups experience different kinds of protections from violence in Canadian society. They questioned whether a quicker police response would have made a difference in saving Riya. Her parental abduction was reported at 6 p.m., but an amber alert was not issued until 11:30 p.m.

Some readers were not happy with this response. For instance, the organization received an email from a woman presumed to be of Italian background (determined by her name in the email). She started by acknowledging that women all over the world are victims of "male violence," but moves between blaming the men themselves and blaming culture for men's violence against women. "It seems some cultures are worse than others in their dominance over women," she said.[3] She noted that Riya had her nails done that morning[4] and wondered if the father felt his daughter was "becoming too westernized." She asserted, "Some people who come to Canada—can't adjust to a free society for women."[5] The author of the email assumed he was from a culture oppositional to "western" views and values, that exerted "dominance over women," "that degrade women—belittle women—reduce women."[6]

Many reports did not specify that Rajkumar was an Indo-Guyanese migrant. Indo-Caribbean-Canadians do not fit neatly into an identity category; each of these terms connote race, ethnicity, and location, yet do not signify a singular appearance or experience. Caribbean people of South Asian descent are as diverse in appearance as the people of the Indian subcontinent; they may be recognized as brown and mistakenly assumed to be from the subcontinent. Brampton, where Rajkumar lived, is also known for having a large South Asian population. Preity Kumar, co-founder and co-facilitator at The Lotus Project in Toronto, said "There is a homogenization of South Asian and Indo-Caribbean, so when you see perhaps, something like honor killing, or one of these things that get taken up in Canadian media, people assume we're from the same community. 'Because you're brown, you're the same kind of people.' There's that stereotype."[7]

The media is an important source of information through which the world becomes known. The media has "a monopoly of knowledge, and through their practices of selection, editing and production, they determine the kinds of news we receive about our nation,"[8] making it the most useful tool for nation-building, for establishing a sense of self and an understanding of the other. Attitudes and beliefs are shaped by the knowledge made public through media, one of the richest and most influential institutions in society.[9] The most dominant images of minorities in the public domain are often based on stereotypes, mainly negative, while other aspects are downplayed or absent.[10] Media depictions of minorities also center the qualities that mark them as different, as "other," as enemy to the defined "us," the West.

How does the death of Riya Rajkumar relate to the 2019 remake of *Aladdin*? The author of the email sent to Lotus based her opinions on media representation of the case and the parties involved. Her response reflects how media representation of people of color has real-life consequences by shaping popular opinion. This chapter explores the symbolic violence of media depictions that conflate and misrepresent brown people, and how this results in structural, systemic, and interpersonal violence. Firstly, the chapter addresses contemporary islamophobia and anti-migrant sentiment in the U.S. and Canada, and its relationship to media portrayals; portraying brown men as villainous, monstrous, backward, and terrorists have resulted in increasing hate crimes against them, while depicting brown women as helpless and trapped in an oppressive culture denies them voice and agency. The 1992 *Aladdin* film is implicated as perpetuating these depictions, while the 2019 *Aladdin* film attempts to nuance them by toning down the allusions to barbaric acts of violence and the exotification of Princess Jasmine, while playing up her defiance. Secondly, this chapter looks at women's agency today through the work of Lotus in the Jane and Finch community in Toronto, a high density, low income, mainly immigrant neighborhood that has been underserved by public services and subject to targeted policing.

PORTRAYING THE EAST THROUGH WESTERN EYES: *ALADDIN* AND CONTEMPORARY ISLAMOPHOBIA

The 2019 remake of the Disney classic *Aladdin* was full of controversy before it even began filming, concerning its casting and setting. Although published in the 1712 version of Antoine Galland's tales *Les mille et une nuit: Contes Arabes (1001 Nights: Arabian Tales)*,[11] the origins of the story are unknown. Galland, a French orientalist scholar and archaeologist, wrote in his diary that he first heard the tale from a Syrian storyteller from Aleppo named Hanna Diyab[12] on May 8, 1709.[13] While the origin of the story remains uncertain, over its many retellings, the multiethnic and cosmopolitan Arab context has been obscured and recoded. As Arafat Razzaque explains, the original tale is set in China, which may have been used symbolically to represent the "far away lands," an abstract, exotic place, from a Middle Eastern perspective. Arabic versions of *Aladdin* denote the sorcerer (Jafar) as a *"maghribi"* or North African, alluding to the Arab world's connections through North Africa and Europe to South Asia and China. Islam is among the religions practiced in these regions. Through religious, economic and political ties, the cities of the Arab world developed as important global centers. Agrabah, where the tale of *Aladdin* is set, has come to be understood similarly, as a thriving port city within the Arab world, with diverse peoples and cultures.

Julie Ann Crommett, Disney's vice president of multicultural engagement, explained the film's dedication to having a cast reflective of the cosmopolitan nature of the Arab world and the Silk Road, inclusive of South

Asia, China, North Africa, and the Middle East. Special consultants were brought in to advise on every detail of the film, as Crommett said, to capture authenticity, regardless of the identity of the cast and crew.[14] *Aladdin* (1992) depicted Orientalist stereotypes of Arab cultures and peoples, portraying men as violent, barbaric, and dangerous, and women as demure, submissive, and exotic.[15] The makers of the 2019 remake were attentive to "moving away from stereotypes and really celebrating the culture in quite a positive way and really depicting it in a way that feels more nuanced and more authentic."[16] The lyrics of Arabian night which opens the movie have been altered, replacing images of barbarism ("where they cut off your tongue to spite your face, its barbaric but hey it's home") to praises of the culture of the city ("where you wander among every culture and tongue, its chaotic but hey its home"). Other creative decisions included having a predominantly Brown cast, reducing allusions to violence, reducing the sexualization of women by dressing them more modestly, and by empowering the princess Jasmine, de-emphasizing marriage and female subservience in her story arc.

One thing they did not change was the use of American accents for the protagonists, Aladdin, Jasmine, and the Genie. Jasmine is played by Naomi Scott, an Anglo-Indian. Aladdin is played by Mena Massoud, of Egyptian origin, raised in Toronto. The iconic genie is portrayed by Hollywood superstar Will Smith. Their accent makes them more intelligible to American viewers and marks them as inherently good. They are symbolically aligned with the West, while the other characters are cultural "others."[17] The protagonist Aladdin embodies western ideals by seeking the actualization of his own personal desires, aided by a magical genie, the "godmother" prototype repeated in the Disney princess films. His accent and western values confirm him as the hero of the film. Similarly, Jasmine's defiance can be read as her westernization, as defiance against the control of women enforced within Middle Eastern and Arab cultures.

Weaponizing Gendered Portrayals of the Arab-Asian

Much of the recent media discourse around Arab-Asian people are shaped by two key news events: the September 11 terrorist attacks and the War on Terror that followed it, and migration stemming from the Syrian civil war. However, Arab-Asian depictions in the media pre-date these recent events and little has been done in Hollywood or in Western news to counter it. In the original *Aladdin* animation, the two major male Arab figures of the Sultan and Jafar represented two contrasting portrayals of Arab masculinity: the wealthy, indulgent, fat, infantile, weak sultan is overpowered by the evil, conniving, and beguiling Jafar, who utilizes dark magic to get his way. These characters embody the stereotypical portrayals of Arab men as described by Jasbir Puar and Amir Rai: the "fag" who is weak, soft, and effeminate (the sultan), versus the "monster-terrorist" (Jafar).[18] Puar and Rai explore how similar portrayals of gender and sexuality have been utilized in propaganda supporting the war on terror, whereby the monstrosity and sexual perversion of the "other" is defeated and redeemed by the aggressive heterosexual patriotism of the West.[19]

A mediated binary around Arab Asian identity begins to shape not just discourse but actions. After the 9-11 attacks on the World Trade Center and the Pentagon, there was a rapid proliferation of mocking images sporting a turbaned Osama bin Laden, either as monstrous terrorist, or being emasculated, for instance being sodomized with the Empire State Building.[20] The nexus of gender, sexuality, and race is where disciplinary action against the terrorist has become situated. The figure of the oppressed Arab woman is used to mobilize hatred for the Arab man, and justify his emasculation by American retaliation for the 9-11 attacks, by treating him as the Taliban treat Afghan women. According to Puar and Rai, "this promise not only suggests that if you're not for the war, you're a fag, it also incites violence against queers and specifically queers of color."[21] There indeed was an upsurge of attacks on queers of color, Middle Eastern, and South Asian people, particularly those wearing religious garb, such as head scarves and turbans. As Jasbir Puar asserts, "the turban is a complicated and ambivalent signifier of both racial and religious community as well as of the power of masculine heteronormativity."[22] Versions of the turban are worn by practitioners of Sikhism, Islam, Judaism, Rastafarianism, and Christianity (such as the Akurinu in Kenya). Interpretations of the racial and sexual differences regarding the wearing of the turban, form part of community and identity formation among South Asian, African, Middle Eastern, and Arab American peoples. But it is also mobilized in discourses pertaining to multiculturalism in the West, symbolizing the patriarchy of the East, of Islam, of the Taliban, and their oppression of women.

Another popular image of bin Laden post 9-11, superimposed his face on to a 7-Eleven convenience store scene as a cashier, similar to Apu from *The Simpsons*. These images caused racist backlash against Arab American and South Asian American communities.[23] Indian and Middle Eastern people who owned and ran convenient stores and other small retail and service businesses, found themselves targeted for acts of Islamophobic violence, vandalism, beatings, and arson. Sikhs were particularly vulnerable as they wore turbans.

Anti-Islamic sentiment has existed for hundreds of years, but the heightened rhetoric since 9-11, the American War on Terror and the painting of the terrorist as Arab, has fueled the propagation of hate speech and acts targeting those perceived to be Muslim. Scholars have offered political readings of the characters of *Aladdin* as reflective of the U.S. imperialist actions within the Middle East.[24] Reading *Aladdin* as a symbol of the West, his achieving power over the Sultan and Jafar, symbolizes the West's triumph over the Arab world. While production of the 2019 *Aladdin* film has been responsive to the xenophobic and anti-Islamic rhetoric of today, the story line has not changed much, following the same general arc. The depiction of Jafar has been toned down, perhaps intending him to be less menacing than the cartoon counterpart and de-emphasizing this character's resemblance to the often potrayed Arab "monster-terrorist." Bigger changes were made to the film's portrayals of Jasmine.

The Damsel Rescues Herself: Female Agency and Empowerment

While Disney's 2019 live-action remake of *Aladdin* attempted to nuance its depictions of the Arab world, it barely addressed issues of "othering" regarding Arab masculinity, but made greater effort to revamp Jasmine and brown femininity. The 1992 animated film's depiction of Jasmine reiterated gender stereotypes of the region. She is an exoticized sexual "other" and an oppressed other. In Disney's films, scholars have noted that heroines of color embody the exoticized "other," and are illustrated to emphasize their sexual maturity above all else, inviting viewers' more voyeuristic gaze.[25] Jasmine's petite frame with an unnaturally narrow waist is dressed in the manner of a belly-dancer. The small bodice exposes her midriff, hugs her mature breasts, and falls suggestively off her shoulders. Her makeup is dark and sultry, calling attention to her exotic features, a small nose and mouth, and large, almond-shaped eyes. The 2019 live-action movie did not replicate these outfit choices, instead dressing the princess in form fitting yet covered outfits in rich colors and fabrics. Her bodices were contoured and structured to accentuate her curves but covered her midriff. Her signature blue and gold outfit had a sheer midsection that tastefully covered the princess's body. She also wears a shawl or veil over her head when outside of her private chambers. On her visit to the market place, her headscarf is of a thicker silk and wrapped more tightly around her face.

The palace symbolizes the private sphere. It is simultaneously, representative of the princess' oppression and Aladdin's aspirations to improve his social status. He does not desire to be a prince until he learns that the girl who he met in the market place is the princess (in the 2019 film). In the 1992 film, Aladdin desires wealth, believing it brings power; he said "the one who has the gold makes the rules." While in the animation, Jasmine longs to leave the palace and be free of other's control over her life, and in the 2019 remake, she primarily longs to be Sultan. She tells Dalia, her handmaiden in the 2019 film, "I was born to do more than marry a useless prince." She wishes to rule, even though the law states only a man, her husband, can rule. Her husband becomes sultan, and she becomes queen. The Sultan also urges her to marry so that she might be cared for when he is gone, emphasizing a woman's need for a man as provider and protector.

Jasmine of the 2019 remake is more multidimensional than the animated film's depiction. Her education through books and maps is reiterated. She is later shown in her room studying maps, looking for Ababwa. "Maps are old and useless and have no practical value," Aladdin says dismissively, trying to take her attention away. "Maps are how I see the world," she replied. "I thought a princess could go anywhere?" he then asks her, now truly interested. "Not this princess," she replies, hinting at a complicated story. Her loving father became over-protective when her mother died, not wanting to risk losing her too. Throughout the movie, Jasmine mentions something she learned from her mother, like the song on the lute, or lessons in diplomacy and leadership, making the mother present in the film, also as a multidimensional female figure. Aladdin coaxed Jasmine onto the magic carpet by offering "a whole world outside of books and maps." At the end of the carpet ride, while gazing at a group of revelers in a courtyard in Agrabah, Jasmine suggests she would like to lead the country. Aladdin is the first male character we see showing her support; he does not wish to rule. When the Sultan gives his blessing for the two to wed, Jasmine seems pleased to marry him, perhaps momentarily accepting that she will have a supportive husband who would allow her more power and opportunity to lead. Earlier, she had suggested her capability to rule by referencing the books, she had been reading on politics and policy; Jafar quickly shuts her down saying "you cannot read experience." Books symbolize education and knowledge; which can be the means for providing women opportunity and advancement today. But even though she may have knowledge, the Sultan cited the laws as the reason why Jasmin could not rule, pointing to structural barriers to women's advancement. Similar to the Taliban's use of law to enforce their own interpretation of Islam that barred girls from schools. Jafar and the Sultan are the enforcers of "culture" and "tradition." Jafar instructs her "Life will be kinder to you once you accept these traditions and know it is better for you to be seen and not heard." The silencing of the princess is symbolic of the culture's silencing of women.

Fittingly, Jasmine's breakout song declared "I won't be silenced, You can't keep me quiet, Won't tremble when you try it, All I know is I won't go speechless." Her finding of voice is quite literal. When Jafar takes power and attempts to imprison her, she uses her words to persuade the Chief of the Guards, Hakeem, to stand up for the people of Agrabah and do the right thing by arresting Jafar for his treason. When Jafar tortures her father, she bravely consents to marry him, but when asked to take the marital vow, she says, "I don't." Her verbal and physical oppositions symbolically represent her rejection of the values and traditions he (Jafar) embodies. By changing the laws to allow Jasmine to be princess, the Sultan shows how culture is socially produced and thus can change. The hard and fast Eastern patriarchy (Jafar) is ultimately outsmarted and defeated by the liberal western patriarchy, symbolized by Aladdin and Jasmin, the female Sultan.

This revision of Jasmine's personality fits a Western interpretation of empowerment. Indeed while the film's cast is far more diverse and representative of the region than the animated original, its script is still written by two white men: Guy Ritchie, its director, and John August, are British and American, respectively. U.S. notions of liberty and happiness are embodied in its anthem as the "land of the free," and other notions of exceptionalism as the home of liberty and freedom, the protector of freedom's abroad and the liberator of oppressed peoples. Likewise, Western interventions into the Arab world, led in the current era by the U.S., have also been framed as liberating Muslim women, much like Aladdin's support gave Jasmine the courage to use her voice.

Associating Jasmine's defiance of Jafar/Arab Asian culture with "Western values" obscures the fact that defiance and resistance occur among Middle Eastern peoples. While taken as universal, liberal theories of freedom result from locally specific historic trajectories;[26] measuring women's freedom and agency based on one society's or group's definition of it, turns a blind eye to the other ways in which women can be agentive and revolutionary. This is worsened for Muslim women who are perceived as constrained by culture and unable to act with agency and autonomy. The various forms of hijab or veiling are seen as symbolic of women's oppression,[27] even though there is evidence of veiled women who are empowered by the practice. Western nations, like France, believe that banning hijab and burka frees women from this religious oppression, but women may feel their freedoms of religion and expression are being curtailed.[28] The role of the burka in aiding anti-colonial efforts in Algeria is implanted in France's nationalist memory, making it a particularly abhorrent symbol of Islam and anti-imperial sentiment. The veil, especially the burka, aided in the surreptitious movement of rebels and their weapons; it was a tool of resistance.[29] Using it instead to represent male oppression of women, justifies demonizing Islam even when practiced in Western cultures that preach religious freedom, yet ban religious practices they determined to be oppressive, such as the wearing of the hijab and burkini. Muslim women have protested the ban on burkinis at French pools and beaches, facing arrest and fines for choosing to wear the garment that covered their entire bodies.[30]

In eastern contexts too, Muslim women have been protesting oppressive political policies. Videos have surfaced on social media with Saudi

Arabian women engaging in restricted activities, such as dancing in public and driving. They have protested being forced to publicly wear the face veil and the abaya, a long gown, by wearing the garments inside-out.[31] Women have also been active in protests throughout South-Asia on child marriage, rape culture,[32] divorce stigma, and menstrual taboos. Muslim women took to the streets of New Delhi in 2017 to protest triple talaq, also known as talaq-e-biddat, instant divorce and talaq-e-mughallazah (irrevocable divorce), forms of Islamic divorce where a man can divorce his wife by saying talaq three times.[33] In the biggest demonstration in Indian history, on January 1, 2019, five million women formed a wall in Kerala to protest their restriction from entering the Sabarimala temple.[34] These women are agentive and seek their own interests regardless of Western propaganda, yet depictions of Arab and South Asian women as vulnerable, oppressed by practices of domination and subordination, are used to maintain their otherness and exclusion within Western societies.

DOING THE WORK WITHIN

Multiculturalism and Muslim Women's Agency in Canada

Another unchanged aspect of the 2019 live-action *Aladdin* remake was Jafar's use of violence and intimidation to force Jasmine to marry him. Despite much of her agency to speak up and her own empowerment song, under threats to her loved ones and her own life, Jasmine is coerced into marrying Jafar. During the forced wedding, notably using modern vows of western society typically used in movies, Jasmine is asked if she takes Jafar to be her husband. She almost agrees until she spots a glimmer of hope in the far distance, and at the last minute grabs the lamp from Jafar's waist and leaps off a balcony landing on the magic carpet. She makes a choice to save herself and her family from Jafar. Jasmine's agency in the remake in saving herself is a reflection of social movements today. This section examines ways in which South-Asian Diasporic women living in Western cultures navigate policies and practices that both harm and help them. Women are at the forefront of social issues, doing the work, bridging generations, locations, and cultures to achieve what independence, strength, and survival means for them.

Lotus: Resilience of Indo-Caribbean Women in Jane–Finch, Canada

Preity Kumar and Suzanne Narain cofounded Lotus in 2016 with Talisha Ramsaroop. Ramsaroop had just learned about the term "Indo-Caribbean" and was discussing it with Narain, then a PhD candidate. The hyphenated identity "Indo-Caribbean" is a scholarly term, but is not used typically by people who are identified by it. As the women discussed what it meant to be Indo-Caribbean, they realized the experience was contextual: What did it mean to be "Indo-Caribbean" in Toronto? What are the experiences of Indo-Caribbean women in their own neighborhood, Jane and Finch? With a small grant from the government of Ontario, Lotus began organizing monthly programs in the community, to create a space in the diaspora for Indo-Guyanese women, and to tackle the problems within the community, including alcoholism, sexual exploitation, gender-based violence (GBV), and displacement, as well as the systemic problems of difficulty accessing housing, food and security. Lacking culturally specific resources and community programs, Lotus chose to draw on the shared, and often unspoken, histories of Indo-Caribbean women to build authentic social connection through art, activism, and solidarity building. According to the organizers, Lotus is the first and only organization of its kind in Canada.

Over just a short time, Lotus built a rapport with the women of the Jane and Finch community, the area with the highest Indo-Caribbean population in the city. According to Narain, by sharing these experiences, the women are "building solidarity and safety with one another. These safe spaces then become sites of survival for women."[35] Some of the past activities put on by the group included sessions documenting and recording oral narratives, folktales, and recipes of the Caribbean, noting how things are orally passed down. They intend to collect the recipes into a book. Preity Kumar described another session where the women discussed how different kinds of religious practices in the Caribbean, whether Muslim, Hindu, or Christian, can create community for sharing resources and food. The workshops were an opportunity for women to share their traumas and pains, build trust, support, and community.

Although Lotus reaches out to the wider community, it is mainly Indo-Caribbean women who regularly attend meetings, particularly elder women. Narain said: "Sometimes they do not speak that much in meetings but they have been the heartbeat and reason we are able to advocate. Nothing passive about them." After the passing of Riya Rajkumar, Lotus felt the women's need for catharsis and healing, as they carried the pain and trauma of their own experiences with gender-based violence. On May 9, they held a support group to discuss gender-based violence (GBV) in their lives, in their colonial histories and in the diaspora. They planned a series of workshops in June and July 2019, hoping to continue the conversation on GBV. In their February release after Riya's death, Lotus referenced Gaiutra Bahadur's work[36] in recovering the stories of indentured South Asian women who went to the Caribbean, providing detailed accounts of the violence they were exposed to within that exploitative labor system. Simultaneously, indentured men were experiencing social, political and economic marginalization under this system. Gender-based violence proliferates under such conditions, which persist even today. Violence against women remains a problem across the region.

Viewing the systemic problem of gender-based violence as an individual issue eclipses its roots in the gender ideologies, socio-economic and political allotments made within the society. As the members of Lotus reflected:

> Sadly, our community is not really open to having conversations about the violence and subsequent deaths that occur as a result of such violence. Such violence is too often interpreted as a normal feature of love, especially in a heterosexual romantic intimate partner relationship. And the violence between parent and child is also seen as part of how one parents, not as a sign of abuse.[37]

Abuse is allowed to continue as "normal," and cycles of violence are perpetuated. Even when migrants enter new environments, the triggers are not removed and the violence persists. Moving from the Caribbean to Toronto adds new pressures of migration, structural inequality, and racism of the new context. Lotus recognized the need to break these cycles of violence that trap Indo-Caribbean men and women, by including men in any solutions.[38] They mentioned holding men accountable, providing for their mental health, creating healthy relationships among couples, families, and communities. Kumar, of Lotus, explained that "when similar violence happens to brown and black women's bodies, it is seen as a cultural problem or a religious problem, not as a deeper structural-mental health-migration-trauma, along with toxic masculinity problem that bleeds into every culture."[39]

In her email to Lotus, the displeased Italian-Torontonian referred to Riya's father, Roopesh, as an "evil prick," "selfish beyond measure," and a "calculating monster." From her perspective, the structural inequalities in Toronto were irrelevant; she could not see how they would foster unhealthy psychologies and behaviors, and instead focused her attention on the man himself and the unspecified oppressive "culture" she believed him to be a part of. Roopesh here is symbolically aligned with Jafar, the violent oppressor, representative of an oppressive culture. At Lotus' suggestion that perhaps the police could have handled the case differently, she wrote:

> Color didn't play a role here. The police worked it for the little girl. Her dark skinned dad was the danger to his beautiful dark skinned girl. Not the multicultural cops. They did the opposite of her father—they tried to save her. Don't blame them. Blame the man who killed his own child. Him only. Him.[40]

She contrasts the father, the symbol of an eastern intolerant and oppressive culture, to the "multicultural cops," the figure of the liberal western state. In Canada, policing has been criticized for its racism. As Tator and colleagues purport, "policing culture and its structures are a composite of ideologies, values, norms, and practices that are deeply connected to and embedded in diverse societal systems,"[41] meaning that racist ideologies are shared across multiple societal institutions that inform and influence each other.

CONCLUSION

Although the 2019 *Aladdin* remake may have missed the mark on its ability to counter Western mediated portrayals of Orientalism and the Arab-South Asian world to a global audience, it has taken steps in the right direction. Their inclusive casting choices and use of cultural consultants have reduced the exaggerations of Arab culture from the 1992 animated feature film, yet the stereotypical depiction of Arab heteropatriarchy remains. They have expanded the role of Princess Jasmine in the story, from exotic prop for Aladdin, to being a heroine in her own way. Viewers see more of her personality, her education, and her training as royalty. She is also no longer the lone female presence, now having a memory of her mother, and a handmaiden with whom she could converse. The film offers a glimpse of the agential brown woman in a male dominated culture, demonstrating how these women may use their skill and knowledge to be defiant against "cultures" that constrain them, whether it is fundamental Islam in the Middle East, post-indenture gender-based violence in the Caribbean, or white settler nationalism in Canada. This chapter underscores how much Jasmine's evolution is a reflection of contemporary discourses and actions pertaining to racialized peoples, including rising Islamophobia, xenophobia, and social justice activism taking place around the world.

The filmmakers recognized their responsibility to more honest storytelling that did not demonize entire cultures. Future filmmakers should be considerate of how their portrayals of people of color influences public opinion of these groups. Blanketed portrayals of colored people flatten the cultural distinctions and diversity that exists even within one ethnic group, far be it from reflecting entire regions with billions of people. A single film cannot cover the breadth of experiences, ideas, and traditions that exist, but over time, responsible filmmaking can present more diverse perspectives that do not repeat the typical white savior or Western-gaze narrative. This includes depicting people of various religions and cultures within Western and non-Western contexts in ways that are fair and honest. Including writers of the cultural background of the film's focus is an important step in shifting the narrative away from these regular tropes, and infusing their stories with more authenticity. Perhaps then people of color would look at these films and see truer representations of themselves and their cultures.

NOTES

1. Lotus, "The Legacy of Violence in the Indo-Guyanese Diaspora: Remembering Riya Rajkumar." *Guyanese Online: Guyana News and News from Guyanese Associations Worldwide*, February 25, 2019. https://guyaneseonline.net/2019/03/08/the-legacy-of-violence-in-the-indo-guyanese-diaspora-by-lotus/.
2. Ibid.
3. Name excluded. Email sent to Lotus. February 26, 2019. Shared with author by Preity Kumar, co-founder of Lotus.
4. Mentioned in Alan Kan, "Riya Rajkumar's Mother Speaks Out After Daughter's Death." *Inbrampton.com*, February 20, 2019, https://www.inbrampton.com/riya-rajkumars-mother-speaks-out-after-daughters-death.
5. Name excluded. Email to author, 2019.
6. Ibid.
7. Preity Kumar, Interview with author, May 22, 2019.
8. Yasmin Jiwani, "The Media, 'Race' and Multiculturalism," A Presentation to the BC Advisory Council on Multiculturalism, March 17, 1995, http://www.harbour.sfu.ca/freda/articles/media.html
9. Ibid.
10. Minelle Mahtani, "Representing Minorities: Canadian Media and Minority Identities," *Canadian Ethnic Studies/ Études Ethniques au Canada* XXXIII, no. 3 (2001): 99–133.
11. Galland translated the Arabic manuscript *Ḥikāyat Alf layla wa layla* ("Tales of 1001 Nights") into French, first publishing his *1001 Nights* in 1704.
12. Diyab worked as translator and servant to French tomb raider Paul Lucas, who brought to France many treasures from the East. In Hanna Diyab's autobiography/travelogue (discovered at the Vatican Library in 1993), Diyab recounts his exploits with Lucas, including one story that could have inspired the tale of Aladdin. Wanting to explore the ruins of a church outside Aleppo, Lucas made a local shepherd go into a vault beneath a rock; the boy returned with an ancient ring and a lamp. Arafat Razzaque mentions a suggestion that Diyab heard the stories from professional storytellers in the coffeehouses and theaters of Aleppo. In his travelogue, Diyab notes that "an old man" who visited him and Lucas inquired into the Tales, and that he had told him the stories that he knew. Diyab placed little importance on the event, and did not even refer to Galland by name. See note 13 below.
13. Arafat A. Razzaque, "Who Wrote Aladdin? The Forgotten Syrian Storyteller," *Ajam Media Collective*, September 14, 2017, https://ajammc.com/2017/09/14/who-wrote-aladdin/.
14. Piya Sinha-Roy, "How Disney Handled the Casting and Cultural Authenticity of Live-Action *Aladdin*," *Entertainment Weekly*, December 21, 2018, https://ew.com/movies/2018/12/21/disney-aladdin-cultural-authenticity/.
15. Vanessa Matyas, "Tale as Old as Time: A Textual Analysis of Race and Gender in Disney Princess Films" (Masters thesis, McMaster University, 2010).
16. Julie Ann Crommett, Disney's vice president of multicultural engagement, quoted in Piya Sinha-Roy, "How Disney Handled the Casting and Cultural Authenticity of Live-Action *Aladdin*."
17. Matyas, "Tale as Old as Time."

18. Jasbir K. Puar and Amit Rai, "Monster, Terrorist, Fag: The War on Terrorism and the Production of Docile Patriots," *Social Text* 20, no. 3, (Fall 2002): 117–148.
19. Ibid.
20. Jasbir Puar, *Terrorist Assemblages: Homonationalism in Queer Times* (Durham: Duke University Press, 2004).
21. Puar and Rai, "Monster, Terrorist, Fag," 126.
22. Ibid., 137.
23. Ibid., 131.
24. Ian Wojcik-Andrews and Jerry Phillips, "Telling Tales to Children: The Pedagogy of Empire in MGM's Kim and Disney's Aladdin," *The Lion and the Unicorn*, Volume 20, 1 (June 1996): 66–89; Yahya R. Kamalipour, ed. *The U.S. Media and the Middle East: Image and Perception* (London: Praeger, 1995).
25. Matyas, 16.
26. Saba Mahmood, "Feminist Theory, Embodiment, and the Docile Agent: Some Reflections on the Egyptian Islamic Revival," *Cultural Anthropology*, 16, no. 2 (May, 2001): 202–236.
27. Yvonne Yazbeck Haddad, "The Post-9/11 Hijab as Icon." *Sociology of Religion*, 68, no. 3, (2007): 253–267, https://doi.org/10.1093/socrel/68.3.253.
28. Amani Hamdan, "The Issue of Hijab in France: Reflections and Analysis." *Muslim World Journal of Human Rights*, 4, no. 2, 1554–4419, doi: https://doi.org/10.2202/1554-4419.1079.
29. Peter Racco, "The Dynamism of the Veil: Veiling and Unveiling as a Means of Creating Identity in Algeria and France," *The Undergraduate Historical Journal at UC Merced*, 1, no. 1, (2014), https://escholarship.org/uc/item/62w625wh.
30. "Muslim Women Challenge Burkini Ban in French Pool," *CNN.com* video, July 25, 2019, https://www.cnn.com/videos/world/2019/06/25/women-protest-burkini-ban-at-pool-mh-orig.cnn.
31. "Saudi Women in 'Inside Out' Abaya Protest," *BBC*, November 15, 2018, https://www.bbc.com/news/world-middle-east-46222949.
32. For example, Nepali women's Rage against Rape. "Women March on Kathmandu Streets to Protest Rising Rape Incidents," Xinhaunet, March 8, 2018, http://www.xinhuanet.com/english/2018-03/08/c_137025294.htm.
33. Saif Khalid, "What Is 'Triple Talaq' or Instant Divorce?" *Al Jazeera*, August 22, 2017, https://www.aljazeera.com/indepth/features/2017/05/tripple-talaq-triple-divorce-170511160557346.html.
34. Snigdha Poonam, "Indian Women Just Did a Remarkable Thing—They Formed a Wall of Protest," *The Guardian*, January 3, 2019, https://www.theguardian.com/commentisfree/2019/jan/03/gender-activism-india-womens-wall-sabarimala-temple-kerala.
35. Suzanne Narain, Interview. May 25, 2019.
36. Gaiutra Bahadur. *Coolie Woman: The Odyssey of Indenture* (Chicago: University of Chicago Press, 2013).
37. Lotus, "The Legacy of Violence in the Indo-Guyanese Diaspora: Remembering Riya Rajkumar," 2019.
38. Lotus, 2019
39. Kumar, Interview, 2019.
40. Name excluded, Email, 2019.

41. Carol Tator, Frances Henry, Charles Smith, Maureen Brown, *Racial Profiling in Canada: Challenging the Myth of "A Few Bad Apples"* (Toronto: University of Toronto Press, 2006), 38.

BIBLIOGRAPHY

Bahadur, Gaiutra. *Coolie Woman: The Odyssey of Indenture*. 2013. Chicago: University of Chicago Press.

"Canada Meets Target to Resettle 25,000 Syrian Refugees." *The Guardian*. March 1, 2016. https://www.theguardian.com/world/2016/mar/01/canada-target-resettle-25000-syrian-refugees.

Haddad, Yvonne Yazbeck. "The Post-9/11 Hijab as Icon." *Sociology of Religion*, 68, no. 3, (Fall 2007): 253–267, https://doi.org/10.1093/socrel/68.3.253.

Hamdan, Amani. "The Issue of Hijab in France: Reflections and Analysis." *Muslim World Journal of Human Rights*, 4, no. 2, (2007) 1554–4419, doi: https://doi.org/10.2202/1554-4419.1079.

Jarmakani, Amira. *Imagining Arab Womanhood: The Cultural Mythology of Veils, Harems, and Bellydancers in the US*. New York: Palgrave Macmillan, 2008.

Jiwani, Yasmin. "The Media, 'Race' and Multiculturalism." A Presentation to the BC Advisory Council on Multiculturalism, March 17, 1995. http://www.harbour.sfu.ca/freda/articles/media.html.

Kamalipour, Yahya R. ed. *The U.S. Media and the Middle East: Image and Perception*. London: Praeger, 1995

Kan, Alan. "Riya Rajkumar's Mother Speaks Out After Daughter's Death." *Inbrampton.com*. February 20, 2019. https://www.inbrampton.com/riya-rajkumars-mother-speaks-out-after-daughters-death.

Lotus. "The Legacy of Violence in the Indo-Guyanese Diaspora: Remembering Riya Rajkumar." *Guyanese Online: Guyana News and News from Guyanese Associations Worldwide*. February 25, 2019. https://guyaneseonline.net/2019/03/08/the-legacy-of-violence-in-the-indo-guyanese-diaspora-by-lotus/.

Mahmood, Saba. "Feminist Theory, Embodiment, and the Docile Agent: Some Reflections on the Egyptian Islamic Revival." *Cultural Anthropology*. 16, no. 2 (May, 2001): 202–236.

Mahtani, Minelle. "Representing Minorities: Canadian Media and Minority Identities." *Canadian Ethnic Studies/ Études Ethniques au Canada* XXXIII, no. 3 (2001): 99–133.

Matyas, Vanessa. "Tale as Old as Time: A Textual Analysis of Race and Gender in Disney Princess Films." Masters thesis, McMaster University, 2010.

Narain, Suzanne. "Indo-Caribbean Women and Social Activism in the Diaspora." *Stabroek News*. November 20, 2017. https://www.stabroeknews.com/2017/features/in-the-diaspora/11/20/indo-caribbean-women-and-social-activism-in-the-diaspora/?fbclid=IwAR1s3CP22c7zOvGeWC2_oqEaAfrl1o5KYnsIciVsOEwILuiNVmmGWTHSoMk.

Puar, Jasbir K. Amit Rai. "Monster, Terrorist, Fag: The War on Terrorism and the Production of Docile Patriots." *Social Text*, 20, no. 3, (Fall 2002): 117–148.

https://www150.statcan.gc.ca/n1/daily-quotidien/170613/dq170613b-eng.htm?HPA=1.

———. *Terrorist Assemblages: Homonationalism in Queer Times*. Durham: Duke University Press. 2004.

Racco, Peter. "The Dynamism of the Veil: Veiling and Unveiling as a Means of Creating Identity in Algeria and France." *The Undergraduate Historical Journal at UC Merced*, 1, no. 1, 2014. https://escholarship.org/uc/item/62w625wh.

Razzaque, Arafat A. "Who Was the 'Real' Aladdin? From Chinese to Arab in 300 Years." *Ajam Media Collective*, August 10, 2017. https://ajammc.com/2017/08/10/who-was-the-real-aladdin/.

———. "Who Wrote *Aladdin*? The Forgotten Syrian Storyteller." *Ajam Media Collective*. September 14, 2017. https://ajammc.com/2017/09/14/who-wrote-aladdin/.

Sinha-Roy, Piya. "How Disney Handled the Casting and Cultural Authenticity of Live-Action *Aladdin*." *Entertainment Weekly*. December 21, 2018. https://ew.com/movies/2018/12/21/disney-aladdin-cultural-authenticity/.

Tator, Carol, Frances Henry, Charles Smith, Maureen Brown. *Racial Profiling in Canada: Challenging the Myth of "A Few Bad Apples."* Toronto: University of Toronto Press. 2006.

Wojcik-Andrews, Ian and Jerry Phillips. "Telling Tales to Children: The Pedagogy of Empire in MGM's Kim and Disney's Aladdin." *The Lion and the Unicorn*, 20, no. 1 (June 1996): 66–89.

III

DECONSTRUCTING PRINCESS NARRATIVES

12

Belle

Beyond the Classic Story for the Modern Audience

Rebecca Weidman-Winter

REVISITING BELLE: WHY BEAUTY IS NOW STRONG

Today it is nearly impossible to avoid the Disney princess culture. With this comes a myriad of gender and cultural stereotypes and, more critically, influences on children as they assimilate this information.[1] A 2016 study of preschool and kindergarten age children found that only 4 percent of girls had never viewed any Disney media and 61 percent of girls played with Disney princess toys at least once a week.[2] Encouragingly, recent Disney productions seem to demonstrate a shift in their presentation of the princess character to expand and diversify gender roles.

One example is the 2017 live-action remake of *Beauty and the Beast*. The original story line alone inherently lends itself to the portrayal of a modern princess, better able to reflect changes in society and accepted gender norms. There are many versions of this story but each, in some form, ends with Belle saving the Beast.[3] Cinderella, Snow White, and Aurora, as scholars have outlined,[4] are passive and, arguably, weak. By contrast, Belle best fits narratives women expect today as her story embodies the theme of a strong, independent woman. Belle as a character ages well to the current times.

In January 2015, Disney announced that Emma Watson had been cast as Belle for their upcoming production of *Beauty and the Beast*. The impact of Disney's choice of actress for Belle cannot be underestimated. For ten years, from 2001 to 2011, Emma Watson played Hermione Granger in eight *Harry Potter* films where she achieved international fame for her portrayal as the smart, independent girl. Hermione was appealing to young girls as she, too, struggled with her insecurities, did not come from a wizarding background like many of the other students, was teased for her looks, and yet was often the smartest student in the room. Watson said of her J.K. Rowling–created character: "Hermione made it OK for girls to be the smartest in the room. To be a leader, the one with the plan."[5]

In 2014, Emma Watson was named a Goodwill Ambassador for the United Nations. On September 20, 2014 she gave a speech promoting gender equality and introduced her campaign HeForShe. U.N. Women described HeforShe as a "social movement campaign . . . through which men and boys become agents of change for the achievement of gender equality."[6] By the start of filming for *Beauty and the Beast*, Emma Watson had almost fifteen years under her belt as a role model for girls and women the world over. Her fans loved not just her characters in film, but what she personally stood for as an influencer. Her activism is neither a distraction. *Beauty and the Beast* (2017) earned $1.264 billion at the box office and ranked as the highest grossing musical at the time.[7]

Upon accepting the role of Belle, Emma Watson stipulated that she would be allowed to work with the director, Bill Condon, in further shaping the character of Belle. Watson helped finalize the details of each of Belle's costumes, especially the clothes she wore every day in the village.[8] The 1991 animation of Belle only hinted at Belle's skills as an inventor. For the 2017 version, it was Emma Watson's idea to add the scene where Belle independently creates her own washing machine.[9] It was important for the 2017 film to clearly show the intelligence and independence of Belle— that her skills were independent of those of her father. In this context, it is not surprising that *Beauty and the Beast* reflects the current climate of empowering women. This chapter examines why it was ultimately so successful as a live-action remake.

EMPOWERING BELLE FOR MODERN AUDIENCES

Although the 2017 remake of the *Beauty and the Beast* closely follows the plot and script of earlier versions, the character of Belle has significantly evolved from the earlier version. Throughout the film are instances where Disney contemporizes the role of Belle as a reflection of today's social constructs. This is particularly apparent regarding the view of women in academia and breaking out of previously constructed gender roles.

The audience first meets Belle in her modest home in a small village. She passes the chickens in her yard and, as she reaches the village, quickly stops to caress the face of a horse and feed a donkey. Belle is kind and compassionate, remembering to care for all animals she encounters. As she begins to sing, the lyrics make it clear Belle resents the predictability of life in the village.[10] The repetition of the lyrics helps to establish the angst Belle feels with the constrictions placed on her life by society. Although the musical impact is not unique to the live-action musical[11] it is an important feature of this film regarding the approach to modern trends.

Belle greets Jean the Potter and mentions she is on her way to return a wonderful book, set in Verona. One of the first things the audience learns about Belle is that she is literate, an unusual circumstance for a woman of this time and place, and she is well read.[12] She enjoys books about faraway places and characters who live a life quite different than her own.[13] A second scene supports this modern view of educating women. Earlier in the film the audience sees a line of boys marching into school. It is a subtle acknowledgment that girls are not permitted to attend school. This becomes more obvious later when Belle is teaching a young village girl to read. The girl's joy and sense of accomplishment is immediately clear until the moment is swiftly destroyed by the headmaster scolding Belle for her actions.[14]

Throughout this chapter are several prominent themes of the remake which will be explored in further detail. In the first theme, the chapter examines women's virtues. It is not only Belle but many of the female characters who represent women of integrity and intelligence. Another theme is challenging norms, as Belle is often stepping outside of the roles prescribed to her by society. She is both resourceful and independent as she navigates her life and defines her role in society. A third is redefining the role of a princess. Belle demonstrates how being a princess requires being a role model, possessing both responsibility and leadership. Finally, the film offers a glimpse of how realism and feminism can coexist within the imaginary world of a fairy tale.

WOMEN OF INTEGRITY AND INTELLIGENCE

We are first introduced to the idea of a strong female character in the opening scenes of *Beauty and the Beast*. An old woman arrives at the castle to request shelter from the storm. The Beast laughs at her, his scorn obvious. Seeing only a haggard, old woman he declines her request. Of course, she is more than an old woman, she is a beautiful enchantress. Here, the enchantress created an opportunity for a shallow, young prince to look past her outward appearances and see her beauty within. Having failed the test, the enchantress casts a spell on the prince and all the occupants in the castle. The spell will last for all of eternity unless the prince can find someone to look past his own exterior, and learn to love him before the last petal of the rose falls from the stem. In just this short scene the audience has seen that the prince is shallow, uncaring, and only concerned with superficial representations of wealth and beauty. The enchantress on the other hand, possesses wisdom, intelligence, and power. When the prince refused to look past her appearance, all of his wealth and prestige was not enough to break the power of her spell.

Gaston, too, is the opposite of Belle.[15] He does not care to read and fails to understand the appeal of reading books.[16] Ironically it is Belle's uniqueness, her intelligence and love of learning, that fuels Gaston's attraction to Belle. When Gaston invites himself to dinner. Belle refuses without apology or excuse. Belle's strong character is a reflection of modern attitudes. In fact, each conversation between Belle and Gaston supports a departure from what would have been an accepted gender role of the time. After an incident with Belle and the headmaster, Gaston leaps in to "save" Belle from the changes she is trying to make. During this conversation Belle admits she is "not ready to have children." This is a shocking admission in a community where women are expected to not only have many children, but to also look forward to having children. In some ways it is their life's goal. Gaston reminds Belle that she should at least make an effort to find a husband. When she counters that she has met all of the men in the village and is uninterested he becomes frustrated. "Do you know what happens to spinsters in this village after their fathers die?"[17] The consequence is that women with no husband will become destitute. There is no possibility of a woman supporting herself or surviving with any sense of independence. Belle's independent and forward thinking has no place in the entire village. No one would allow her or her ideas[18] and efforts to flourish. The insinuation is that she is only able to live as she does because her father is still alive to protect her. The musical interlude serves to reinforce Belle's disgust at the idea of marrying Gaston.[19] She knows the consequences of her decisions and remains adamant that she longs for "more than this provincial life."

Mrs. Potts and Agathe are two more links in the chain of indomitable women in *Beauty and the Beast*. Although Mrs. Potts, like all the other castle staff, is a prisoner in the castle, she will not leave herself to whatever fate has planned for her. She will lead the destiny of herself as well as her son, Chip. At one point, Cogsworth, Lumiere, and Chip all express frustration and discouragement that they will never be free. Mrs. Potts, surely, must share the same fear, but it is she who comforts and encourages everyone that there is still time for the spell to be broken.[20] Her spirit and courage are a beacon of hope for everyone else in the castle. Meanwhile, it is Agathe who comes to Maurice's aid in the forest. She frees him from his bonds and then nurses him back to health. Although her circumstances are lacking in advantages, she ultimately saves Maurice out of a love and compassion for others.

BELLE IS RESOURCEFUL AND INDEPENDENT

Another theme in *Beauty and the Beast* is that Belle is different. She doesn't fit in with the rest of the villagers who feel "she is nothing like the rest of us."[21] As Belle talks with her father, he reminds her they live in a small village, both in size and in thinking. Small is safe, but he recognizes that this is not Belle. She is "fearless" like her mother who was also viewed by her community as different. Maurice hints at the struggle this caused for Belle's mother until one-day people began to admire her. As Maurice is repairing a windmill, Belle repeatedly hands him the tool he needs before he has an opportunity to ask. At one point he questions her choice of tool before agreeing that she was correct all along. Belle is just as competent in the understanding of mechanics as her father. Later, Belle creates a washing machine using a barrel, soap, water, and a donkey. Maurice supports his daughter, however unconventional she may be, and advises her never to change. The role of Maurice is crucial in breaking down previous princess stereotypes. Maurice's character also departs from the traditional gender roles of a time when a father figure would have expected, if not demanded, that his daughter conform to the expectations of the time. These, too, are reflections of audiences today, and a subtle acknowledgment that women can possess the same skills as men by understanding mechanics and creating inventions of their own. Even though her path will be difficult she can take comfort in the support of her father.

Belle exhibits independence in all of her daily activities.[22] When Belle is left alone for days as her father conducts business out of town, she shows no fear or concern for herself. Instead she is more concerned for her father's well-being, imploring him to "stay safe." When their horse returns home without Maurice, Belle immediately jumps into action and leaves to save her father. She gives no apparent thought to her own safety, or fear of what she may be headed into. Neither does she ask for help from any of the other villagers. She heads off alone and relies on her own resourcefulness.

When Belle eventually finds Maurice, he is quick to tell her to go. She refuses because she can not leave her father to unknown danger. She is a strong and courageous young woman. When the Beast relays the crimes of her father[23] Belle is quick to take responsibility for her father's actions in order to give him a chance at freedom. Even when Maurice explains to Belle this punishment is forever, Belle does not relent. She is not afraid of the Beast. She demands that he step into the light. When he doesn't, she grabs a candle and walks toward him. Even when she must be facing fear, she comforts her father by agreeing to leave. She can see that he is sick and does not want to burden him. However, she has planned a way to save Maurice on her own. She does not ask permission for her actions.

She takes control of the situation, kissing her father good-bye, and pushing him out of the cell. This is a pivotal moment in the film. Maurice has always cared for his daughter and kept her safe. He left his wife to die, alone, in order to save their daughter. He had raised Belle on his own her entire life. Given a choice he would have gladly stayed prisoner in the castle so that Belle could be free. He too is selfless in his love, he doesn't want Belle to feel any guilt. Belle knows all of this and still follows through in her plan without hesitation. She is in control of her destiny. As Maurice leaves, she seeks only to offer him comfort and hope: "I'm not afraid. I will escape." Even as the Beast drags her father away, she is looking out for the well-being of others.[24]

Upon seeing her new room, Belle admits that it is beautiful. However, rather than perpetuate the princess myth of beautiful clothes and surroundings, Belle is almost disgusted by the idea of being referred to as a princess. It is of no consequence to have a comfortable, well-appointed room, with friends who endeavor to dress her in fine clothes. Instead Belle looks out the window, down several stories to the ground. She is focused on her eventual escape. She is not daunted by the seemingly insurmountable odds. In fact, there are multiple scenes throughout the film where the castle is shown. It is vast, desolate, empty. The castle is not portrayed as a magical creation, or a sort of utopia. This is not a place to choose to be because life as a princess is easy.

RESPONSIBILITY AND LEADERSHIP

Another theme explored in *Beauty and the Beast* is a princess as a leader or role model. As the film progresses, so too does Belle. She develops a greater maturity and understanding of the world around her. Before coming to the castle, her knowledge of the world around her was limited to what she read in books.[25] Now she is beginning to see that things are much more complex, particularly as she struggles to understand why Mrs. Potts and the others don't feel trapped. It seems to Belle that they have accepted their circumstances and have given up fighting. Belle, however, attempts her escape by riding into the forest where she encounters the wolves. Outnumbered and without a means of defense, Belle fends off the wolves with a tree branch. Even in mortal danger Belle first tries to protect her horse, who is the most vulnerable. The Beast comes to her rescue, but he is gravely injured in the fight. Belle's escape is now clear. Depth of character is important in this rendition of a modern princess. Bravery is not enough because a princess is nothing if she is not compassionate, seeking to alleviate the suffering of another. As such, she does not take her chance at freedom, instead she chooses to save the Beast.

As Belle nurses the Beast back to health they finally begin to communicate. It is here the audience sees Belle and the Beast as equals. Unlike other princess tales, Belle cannot give up who she is for a life with a prince. If Belle and the Beast are to develop a relationship it must be on equal footing with both parties contributing to the tangent of events. They compare Shakespeare. This is the first time Belle has met an intellectual equal. She is almost shocked when the Beast has an opinion on a book she's read and that they are able to further converse, sharing opposing ideas. Then the Beast gives Belle the gift of her dreams; access to his substantial library. Belle is a reflection of the ideals of a modern woman. She is not interested in clothes, a castle, or things. Her greatest wealth is knowledge. Belle and the Beast continue to read and share poetry or observations of what they have read. This serves to further emphasize the value of literacy, education, and critical thinking.

We see Belle developing into a true princess through her relationship with the Beast. While Belle and the Beast eat their meals in a formal setting, the Beast is no longer able to observe traditional etiquette in dining. His hands are no longer able to handle eating with silverware. He must slurp his soup straight from the bowl. Belle sees that he is embarrassed, but she does not want to call attention to his insecurities. Rather she attempts to put him at ease by drinking her soup straight from the bowl.[26] The lyrics "he's no Prince Charming" addresses Belle's developing maturity from earlier in the film. She is less concerned with the tales of princes that she enjoys reading. She has come to the realization that the idea of Prince Charming is a myth and is, perhaps, not as appealing as she previously thought.

Another important scene is when Belle and the Beast are ready for the ball. Often Disney movies portray the male character at the bottom of the stairs as they wait to "collect" the princess at the end of her descent from the formal staircase, like in *Cinderella*. This is not the case in *Beauty and the Beast* as both characters descend the stairs from the East and West wings to meet in the middle and then continue down the remaining stairs together. This is a lovely use of imagery to represent their two distinct lives, independent of one another, joining together as equals.

REALISM WITHIN A FAIRY TALE

One of the things that makes Disney's movies so appealing, but also steeps young girls in the princess myth is their trademark fairy-tale magic. The princesses are shown at their best with dramatized clothing, hair, and accessories. *Beauty and the Beast* offers a refreshing, but still lovely, departure from this tradition. It is true that Belle's ball dress is beautiful, but it is something contemporary audiences can imagine themselves wearing. As a benefit of the live-action musical, Belle's dress cannot be made into something magical, unreal, or imaginary. Unlike *Cinderella* (2015) where the entire dress and transport to the ball is magically created through a temporary spell, Belle's is realistic. She has not been transformed into something she is not. This is a crucial departure from previous imaginations of princesses to a reimagined and realistic princess who is relatable to audiences today. In fact, the entire movie has led to this point. At every prior scene in the film Belle is wearing everyday, unremarkable clothes. At all times she is portrayed as a regular person rather than as a fairy-tale princess. Of further note, Disney's animated films tend to alter the physical appearance of princesses, making them unrealistic. In the live-action, Belle's appearance is authentic allowing her character to reflect the average young woman.

Beauty and the Beast also addresses contemporary issues of freedom, independence, and relationships built on trust and respect. At one point, the Beast asks Belle is she could ever be happy with him. She possesses the maturity to realize these are two separate issues. Yes, she does enjoy the company of the Beast and he does make her happy, however it is impossible for anyone to truly be happy if they aren't free. She cannot be complete if her life is not her own. It is a significant act for the Beast to encourage Belle to go save Maurice. The consequences are devastating for the Beast, but like Belle, he never hesitates when faced with difficult decisions. He encourages her to leave and to go to her father. It is important to note that he does not "set her free." He supports her departure recognizing that Belle was never really a captive. The Beast would not have stood in her way if she had chosen to leave earlier. This is thematically important and also a departure from earlier films where the princess is under the control of someone else. Belle has never been controlled by the Beast.

When Belle rides back to the village to save Maurice, she is met with an angry mob. The townspeople have already imprisoned Maurice in the back of a carriage, and they are ready to do battle with the Beast. It would be easier for Belle to agree that he is a beast, but instead she defends the Beast as being kind.[27] In the final moments of the film it is Belle who saves the Beast and by extension everyone who had been imprisoned in the castle. As the spell is broken, Belle and the Beast are wearing very simple clothes. It is their beauty from within that shines through and their appearances are not obscured by fancy clothes. Even at the beginning of the celebration all the other guests are dressed in fancy clothes, but Belle and the Beast are still dressed simply. In this way the audience understands that true royalty leads from within.

REVISITING TALES AS OLD AS TIME

Disney's decision to remake or reimagine its classics as live-action or CGIs allows audiences to develop modern connections to timeless stories. It is not just the redefining of a princess that is accomplished through the medium of a live-action musical; the creators of the live-action expanded the earlier work by its representation of people of color, interracial couples, and LGBTQ characters.[28] These changes were more subtle in their presentation, but are significant as they are almost completely absent in all previous Disney films. Even in *Cinderella*'s 2015 remake, the prince's best friend and trusted guard is Black, and one of his potential love interests appears to be from a Spanish kingdom. The world of Agrabah in 2019's *Aladdin* includes all the ethnic groups along the Silk Road ranging from North African, through the Middle East, South Asia, and China. And of course 2019's Genie is Black, played by Will Smith. In *Beauty and the Beast*, this new diverse world may be easy to miss, and yet, it is obvious, as the creators of the new remakes do not over emphasize them because they want audiences to see the diverse worlds of the princesses as common. In revamping these princess narratives, Disney is portraying a diverse world it wishes to not just entertain, but market its brand to.

It is this and countless other examples of expression and interaction among the characters that successfully develops this classic's modern themes, especially Belle as a reflection of current social movements for women. Feminism, empowering women, equality of women and men, and education for girls are all championed in this 2017 film. The subtleties inherent in human expression and interaction had not been fully relayed through the two-dimensional animation. *Beauty and the Beast* incorporates significant issues relevant to girls through an age appropriate medium. However, the film is limited to the structure of a princess story line. In the end, someone falls in love. As the last petal falls from the rose the spell, the stereotypical princess can be broken. The relevant discussion on what defines a princess in our society today is just beginning.

NOTES

1. Sarah M. Coyne, Jennifer Ruh Linder, Eric E. Rasmussen, David A. Nelson, and Victoria Birkbeck, "Pretty as a Princess: Longitudinal Effects of Engagement with Disney Princesses on Gender Stereotypes, Body Esteem, and Prosocial Behavior in Children," *Child Development* 87, no. 6 (2016): 1912. In Aurora M. Sherman, and Eileen L. Zurbriggen, ""Boys Can Be Anything:" Effect of Barbie Play on Girls' Career Cognitions," *Sex Roles* 70, no. 5–6 (2014): 195–208, the authors conclude "playing with gendered toys, particularly those associated with a movie

franchise, may also promote internalization of gender-stereotypical expectations in early childhood."

2. Sarah Coyne et al., "Pretty as a Princess: Longitudinal Effects of Engagement With Disney Princesses on Gender Stereotypes, Body Esteem, and Prosocial Behavior in Children," 9.

3. Gabrielle-Suzanne Barbot de Villeneuve, "La Belle et la Bête," in *La Jeune Américaine*, 1740. Villeneuve's is considered to be the original version of the tale. Jeanne Marie Leprince de Beaumont edited and abridged the story which appeared in *Magasin des Enfants* in 1756. Beaumont's was much more popular due to the simplified story line and reduced length. In 1889 Andrew Lang published an English version of *Beauty and the Beast* in *The Blue Fairy Book*. In each of these three versions Belle saves the Beast by splashing water from a nearby by spring onto his face. In the Disney version Belle's kiss saves the Beast.

4. Lori Baker-Sperry, Lori, and Liz Grauerholz, "The Pervasiveness and Persistence of the Feminine Beauty Ideal in Children's Fairy Tales," *Gender & Society* 17, no. 5 (2003): 711–726; Marcia R. Lieberman, ""Some Day My Prince Will Come:" Female Acculturation through the Fairy Tale," *College English* 34, no. 3 (1972): 383–395.

5. Tom Bacon, "Hermoine Granger Voted the Best Hollywood Female Character of All Time!" Geeks, 2017, accessed March 30, 2019, https://geeks.media/hermione-granger-voted-the-best-hollywood-female-character-of-all-time.

6. United Nations Women, "HeForShe," accessed March 30, 2019, https://www.unwomen-usnc.org/advocacy-3.

7. Box Office Mojo, "Musical. 1974-Present Live action only," accessed March 30, 2019, https://www.boxofficemojo.com/genres/chart/?id=musical.htm; Box Office Mojo, "Beauty and the Beast 2017," accessed March 30, 2019, https://www.boxofficemojo.com/movies/?id=beautyandthebeast2017.htm.

8. Stephen Milton, "Emma Watson: I've Always Said, 'Forget the Engagement Ring, Build Me a Library!'" March 19, 2017, https://www.independent.ie/style/celebrity/celebrity-features/emma-watson-ive-always-said-forget-the-engagement-ring-build-me-a-library-35534318.html.

9. Stephen Milton, "Emma Watson: I've Always Said, 'Forget the Engagement Ring, Build Me a Library!'" Emma Watson specified the boots Belle should wear and also that her dress must have pockets.

10. *Beauty and the Beast*, 2017. USA: Walt Disney Pictures. "There goes the baker with his tray like always. The same old bread and roles to sell." —Belle

11. *Beauty and the Beast*, directed by Jean Cocteau. 1991. USA: Walt Disney Animation Studios. The 1991 film won multiple awards for Best Music, Original Song and Best Music, Original Score. (1992 Oscar, Golden Globe, and ACCA for both.) Therefore, the musical impact is not unique to the 2017 version; having played a significant role in the animated version.

12. *Beauty and the Beast*, 2017. Père Robert states that Belle is "the only bookworm in town" and has read the entire library available.

13. *Beauty and the Beast*, 2017. "Your library makes our small corner of the world feel big." For the people of this time traveling to the next village would be significant. Belle realizes there is a world far beyond the next village.

14. *Beauty and the Beast*, 2017. "Teaching another girl to read? Isn't one enough?" —Headmaster

15. *Beauty and the Beast*, 2017. LeFou describes Belle as "well read" and Gaston as "athletic."
16. *Beauty and the Beast*, 2017. Belle asks if Gaston has read her book. "Well, not that one, but you know, books . . ."
17. *Beauty and the Beast*, 2017, Gaston.
18. *Beauty and the Beast*, 2017. Belle admits that she may be a "farm girl," but she is not "simple."
19. *Beauty and the Beast*, 2017. Belle describes Gaston as "boorish" and "brainless."
20. *Beauty and the Beast*, 2017. They should not be overcome with despair, because Chip will have his ". . . days in the sun again. You just leave it to me." —Mrs. Potts.
21. *Beauty and the Beast*, 2017. Lyrics of "Belle" sung by the women doing the wash in the village.
22. *Beauty and the Beast*, 2017. Going to town, speaking with various townspeople, going to the library, doing the washing.
23. *Beauty and the Beast*, 2017. The Beast claims Maurice is a thief who has stolen a rose.
24. *Beauty and the Beast*, 2017. Belle shouts to the Beast, "Don't hurt him."
25. *Beauty and the Beast*, 2017. For all of her independence and forward-thinking Belle first sings about a book she is reading for at least the second time. What strikes her as noteworthy is the scene where "she meets Prince Charming, but she won't discover that it's him 'til Chapter 3." As the film progresses, Belle discards this notion of finding a mythical Prince Charming.
26. *Beauty and the Beast*, 2017. The Beast previously drank his soup with his face in the bowl. Belle's gesture is not only kind but also demonstrates another option: even if the Beast's hands can't manage a spoon, his hands can pick up the bowl like a cup.
27. *Beauty and the Beast*, 2017. Belle tells the townspeople "Don't be afraid. He's gentle and kind."
28. *Beauty and the Beast*, 2017. The dancers in the opening party at the castle of the young Prince offer a refreshing diversity of cast: two couples: Plumette/Lumière and Maestro Cadenza/Madame Garderobe. In the pub LeFou sings in reference to Tom, Dick, and Stanley, "and they'll tell you whose team they prefer to be on." During the final battle at the castle Madame Garderobe crossdresses Tom, Dick, and Stanley in elaborate, beautiful dresses to which they cheer in excitement.

BIBLIOGRAPHY

Bacon, Tom. "Hermoine Granger Voted the Best Hollywood Female Character of All Time!" Geeks, 2017. Accessed March 30, 2019. https://geeks.media/hermione-granger-voted-the-best-hollywood-female-character-of-all-time.

Baker-Sperry, Lori, and Liz Grauerholz. "The Pervasiveness and Persistence of the Feminine Beauty Ideal in Children's Fairy Tales." *Gender & society* 17, no. 5 (2003): 711–726.

Beaumont, Jeanne Marie Leprince de. *Magasin des Enfants*. 1756.
Box Office Mojo. "Beauty and the Beast 2017." Accessed March 30, 2019. https://www.boxofficemojo.com/movies/?id=beautyandthebeast2017.htm.
———. "Musical. 1974–Present. Live action only." Accessed June 29, 2019. https://www.boxofficemojo.com/genres/chart/?id=musical.htm
Candy, Lorraine. "Emma Watson, The December 2014 ELLE Cover Interview." *Elle*, June/July, 2015.
Coyne, Sarah M., Jennifer Ruh Linder, Eric E. Rasmussen, David A. Nelson, Victoria Birbeck. "Pretty as a Princess: Longitudinal Effects of Engagement With Disney Princesses on Gender Stereotypes, Body Esteem, and Prosocial Behavior in Children." *Child Development* 87, no. 6 (2016): 1909–1925.
The Disney Blog. "Emma Watson cast as Belle in Disney's live-action Beauty and the Beast movie," Accessed March, 20 2019. https://thedisneyblog.com/2015/01/26/emma-watson-cast-as-belle-in-disneys-live-action-beauty-and-the-beast-movie/
The Hollywood Reporter. "Hollywood's 50 Favorite Female Characters." Accessed March, 20 2019. https://www.hollywoodreporter.com/lists/50-best-female-characters-entertainment-industry-survey-results-951483/item/juno-juno-50-favorite-female-characters-951484.
Lang, Andrew. *The Blue Fairy Book*. London: Longmans, Green, and Co., 1889.
Lieberman, Marcia R. "Some Day My Prince Will Come:" Female Acculturation through the Fairy Tale." *College English* 34, no. 3 (1972): 383–395.
Milton, Stephen. "Emma Watson: I've Always Said, 'Forget the Engagement Ring, Build Me a Library!'" March 19, 2017, https://www.independent.ie/style/celebrity/celebrity-features/emma-watson-ive-always-said-forget-the-engagement-ring-build-me-a-library-35534318.html.
Sherman, Aurora M., and Eileen L. Zurbriggen. ""Boys Can Be Anything": Effect of Barbie Play on Girls' Career Cognitions." *Sex Roles* 70, no. 5–6 (2014): 195–208.
United Nations. "The United Nations Live & On Demand," Accessed March, 20 2019. http://webtv.un.org/watch/launch-of-the-heforshe-campaign-special-event/3797140848001
United Nations Women. "HeForShe." Accessed March 30, 2019, https://www.unwomen-usnc.org/advocacy 3.
Villeneuve, Gabrielle-Suzanne Barbot de. *La jeune américaine, et les contes marins*. 1740.
Villeneuve, Nicole. "Emma Watson Helps Launch the Time's Up Movement in the UK With a $1.4 Million Donation." Accessed June, 29, 2019. https://www.brit.co/emma-watson-times-up-uk-donation/
The Walt Disney Company. "Disney Celebrates Cinderella, Announces Beauty and the Beast." Accessed March, 20 2019. https://www.thewaltdisneycompany.com/disney-celebrates-cinderella-announces-beauty-and-the-beast/.
Walt Disney Pictures. *Beauty and the Beast*, directed by Bill Condon. 2017. USA. DVD.

13

✣

"Let It Go" as Radical Mantra

Subverting the Princess Narrative in Frozen

Susanne R. Hackett

The number one animated film to date, Disney's *Frozen*, is about two young women—sisters—who save each other and learn the true meaning of love. The film not only shattered the 2013 box office ($1.276 billion);[1] it became Disney's highest grossing animation since its Renaissance in the nineties, surpassing *The Lion King* (1994). Its success was predicated on breaking every model to which Disney princess narratives had previously adhered.[2] In the absence of their deceased parents, two princesses have to forge their own destiny, in the setting of their own kingdom (or "princess-dom"? or "queen-dom"? is it still a "kingdom" if there is no king?). Going against the model of previous Disney princess stories, there is no wedding at the end; while there is an implied "happily ever after," it is the result of the restored bond of love between the two sisters, and not a result of any heteronormative matrimonial union. The salvific "act of true love" that would "thaw a frozen heart" comes not through romantic love—e.g., "true love's kiss"—but instead through sacrificial sisterly love, wherein one sister sacrifices herself to save the other. And yet, the narrative self-consciously plays with and speaks to traditional princess tropes, subverting the viewer's expectations in the final outcome.

Frozen's adaptation of the original Snow Queen story by Hans Christian Andersen sets both sisters on a character journey, each with a different lesson to be learned about love. Elsa learns to embrace love and to "let go" of fear of her own power; Anna learns to "let go" of false preconceptions of romantic love, born out of her adolescent isolation. This film arrived at a distinct cultural moment for women and women's movements and became a flashpoint in popular culture precisely because it rejected long-held heteronormative standards. This chapter examines how the narrative journeys the two princesses undergo in the film mirror synchronous shifts in perceptions of a woman's place in society and the role of love in her life.

ELSA AND ANNA: TODAY'S "PRINCESSES"

Elsa's Journey

Through both story and song, screenwriter Jennifer Lee along with her co-director Chris Buck and songwriting team, Robert Lopez and Kristen Anderson-Lopez, reveal the complexity of female power through Elsa's experience. In the film's opening scene, however, it is a chorus of strong men, doing men's work, who sing "Beautiful, Powerful, Dangerous, Cold"[3] of the curious and strangely powerful force of ice, which serves as a metaphor for Elsa and her powers. They chant:

> Ice has a magic can't be controlled
> *Stronger than one! Stronger than ten!*
> *Stronger than a hundred men!*[4]

The combination of Beautiful-Powerful-Dangerous-Cold is what makes Elsa's power so foreboding, not to *her* per se, but to a society that tells her to "conceal it." The adjective "cold" is frequently used to describe powerful women; women who are sexually unavailable to men or uninterested in sex are often called "frigid." Sometimes women's strongest power within heteronormative, patriarchal structures is the power to withhold—particularly to withhold love, sex, nurturing, or intimacy. In Elsa's case, her "coldness" is not only undesirable; it is dangerous.

The first man to tell Elsa to conceal and suppress her powers is her father, though his intention is to protect her and Anna from its potential harms. He takes his precautions a step further by closing off the kingdom's castle entirely to the outside world. Upon consulting the wise old male troll after Elsa accidentally injures young Anna, the elder patriarch tells a frightened young Elsa, "Your power will only grow. There is beauty in it, but also grave danger. You must learn to control it. Fear will be your enemy." Paradoxically, he is teaching her to fear her own power, at the same time that he is telling her that fear is her worst enemy.

Other male characters in *Frozen* seek to undermine or suppress Elsa's power, though with more sinister motives than protecting her. The Duke of Weselton, a man looking to exploit her for the economic power she holds as head of her kingdom, calls her a "monster" after her public display of her magical freezing powers, decrying it as "sorcery." He leads the rallying call to, as it were, "Lock her up" when she proves too dangerously powerful to be let loose in society. Finally, it is Prince Hans who attempts to destroy this powerful woman, after her sister leaves him in charge of the kingdom, with his covert plan to marry her sister and stage an unfortunate "accident" that will allow him to become king. From a patriarchal point of view, Elsa and her magical "powers" are dangerous, and thus must be controlled, concealed, locked away, and ultimately destroyed.

Letting Fear Go

These powers also protect Elsa and give her agency to evade or defend herself against those who wish her harm. Her freezing powers enable her to literally walk on water (divinity), yet those same powers lead to accusations of being a monster, not unlike countless women throughout history who have been accused of being "witches" for exercising powers, supernatural or otherwise, outside of their prescribed social roles in the patriarchy. Elsa's supernatural powers force her to walk a fine line between divinity and demonization.

She exerts another kind of power, that of self-suppression, in attempting to control her magical powers. Elsa's mantra, as taught to her by her father, is "Conceal, don't feel." In her songs, this line is frequently accompanied by, "Be the *good girl* you always have to be." For Elsa, Coronation Day means facing her own power—both her political power, as future Queen, and her magical powers over which she is terrified of losing control. While her younger sister dances around fantasizing about opening the castle gates for the coming party, Elsa prepares to "put on a show" for her subjects, of whom she is also terrified, lest they discover her secret.

For Elsa, fear and power go hand in hand. As the wise old troll predicted, fear is her enemy in that it allows her magical powers to take over, to effectively *disempower* her by taking away her (self-)control over her body and the magical freezing power it emanates. On Coronation Day, it is at the very moment when she is presented to the people as Queen that her magical freezing powers are first activated in public, and she quickly puts her gloves back on to conceal it. It is as if one form of "power" triggers another: the fears associated with her assumption of political power and its inherent scrutiny triggers the very fear that activates her "magic" powers of freezing.

Her gloves act as a kind of mask. We first see her don them as a child with her father saying, "Here, these will help." Elsa and Anna's confrontation at the Coronation ball reaches a climax when Anna grabs one of Elsa's gloves, forcing her to remove it, not understanding her need to constantly wear them ("She wore the gloves all the time, so I just thought maybe she has a thing about dirt," she tells Kristoff later). It is notable that while singing the song "Let It Go" Elsa casts off her one remaining glove, along with her cape, while confidently proclaiming, "the cold never bothered me anyway." The casting off of her gloves represents a rejection of the mandate to both conceal and not to feel (and by extension, the mandate to be a "good girl"), as the gloves not only help her conceal her powers, but also keep her hands from "feeling" the world unmediated by a protective layer of fabric.

As she sings "Let It Go" while creating her ice palace, Elsa indulges in her very own party of one—a celebration of her magical powers. Compared to the Coronation Day celebration that she has just fled, where she was constricted and weighted down by the demands of her impending queendom and its attendant judgment and scrutiny, in her ice palace she exhibits the joy and freedom that she could never express in the confines of the royal palace while surrounded by her subjects. Not only is she accepting her powers in the "Let It Go" scene, she is *delighting* in them as she builds the ice palace around herself, singing, "My power flurries through the air into the ground / My soul is spiraling in frozen fractals all around." Her physical transformation is complete when she uses her powers to change her dark and heavy Queen of Arendelle clothes into a glittering gown and sparkling cape befitting an ice queen. Elsa is experiencing self-love for the first time, and the song closes with her meeting the dawn of a new day, both literally and figuratively. "Let the storm rage on," she concludes, "the cold never bothered me anyway."

No Escape from the Storm Inside

However, although her ice palace provides her with escape from the social pressures of being Queen, the notion that she has resolved all of the problems caused by her magic powers by isolating herself on this distant mountain is shattered when Anna visits her and informs her of the "eternal winter" that is plaguing Arendelle. To her dismay, Elsa realizes that "Turn away and slam the door" is not the solution she thought it was. Once again, Elsa reacts out of fear of her powers, pushing her sister away, as snowflakes begin to whirl around her—the storm inside, catalyzed once again by fear, erupts like Pandora's box and literally morphs into a snow monster that chases Anna and Kristoff off the mountain. In Elsa's defensive reaction, she inadvertently strikes Anna's heart and freezes it, echoing their childhood accident.

As Elsa sings about the fear that overwhelms her, and all those around her, she laments in anguish that there is "No escape from the storm inside." The storm, now external and seemingly beyond her control, reaches its apex in the climactic scene at the very end of the film: the "swirling storm" which had previously been trapped inside of Elsa has been fully released into the world, uncontrollable. In the narrative climax it now surrounds all of the main characters, who meet for a final encounter on the frozen fjords.

Anna's Journey

From early childhood, Anna seeks connection with others, and particularly with Elsa. "Do you wanna build a snowman?" is initially spoken as an invitation by Anna for Elsa to exercise her magic powers, a strategic invitation that she knows will rouse sleepy Elsa from her warm bed in the middle of the night to play. As children, until the fateful "accident," the sisters delight in Elsa's power. However, following the accident, in which Elsa strikes Anna's head with her freezing powers, their parents react by taking all possible measures to repress Elsa's power, down to erasing Anna's memories of it and shutting the palace to the outside world.

Both sisters have been marked by the traumatic incident in their childhoods, but in opposite ways. Anna has been literally "marked" with her streak of white hair ("I dreamt I was kissed by a troll," she tells Prince Hans by way of explanation); Elsa's manifestations of the trauma are inward and expressed through her behavior—shutting herself away in her bedroom, and closing herself to love and connection, even from her sister. With Anna's memory having been erased by the wise old troll, she is given no explanation for the abrupt withdrawal of Elsa's companionship and their parents' decision to shut the palace to the outside world. As she will sing later to Hans, "All my life has been a series of doors in my face."

The trauma of the accident is compounded by the death of their parents, which Anna experiences as yet another abandonment on top of Elsa's. As their death occurs three years before Elsa "comes of age" to be queen, we witness how they are forced to "grow up too fast," orphaned and isolated in the royal palace. For Anna, Elsa's continued rejection only underscores the neglect and abandonment she feels at the loss of their parents. Plaintively, she repeats the line, "Do you wanna build a snowman?" outside Elsa's locked door, as the years pass, until she gives up altogether, recognizing the futility. The phrase gradually morphs from a clever ploy to lure Elsa into engaging with her, to become an expression of Anna's loneliness and unfulfilled desire for connection.

It is no wonder then, that for Anna, the definition of love itself is reduced to "love is an open door," regardless of who it is that opens or passes through that door, and what his or her intentions are in crossing the threshold. This yearning for love, in the form of *any* "open door," is what leaves her vulnerable to the opportunistic and predatory machinations of Prince Hans.

Looking for Love in All the Wrong Paintings

Anna's anticipation of the Coronation Day festivities is diametrically opposed to Elsa's trepidation; she practically can't contain her excitement and yearning for social contact to break her isolation ("Don't know if I'm elated or gassy, but I'm somewhere in that zone!" she sings). At the same moment that Anna cannot wait to fling open the doors of Arendelle to engage with the people, Elsa is literally saying to herself, "Don't let them in, don't let them see."

Anna's yearning for social contact and connection transitions easily into a desire for romantic love and connection. Her naiveté about love in all its various forms is revealed during her song "For the First Time in Forever" when she immediately jumps from "I can't wait to meet everyone" to "What if I meet *The One*?" In a sense, the viewer is being narratively primed for her encounter with Hans, her "Prince Charming." Dancing through the palace hallways, she wraps herself in the red drapes, as if it were an evening gown, fantasizing about her own "coming of age" in the form of being an eligible bachelorette awaiting her first suitor(s). The red drape as elegant evening gown seems to symbolize her nascent sexuality and desire for romantic love.

As Anna dances through palace rooms covered in classical paintings, she mirrors the female poses in the images depicting courtship, physically acting out her idea of what she expects love and romance to be. Her knowledge of romantic love, with the exception of her childhood exposure to her parents' partnership, appears to be informed solely by these images. These paintings serve as "the media" of her time and place that inform her what life and love are about. We already know this from her earlier snowman song, when she sings to Elsa, "I think some company is overdue / I've started talking to the pictures on the walls," punctuated by a "Hang in there, Joan!" spoken to a painting of Joan of Arc.

The classic princess trope espouses the idea that romantic love is "meant to be" and that it involves finding "The One." Anna enacts this fantasy with Hans at the party, as they sing their duet "Love Is an Open Door." At this point in the story, the viewer is just as unwitting as she is as to the real motivations behind Prince Hans' courtship and marriage proposal. Another element of the classic princess narrative is that when she finds "The One," she finds "True Love." Anna uses this phrase in her argument with Elsa about marrying Hans. When Elsa chides her, "You can't marry a man you've just met," Anna responds, "You can, if it's True Love."

In their courtship scene outside the Coronation Day party, there is a brief foreshadowing of Prince Hans' real motivations at the beginning of their duet "Love Is an Open Door." When he sings to her, "I've been searching my whole life to find my own place," he gestures toward the kingdom of Arendelle in view from the balcony they are on. At that moment he has already revealed that as an "invisible" thirteenth brother among princes, there is no legitimate space for him to hold power back home in the Southern Isles. His "love" masks his naked opportunism in pursuing Anna. His true intentions are revealed only at the end of the story. Just at the moment that Hans is about to deliver what we think is going to be the "True Love's Kiss" that saves Anna, he abruptly stops and remarks, "Oh Anna, if only there was someone who loved you." It is at this moment that Hans' true character is revealed: that he has *not* been motivated by love, but by greed.

The Anna–Kristoff Story Line

The story line between Anna and Kristoff serves several purposes. Firstly, it provides a more realistic depiction of romantic love than the idealized version that is initially enacted between Anna and Hans. Second, it provides the second "expected" heteronormative outcome, after Hans is revealed *not* to be the Prince Charming that Anna thought he was, and Kristoff turns around and races back to the castle to save Anna with a "True Love's Kiss." As he turns around to return to save Anna, the viewer is made to think *this* is the moment in the narrative when it becomes evident that *Kristoff* has been the "true love" all along, and his act of returning to Arendelle (and presumably, delivering the kiss that Hans reneged on) is what will finally thaw Anna's frozen heart.

Prior to this, when Kristoff brings Anna back to the castle to return her to the people of Arendelle and to Hans, the doors to the castle close in his face, a fitting echo of the theme of "my life has been a series of doors in my face." It's as if the castle door that closes between them represents the social class distance between Anna and Kristoff. Narratively, the viewer is being led to question whether the "true love" Anna needs is really Kristoff, and not Hans as they believe. The viewer is being set up to suspect that it is false notions of social class barriers that are keeping Anna from the "true love" she needs. A princess has to marry a prince, after all, right? No longer in the ruggedness of nature, where Anna and Kristoff were equals, the class difference between the two is made starkly clear upon the closing of the castle gates, leaving Kristoff outside of Anna's privileged world.

Yet, even after the final resolution, after the anticipated "Act of True Love" that saves Anna's life transpires between the two sisters, and *not* in any heteronormative or romantic sense, there is still an implied romantic potential between Anna and Kristoff. After the resolution of the central conflict, in the "afterwards" scene, Anna gifts Kristoff a new sled, and in his bumbling gratitude, he kisses her awkwardly. We are left with the expectation that theirs is a more "real" relationship, the alternative to the perfect Prince Charming narrative. Theirs is a love that crosses lines of class and life experience, but its basis in honesty and true partnership makes it more tenable than the ideals Anna falsely held at the beginning of the story.

Like with a "real" and so-called "healthy" romantic relationship, Anna is able to grow as a person and learns how to express her agency in shaping her own destiny. Anna finds her authoritative voice in dealing with Kristoff, after their initial meet-(not so?)-cute at Wandering Oaken's Trading Post and Sauna, when she compels him to join in her quest to find Elsa, though we as viewers are privy to the fact that her bravado is tinged with self-doubt. Her quest to find her sister—one driven by love—leads to her finding her voice of authority, as well as finding her romantic partner. In terms of the message conveyed to young Disney viewers, it appears to be a conscious rejection of the classic princess narrative, and a more realistic and accurate depiction of a bond of romantic intimacy forming between two people through shared experience and struggle.

There are also several moments between Anna and Kristoff in which traditional gender roles are called into question. As Anna and Kristoff escape the wolves chasing them, it is *Anna* who saves Kristoff from falling off a cliff. At the sight of Elsa's magnificent ice palace, Kristoff (who mines and sells ice for a living) remarks, "Now *that's* ice . . . I might cry," to which Anna responds, "Go ahead. I won't judge." Implicit in this exchange is the message that it is okay for boys or men to cry. Lastly, in the film's final resolution, Anna stops Kristoff from confronting Hans, as if to say, "I can handle this one myself." Anna does not need another man (Kristoff) to confront the man who has deceived her (Hans). Then, as if to bookend their initial meet-cute on the docks of the fjord on Coronation Day, she punches Hans, knocking him off the deck of the ship into the water once again.

LOVE CONQUERS FEAR

Frozen asks the eternal question, "what is love?" and provides a spectrum of answers in return, from self-love to sisterly love to romantic love. When Olaf says to Anna, sitting before the fireplace, "Some people are worth melting for," this is a nod to the idea of self-sacrifice as an act of true love. He tells her, "Love is putting someone else's needs before yours." When Anna does just that by putting herself between Hans' sword and Elsa, finally, this is the "act of True Love" needed to thaw her frozen heart, and its power ripples across the kingdom, thawing the ice and returning summer to Arendelle. Even Kristoff has a "love journey," in learning to love people as much as he loves his reindeer Sven. He goes from singing, "Reindeers are better than people . . ." to forging a legitimate bond of trust and affection with Anna.

The final credits reveal that the story was inspired by the classic fairy tale "The Snow Queen" by Hans Christian Andersen. One noteworthy change from the original is that in *Frozen* the Trolls are no longer evil, but rather, benevolent forces of wisdom and primordial knowledge. For example, after the initial childhood accident in which Elsa "freezes" Anna's head, the wise old troll patriarch offers this piece of wisdom: "The heart is not so easily changed; but, the head can be persuaded." Later, when Anna and Kristoff join forces to find Elsa and save the kingdom, we learn that Kristoff's friends who are "love experts" are these very same trolls.

By learning to embrace her powers rather than fearing them, Elsa finds the balance and resolution that heals the trauma from her childhood. In the absence of fear, her powers become a welcome and delightful gift again, like they were when she and Anna were small children. In the closing scene, Elsa uses her powers to turn the palace courtyard into an ice skating rink, upon which the citizens of Arendelle joyously skate. For the first time in the narrative, both summer and winter are able to coexist harmoniously in the same space. Elsa's powers are even able to resolve Olaf's dilemma as a summer-loving snowman, by creating his very own personal snow flurry that hovers over and follows him, keeping him frozen and intact, yet still able to smell the flowers of springtime.

Love, acceptance, open gates and open hearts—these are the answers the two sisters have been seeking on their individual yet intertwined journeys. "I like the open gates," Anna says to Elsa, who responds, "We are never closing them again." The concluding message is that fear shuts down possibilities for joy, whereas love opens up the infinitely possible.

FROZEN'S PLACE IN POPULAR CULTURE

Frozen became a site for multiple readings, with audiences projecting varied interpretations onto the film's anthem "Let It Go." In a film that featured not one, but two female leads, it developed a fandom that generated discourse around queer identity, the patriarchy and toxic masculinity, and female solidarity. Jennifer Lee, the film's screenwriter, commented on fans' interpretations of the first film, saying that "We know what we made. But at the same time, I feel like once we hand the film over, it belongs to the world, so I don't like to say anything, and let the fans talk. I think it's up to them."[5]

Many viewers saw in Elsa's journey a metaphor for being queer and coming out of the closet to embrace one's true self. When the wise old troll asks, regarding Elsa's powers, "Born with it or cursed?" this evokes discourses around LGBT and queer identity, and the question of whether one is born gay or "chooses" to be gay or queer. In answer to this question, many fans of *Frozen* saw in Elsa's journey a manifestion of Lady Gaga's rallying cry: "Baby I was born this way!" And not apologizing for it.

#GiveElsaAGirlfriend

When a sequel for *Frozen* was announced, the hashtag #GiveElsaAGirlfriend trended. It was first started by Twitter user Alexis Isabel Moncada who noted, "imagine how iconic that would be."[6] Another popular Twitter account for all things Disney posted in 2016, "Spoiler alert: Frozen was a metaphor for a closeted person learning to love herself and your children adored it. #GiveElsaAGirlfriend."[7] Fans launched Pride Month posters for *Frozen II* using the hashtag[8] and dedicated blogs and fan art to lobby Disney to respond to the online campaign.

Most fans believed Disney didn't have the courage to take its most successful animation to date and follow it up with a queer relationship for its lead character. Other fans argued they wanted her journey of self-discovery not to revolve around romantic love, but just self-acceptance, queer or straight. One fan posted about the 2019 sequel: "I'm a lesbian but honestly I would rather the film has no romance instead of hearing rants about who Disney makes her fall in love with from both sides."[9] Like many other women who hold political power, the question remains open as to whether powerful women can or should be defined by their love lives and romantic choices. Can a queen just be a queen, regardless of whether or not she has a partner, male or female? Perhaps again the answer lies in another line from Lady Gaga's aforementioned anthem: "Don't be a drag, just be a queen."

Toxic Masculinity and *Frozen*

Romantic relationships aside, in *Frozen*, the sisters upend traditional interactions between men and women, interrogating male power and aspects of toxic masculinity. One Twitter user proclaimed "hans from frozen IS toxic masculinity."[10] Other users have used *Frozen* memes to troll President Donald Trump, whom they consider an example of toxic masculinity.[11] At the end of *Frozen*, Elsa proceeds to rule, not needing anyone at her side other than her sister. They both challenge the patriarchy they inherit and fans have found inspiration in their story in viral ways beyond the context of the film.

Interestingly enough, male fans have engaged with *Frozen* in the context of breaking down toxic masculinity. Many fathers have posted videos on YouTube and other social media platforms of them dressed up as Elsa with both daughters and sons.[12] Norwegian dad and comedian Ørjan Burøe appeared on *Good Morning Britain*, dressed in his Elsa costume and explained to host Piers Morgan why he bought the dress on eBay. When he wore the dress, his son, who he said also likes to dress as Spiderman, saw his father and said, "Aww, we have two superheroes now." As a young boy, his son recognized Elsa also as having powers, and likened her to Spiderman, a typical superhero marketed to boys. When Morgan asserted that Elsa cannot be equated to Spiderman, Burøe countered him: "What? She is a superhero. She is the first lady actor in a cartoon that is a hero. That goes away from all the . . . she don't need a prince and everything, so I think that Elsa is ah, important."[13] Burøe echoed another father on Twitter who posted an image of his injured hand with a Frozen bandage on it and tweeted: "Fellas if you got cut and the only bandaid in the house is Frozen themed, would your toxic masculinity prevent you from covering your wound with it [blush emoji]."[14]

Women Supporting Women

In the final climax of *Frozen*, Anna literally has Elsa's back. In an era of many movements led by women, fans of the film acknowledge its importance for advocating female solidarity against various forms of oppression. One Twitter user noted that "Frozen was so important because the idea of women supporting women is such a necessary lesson to teach young kids."[15] One Women's Emergency shelter held a *Frozen* themed Christmas party to reflect how such resources support women in crises.[16]

Yet, despite what *Frozen* brings to our popular culture in positive ways, it also lacks in other ways. The world of Anna and Elsa is primarily a white one; we do see a few people of color among the Coronation Day attendees, but all main speaking characters are white, with the exception of the trolls (who, it could be argued, act as a symbol of Blackness in the film, with their gospel style singing and other characteristics). As with feminist movements more generally, the intersectional critique is that they have often been framed through the eyes and lived experiences of white women. The privilege of Elsa and Anna is clear—they are royalty. Like white women, their privilege also means that many of the intersectional structures that impeded women of color are absent for white women. Today, it is often women of color who continue fights against oppression that in some instances are obstructed by white women. In expanding stories about womanhood, the stories of women of color are often marginalized or invisible. *Frozen* may have given one spectrum of women's stories, but there are still many more out there to be told.

CONCLUSION

Frozen was a cultural flashpoint that not only officially marked a change in Disney's take on princesses, it cemented it. In taking on a life of its own, the film's social commentary became part of the lexicon of popular culture in an era of social media. It found its ways into the language of activism and into ordinary popular references, all connected to women's empowerment and to challenging patriarchy.

Long before Marvel and DC Comics brought women with supernatural powers to the big screen, there was Elsa. She represented all the complexities of a woman with power, both in her capacity to lead and her capacity to love. She also represented how easily powerful women can be hated, feared, and rejected and how important female solidarity is to the larger fight against the oppression of women. Both Elsa and her sister Anna present a spectrum of what it means to be a woman, to have power as a woman, and to experience love as a woman.

NOTES

1. "Frozen," Box Office Mojo, accessed July 15, 2019, https://www.boxofficemojo.com/movies/?id=frozen2013.htm.

2. Scholars have examined ways in which *Frozen* was a shift for Disney princess films: Benjamin Hine, Dawn England, Katie Lopreore, Elizabeth Skora Horgan, and Lisa Hartwell, "The Rise of the Androgynous Princess: Examining Representations of Gender in Prince and Princess Characters of Disney Movies Released 2009–2016," *Social Sciences* 7, no. 12 (2018): 245; Benjamin Hine, Katarina Ivanovic, and Dawn England, "From the Sleeping Princess to the World-Saving Daughter of the Chief: Examining Young Children's Perceptions of 'Old' Versus 'New' Disney Princess Characters," *Social Sciences* 7, no. 9 (2018): 161; Svenja Hohenstein, *Girl Warriors: Feminist Revisions of the Hero's Quest in Contemporary Popular Culture* (Jefferson, NC: McFarland, 2019); Sabine Krouwels, "Let It Go: A New Way of Looking at Gender Discourse by Breaking the Disney Formula," Master's thesis, Leiden University, 2016; Michelle Law, "Sisters Doin' It for Themselves: *Frozen* and the Evolution of the Disney Heroine," *Screen Education* 74 (2014): 16; Auba Llompart, and Lydia Brugué, "The Snow Queer? Female Characterization in Walt Disney's *Frozen*," *Adaptation* (2019); Madeline Streiff and Lauren Dundes, "*Frozen* in Time: How Disney Gender-Stereotypes Its Most Powerful Princess," *Social Sciences* 6, no. 2 (2017): 38.

3. *Frozen*, Walt Disney Studios Home Entertainment, directed by Jennifer Lee and Chris Buck, starring Idina Menzel, Kristen Bell, Jonathan Groff, Josh Gad, 2014, 102 minutes, digital copy.

4. *Frozen*, Walt Disney Studios Home Entertainment, digital copy.

5. Madie, "Why Do We Want to Give Elsa a Girlfriend," PlannedParenthood.org, April 27, 2016, https://www.plannedparenthood.org/planned-parenthood-south-east-north-florida/blog/why-do-we-want-to-give-elsa-a-girlfriend.

6. Hollee Actman Becker, "This Is Why #GiveElsaAGirlfriend Is a Thing," Parents.com, accessed July 15, 2019, https://www.parents.com/toddlers-preschoolers/everything-kids/this-is-why-giveelsaagirlfriend-is-a-thing/; Alexis Isabel, Twitter, accessed July 15, 2019, https://twitter.com/lexi4prez?ref_src=twsrc%5Etfw.

7. The Volatile Mermaid, @OhNoSheTwitnt, "Spoiler Alert: Frozen is a Metaphor for a Closeted Person Learning to Love Herself and Your Children Adored It. #GiveElsaAGirlfriend," Twitter, May 3, 2016, 8:40 a.m, https://twitter.com/OhNoSheTwitnt/status/727523286083620865.

8. Karin Khaotic, @KarinKhaotic, "Yes please #Frozen2 #GiveElsaAGirlfriend," Twitter, July 21, 2019, 12:08 p.m, https://twitter.com/KarinKhaotic/status/1153018932623740932.

9. Melissa, @kuzr0nk, "I'm a lesbian but honestly I would rather the film has no romance instead of hearing rants about who Disney makes her fall in love from both sides. #GiveElsaAGirlfriend," Twitter, February 13, 2019, 7:52 a.m., https://twitter.com/kuzr0nk/status/1095712238210437120.

10. Virgo Who Can't Drive, @_lanabelle, "hans from frozen IS toxic masculinity!!" Twitter, June 30, 2019, 2:25 p.m., https://twitter.com/_lanabelle/status/1145443174711775233.

11. Averie Maddox, @RABBITISH1, "They're making a Frozen 2. This one is about Donald Trump's heart," Twitter, January 21, 2016, 8:32 p.m., https://twitter.com/RABBITISH1/status/690361488696016896.

12. *Good Morning Britain*, "Video of Father and Son Dancing as Elsa from *Frozen* Goes Viral," YouTube video, 4:55, posted January 28, 2019, https://youtu.be/BI7X8C-sLsw.

13. Ibid.

14. L, @bean_supreme, "Fellas if you got a cut but the only bandaid in the house is Frozen themed, would your toxic masculinity prevent you from covering your would with it [blush emoji]," Twitter, May 5, 2019, 9:34, a.m. https://twitter.com/bean_supreme/status/1125076369682124800.

15. OliVia, @Oliviadesmith, "Frozen was so important because the idea of women supporting women is such a necessary lesson to teach young kids," Twitter, October 19, 2015, 6:23 a.m. https://twitter.com/Oliviadesmith/status/656098248126541824.

16. Debraross, @debraross7, "Frozen Christmas supporting YYC Women's Emergency Shelter. @TJAndersonYYC @EndAbuse @JOELLESNOELLE," Twitter, December 5, 2014, 11:39 p.m. https://twitter.com/debraross7/status/541134811327242240.

BIBLIOGRAPHY

Averie Maddox, @RABBITISH1. "They're making a Frozen 2. This one is about Donald Trump's heart." Twitter. January 21, 2016, 8:32 p.m. https://twitter.com/RABBITISH1/status/690361488696016896.

Becker, Hollee Actman."This Is Why #GiveElsaAGirlfriend Is a Thing." Parents.com. Accessed July 15, 2019. https://www.parents.com/toddlers-preschoolers/everything-kids/this-is-why-giveelsaagirlfriend-is-a-thing/; Alexis Isabel,

Twitter, accessed July 15, 2019, https://twitter.com/lexi4prez?ref_src=twsrc%5Etfw.

Debraross, @debraross7. "Frozen Christmas supporting YYC Women's Emergency Shelter. @TJAndersonYYC @EndAbuse @JOELLESNOELLE," Twitter. December 5, 2014, 11:39 p.m. https://twitter.com/debraross7/status/541134811327242240.

"Frozen." Box Office Mojo. Accessed July 15, 2019. https://www.boxofficemojo.com/movies/?id=frozen2013.htm.

Frozen. Walt Disney Studios Home Entertainment. Directed by Jennifer Lee and Chris Buck, starring Idina Menzel, Kristen Bell, Jonathan Groff, Josh Gad, 2014. 102 minutes. Digital copy.

Good Morning Britain. "Video of Father and Son Dancing as Elsa from Frozen Goes Viral." YouTube video, 4:55. Posted January 28, 2019. https://youtu.be/BI7X8C-sLsw.

Hine, Benjamin, Dawn England, Katie Lopreore, Elizabeth Skora Horgan, and Lisa Hartwell. "The Rise of the Androgynous Princess: Examining Representations of Gender in Prince and Princess Characters of Disney Movies Released 2009–2016." *Social Sciences* 7, no. 12 (2018): 1–23.

Hine, Benjamin, Katarina Ivanovic, and Dawn England. "From the Sleeping Princess to the World-Saving Daughter of the Chief: Examining Young Children's Perceptions of 'Old' Versus 'New' Disney Princess Characters." *Social Sciences* 7, no. 9 (2018): 1–15.

Hohenstein, Svenja. *Girl Warriors: Feminist Revisions of the Hero's Quest in Contemporary Popular Culture.* Jefferson, NC: McFarland, 2019.

Karin Khaotic, @KarinKhaotic. "Yes please #Frozen2 #GiveElsaAGirlfriend." Twitter. July 21, 2019, 12:08 p.m. https://twitter.com/KarinKhaotic/status/1153018932623740932.

Krouwels, Sabine. "Let It Go: A New Way of Looking at Gender Discourse by Breaking the Disney Formula." Master's thesis. Leiden University, 2016.

Law, Michelle. "Sisters Doin' It for Themselves: Frozen and the Evolution of the Disney Heroine." *Screen Education* 74 (2014): 16.

Llompart, Auba, and Lydia Brugué, "The Snow Queer? Female Characterization in Walt Disney's Frozen." *Adaptation* (2019). https://doi.org/10.1093/adaptation/apz019.

L, @bean_supreme. "Fellas if you got a cut but the only bandaid in the house is Frozen themed, would your toxic masculinity prevent you from covering your would with it [blush emoji]." Twitter. May 5, 2019, 9:34, a.m. https://twitter.com/bean_supreme/status/1125076369682124800.

Madie. "Why Do We Want to Give Elsa a Girlfriend." PlannedParenthood.org. April 27, 2016. https://www.plannedparenthood.org/planned-parenthood-south-east-north-florida/blog/why-do-we-want-to-give-elsa-a-girlfriend.

Melissa, @kuzr0nk. "I'm a lesbian but honestly I would rather the film has no romance instead of hearing rants about who Disney makes her fall in love from both sides. #GiveElsaAGirlfriend." Twitter. February 13, 2019, 7:52 a.m. https://twitter.com/kuzr0nk/status/1095712238210437120.

OliVia, @Oliviadesmith. "Frozen was so important because the idea of women supporting women is such a necessary lesson to teach young kids." Twitter, October 19, 2015, 6:23 a.m. https://twitter.com/Oliviadesmith/status/656098248126541824.

Streiff, Madeline, and Lauren Dundes, "Frozen in Time: How Disney Gender-Stereotypes Its Most Powerful Princess." *Social Sciences* 6, no. 2 (2017): 38. https://doi.org/10.3390/socsci6020038.

The Volatile Mermaid, @OhNoSheTwitnt. "Spoiler Alert: Frozen is a Metaphor for a Closeted Person Learning to Love Herself and Your Children Adored It. #GiveElsaAGirlfriend." Twitter. May 3, 2016, 8:40 a.m. https://twitter.com/OhNoSheTwitnt/status/727523286083620865.

Virgo Who Can't Drive, @_lanabelle. "hans from frozen IS toxic masculinity!!" Twitter. June 30, 2019, 2:25 p.m. https://twitter.com/_lanabelle/status/1145443174711775233.

14

✢

Shuri of Wakanda, the People's Princess

Charity Clay

Just days after the February 18, 2018, United States theatrical release of Marvel's *The Black Panther*, social media erupted over the conversation of whether or not Princess Shuri of Wakanda could be a "Disney princess." The same day the film debuted in the United States, acclaimed Black woman illustrator Vashti Harrison posted an illustration of Shuri on her Instagram account with the caption "Nothing but respect for my Disney princess #shuri #blackpanther @letitiawright."[1]

The quickly growing number of Shuri fans argued that since Disney owns Marvel, and Shuri is an actual princess in the Marvel Cinematic Universe, she "technically" *is* a Disney princess. Fans expressed excitement at the possibility that Disney could possibly recognize an African princess of a technologically advanced kingdom alongside characters like Cinderella and Snow White.

Although, the court of public opinion has rendered the verdict and crowned Shuri as a Disney princess, there has been no official word from Disney, to date. Unbeknownst to most, there is a criterion used to determine the characters officially recognized as part of the Disney princess franchise created by Andy Mooney in the early 2000s. A criterion that is based in a marketing formula intended to maximize profitability of the princesses more than to empower young girls.

The first Disney princesses included Cinderella, Aurora of *Sleeping Beauty*, Belle from *Beauty and the Beast*, Ariel from *The Little Mermaid*, Jasmine from *Aladdin*, Pocahontas, and Mulan. Although Jasmine is not the main character and Mulan and Pocahontas are not technically princesses, they were added to the franchise due to what Disney reporter Jim Hill called a "sensitivity [of], 'how many white blond women can we have in this group? We need to bring in some people of color."[2] Since the initial release of Disney princesses, there have only been four additions, Rapunzel from *Tangled*, Tiana from *The Princess and the Frog*, Merida from *Brave*, and Moana in 2019.[3] Each princess has her own webpage with games, crafts, quizzes, and of course merchandise featuring her animated likeness.

While many of the other princesses saw their fate start and end with one film, Shuri has two stories; one that spans multiple films and another that exists in the comics. With regards to both Marvel Cinematic and Comic Universes, Shuri's story is PG-13 whereas the primary consumer for the Disney princess franchise is the G-rated moviegoer. These barriers to Shuri's inclusion into the Disney princess franchise lead Hill to conclude the following about Disney's plan for Shuri and the other women of Wakanda: "Screw folding them into the Disney princesses. This is a franchise all by itself."[4] Hill is right.

This chapter specifically argues that calls for Shuri being presented as "technically" a Disney princess, marks a shift for counter-narratives of Black womanhood in the center of mainstream media resulting in not only a new role model for Black girls, but new representation of Black girls. The chapter also argues that Shuri becoming "officially" a Disney princess would require a whitewashed version of her character determined by market research to be most profitable and the least risky. Thus it fits her into more commonly acceptable Disney princess caricature that ultimately undermines Shuri's potential to transform social perception, but maximizes her profitability for Disney and its beneficiaries. Ultimately, the chapter argues against Shuri being added to the Disney princess franchise. Her popularity indicates that Disney should add an African princess soon while leaving Shuri to evolve in the Marvel Comic and Cinematic Universes.

HOLLYWOOD STEREOTYPES OF BLACK WOMEN AND ADULTIFICATION OF BLACK GIRLS

In 2015, Twitter user @ReignofApril introduced the hashtag #OscarsSoWhite after noticing that all twenty of the nominees for lead and supporting acting categories were white.[5] Increased calls for diversity in the Hollywood academy seems like progress to some, it must be considered that negative misrepresentations of non-white characters are intentional and tantamount to maintaining white supremacy. Thus, simply increasing the number of non-white people participating does not equate to structural change. In fact, token successes are often celebrated to cover continued oppression. And regardless of the members of the academy, the stereotypical portrayals still operate as Hazel Carby notes, "not to reflect or represent a reality but to function as a disguise, or mystification, of objective social relations."[6] Specifically in the case of Black women, Patricia Hill Collins writes:

> Portraying African American women as stereotypical mammies, matriarchs, welfare recipients, and hot mommas helps justify U.S. Black women's oppression. . . . These controlling images are designed to make racism, sexism, poverty, and other forms of social injustice appear to be natural, normal and inevitable parts of everyday life.[7]

Collins identifies five main "controlling images" of Black womanhood as: Mammy (happy domestic servant), Matriarch (Emasculating unfit mother), Welfare Mother (Materialistic, neglectful single mother), Black Lady (Professionally successful but personally damaged single woman) and Jezebel (sexually promiscuous). Collins writes that these images "represent elite white male interests in defining Black women's sexuality and fertility."[8]

These interests are served through social structures that create policies that control Black women's bodies. In addition to the controlling images that Collins recognizes, other scholars have added the Sapphire, Tragic Mulatto, and the Magical Negress.[9] The Sapphire is considered to be connected to the Matriarch but does not always have children, the Tragic Mulatto is a specific type of Jezebel who uses the physical attractiveness associated with her Eurocentric features to lure and seduce men, and the Magical Negress has supernatural abilities but is akin to the Mammy because she only uses these abilities in service of whites, never to improve her own plight.

Whereas these controlling images in some way center on either Black motherhood or Black women's sexuality, there is also a set of characteristics applied to Black girls that serve as controlling images. The two most prominent that operate as a binary often prevail; one is the "fast girl" who is hypersexualized, the other one is the "tomboy" who is masculinized. A 2017 survey conducted of 325 adults, 74 percent white, 65 percent female, and 69 percent degree holders reported the following general perceptions of Black girls as compared to white girls:

- Black girls need less nurturing
- Black girls need less protection
- Black girls need to be supported less
- Black girls are more independent
- Black girls know more about adult topics
- Black girls know more about sex[10]

These perceptions support the claims of the binary characteristics of controlling images for Black girls. Needing less nurturing and needing to be supported less reflect the masculinization of Black girls; knowing more about adult topics and knowing more about sex reflect the hypersexualization; and needing less protection and being independent reflect both masculinization and hyersexualization.

The authors of the above study, in analysis of their findings use the term "Adultification" to describe a social or cultural stereotype that is based on how adults perceive children; in the absence of knowledge of children's behavior and verbalizations.[11] This definition of adultifcation is considered significantly different from the initial term that was introduced by Linda Burton's conceptual model in 2007. Burton's definition referred to "A process of socialization, in which children function at a more mature developmental stage because of situational context and necessity, especially in low-resource community environments."[12]

Burton's initial conceptualization of adultification will be addressed later within the context of Black women's sacred texts and Womanist counter-narratives. Here however, I focus on the application of adulting stereotypes acknowledged in the 2017 study and the negative impact on Black girls' well-being. The ultimate result of the social and cultural stereotypes that support adultification of Black girls is that as one of the report's authors exclaimed: "Black girls are not getting the benefits of being viewed as innocent."[13] The authors show how these findings have implications for both the education and juvenile justice systems that have been found to punish Black girls at higher rates and more severely than their white girl peers.[14]

Media is essential to the adultification of Black girls because the stereotypes exist absent the understanding of motivations behind Black girls' words and actions. So, although there are not specific archetypes for the controlling images for Black girls, they are either masculinized as "tomboys" or sexualized as "fast girls." In Hollywood films, Black girls are negatively portrayed by simplifying their behaviors in ways that suggest that they are inherently "bad" to justify the perception by mainstream audiences like those who completed the survey that fail to consider that these girls' behavior is learned, not innate.

Hollywood has become a primary site for these controlling images to be produced, disseminated, and celebrated. In the ninety-one years of the Academy of Motion Picture Arts and Sciences awards, known as "The Oscars" all Black women nominated for the Best Actress award fit into these controlling images and stereotypes, most notably:

- Dorothy Dandridge's nomination in 1954 for the jezebel character Carmen in the film *Carmen Jones*[15]
- Diahann Carroll's nomination in 1974 for the welfare mother character Claudine in the film *Claudine*[16]

- Halle Berry's win in 2001 for the tragic mulatto, jezebel/Matriarch character Leticia Musgrove in the film *Monster's Ball*[17]
- Viola Davis' 2011 nomination for the Mammy-like character Aibileen Clark in the film *The Help*[18]

It is important to acknowledge that it is the industry and mainstream audiences that recognize these roles only within the context of controlling images. Similar to the celebrated roles for Black women, the actresses portraying Black girls nominated for the same awards are prime examples of the adultification of Black girls:

- Whoopi Goldberg's 1985 nomination for playing sexually abused fourteen-year-old child bride Celie Johnson in *The Color Purple*
- Gabourey Sidibe's 2009 nomination for playing the developmentally challenged, sexual abuse victim Claireece "Precious" Jones in the film *Precious*
- Quvenzhané Wallis' 2012 nomination for playing six-year-old Hushpuppy, who lives in poverty with her father and is forced to navigate a world-ending storm in the midst of his disappearance[19]

It is important to note here that the Hollywood film portrayals of Black girls taken from novels written by Black women, *The Color Purple* and *Precious*, which is an adaptation of the novel *Push*, remove the depths that the characters are written, so that they fit neatly into existing stereotypes. This is particularly bothersome because the purpose of these novels is to provide counter-narratives of mainstream stereotypes. Both novels *Push* and *The Color Purple* are originally counternarratives that show Black girls persevering through being robbed of their innocence and girlhood by abusive adults and dire circumstances as opposed to them being considered innately bad. Mainstream audiences however, do not see the depths and nuances of these characters, they only see the representations as justification for the stereotypes they already hold of Black girls being innately more sexual, more independent, less loveable, less innocent, and less needing of support and protection. With these portrayals prevailing in Hollywood, and being most commonly recognized and awarded, Shuri and the other women of Wakanda stand out as refreshing to see in a major Hollywood film.

Ryan Coogler's Womanist Wakanda

Citizens of Ryan Coogler's Wakanda may bow to T'Challa the Black Panther as its king, but it's clearly a country run by women. During the film, Wakanda goes through many changes, but throughout, T'Challa is supported by Wakandan women that provide representations of Black women never before seen in such a major film, namely; Queen Mother

Ramonda, Okoye, Nakia, and Shuri. The genius of these portrayals is that they may appear on the surface to be similar to existing controlling images, but as the characters are introduced, moviegoers are immediately exposed to women characters that steal scenes from T'Challa and pique curiosity into their backstories. These four characters introduce archetypes of Black women that center and celebrate Black women as a balance of beauty, strength, intelligence, humor, loyalty, compassion, nurturing, and courage.

We are first introduced to Okoye, general of the all-woman Wakandan royal army known as the Dora Milaje. Although she is first seen meditating, she is a fearless and highly skilled warrior who is fiercely loyal to the throne of Wakanda, but at the same time kind-hearted, loving, and nurturing. Next is Nakia, member of the Wakandan war-dogs, the title bestowed on the international spies that Wakanda has placed across the globe to protect Wakandan interests. While she is supposed to focus on protecting Wakanda abroad, Nakia also engages in human rights missions like saving victims of civil wars across Africa. She is also weapons trained and highly skilled and has an on-again, off-again romance with T'Challa that centers on her not wanting to give up her life's work to become queen.

There is Queen Mother Ramonda played by Angela Bassett who is a staple of womanhood within Black American cinema playing iconic characters like Tina Turner, Betty Shabazz, and Voletta Wallace.[20] Ramonda provides guidance and support as T'Challa questions his capabilities as king and she nurtures Shuri's rebellious spirit and technological genius while teaching her traditions and encouraging her to be respectfully creative in her self-expression. When we are finally introduced to princess Shuri, it is through a seemingly insignificant jab she takes at her brother T'Challa after he and Okoye have returned with Nakia for his coronation ceremony when she asks Okoye, "Did he freeze?" in reference to T'Challa being distracted upon sight of his love interest Nakia. Initially, she is portrayed as innocent, a younger sister making light of her older brother being in love but her lightheartedness shifts very quickly as she begins to seriously question T'Challa about how well the gadgets she made performed for him during his mission. In this exchange, it becomes clear that Shuri is more than a static character and Black moviegoers begin to recognize her #BlackGirlMagic while others begin to appreciate her #GirlPower.

Princess Shuri's #BlackGirlMagic vs. "GirlPower"

In 2013, blogger Cashawn Thompson created the hashtag #BlackGirlsAreMagic and later the more popular #BlackGirlMagic hashtag to celebrate the accomplishments of Black women across various social media platforms. Many of the posts using the hashtag included present day accomplishments of Black women and to highlight Black women throughout history.[21]

In addition to providing a positive representation, Shuri also serves #BlackGirlMagic and becomes an easy way to introduce real African royalty like Queen Nefertiti, Amina, Sheeba, and Nandi. Her job as a scientist and engineer becomes easy ways to introduce contemporary Black women like Mae Jemison and Katherine Johnson.

For her first appearance on camera, before she speaks, she is presented as impeccably stylish in a way that combined traditional African fashion with modern influences in a seamless way that was noticeable by those familiar with African culture, but not so much so to be considered "too ethnic" for those unfamiliar or unappreciative. Her initial outfit features a jersey style crop top sweater with buckles on the sleeves, something you would expect to see on a winning design on an episode of *Project Runway*. Front and center of the outfit is an Adinkra symbol. Adinkra symbols are believed to have originated in Gyaman, a former kingdom of current day Côte d'Ivoire that was defeated by the Asante Kingdom. The symbols are culturally significant with meanings that express different African values and depict significant historical developments. As such, new symbols are created as Ghanian history and culture evolve, new signs are created to reflect the evolution.[22] Currently there are at least sixty-three known symbols.[23] The symbol on Shuri's top is known as the Wawa Aba or "Seed of the Wawa tree." In a *Vanity Fair* video, multiple award-winning costume designer Ruth Carter, who became the first Black woman to win an Oscars for Best Costume Design for this film, explained the Adinkra Symbol Shuri is wearing claiming that it "means purpose, and she certainly has a purpose in Wakanda."[24] Additionally, Carter points out that Shuri's fashionable necklace also has African historical significance adding that, "These little puka [also known as cowrie] shells, were used as trading, they represented wealth."[25] Shuri's introductory outfit also contains stylish shoes that are a cross between sneakers and combat boots, and a hairstyle reminiscent of Princess Leia's two spiral buns with an update of asymmetrical parts in the back.

Shuri's outfits throughout the film have inspired numerous social media and blog posts from stylists and designers attempting to provide shoppers with similar outfits for every budget. *College Fashion*, a blog whose content caters primarily to an audience of white college age women even featured Shuri's outfits and called her character "a role model for young girls."[26] While highlighting her humor, charisma, intelligence, and evolution, they do not recognize any of the African elements in any her outfits as they provided their audience with ways to imitate her style. This embrace of Shuri's universal girl power is seemingly enhanced by the erasure of her African influences and complicates the claims that Shuri's embrace can lead to a greater appreciation for Black girls and women. In some ways, while Black girls and women see themselves in Shuri, the rest of the world sees her as an outlier, a unique princess that is not representative of the everyday Black girl, rather one who only exists in the fictional African country of Wakanda.

As princess of Wakanda, Shuri is respected; her tribe rules Wakanda and being the Black Panther is her family tradition. Shuri is also seriously protected by the Dora Milaje who not only protect the king of Wakanda but also the royal family. Shuri is also supported in her scientific endeavors, is considered smarter than both Tony Stark (Ironman) and Bruce Banner (The Hulk) and at sixteen years old, has her own science and technology lab where she is free to create and experiment. While most girls, and specifically Black girls are discouraged from pursuing STEM careers, Shuri's purpose in Wakanda as chief scientist and engineer may be considered one of the most important in the country because of its dependence on the ability to sustainably harness and utilize the power of vibranium.

Shuri is also nurtured not only in her technological pursuits but in her growth and development as a young woman. It is clear that there are some issues with her departure from traditional Wakandan ways; M'Baku claims that she is a "child who scoffs at tradition"[27] and T'Challa joked about being excited to see the changes she would make to her "ceremonial outfits."[28] Later, Shuri publicly proclaimed that the corset that was part of her ceremonial garment at challenge day was "really uncomfortable."[29] However, Shuri is never embarrassed or punished for being outspoken, she is allowed by all in the kingdom to be herself and is only slightly chided by her mother, Queen Ramonda. While Shuri is given the freedom to be herself as princess of Wakanda, she is also surrounded by amazing women who inspire her by providing varied examples of greatness that she is undoubtedly expected to follow, even if in her own way.

While Shuri may be considered a great representation of #BlackGirlMagic, she is far from the underclass Black girl routinely portrayed in Hollywood films. She is African royalty from a fictionalized country with no integration with the outside world. Whereas all African countries have had to defend against European colonialism, Wakanda is conceptualized as a nation free of Western imperialist influences and therefore authentically and uniquely African. Many consider Wakanda to be an idealization of what African countries would've developed into had they not been colonized.[30] While Wakanda is considered authentically African and Blackness there is not constructed by the white gaze, Shuri, especially, is very aware of Western popular culture which is evident by her references to

"Coachella and Disneyland" and the viral video that asked the question "What are those?" These seemingly small acts connect her with Western culture in ways that allow her to connect with non-Black audiences. More significantly, Shuri is the one who embraces interracial alliances. While she initially refers to Agent Ross as "another white boy to fix"[31] and a "colonizer," she does so in English, the same language spread throughout Africa as a result of colonization. In an earlier exchange between Okoye and Agent Ross where Okoye speaks to T'Challa in their native language and Ross questions "does she speak English?" Okoye's reply being "when she wants to" shows her as being resistant to Western influence, thus further endearing non-Black audience to Shuri by comparison. Not only does she heal Agent Ross but she trusts him to carry out a most important mission of shooting down Wakandan planes sent by Killmonger to distribute vibranium-powered weapons intended to aid oppressed Black communities across the globe. In conversations with Agent Ross, Shuri also seemingly rejects the magic of Wakanda by explaining to him that bullet wounds heal in a day in Wakanda "not by magic, by technology."[32] It is these moments in the film that highlight Shuri's "girl power" over #BlackGirlMagic that shows her relatability to non-Black audiences, it also brings some to question what about Shuri is being embraced, on what terms, and what is the impact on everyday Black girls and women. Shuri's uniqueness lies in her committed character creation and development by Black writers Coogler, Joe Robert Cole, Ta-Nehisi Coates, and Roxane Gay.

PROTECTING SHURI FROM HOLLYWOOD COOPTATION

Characters like Shuri have always existed within what Ann duCille refers to as "sacred texts."[33] Works written by Black women, primarily for Black women that express the myriad of manifestations of Black womanhood as resistance to controlling images, have dominated the mainstream since the existence of American media and academia. One aspect of critical race theory that places it with the traditions of womanism and Black feminism is the emphasis on fiction and narrative as "text." Recognizing the history of exclusion within the academy that prevented marginalized groups from contributing to scholarship, critical race theory looks at other forms of literature as empirical evidence providing detailed documentation of the life experiences of marginalized people.

For generations Black women have been writing to and for Black girls and women to provide survival guides to be used and shared as needed from childhood to elder adulthood. In her book *In Search of Our Mother's*

Gardens, Alice Walker introduced the term womanism, claiming it derived from womanish, and defined it as:

> ([Opposite] of "girlish", i.e. frivolous, irresponsible, not serious) . . . From the black folk expression of mothers to female children, 'you acting womanish,' i.e. like a woman. Usually referring to outrageous, audacious, courageous or *willful* behavior. Wanting to know more and in greater depth that is considered 'good for one.' Interested in grown up things. Acting grown up. Being Grown up. Interchangeable with another black folk expression: 'you trying to be grown.' Responsible. In charge. Serious.[34]

While this definition may seem to fit within the damaging concept of adultification referenced earlier, it relates more so to Burton's original concept of adultification that acknowledges that children, in this case Black girls, are socialized to be more mature in order to adapt to their surroundings. In this way, the characteristics of womanist become synonymous with those needed for Black girls' survival. Through the power of narrative as text; essays, plays, and novels provided the truths about Black women's lives in ways where "fictional" characters became women we knew or wished we knew, women wished we were, women we were, or women we wished we weren't. These stories have empowered girl children to fight because they "ain't safe in a family of men";[35] are poetry demanding we find God in ourselves and "love her fiercely";[36] are essays warning us that the alternative to self-definition is being "eaten alive"[37] and is dialog encouraging us to "give up pain and hurt and make room for lovely things."[38]

While these writings remained sacred texts among Black women, they have remained largely unknown to others. To appeal to wider audiences, some of these sacred texts have been adapted for the silver screen but with little success. In fact, films like *The Color Purple, Beloved, Their Eyes Were Watching God,* and *For Colored Girls* have all been heavily critiqued for the way that the films left essential elements of the literature out of the movies in perceived attempts to appeal to white audiences. Even the most successful of the aforementioned examples, *The Color Purple,* that earned both actress Oprah Winfrey and director Steven Spielberg awards nominations caused a rift within the Black community due to its portrayal of Black men as abusive. While Alice Walker's novel of the same name focuses on the ways that Black girls and women survive and triumph over abusive situations, the film left out much of the importance on sisterhood and intimate friendships among Black women. The film did however, provide vivid scenes based on the narratives of abuse that the Black girls and women in the film suffered at the hands of Black men. The film raised the question within the Black community of whether Black women's stories should be told to white audiences when they portrayed Black men negatively; especially when the efforts were headed by Black women in collaboration and with backing by white men. Similar conversations around movies like *Waiting to Exhale* would soon follow. This viewpoint removes Black women from the center of their own stories and relegates them to being tools used by the white power structure to cast Black men as villains and to simplify the source of Black women's trauma.

In addition to the inability of most to understand Black women characters outside of a very narrow Eurocentric view, such adaptations of Black women's sacred texts resulted in a patriarchal gaze that profits the most from Black women's hypervisibility and misrepresentation. In *Black Looks*, bell hooks writes about the "commodification of otherness" and how it allows whites not only to enjoy "Black culture" but to profit from it while systems of oppression continue to limit ways that Black people are credited and compensated for the cultural artifacts they produce and give value to. DuCille specifically acknowledges that

> Where gender and racial difference meet in the bodies of Black women, the result is the invention of an Otherness, a hyperstatic alterity. Mass culture . . . promotes, and perpetuates the commodification of Otherness through the exploitation of the Black female body.[39]

In this way, even Black female characters that are created outside of and in resistance to controlling images get packaged in ways that reduce them to those images and narratives. White audiences feel safe to pay for the perceived opportunity to experience what is being marketed to them as authentic Blackness. Hollywood can then also simultaneously profit from Black audiences that support these portrayals because it is rare that they see faces that look like them in mainstream Hollywood films.

Unfortunately, none of this improves conditions for Black women, instead white industries profit and Black men and white women, historically become experts who are credited with "discovering and analyzing" Black women's already existing work.[40] The message to Black women in all of this, was to keep sacred texts, their characters and their stories protected by remaining outside of the mainstream; within the community of Black women, to be passed down through generations, each one adding their own texts to this protected canon. So, while Shuri's embrace has caused some to reconsider that mainstream audiences may be ready for more dynamic representations of Black girls and women on screen, others view her recent character most deserving of protection within the canon of Black women's sacred texts, in a land far far away from the Disney princess franchise.

THE FUTURE OF SHURI OF WAKANDA: PRINCESS OR SACRED TEXT

From the moment moviegoers saw her on screen in *Black Panther*, Shuri of Wakanda captivated audiences as the highly intelligent, quirky, confident, stylish, warrior princess. In such, she provided a representation of Black girlhood and womanhood free of controlling images that masculinize and hypersexualize Black female bodies. Moviegoers and cultural critics applauded Marvel, Ryan Coogler, and Letitia Wright for successfully introducing a character that was so deeply rooted in her African heritage but universally relatable at the same time. Unexpectedly, her popularity among young moviegoers transcended both race and gender with girls of all races and ethnicities wanting not only to dress up as Shuri but wanting to be STEM geniuses and boys wanting to fight side-by-side with her as they fight to save the world instead of wanting her to stay at home cheering them on. For children introduced to Black female representation through *Black Panther*, it may be more difficult for them to accept the controlling images of Black women that portray them as hypersexual, unintelligent, emasculating, and unattractive. The hope is that, characters like Shuri represent a shift in mainstream media representation of Black girls and women that expands beyond controlling images and contributes to socializing a generation that values Black girls and women in real life and not just on screen.

For Disney however, any decision to make Shuri a Disney princess is about profitability even when considering the positive impact of new representations within the franchise. Beyond the obvious barriers to Shuri being a Disney princess, like her not having her own feature film, not being introduced initially as an animated character, and being a from a Disney subsidiary (Marvel) and not birthed in the Disney kingdom, this designation would be disappointingly limiting for the character. It is true that Disney princesses are beginning to be presented as more assertive, and rejecting the damsel in distress narrative. However, Disney princesses are static characters who are fixed in the time of their feature length films, with only four having sequels, mostly relegated to VHS releases. What fundamentally excited fans about Shuri is the potential of watching her character grow through roles in successive films. As we leave her in *Black Panther*, she is the newly appointed director of the science and information exchange at the First International Wakanda Outreach center in Oakland.[41] At sixteen years old, she is just growing into her womanhood, something that she would not be allowed to do if brought into the Disney princess franchise.

Ultimately, I agree with Jim Hill's claim that Shuri, and the other featured women of Wakanda are a franchise on their own. Just a month after the release of *Black Panther*, Marvel announced a three-issue comic miniseries focusing on the Women of Wakanda where they team up with other heroes of the Marvel Comic Universe with the first issue being titled *Wakanda Forever: The Amazing Spider-Man*.[42] Additionally, in October 2018, Marvel released the first issue of Shuri's self-titled feature also written by Nnedi Okorafor[43] with the cover art for the issue released June 19, 2019, featuring Shuri as the Black Panther, leading the Dora Milaje.[44] In this way, especially with Okorafor writing the story, Shuri can remain protected in a "sacred text" of the comic world, written by Black women for Black women. Okorafor is an award-winning writer likened most often to Octavia Butler and Nalo Hopkinson for her Afro-futurism, and women-centered work. In just nine short issues, the Shuri comic shows the character's evolution beyond anything that Disney has allowed for any of their princesses to date.

So while Shuri is not the best fit and serves better as the "People's Princess," her largescale embrace shows Disney that its audience is ready for an African Princess to be added to the franchise. Many of Disney's princess movies are adaptations of existing fairy tales, and more recently, many of them are being rewritten and remade as live-action to update narratives that are now viewed as demeaning to girls. Adding an African princess to the Disney franchise eliminates the need to rewrite existing narratives because there are plenty of African folk tales and real-life princesses to add to the franchise that would celebrate the values of African culture and the beauty of African girlhood and womanhood in ways that empower girls to be strong, courageous, smart; and that shift conventional notions of beauty.

NOTES

1. Vashti Harrison, "Nothing but respect for my Disney princess #shuri #blackpanther @letitiawright," *@Vashtiharrison*, Instagram, February 16, 2018, https://www.instagram.com/p/BfSPS3HFuKV/.

2. Jessica M. Goldstein, "Is Shuri Better off Without the Disney Princesses?" *Think Progress,* February 27, 2018, https://thinkprogress.org/wakanda-magic-kingdom-shuri-disney-princess-0b65ee1be2e2/.

3. Ibid.

4. Ibid.

5. April Reign, "#OscarsSoWhite Is Still Relevant This Year, *Vanity Fair,* March 2, 2018, https://www.vanityfair.com/hollywood/2018/03/oscarssowhite-is-still-relevant-this-year.

6. Hazel Carby, "It Jus Be's Dat Way Sometime: The Black Sexual Politics of Women's Blues," in *The Jazz Cadence of American Culture,* ed. Robert G. O'Meally (New York: Columbia University Press, 1998).

7. Patricia Hill Collins, "Mammies, Matriarchs, and Other Controlling Images," *Black Feminist Thought: Knowledge, Consciousness and the Politics of Empowerment*, (New York: Routledge, 2000), 69.

8. Ibid., 84

9. Krin Gabbard, "Black Angels in America: Millennial Solutions to the 'Race Problem,'" *Black Magic: White Hollywood and African American Culture* (Piscataway: Rutgers University Press, 2004), 154.

10. Rebecca Epstein, Jamilia J. Blake, and Thalia González, "Girlhood Interrupted: The Erasure of Black Girls' Childhood," *Georgetown Law Center on Poverty and Inequality*, 2017, accessed May 10, 2019, https://www.law.georgetown.edu/poverty-inequality-center/wp-content/uploads/sites/14/2017/08/girlhood-interrupted.pdf.

11. Ibid.

12. Linda Burton, "Childhood Adultification in Economically Disadvantaged Families: A Conceptual Model," *Family Relations* 56, no. 4 (2007): 329. https://onlinelibrary.wiley.com/doi/abs/10.1111/j.1741-3729.2007.00463.x.

13. Rebecca Epstein, Jamilia J. Blake, and Thalia González, "Girlhood Interrupted: The Erasure of Black Girls' Childhood."

14. Ibid.

15. *Carmen Jones'* title character fits the Jezebel stereotype mainly because she seduces a soldier to leave his fiancé, only to leave him for another man. This fits into the characterization of the Jezebel as so powerful in her seduction that she drives men to commit irrational and criminal acts.

16. Although, within the Black community, Claudine is viewed as an accurate portrayal of the struggles that working class and impoverished Black couples had to endure to navigate the constraints of many oppressive social structures, white audiences, unable to adopt this lens, applauded the portrayal of Claudine because it fit the Welfare Mother stereotype.

17. A film about a Black woman, Leticia Musgrove falls in love with her husband's white executioner Hank Grotowski. The film presents Musgrove as a Tragic Mulatto character who is constantly indecisive and victimized by her circumstances. The interracial dynamics of this film contribute to it fitting stereotypical characterizations of Black women.

18. Within the Black Community, *The Help* is viewed as a counternarrative showing how Black women domestic servants in the South were not only aware of the way whites viewed them, but exploited the whites' own prejudices to successfully navigate their work, home, and community lives. However, the character of Aibileen is praised by whites in the academy because it aligns with their characterization of a Mammy character, happily serving her white family.

19. *Beasts of the Southern Wild* is adapted from a screenplay where the character Hushpuppy is initially cast as a boy. In the film, Hushpuppy played by Quvenzhané Wallis is portrayed as very mature for a six-year-old whose father is dying and mother is absent. She is not seen as even aware that her familial situation is not ideal and instead focuses on solving problems for not only herself but her community. When the woman she believes to be her mother doesn't recognize her and when she he has to bury her father, she shows little emotion and continues

life as if these occurrences are normal. This portrayal supports white audiences view that Black girls need less nurturing, protection, and support.

20. IMDb, "Angela Bassett," accessed March 20, 2019, https://www.imdb.com/name/nm0000291/.

21. Dexter Thomas, "Why Everyone's Saying 'Black Girls Are Magic,'" *The Los Angeles Times*, September 9, 2015, https://www.latimes.com/nation/nationnow/la-na-nn-everyones-saying-black-girls-are-magic-20150909-htmlstory.html.

22. "Adinkra—Cultural Symbols of the Asante People," accessed June 1, 2019, http://www.stlawu.edu/gallery/education/f/09textiles/adinkra_symbols.pdf.

23. "West African Wisdom: Adinkra Symbols and Meanings," Adinkra.org, accessed June 1, 2019, http://www.adinkra.org/htmls/adinkra_index.htm.

24. "Black Panther Costume Designer Breaks Down T'Challa's Entrance Scene," *Vanity Fair videos*, May 8, 2018, https://video.vanityfair.com/watch/black-panther-s-costume-designer-breaks-down-t-challa-s-entrance-scene.

25. Ibid.

26. Paloma, "Heroic Styles: Shuri (Black Panther)," CollegeFashion.net, accessed May 15, 2019, https://www.collegefashion.net/inspiration/shuri-style-black-panther/.

27. Ibid.

28. Ibid.

29. Ibid.

30. Agunda, Okeyo, "Wakanda: A Nation Without Chains," Progressive, February 23, 2018, https://progressive.org/dispatches/black-panther-wakanda-a-model-for-the-world-180223/.

31. Shuri makes this comment in reference to her being the one who healed Bucky Barnes the Winter Solider in an after credits scene of *Captain America: Civil War*. Shuri's ability to singlehandedly heal Bucky from the brainwashing done by Hydra elevates her status of science genius above that of Tony Stark, Bruce Banner, and Dr. Strange.

32. Coogler, *Black Panther*.

33. Ann duCille, "The Occult of True Black Womanhood: Critical Demeanor and Black Feminist Studies," *Signs* (1994), 591.

34. Alice Walker, *In Search of Our Mothers' Gardens: Womanist Prose* (New York: Houghton Mifflin Harcourt, 1983).

35. This refers to a monologue from the Oprah Winfrey's character Ms. Sofia in Alice Walker's 1982 novel *The Color Purple*.

36. This refers to a monologue from the "Lady in Red" character from Ntozake Shange's 1976 choreopoem "For Colored Girls Who Have Considered Suicide/When the Rainbow Is Enuf."

37. This refers to a 1982 address delivered by Audre Lorde entitled "Learning from the 60s" that was later published in her 1984 collection of *Sister Outsider: Essays and Speeches by Audre Lorde*.

38. This refers to a question the character Minnie Ransom asks Velma Henry, the protagonist in Toni Cade Bambara's 1980 novel *The Salt Eaters*.

39. DuCille, *Signs*, 592.

40. Ibid.

41. Coogler, *Black Panther*.

42. Alanna Vagianos, "Ryan Coogler Would Love to See a Woman of Wakanda Spinoff," *Huffington Post*, Updated May 15, 2018, https://www.huffpost.com/entry/ryan-coogler-would-love-women-wakanda-spinoff_n_5af990f9e4b032b10bfcf692.

43. "Nnedi Okorafor: Comics."

44. Nnedi Okorafor: "#9,"*Shuri*, Marvel, 2019.

BIBLIOGRAPHY

Adinkra. "West African Wisdom: Adinkra Symbols and Meanings." Adinkra.org. Accessed June 1, 2019. http://www.adinkra.org/htmls/adinkra_index.htm.

"Adinkra—Cultural Symbols of the Asante People." Accessed June 1, 2019, http://www.stlawu.edu/gallery/education/f/09textiles/adinkra_symbols.pdf.

Agunda, Okeyo, "Wakanda: A Nation Without Chains." Progressive, February 23, 2018, https://progressive.org/dispatches/black-panther-wakanda-a-model-for-the-world-180223/.

Burton, Linda. "Childhood Adultification in Economically Disadvantaged Families: A Conceptual Model," *Family Relations* 56, no. 4 (2007): 135. https://onlinelibrary.wiley.com/doi/abs/10.1111/j.1741-3729.2007.00463.x.

Carby, Hazel. "It Jus Be's Dat Way Sometime: The Black Sexual Politics of Women's Blues," in *The Jazz Cadence of American Culture*, ed. Robert G. O'Meally. New York: Columbia University Press, 1998.

duCille, Ann. "The Occult of True Black Womanhood: Critical Demeanor and Black Feminist Studies," *Signs* (1994), 591.

Epstein, Rebecca, Jamilia J. Blake, and Thalia González, "Girlhood Interrupted: The Erasure of Black Girls' Childhood." *Georgetown Law Center on Poverty and Inequality*, 2017. Accessed May 10, 2019, https://www.law.georgetown.edu/poverty-inequality-center/wp-content/uploads/sites/14/2017/08/girlhood-interrupted.pdf.

Essence. "Essence Celebrates #BlackGirlMagic Class of 2016 on February Cover," *Essence*, January 6, 2016, https://www.essence.com/celebrity/essence-celebrates-blackgirlmagic-class-2016-february-cover/.

Gabbard, Krin. "Black Angels in America: Millennial Solutions to the 'Race Problem,'" *Black Magic: White Hollywood and African American Culture*. Piscataway: Rutgers University Press, 2004.

Goldstein, Jessica M., "Is Shuri Better off Without the Disney Princesses?" *Think Progress*, February 27, 2018. https://thinkprogress.org/wakanda-magic-kingdom-shuri-disney-princess-0b65ee1be2e2/.

Graphic Novels. "Ta-Nehisi Coates." Accessed March 10, 2019. https://ta-nehisicoates.com/graphic-novels/.

Harrison, Vashti. "Nothing but respect for my Disney princess #shuri #blackpanther @leticiawright," *@Vashtiharrison*, Instagram. February 16, 2018. https://www.instagram.com/p/BfSPS3HFuKV/.

Hill Collins, Patricia. "Mammies, Matriarchs, and Other Controlling Images," *Black Feminist Thought: Knowledge, Consciousness and the Politics of Empowerment*, New York: Routledge, 2000.

IMDb, "Angela Bassett." Accessed March 20, 2019, https://www.imdb.com/name/nm0000291/.

Marvel. "Nnedi Okorafor: Comics." Accessed March 1, 2019. https://www.marvel.com/comics/creators/13208/nnedi_okorafor.

Marvel Studios. *Captain America, Civil War*. Directed by Anthony Russo and Joe Russo, 2016, DVD.

———. *Black* Panther. Directed by Ryan Coogler, 2018, DVD.

Okorafor, Nnedi. "#9,"*Shuri*." Marvel, 2019.

Paloma. "Heroic Styles: Shuri (Black Panther)," CollegeFashion.net. Accessed May 15, 2019. https://www.collegefashion.net/inspiration/shuri-style-black-panther/.

Reign, April. "#OscarsSoWhite Is Still Relevant This Year, *Vanity Fair*, March 2, 2018, https://www.vanityfair.com/hollywood/2018/03/oscarssowhite-is-still-relevant-this-year.

———. @ReignofApril, Twitter post, *@ReignofApril*, January 23, 2018, 6:48 a.m., https://twitter.com/ReignOfApril/status/955814462920904709.

Thomas, Dexter. "Why Everyone's Saying 'Black Girls Are Magic.'" *The Los Angeles Times*, September 9, 2015. https://www.latimes.com/nation/nationnow/la-na-nn-everyones-saying-black-girls-are-magic-20150909-htmlstory.html.

Vagianos, Alanna. "Ryan Coogler Would Love to See a Woman of Wakanda Spinoff." *Huffington Post*, Updated May 15, 2018. https://www.huffpost.com/entry/ryan-coogler-would-love-women-wakanda-spinoff_n_5af990f9e4b032b10bfcf692.

Vanity Fair. "Black Panther Costume Designer Breaks Down T'Challa's Entrance Scene," *Vanity Fair videos*, May 8, 2018. https://video.vanityfair.com/watch/black-panther-s-costume-designer-breaks-down-t-challa-s-entrance-scene.

Walker, Alice. *In Search of Our Mothers' Gardens: Womanist Prose*. New York: Houghton Mifflin Harcourt, 1983.

Walt Disney Animation Studios. *Ralph Breaks the Internet*. Directed by Phil Johnston and Rich Moore, 2018. DVD.

15

Maleficent

Rape, Wrath, and the Feminine Divine

Sarah A. Clunis

Disney's 2014 film *Maleficent* was a game changer in the world of fairy tales. Not since Disney's 1996 live-action *101 Dalmations*, had Walt Disney Studio featured a villain as the lead, with Glenn Close taking on the role of Cruella de Vil. But the film was not named after Cruella, as Maleficient's was, it was named after the puppies, the subject for which the creators wanted audiences to direct their sympathies and compassion toward, and not the villainess. Thus, it was Disney's intention to make Maleficent[1] the object of audiences' attention, by offering up an anti-hero and revisiting its lack of character development around its princess villains. The words of *Maleficent*'s screenwriter Linda Woolverton indicated the objective of the film: "Let us tell an old story anew and see how well you know it."[2] This is the first line of the film.

The original personification of the villainess, Maleficent in Disney's 1969 animated film *Sleeping Beauty* is probably the most evil Disney villain ever portrayed. In the 2014 film, however, Maleficent's story is a subverted one about rape. It is in the mining of both ancient mythology and European renaissance folktales of Sleeping Beauty that we find evidence and perpetuation of a deeper more insidious culture of rape that is further aggrandized within both art history and in popular culture. This chapter marries both the social life of objects and images with the stories that illuminate their meaning. It sheds light on a number of formative tales about the feminine divine as portrayed as arrogant, evil, and defiled and grounds the phenomenon of the current #MeToo social movement as a way of reflecting on the gravitas of this iconographic comparison and how it acts as an agent of social control in the here and now.

There is no dearth of stories about rape in ancient mythology and this chapter will focus in particular on one Mesopotamian myth and a number of other related myths of antiquity that helps to elucidate Disney's iconographic depiction of the villainess, Maleficent.[3] This analysis will frame the iconography of the Mesopotamian goddess, Inanna[4] as an iconography that continues to influence the quintessential depiction of an evil feminine force in the Western world.[5] The specific hybrid iconographic properties of Mesopotamian goddesses can be compared to a variety of depictions of other ancient goddesses and other fantastic bestial hybrid beings from the ancient world. Disney's portrayal of Maleficent will demonstrate how these iconographic properties are used effectively to communicate "the fallen woman," and how this relates to current issues concerning the #MeToo social movement and its epistemological argument with the media's representation of victims of sexual assault as deceitful, wrathful, and scorned. Both in antiquity and today there are ubiquitous examples of survivors of rape exhibiting hysterical and deviant behaviors. These behaviors ultimately are used to discredit testimonies of rape, harassment, and other forms of sexual violence. We will see how these behaviors transform the female body from a body that is considered beautiful into a body that is considered grotesque, both figuratively and metaphorically.

VILLAIN-IZING WOMEN'S TRAUMA

Disney's 2014 film *Maleficent* was greeted with mixed reviews, even though it was the fourth highest grossing film of that year and Angelina Jolie's highest grossing film.[6] Discussions of the film focused on a number of issues including industry, colonization, patriarchy, and the overall exploitation of others in the name of greed. In his quest to marry the princess of the human kingdom and therefore occupy the throne, the protagonist, Stefan, seduces the benevolent fairy Maleficent and drugs her and then cuts off her glorious wings while she sleeps. When she wakes up and finds out what he has done she is at first consumed with mourning and then transformed from a trusting and powerful force of good to a wrathful, vengeful, and incredibly traumatized force of evil. The Moors, where she lives, once bright and whimsical, turn into a lacework of tangled branches, darkness, and desolation.

There is much in this tale that is both similar and familiar. But it is our current increasing social concerns about sexual violence that is most evident in the way that Maleficent was not only conceived but perceived. Both Angelina Jolie and Woolverton acknowledge that the intent of Maleficent's violation was to provide an allegory for rape within a children's film.[7] Although the film's creation and release was ahead of Hollywood's use of the #MeToo hashtag, discourse and activism around women and girl's sexual assault had already been underway, particularly in communities of color.

The #MeToo movement started in 2006 by Tarana Burke to help young women of color who were victims of sexual violence. The concept of "Me Too" was meant to emphasize the prevalence of sexual violence and to help survivors feel that they were not alone.[8] And although a movement with a focus on empathy is admirable, the fact that most survivors of sexual assault face skepticism in the public arena adds to the trauma of rape and can increase not only feelings of isolation but also of anger and mania. Survivors of sexual assault whether intoxicated, unconscious, or juvenile when the violation occurs are publicly blamed and doubted when they seek justice through many global legal systems. Emily Crockett states:

> Female hysteria is another deeply rooted stereotype, and it tells us that women can't even be trusted to know their own feelings. These stereotypes cause doctors to ignore women's symptoms of pain, and they inspire lawmakers to pass abortion waiting periods because they don't think women consider their decision carefully enough. . . . Our society . . . has created a perfect storm of reasons to dismiss rape victims.[9]

If there is one thing that the #MeToo movement has illuminated, aside from the pervasiveness of rape, it is the way that women who speak out about their rape are treated and disbelieved. Ever since 2016 in particular, the #MeToo movement has exposed the deep distrust our society has for the legitimacy of women's testimonies. All of it culminates in the observed phenomenon that women cannot be believed to either remember facts correctly or make intelligent decisions. Ultimately because of this disbelief women are considered untrustworthy, especially when it comes to making choices about their own bodies. It is instead assumed that "any explanation other than rape, however implausible, must be the correct one."[10]

All we have to do is look at the nineteenth-century example of the diagnosis of female hysteria to see how even with outstanding evidence of childhood sexual abuse, women's voices were silenced. In Freud's 1896 paper, *The Aetiology of Hysteria*,[11] we see a connection made between early childhood sexual violence and certain behaviors linked specifically to women involving anxiety, nervousness, irritability, and sexually forward behavior.[12]

We can make connections between this type of behavior exhibited by women both in the nineteenth century and today with a form of trauma that comes from sexual assault. This trauma is expressed in a form of mania that embodies both hysteria and wrath. We can also see evidence of this in mythologies of the ancient world that involve rape, abduction, and an overall violation of women's bodies.

ANCIENT MYTHOLOGIES OF MALEFICENT'S TRAUMA

Wrathful female deities in ancient Mesopotamia are evoked in cosmological stories with a number of corresponding circulated images with related iconographies. These iconographies are not exclusive to feminine deities but for our purposes we will focus on representations of Inanna, the Sumerian goddess of love, war, justice, and a plethora of other fantastic attributes. Horned, winged, and often in the company of a serpent,[13] three of the most famous Sumerian myths featuring the goddess are *Inanna's Descent into the Underworld*, *Inanna and the Huluppu Tree*, and *Inanna and Šukaletuda*. The myth that we will give the most attention to is the myth of *Inanna and Šukelatuda*, a story of the rape of Inanna followed by an ecological disaster not unlike the Demeter/Persephone myth in Ancient Greek mythology.

There are a number of ancient images of the goddess Inanna, archaeological artifacts, cylinder seals in particular, that we know for certain represent Inanna or her Akkadian counterpart Ishtar. In these images she is always represented with the same iconography featuring wings, horns, and often in the company of a lion, sometimes also a serpent. But one Mesopotamian artifact in particular, the *Burney Relief* also called *Queen of the Night* has long been the subject of dispute. Many strong arguments exist for who the Burney relief represents.[14] It has been suggested that the relief represents the demoness Lillith, the goddesses Innana, or her sister Ereshkigal, and arguments for these designations have all been eruditely explored.[15]

Thorkild Jacobsen (1987) notes in Domonique Collon's book that the *Queen of the Night Plaque* is a representation of Inanna in her role as the patron goddess of harlots. Much of Jacobsen's argument centers on the representation of the owl in the plaque.[16] Jacobsen writes:

> The Akkadian word for owl, *eššebu* corresponds to Sumerian ninna 'owl' and also to nin-ninna 'Divine Lady Owl,' that is owl goddess. This owl goddess Nin-ninna, however, is Ishtar, the Akkadian name of Inanna. Besides the translation *eššebu* 'owl' the ancient lexical texts give for Nin-ninna also *kilili* which likewise is known to be a name for Inanna/Ishtar as was shown first by Zimmerman who many years ago pointed to an incantation reading 'Exalted Lady, Kilili who has rushed at me, great Ishtar who has flung her limbs at me.[17]

Jacobsen goes on to explain that the name Kilili signifies the harlot who comes out at night just like the owl comes out at dusk. In Sumerian, Kilili

Figure 15.1. Akkadian and Funerary Siren, Myrina, 1st Century B.C. Left image: "Funerary siren raising a hand to her breast and another hand to her hair, two typical gestures of distress and mourning," Terracotta, Myrina, 1st century B.C., accessed May 25, 2019, https://commons.wikimedia.org/wiki/File:Funerary_siren_Louvre_Myr148.jpg; Right image: "Ishtar on Akkadian seals, Akkadian antiquities in the Oriental Institute Museum," Image by Sailko, accessed May 25, 2019, https://commons.wikimedia.org/wiki/File:Periodo_accadico,_sigillo_in_calcare_nero_con_ishtar_con_piede_su_schiena_di_leone_e_una_devota,_2350-2150_ac_ca.jpg.

is *Abashushu* which literally means "one who leans out of the window," as in the harlot who leans out of the bordello window beckoning customers. Jacobsen also points out that there is evidence that Inanna had an aspect of her as a goddess of harlots which is featured in a Sumerian hymn which states:

> Harlot, you go down to the alehouse
> Inanna, you are turning into one leaning
> Out of the window lifting up your voice . . .[18]

It is important then to identify the *Queen of the Night* as Inanna so that we can compare the iconography of the goddess with how Maleficent is constructed by Disney. In the original 1959 *Sleeping Beauty*, Maleficent is figured as a horned figure with a crow named Diablo for a companion. Her skin appears grayish with a green tinge and yet she is not rendered unattractive. Her character, however, is unbelievably evil. She curses an infant to likely death because she did not receive an invitation to the christening. And at the end of the film she transforms into a dragon in an attempt to murder Prince Phillip who is determined to deliver true love's kiss. No explanation is given for her evil and frankly none is needed. Her iconography is enough to explain her evil. She has horns, she has a pet raven named Diablo, and she transforms into the iconic symbol of the devil, a dragon. So, we are good. We know she's the bad guy.[19]

Inanna and Šukaletuda

In Disney's 2014 *Maleficent*, the evil fairy is portrayed as a whimsical winged and horned little girl who lives in a magical fairyland called the Moors. She sleeps in a tree and flies over the mountains overseeing the lifecycle of the Moors, ensuring that all is well. She makes friends with a greedy, stupid little human thief called Stefan and they form a life-long friendship. That is until he drugs her and violently cuts off her wings so that he can be king.

In the Mesopotamian myth, *Inanna and Šukaletuda,* Inanna is described as departing from the sky and the earth and arriving in the mountains in order to bestow justice. In a garden on earth there is a gardener Šukaletuda who is doing a terrible job of gardening. All his plants are either uprooted or dead, except for a beautiful poplar, which Inanna has fallen asleep under because she is completely exhausted from her travels. When Šukaletuda sees the goddess sleeping under the tree he is amazed at her beauty, removes her divine garments and has intercourse with her while she is sleeping.[20] When Inanna wakes up she inspects herself and understands that she has been violated and is immediately outraged asking "What should be destroyed on account of my vulva?"[21] Inanna, consumed with outrage then proceeds to "strike the land with a series of plagues filling all the wells and waterways with blood, designed to punish and force the country into revealing the person responsible for this heinous act."[22] Wells are filled with blood, then storms are set upon the land, and finally all the roadways are blocked preventing travel.[23] In each of these instances the father of Šukaletuda advices him to hide "in the city."[24] Šukaletuda is finally revealed after Inanna appeals to the god Enki and the angered goddess then sentences the gardener to death and a millennia of humiliation as his transgression will live forever in the form of this myth.[25]

The myth of *Inanna and Šukaletuda* mirrors the transformation of Maleficent after her wings have been taken from her body and she is mutilated, wounded, and outraged. The Moors become desecrated and demolished and an ecological disaster mirrors the violation of the fairy's body while she was sleeping by someone she trusts. Here, however, the violation is not one that we can specifically ascribe to lust or a wild and uncontrollable desire nor to the idle and terrible curiosity that we see with Šukaletuda. Instead, Stefan's motives are material, as were his motives as a young boy stealing things from the Moors at the beginning of the film. So, in many ways both *Maleficent* and the Inanna myth also speak of a knowing human destruction of the land that is related to rape. In fact, all of the mythological and folk tales told here tell a story of rape that ultimately leads to a second iteration of violence in some form. This recalls the most ancient of stories about the interconnectedness of the feminine divine to the earth, to sexuality, to nurturing, and to death.

From Woman to Monster

In her discussion of the depiction of female grotesques Mary Russo argues that, "The grotesque body is the open, protruding, extended secreting body, the body of becoming, process and change . . . opposed to the classical body, which is monumental static, closed, and sleek."[26] The grotesque body is the body transformed, possibly hybrid, but definitely fantastic. This body is both beast and human, offensive and frightening to the naked eye, an example of a human body that cannot contain the animal and therefore seeps. We see these human animal hybrids throughout history and in the case of the feminine form either human or divine, we often see a transformation related to the sexuality or sexual violation of the protagonist. Sex does have a way of "opening" the body, making the body protrude and secrete. The most obvious way that we equate the transformation of the female body with sex is with the progression of pregnancy but it can be observed in other ways, and with much visual and literary evidence from the ancient world, we see that there is a direct correlation or relationship between sexual violence and the transformation of women into monsters.

Tales from Ovid's *Metamorphoses*[27] and other related ancient mythologies reflect this phenomenon of monstrous transformation. Ovid tells the story of many myths in his *Metamorphoses* and the subject of rape is ubiquitous throughout the manuscript. In her analysis of this work, Nikki Bloch has this to say:

> The metamorphoses of female victims of rape in Ovid's epic are representations of the victims' emotional trauma, even for those that are able to evade rape. The metamorphoses of the male perpetrator symbolize their brutishness and unrefined power in committing acts of rape. Ovid further expounds the suffering of female victims in his depictions of victim blaming and secondary victimization at the hands of the goddess. Ovid reexamines rape in these myths in depicting the ongoing torment victims of rape endure and the inexcusable injustice of rape itself.[28]

In Hesiod's *Theogony*, he describes the first woman as a *kalon-kakon*, "a beautiful-evil thing,"[29] one who is essentially evil but is disguised by her beauty. We can see evidence of this theory in the works of other writers such as Ovid in his *Metamorphoses*, when Medusa is described by Perseus as "very lovely once," and "of all her beauties her hair most beautiful."[30] Poseidon[31] enthralled with Medusa's beauty, rapes and impregnates her as she is giving an offering in the temple of Athena. Poseidon's rape of Medusa in Athena's temple speaks of a violation of both Medusa's body and Athena's sacred space and invokes the goddess' wrath. Unable to seek vengeance on a deity as powerful as Poseidon, Athena displaces her anger on Medusa and transforms her into a snake-haired monster as a punishment. In archaic depictions of Medusa she is shown winged with serpents for hair but in later depictions her wings are added to her hair and are so tiny they almost resemble horns.

Because of her rape, Medusa is alienated from society. She is forced to live far away from any living creature that could be turned to stone by her gaze. Her personal transgression is still unclear but her tragic tale continues when the Greek hero, Perseus decapitates her with Athena's assistance, and her children, the winged stallion Pegasus and the boy Chrysaor, emerge from her neck. In Ann Stafford's 1977 poem "Medusa," the gorgon describes her own transformation after she is raped by Poseidon:

> My hair coiled in fury; my mind held hate alone. I thought of revenge, began to live on it.
> My hair turned to serpents, my eyes saw the world in stone.
> Whatever I looked at became a wasteland.[32]

The Greek goddess Demeter has an eerily similar story as Medusa. While she is desperately searching for her missing daughter Persephone, she too is pursued by the lustful Poseidon. She transforms into a mare to escape him and Poseidon then transforms into a horse in order to rape her. After Poseidon's violation, Demeter becomes wrathful and chthonic and in this form she is worshipped in the form of an *Erinys*,[33] and is described in multiple sources as a monster with serpent-hair.

After her rape Demeter gives birth to a horse deity, Areon and a daughter, Despoina.[34] We can speculate that possibly the story of Medusa is the same as the myth of Demeter-Erinys, the snake-haired goddess, in her Arcadian form, whom Poseidon raped resulting in the birth of twin children, one of them a horse. Demeter's wrath is most often discussed as a symbol of the destructive aspect of nature, exemplified during the fruitless winter and is rationalized as either anger for her own rape or anger at the rape and abduction of her daughter, Persephone, by Hades.[35] In terms of iconography, Demeter herself has no wings but she transforms Persephone's handmaidens, the sirens, into winged beings in order to find her daughter after she is abducted by Hades.

In Ovid's *Metamorphoses*, the story of Philomela, Procne, and Tereus is terrifying in its brutality. After Philomela is brutally raped by Tereus, her sister Procne's husband, she threatens to expose what he has done. Tereus then cuts out her tongue and rapes her again to silence her. With vengeance and wrath Procne kills her son by Tereus, Itys and feeds him to Tereus, in an act of gruesome infanticide and cannibalism. All these protagonists are consumed with rage and anger and as Tereus chases the sisters they are transformed into birds. These physical transformations of woman into animal or hybrid entities work as metaphors for the transformation of a woman into a hysterical, angry, vengeful and ultimately wicked creature. Rape therefore can be seen as a catalyst for the release of the most base and animalistic qualities in a human being (or goddess), all of which constitute a transformation into the monstrous.

Renaissance Era

In the rebirth of the ancient world, the Renaissance, we find that the original Sleeping Beauty tale surprisingly features elements of rape and infanticide as well. In Giambatista Basile's *The Pentameron*[36] a story entitled, *Sun, Moon and Talia* tells the tale of the birth of a baby girl, Talia, whose father receives a dire prophecy that she would be put in grave danger from a splinter of flax. As a result her father, a great lord, forbids any flax be brought into their home. As a young woman, however, Talia sees a spindle in the hands of a passing peddler, an old woman who offers it to the girl to inspect as she had never seen such an instrument before.

Immediately a splinter of flax pierces the skin under her nail and she falls into a deep sleep from which she cannot be roused. Struck with grief, Talia's father turns one of his country mansions in the woods into her tomb and closes the doors and abandons his daughter forever. Sometime later, a king from a nearby kingdom out on a hunt discovers Talia in the house. He does his best to wake her and finding her unmovable but still entranced by her beauty he makes love to her while she is asleep. The story says as much when Basile writes:

> ... and he called her but she remained unconscious. Crying aloud, he beheld her charms and felt his blood course hotly through his veins. He lifted her in his arms and carried her to a bed, where he gathered the first fruits of love. Leaving her on the bed, he returned to his own kingdom, where in the pressing business of his realm, he for a time thought no more about the incident.[37]

So after nine months Talia miraculously gives birth to twins, aided by two fairies and in an attempt to nurse from her breast the newborns instead suck on her fingers and dislodge the splinter which awakens Talia. The king suddenly remembers Talia and hurries to the woods only to find her with the two babies and is overjoyed. The king's wife finds out about his other family and scorned and furious she sends an order to invite the children (Sun and Moon) to the castle where she orders the cook to make the children into several delicious dishes, which she will feed to the king. The cook hides the children and prepares two lambs instead and the king exclaims at how deliciously prepared the meal is.[38] The Queen then makes plans to murder Talia by throwing her into a fire even while Talia protests that "it was not her fault because the king had taken possession of her territory when she was drowned in sleep." The story continues with the king throwing his ill-intentioned wife into the fire, rewarding the cook, and marrying Talia, where of course everybody is presumed to live happily ever after. The story ends with the following proverb:

> Those whom fortune favors
> Find good luck even in their sleep.[39]

The nineteenth century Brothers Grimm version of Sleeping Beauty, *Little Brier-Rose* (1812),[40] is what the original Disney animated film *Sleeping Beauty* is based on. This version does not include either the evil ogress or the cannibalism of the Basile or the Perrault (1697) tales quite possibly because the death of children has no place in fairy tales.[41] While the Basile tale is both grotesque and unrealistic, both the Grimm *Brier Rose* fairy tale and Disney's *Sleeping Beauty* also feature an unconscious woman kissed without consent which continues to provide a problematic example of romantic engagement for children.[42]

CONCLUSION

Disney's *Maleficent* is a tale of ecological disaster, imperialism, and colonization, hunger, haughtiness, and greed all perpetrated by an age-old tale involving sexual assault, infanticide, and monstrous transformation. Ultimately this is a tale about the betrayal of goodness and an acceptance of evil as appropriate coping mechanisms for trauma. But this tale is transforming, because what *Maleficent* does do is exemplify the way that women, like nature, are cast as something broken that can be fixed by power and ownership. Unless they refuse to be "fixed," they instead become monstrous, a metamorphosis catalyzed by rape.

Ancient mythologies suggest that a woman can be blamed for her rape because of her beauty, she in turn becomes a *casus belli* as in the case of Helen of Troy or even Philomela (because what is an act of infanticide if not an allegorical act of war?). But ultimately war is caused not by beauty but by *atë*, the Greek word for folly, mania, madness, and possession. It is a word that implies a blind infatuation, a rashness and ruin, a disaster which consumes both victim and agent where both the crime and the punishment are the same. The scholar Michael Kinnucan in his discussion of the house of Atreus in Greek mythology states:

> . . . *atë* consumes everything it touches; it renders both victim and criminal unclean, it erases the distinction between avenger and avenged, between aggressor and victim. Atreus' crime is so terrible that neither he nor his enemy will live it down. Such acts will not be forgotten, will not exhaust themselves in the moment of action; they expand outward to contaminate observers, bloodlines, cities.[43]

It is not the victims of rape that ultimately embody this madness and mania that fuels their transformation into monsters. It is ultimately the perpetrators of sexual violence that engage with *atë* and it is their impulse and folly that affects our transformative potentials still. An act of rape is the *casus belli* and the war it ignites is a perfect storm indeed.

Five thousand years ago the poet who wrote *Inanna and Šukaletuda* knew this when he embedded an allegory for the planet Venus' movements across the sky into his prose. When we are not careful with our actions, deliberate and gentle with our intentions, both with the earth and with other human beings, we create monsters.

And these monsters do not sleep.

NOTES

1. Maleficent, Walt Disney Pictures film still, 2014, accessed May 20, 2019, https://www.awn.com/vfxworld/mpc-brings-us-magic-maleficent.

2. Kevin Fallon, "The 'Maleficent' Screenwriter Also Wrote 'The Lion King' and 'Beauty and the Beast,'" *The Daily Beast*, updated July 12, 2017, https://www.thedailybeast.com/the-maleficent-screenwriter-also-wrote-the-lion-king-and-beauty-and-the-beast.

3. Both in the original animated movie, *Sleeping Beauty* (1959), as well as in the live-action film *Maleficent* (2014).

4. Inanna is also known as Ishtar, sometimes Astarte. The myths and visual representations of her featured in this chapter are also attributed to the other goddesses with subtle differences. Analysis of those differences is beyond the scope of this chapter and therefore for clarity, she will always be referred to as Inanna. The spelling of her name in various writings about her also differs. I have maintained one spelling throughout.

5. Reasons for Inanna's iconography, functioning as an iconography for evil, are manifold. She was much-loved by the Sumerians and Mesopotamian cultures in general and there is much evidence for this. She is also feared as a deity that is easily angered and that provokes warfare, but she becomes maligned primarily through the Bible in her form of Astarte (also translated as Astoreth) and in references to her as the "Queen of Heaven," (Jeremiah) where when she is worshipped she evokes the wrath of God (see Kings, Samuel, Judges).

6. Box Office Mojo, "Angelina Jolie," accessed May 1, 2019, https://www.boxofficemojo.com/people/chart/?view=Actor&id=angelinajolie.htm.

7. Nina Bahadur, "Angelina Jolie: 'Maleficent' Scene Is a 'Metaphor for Rape,'" *Huffington Post*, June 11, 2014, https://www.huffpost.com/entry/angelina-jolie-maleficent-rape-scene_n_5485633.

8. Sandra E. Garcia, "The Woman Who Created #MeToo Long before Hashtags," *The New York Times*, October 20, 2017, accessed June 12, 2019. https://www.nytimes.com/2017/10/20/us/me-too-movement-tarana-burke.html.

9. Emily Crockett, "Rape and Sexual Assault Are Common. So Why Don't We Believe Victims?" *Vox*, October 17, 2016, accessed June 27, 2019, https://www.vox.com/2016/5/1/1153848/belive-rape-victims.

10. Ibid.

11. Sigmund Freud, "The Aetiology of Hysteria," in *The Standard Edition of the Complete Psychological Works of Sigmund Freud, Volume III (1893–1899)*, 187–221 (Early Psycho-Analytic Publications, 1962).

12. Frank Sulloway, *Freud, Biologist of the Mind: Beyond the Psychoanalytic Legend* (Cambridge, MA: Harvard University Press, 1992), 513–515.

13. These images, based on date and location, most likely represent Ishtar, the name of Inanna in Akkadian.

14. See Pauline Albenda (2005), Dominique Collon (2005, 2007), and Thorkild Jacobsen (1987), among others, but these scholars provide the strongest arguments.

15. In the Sumerian poem, *The Descent of Inanna* (1900–1600 BCE) when Inanna arrives at the gates of the underworld, she is required to shed one item of her royal garment at each gate. By the time she reaches the throne room of her sister Ereshkigal, she is completely naked. It is probably in this state that she is represented on the *Burney Relief* and if not a representation of her, then it is most likely a representation of her sister, Ereshkigal, queen of the underworld, holding two

rod and ring symbols (one of which would have been taken from Inanna during her descent. See Jacobsen (1987) for alternate theory.

16. Interestingly enough the owls are what Albenda argues are reason to believe that the plaque is indeed not authentic because of the lack of owl symbolism found in Mesopotamian art, as well as the absence of skill in their rendering. See Pauline Albenda, "The 'Queen of the Night' Plaque: A Revisit," *Journal of the American Oriental Society*, 125, no. 2 (Apr.–Jun., 2005): 171–190. It is also important to note here that Assyriologist Niek Veldhuis argues that the *eššebu* is more likely a harrier, and not an owl. For this discussion see Niek Veldhuis, *Religion, Literature and Scholarship: The Sumerian Composition Nanše and the Birds* (Leiden: Brill/Styx, 2004), 272–274.

17. Thorkild Jacobson, "Pictures and Pictorial Language (The Burney Relief)" in *Figurative Language in the Ancient Near East*, edited by M. Mindlin, M. J. Geller, and J. E. Wansbrough (London: School of Oriental and African Studies, University of London, 1987), 4.

The original reference was published by Zimmern OLZ 31, 1928 1ff. The passage was published by Ebeling MVAG 23/2, 22 line 45.

18. Ibid, 19.

19. Maleficent's transformation into a dragon in *Sleeping Beauty* and then Diaval's transformation into a dragon in *Maleficent* can be related to other myths of Inanna where both her and her consort Dumuzid are called *ama-ushumgal-an-na*, "the mother is a great serpent of heaven." See Walter R. Mattfeld, *The Garden of Eden Myth: Its Pre-Biblical Origin in Mesopotamian Myths* (Lulu.com, 2010).

20. Jeffrey L. Cooley, "Inanna and Šukaletuda: A Sumerian Astral Myth," *KASKAL: Rivista di storia, ambientie culture del Vicino Oriente Antico*, 5 (2008): 162.

21. Judy Grahn, "Ecology of the Erotic in the Myth of Inanna," *International Journal of Transpersonal Studies*, 29, no. 2 (2010): 60.

22. Cooley, "Inanna and Šukaletuda."

23. Judy Grahn has suggested that all of these actions are related to cultural taboos during a woman's menstrual cycle in the Sumerian culture. See Grahn, 62.

24. Cooley, 162.

25. Ibid., 163.

26. Mary Russo, "Female Grotesques: Carnival and Theory," in *Feminist Studies/Critical Studies*, edited by Teresa de Lauretis (London: Macmillan, 1988), 219.

27. Ovid, *Metamorphoses*.

28. Nikki Bloch, "Patterns of Rape in Ovid's Metamorphoses," *Undergraduate Honors Theses* (Colorado: unpublished, 2014), Abstract, 2, accessed May 30, 2019, https://scholar.colorado.edu/honr_theses/48.

29. Bettany Hughes, "Would You Be Beautiful in the Ancient World," *BBC.com*, January 10, 2015, https://www.bbc.com/news/magazine-30746985.

30. It should be noted that Ovid gives a sympathetic view of the rape of women in *Metamorphoses*. Bloch, 36.

31. The original retelling of the myth by Ovid used the Roman equivalents of Poseidon and Athena, which are Neptune and Minerva respectively. For clarity, I am keeping the Greek names instead of the Roman designations.

32. Maxine Scates and David Trinidad (editors), *Holding Our Own: The Selected Poems of Ann Stanford* (Port Townsend, Washington: Copper Canyon Press, 2001), 114.

33. She is worshipped in this form in the region of Arcadia. "Erinyes 5," Theoi .com, accessed May 30, 2019, https://www.theoi.com/Khthonios/Erinyes5.html.

34. Pausanias, *Pausanias Description of Greece with and English Translation by W. H. S. Jones, Litt. D., and H. A. Ormerod, M. A, in 4 Volumes* (reprint Cambridge, MA: Harvard University Press; London: William Heinemann Ltd., 1918), 8.25.3 and 8.42.1.

35. Ibid.

36. Giambattista Basile, *The Pentameron* (London: Spring Brooks, 1955), accessed June 22, 2019, http://www.pitt.edu/~dash/type0410.html#basile, 2.

37. Giambattista Basile, *The Pentameron*, 2.

38. All the time his wife murmurs, "Eat, eat, you are eating your own," Giambattista Basile, *The Pentameron*, 3.

39. Ibid., 4.

40. Jacob Grimm and Wilhelm Grimm, *Kinder-und Hausmarchen*, First Edition, volume 1, no 50 (Berlin: Realschulbuchhandlung, 1812): 225–229.

41. It is interesting to note, however, that the Grimm Brothers did include these elements in their tale of Hansel and Gretel, including both evil stepmother and cannibalistic witch, intending to eat children.

42. Snow White also gets kissed while she is unconscious and Belle in *Beauty and the Beast* (2017) is kidnapped and held captive.

43. Michael Kinnucan, "Incest, Cannibalism and the Goods: The Rise of the House of Atreus," *Hypocrite Reader*, 4; "The Progress of Memory," May 2011, accessed July 1, 2019. http://hypocritereader.com/4/incest-cannibalism-and-the-gods.

BIBLIOGRAPHY

Albenda, Pauline. "The 'Queen of the Night' Plaque: A Revisit." *Journal of the American Oriental Society* 125, no. 2 (Apr.–Jun., 2005): 171–190.

Bahadur, Nina. "Angelina Jolie: 'Maleficent' Scene Is a 'Metaphor for Rape.'" *Huffington Post*, June 11, 2014. https://www.huffpost.com/entry/angelina-jolie-maleficent-rape-scene_n_5485633.

Basile, Giambattista. *The Pentameron*. London: Spring Brooks, 1955. Accessed June 22, 2019, http://www.pitt.edu/~dash/type0410.html#basile.

Bloch, Nikki. "Patterns of Rape in Ovid's Metamorphoses." Undergraduate Honors Theses. Colorado: unpublished. 2014. Accessed May 30, 2019. https://scholar.colorado.edu/honr_theses/48.

Box Office Mojo. "Angelina Jolie." Accessed May 1, 2019, https://www.boxofficemojo.com/people/chart/?view=Actor&id=angelinajolie.htm.

Cooley, Jeffrey L. "Inanna and Šukaletuda: A Sumerian Astral Myth," *KASKAL: Rivista di storia, ambientie culture del Vicino Oriente Antico*, 5 (2008): 162.

Crockett, Emily. "Rape and Sexual Assault Are Common. So Why Don't We Believe Victims?" *Vox*, October 17, 2016. Accessed June 27, 2019. https://www.vox.com/2016/5/1/1153848/belive-rape-victims.

"Erinyes 5," Theoi.com. Accessed May 30, 2019. https://www.theoi.com/Khthonios/Erinyes5.html.

Fallon, Kevin. "The 'Maleficent' Screenwriter Also Wrote 'The Lion King' and 'Beauty and the Beast,'" *The Daily Beast*, Updated July 12, 2017, https://www.thedailybeast.com/the-maleficent-screenwriter-also-wrote-the-lion-king-and-beauty-and-the-beast.

Freud, Sigmund. "The Aetiology of Hysteria," in *The Standard Edition of the Complete Psychological Works of Sigmund Freud, Volume III (1893-1899)*, 187–221. Early Psycho-Analytic Publications, 1962.

Garcia, Sandra E. "The Woman Who Created #MeToo Long before Hashtags." *The New York Times*, October 20, 2017. Accessed June 12, 2019. https://www.nytimes.com/2017/10/20/us/me-too-movement-tarana-burke.html.

Grahn, Judy. "Ecology of the Erotic in the Myth of Inanna." *International Journal of Transpersonal Studies* 29, no. 2 (2010): 60.

Grimm, Jacob, and Wilhelm Grimm. *Kinder-und Hausmarchen*. First Edition 1, no. 50. Berlin: Realschulbuchhandlung, 1812.

Hughes, Bettany. "Would You Be Beautiful in the Ancient World," *BBC.com*, January 10, 2015. https://www.bbc.com/news/magazine-30746985.

"Ishtar on Akkadian Seals." Akkadian Antiquities in the Oriental Institute Museum. Accessed May 25, 2019, https://commons.wikimedia.org/wiki/File:Periodo_accadico,_sigillo_in_calcare_nero_con_ishtar_con_piede_su_schiena_di_leone_e_una_devota,_2350-2150_ac_ca.jpg.

Jacobson, Thorkild. "Pictures and Pictorial Language (The Burney Relief)." In *Figurative Language in the Ancient Near East*. Edited by M. Mindlin, M. J. Geller, and J. E. Wansbrough. London: School of Oriental and African Studies, University of London, 1987.

Kinnucan, Michael. "Incest, Cannibalism and the Goods: The Rise of the House of Atreus," *Hypocrite Reader*, 4, "The Progress of Memory," May 2011. Accessed July 1, 2019. http://hypocritereader.com/4/incest-cannibalism-and-the-gods.

Mattfeld, Walter R. *The Garden of Eden Myth: Its Pre-Biblical Origin in Mesopotamian Myths*. Lulu.com, 2010.

Ovid. *Metamorphoses*. 1, 8 AD. A.C.E. Accessed July 30, 2019 http://classics.mit.edu/Ovid/metam.html.

Pausanias. *Pausanias Description of Greece with and English Translation by W. H. S. Jones, Litt. D., and H. A. Ormerod, M. A, in 4 Volumes*. Reprint Cambridge, MA: Harvard University Press; London: William Heinemann Ltd., 1918.

Russo, Mary. "Female Grotesques: Carnival and Theory." In *Feminist Studies/Critical Studies*. Edited by Teresa de Lauretis. London: Macmillan, 1988.

Scates, Maxine, and David Trinidad (Eds.). *Holding Our Own: The Selected Poems of Ann Stanford*. Port Townsend, Washington: Copper Canyon Press, 2001.

Sulloway, Frank. *Freud, Biologist of the Mind: Beyond the Psychoanalytic Legend*. Cambridge, MA: Harvard University Press, 1992, 513–515.

Terracotta, Myrina, 1st century B.C. Accessed May 25, 2019, https://commons.wikimedia.org/wiki/File:Funerary_siren_Louvre_Myr148.jpg.

The Pentameron of Giambattista Basile. Translated Richard F. Burton (privately printed 1893) Day 5, Tale 5. Accessed May 30, 2019, http://www.pitt.edu/~dash/type0410.html#basile.

Veldhuis, Niek. *Religion, Literature and Scholarship: The Sumerian Composition Nanše and the Birds*. Leiden: Brill/Styx, 2004.

IV

EMBEDDING SOCIAL DISCOURSE AROUND THE DISNEY HEROINE

16

Disney's Social Consciousness

Explaining #BlackLivesMatter through Zootopia

Ahli Chatters and Shearon Roberts

In 2016, Walt Disney Animation Studios released *Zootopia*. The film adopts the easily recognizable and accessible traits that have become Disney's successful animation formula. It also departs from this formula in its problematized exploration of race, marginalization, and otherness in what is supposed to be a utopic society. This chapter critically examines *Zootopia*, and argues that the film is part of a socially conscious, narrative evolution by Disney Animation Studios in a post–Walt Disney Revival era. In correcting historical overlooks in earlier Disney Animation works, particularly on the treatment of race and society, *Zootopia* goes beyond the recent releases in the 2000s of Disney Animation films where the journeys of female protagonists are not merely love stories but critical encounters with realism that asks tough questions about the world around them. In this chapter, we de-construct both characterization and narrative in *Zootopia* to examine how Disney employed anthropomorphism for teaching children and families, Disney's primary audience, about #BlackLivesMatter, as a naive police officer bunny wrestled with prejudice, bias, and stereotyping for those she considered "others."

DISNEY ANIMATIONS' SECOND RENAISSANCE

The Disney Golden Age set the standard for the Disney princess, beginning with *Snow White and the Seven Dwarfs*, where a princess sings that "some day her prince will come." This era reflected the aesthetic of the studio's founder Walt Disney.[1] With the death of both Disney brothers

Walt and Roy, the studio lost its way, produced an era of box office flops described by scholars as a dark age for the studio.[2] The successful Renaissance era followed (1989–1999; from *The Little Mermaid* and *Beauty and the Beast*, to *Pocahontas* and *The Lion King*). As much as the studio returned to its aesthetic acclaim and box office records, critics deplore depictions of race, gender, class, and society.[3] Scholars noted that the studio sought to delve into realism in its narratives in the era that followed, but that those works, *Dinosaur* (2000) to *Meet the Robinsons* (2007), for example, seemed obscure, did not resonate with audiences, or lacked a coherent feel to the brand, as it did during the Renaissance period.[4] Disney's films during the early 2000s did however show early signs of the studio's desire to experiment with storytelling, both technically and in narrative.[5] Despite Disney animation's lack of dominance at the box office in the early 2000s, the studio laid the groundwork for an aesthetic and narrative comeback.

Zootopia is a product of this evolution that began in the early 2000s. It merged the successful creative efforts of the studio's comeback Renaissance era with films like *The Lion King* (1994), with the critical narratives of the post-Renaissance era that failed to catch on at the box office. *Zootopia*'s strong social critique advances this shift in this current era taking audiences out of fairy-tale worlds[6] into a modern backdrop like *Big Hero 6* (2014) another contemporary narrative in the current Disney era. And while *Big Hero 6* features diverse characters in a good-versus-evil story arch that examines the purpose and uses of science, *Zootopia*'s modern story delves deeper into a larger social critique of our modern world.

Both the narrative and the character arches of *Zootopia* are a turning point for Disney Animations, because of its explicit and implicit treatment of diversity, specifically of race and race relations in its story line. It reflects a social consciousness brewing in Disney's creative forces that reflects the reality of the times. For *Zootopia*, audiences meet a naïve cop bunny and a sly, street-smart fox, with a criminal record. Both sides do not trust each other, come from different worlds that reinforce their otherness and distrust for animals not like them. *Zootopia*'s story line allows both crime and politics headlines: from Trayvon Martin's death and other young Black men like him to bleed into its plot.

Disney's legacy of influencing cultural norms has been well documented by scholars, particularly its moral of "happily ever after."[7] *Zootopia* peels away at the "happily ever after" world, that seems fine on the surface, but plagued by injustices and suspicions. In examining *Zootopia*, we outline precisely how Disney attempts to achieve this in its current revival, on the issue of race.

RACE AND DIVERSITY IN THE DISNEY ANIMATED FILM

Disney Animations classics have had diverse leads, but scholars have critiqued the racist representations of heroines, sidekicks, and villains.[8] While some of these films are still remembered for their racist elements, the company took a new creative turn in the 1990s, producing four animated features depicting racial otherness: *Aladdin* (1992), *The Lion King* (1994), *Pocahontas* (1995), and *Mulan* (1998).[9]

Scholars noted that Disney's attempts early on at diverse representations was more an exercise in multiculturalism that was politically correct, than it was a case of critical race representations.[10] It was also diversity without inclusion. Disney plays a powerful role in constructing hierarchies around racial identity.[11] In establishing "constructs related to gender, race, ethnicity, class and sexuality, Disney reigns supreme, and part of that supreme reign is an unquestionable privilege of patriarchy and whiteness."[12]

This is why *Zootopia*'s narrative and characterization is worthy of study. It attracts the typical Disney audience with the promise of high quality entertainment that becomes a social classroom that addresses political correctness.

Teaching #BlackLivesMatter in *Zootopia* through Anthropomorphism

The Black Lives Matter movement became a globally known hashtag when George Zimmerman was acquitted in July 2013 in the shooting death of Trayvon Martin. In a tweet shared between two of the three women behind the movement, the hashtag #BlackLivesMatter was first used. Alicia Garza, one of the three founders of the movement, wrote of that moment in an edited volume that "it was a response to the anti-Black racism that permeates out society."[13]

> Black Lives Matter is an ideological and political intervention in a world where Black lives are systematically and intentionally targeted for demise. It is an affirmation of Black folks' contributions to this society, our humanity, and our resilience in the face of deadly oppression.[14]

Garza called the movement one that connected people against injustice and one that "created space for the celebration and humanization of Black lives." In using social media, the movement's leaders could speak and organize in a way that a new generation did and understood.[15] #BlackLivesMatter was not only about shootings or fear of unarmed young Black men, but rooted in these shootings and suspicion, it was a rallying cry that called attention to the wider, systematic—seen and unseen—discrimination, isolation, and fear of Blackness and Black lives.

#BlackLivesMatter sought to humanize Black people in America. And in reducing its characters to animals in *Zootopia*, who possessed anthropomorphic features, *Zootopia* presented viewers with an apt view of how as humans, we do not always see the humanity in each other. Instead, we as humans resort to primal instincts, distinguishing ourselves through sensory fear of our differences, masked by our shared agreement that in a society, we must be civil. But in being civil we fail to see how our society had become siloed. As Garza writes "suddenly, we began to come across varied adaptations of our work—all lives matter, brown lives matter, migrant lives matter, women's lives matter, and on and on."[16] The movement saw itself in solidarity with others fighting discrimination or other forms of oppression and marginalization.[17] But it saw the movement as lifting up society as a whole, that "when black people get free, everybody gets free."[18] For in having an open, progressive look at the state of Black lives, Garza wrote that "our collective future depends on it."[19]

This is not to assume that the creators of *Zootopia* explicitly set out to make a film about #BlackLivesMatter, but the script underwent its biggest narrative change around November 2014, with only a year to go before the film's release. *Zootopia*'s creators initially had decided to have fox Nick Wilde as the lead character with Judy Hopps as the secondary lead character. This had been the plan for years over the life of the film's development. In one interview, *Zootopia*'s director Byron Howard explained this change.

> We're telling a story about bias, and when you have the Nick character starting the movie, through his eyes the city was already broken. . . . He didn't like Zootopia. . . . We asked 'What are we saying with the movie?' If we're telling this movie about bias—something that is everywhere and in all of us, whether we want to admit it or not—the character that's going to help us tell that message is Judy, an innocent, [who comes] from a very supportive environment where she thinks everyone is beautiful, everyone gets along. . . . Then let Nick, this character who knows the truth about the world, bop up against her and they start to educate each other. When we flipped that, it was a major flip, but it worked so much better.[20]

The directors of the film were also sensitive to the approach to the movie, working to ensure the narrative's key themes of "inclusion and harmony" gelled with creative aesthetics that make Disney films appealing and successful at the box office. In masking key characters in anthropomorphic disguise, the film's creators also employed a tested

Disney technique in creative storytelling: the character journey.[21] Director Howard noted in the interview that:

> We never wanted this to be a message movie. We always wanted it to be this great piece of entertainment, great emotion, great storytelling, but it's never, ever supposed to be in-your-face with the message of the movie. Just letting Judy learn that and seeing her progress grow and grow, it became sort of a personal story between the two of them and helped us in a huge way.[22]

Regardless of whether *Zootopia's* directors and writers intended to create an overt "message movie," scholars who look back at the impact of successful Disney animations point to both the characters and the narratives affecting popular culture, particularly among its youngest audiences.[23] In describing animations as "agents of socialization" scholars[24] view animations as "'portable professors' of a sort, offering diagnoses of culture for adults even as they enculturate children."

In reading #BlackLivesMatter in *Zootopia*, we implore Henry Giroux and Grace Pollack's view of the messages embedded in animations as "regulating culture."[25] Giroux and Pollack added that animated movies have transcended cinema to resonate within our popular culture as an "educational force" about our values and our norms and explains what it means to be "male, female, white, black, citizen and noncitizen."[26] In calling animation "edutainment" Giroux equates the animated movie to that of traditional teaching with its technological aspects having transformative staying power with the receiver, mainly young audiences.

In examining the "educational force" of *Zootopia*, we are guided by Janet Wasko's examination of approaches to interpreting Disney animation content in her 2001 work *Understanding Disney*.[27] Scholars have either conducted a political economic analysis of Disney products or a cultural analysis of Disney products.[28] In interpreting the political economic impact of a Disney film, Wasko points to a "systems approach" in which scholarship looks at both the production and consumption of a film.[29]

For the purpose of reading #BlackLivesMatter, we have acknowledged some of the creative process above and next take a cultural analysis approach. Although Wasko has cautioned that such a reading, without an examination of political economic factors is subjective, we have outlined above how the creators of *Zootopia* were as much interested in blockbuster success as they were in enshrouding a "message movie" with technological achievements in animation and aesthetic achievements in storytelling. Therefore, we wish to uncover the message buried within this subversive film to examine to what degree Disney exhibited a measure of social consciousness in "edutainment" that provides lessons about race and race relations.

READING *ZOOTOPIA*: A CRITICAL ANALYSIS APPROACH

Wasko outlined four areas that are signature to the Disney animation and that have been examined in readings of films.[30] These are style, story, characters, and themes/values. Style is Disney's use of music, light entertainment, and humor, while story is Disney's use of folklore and fairy tales or well-used Hollywood cinematic models. Character treatments in Disney films are anthropomorphic animals, heroes, villains, and sidekicks, as well as the studio's interpretations of race and gender. Finally Disney classic themes have typically included mainstream American values: fantasy, innocence, romance, and good versus evil.[31]

Therefore we examined the characters' stereotypes in tandem with the narrative themes of each scene. We adapted Smith's[32] coding sheet for characters and scenes from Katz and Braly's work on stereotype research.[33] Character traits like (jovial, ignorant, deceitful, lazy, athletic, musical, and aggressive) originally identified in Katz and Braly's work, are often stereotypical depictions for black characters.[34] Traits such as (intelligent, honest, industrious, loud, witty, and arrogant) are often not associated with African American characters.[35]

In our analysis, we identify first how character traits are represented in various scenes for six acts in *Zootopia* using this construct for stereotype research. Secondly, we examine the context in which these traits are presented in the scenes for each act. Therefore, we do not merely present whether *Zootopia's* creators use racial stereotypes, but we contextualize the use of these stereotypes for a larger understanding of the work's themes and values. Finally, we identify discourse on #BlackLivesMatter by characters in the various scenes of the six acts.

ANALYSIS AND DISCUSSION

Zootopia's Characterization

The film was divided into main story arches (acts) as outlined in Table 16.2. The full definition for each character trait can be found in Smith's coding sheet.[36] For this content analysis we focused on the main characters for scenes in each act of the film. Table 2 lists characters in the order they were introduced. The coding of character traits also demonstrates that the film's first three acts maintain traditional stereotypes for characters. As the film's plot reaches its turning point around the fourth act, character traits begin to swap among different groups. Officer Judy Hopps' portrayal was characterized by her intellect and determination to succeed as a police officer, while fox Nick Wilde was characterized as

Table 16.1. The Development of Main Character Traits in Zootopia

	Act 1 Description Timecode	Act 2 Description Timecode	Act 3 Description Timecode	Act 4 Description Timecode	Act 5 Description Timecode	Act 6 Description Timecode
	Judy's Childhood 0:00–5:48	Judy Becomes a Police Officer 5:49–21:43	Judy catches Weaselton 21:44–30:37	Search for Otterton 30:38–57:43	Predator vs Prey 57:44–1:17:05	Reuniting Zootopia 1:17:06–1:36:08 (before credits)

Characterizations

Main Characters						
Judy Hopps	Intelligent, industrious	Industrious	Industrious	Intelligent, Industrious	Ignorant/Naive	Witty
Gideon Grey	Aggressive/ Quick-tempered					Honest
Stu Hopps	Ignorant/Naive	Ignorant/Naive	Ignorant/Naive			Honest
Bonnie Hopps	Ignorant/Naive	Ignorant/Naive	Ignorant/Naive			Honest
Drill Sgt. Polar Bear		Loud/Talkative				
Mayor Lionheart		Arrogant/ Boastful			Deceitful/ Lawbreaking/ Dishonest	Honest
Assistant Mayor Bellwether		Honest		Jovial/ Happy	Industrious	Deceitful/ Lawbreaking/ Dishonest
Officer Clawhauser		Jovial/Happy		Jovial/Happy	Sad/Defeated	Jovial/Happy

(continued)

Table 16.1. (continued)

	Act 1 Description Timecode	Act 2 Description Timecode	Act 3 Description Timecode	Act 4 Description Timecode	Act 5 Description Timecode	Act 6 Description Timecode
	Judy's Childhood 0:00–5:48	Judy Becomes a Police Officer 5:49–21:43	Judy catches Weaselton 21:44–30:37	Search for Otterton 30:38–57:43	Predator vs Prey 57:44–1:17:05	Reuniting Zootopia 1:17:06–1:36:08 (before credits)

Main Characters | | | *Characterizations* | | | |

Police Chief Bogo		Aggressive/ Quick-tempered		Aggressive/ Quick-Tempered	Honest	
Nick Wilde			Deceitful/ Lawbreaking/ Dishonest	Witty	Honest	Intelligent/Witty
Finnick			Deceitful/ Lawbreaking/ Dishonest	Deceitful/ Lawbreaking/ Dishonest		
Duke Weaselton			Deceitful/ Lawbreaking/ Dishonest			Honest
Mrs. Otterton				Honest		
Yax				Honest		
Flash				Jovial/Happy		
Mr. Big				Helpful		
Renato Manchas				Aggressive/ Quick-tempered/ Argumentative		
Gazelle					Honest	

Table prepared by Shearon Roberts

being a deceitful lawbreaker. As the two character's paths converge to solve a disappearance of Mr. Emmitt Otterton, their character traits begin to swap. Judy Hopps displays her ignorance and naiveté about people, while it is Nick Wilde who is trustworthy, loyal, and industrious to support Judy in solving this case.

Among characters who held office in Zootopia (politicians): Mayor Lionheart and Assistant Mayor Bellwether, Lionheart is portrayed as a stereotypical dominant alpha politician who is boastful and brash. While Bellwether appears trustworthy, fighting for noble causes like more diverse representation in the police force through supporting Judy Hopps' quest to become an officer. However, as the story reaches its resolution, we learn that the politician who seemed initially to be supportive of noble causes was in fact a deceitful character and that Judy Hopps had misread Mayor Lionheart.

Zootopia's Discourse

In the first act we learn about the world that Judy Hopps is socialized in as we are introduced to Gideon Grey with a rural country accent, wearing overalls. This world is distinct as a backdrop on the school stage showcases the sparkling slogan "Zootopia! Where anyone can be anything." Judy's parents actively discourage her from her future goals as she wears a police officer costume at the farmer's market. Judy spies trouble and pursues Gideon and his friend Travis, out of suspicion. She is attacked by Gideon, whose claws scratch across her face. Judy and her two sheep friends cower as victims, helpless from the attack by Gideon. This is the foundation of Judy's interpretation of who is hostile (fox) and who is not (sheep).

We see early on discourse surrounding #BlackLivesMatter. In the first few minutes of the film, social differences are established, and fear of difference is explained as Judy narrates during her performance for her school play that

> Fear, treachery, blood, lust. Thousands of years ago, these were the forces that rule our world. A world where prey were scared of predators, and predators had an uncontrollable, biological urge to maim, and maul, and . . . Blood, blood, blood![37]

Judy continues:

> Back then, the world was divided into two. Vicious predator or meek prey. But over time, we evolved. And moved beyond our primitive, savage ways. Now predator and prey live in harmony. And every young mammal has multitudinous opportunities.[38]

Judy decides she can seek out any opportunity she wants and decides she can achieve anything by moving to the city to become a police officer. She tells Gideon Grey, a male red fox in her town: "I can make the world a better place. I am going to be a police officer!"[39] Grey laughingly tells Judy: "Bunny cop? That is the stupidest thing I have heard."[40] This may be the shortest act as the exposition of Judy and her background and worldview is introduced to the audience. However it is the most telling of how "preys" like Judy see police work as doing good, even though she views the world as a form of utopia, with equal opportunities for anyone who wishes to pursue a dream. On the other hand, Gideon Grey, a fox (a traditional predator) living among prey, sees an oxymoron about a "bunny cop." The two words for Grey are a combination of inherent contradictions, with both "bunnies" and "cops" both being forces behind privilege and systemic oppression.

In Act Two Mayor Lionheart announces that his "Mammal Inclusion Initiative" has produced the first "rabbit officer Judy Hopps." Bellwether, the assistant mayor, lets Judy know in solidarity that "it's a real proud day for us little guys."[41] Judy's parents remind her that as a police officer, who is a "bunny," she must have fear. Her father reminds her "we have bears to fear, too. Say nothing of lions and wolves, weasels."[42] Ironically, Mrs. Hopps reminds her own husband "you play cribbage with a weasel."[43] In this exchange the characters hold stereotypes but ironically have close relationships with people outside of their animal groups, those they have taken the time to know intimately.

The most telling signs of distrust come when Judy's parents, as they prepare to leave, give Judy a package of repellent spray labeled "Fox Away," a fox taser that carries an important plot point in the second half of the story.

We learn about privilege among groups in the third act when street-smart fox Nick Wilde and Judy join forces as Judy aims to crack a case of a missing prey Mr. Otterton. Nick and Judy trade stereotypes of each other along the scenes but Nick explains to Judy why he is unable to catch a break. At the 24:32 mark in the film he tells Judy:

> Okay. Tell me if this story sounds familiar. Naïve little Nick with good grades and big ideas decides, "Hey look at me! I'm gonna move to Zootopia where predators and prey live in harmony and sing 'Kumbaya'" only to find, whoopsie, we don't all get along. And that dream of becoming a big city cop? Double whoopsie. . . . and soon enough dreams die.[44]

The irony is that it was through a mayor's office inclusive initiative that Judy is able to get a spot into the academy. Sure enough, she uses her wit and is able to become the first bunny graduate. We do not learn why Nick's dream did not materialize, but when it does not, he turns to petty crime. Both Nick and Judy carried the same dreams, came to a big city and only one succeeded with support from the system: Judy. We see here how the system made a young, female bunny gain access to a "noble" profession, while Nick, who also carried great promise and potential when he arrived in Zootopia, is unable to get a break, or a leg up.

In the fourth act, Judy uses Nick's abilities to help her advance in the police force, hoping that in solving the case of the missing otter, she would be considered more than just a meter maid by her macho peers. She books Nick for a felony tax evasion charge so that he can have his slate wiped by helping her navigate the crime world for clues to solve the disappearance of the otter. She therefore uses the system against Nick, giving him little alternatives but to help her. She has Nick trespass and commit other misdemeanors on her behalf to gain access to the crime world to solve her case. Nick has few options, knowing that she has cornered him to help her in the case, if he wants to not face being arrested.

He ultimately genuinely becomes her ally and agrees to help her but in the fifth act we learn that all Nick has ever wanted was to be accepted. In a flashback to Nick as a young fox, young kids of a different animal group bully a young Nick Wilde telling him "if you thought we would ever trust a fox without a muzzle, you're even dumber than you look."[45] Nick tells Judy about how much he desired to fit in with the Junior Ranger Scouts, even if he was the only fox in the troop. After this childhood trauma of being teased for his difference, he rationalizes "If the world's only gonna see a fox as shifty and untrustworthy thieves, no point in trying to be anything else."[46] Here we learn about why Nick Wilde has turned to a life of petty crime. His rejection as the only fox in his troop as a child, and his failure to "make it" in Zootopia double his feeling of otherness and reinforced that he could not "fit in." It reinforced his social status and that the system does not work for foxes.

However, Nick's honesty in sharing his background does little to educate Judy to her own implicit biases. As she begins to gain media attention for her breakthrough in the case on the missing otter, Nick confronts her on how she portrays "traditional predators" to the media. The following exchange outlines Judy's defensiveness about being challenged on her implicit bias:

Judy: "Nick stop it! You're not like them."

Nick: "Oh, there's a 'them' now."

Judy: "Ugh, you know what I mean, you're not that kind of predator."

Nick: "So let me ask you a question. Are you afraid of me? Do you think I might go nuts? Do you think I might go savage? Do you think I might try to eat you? Just when I thought somebody actually believed in me, huh. Probably best if you don't have a predator as a partner."[47]

During this exchange, as Nick becomes more upset, Judy clutches her Fox repellant spray.[48] The action signals to Nick that Judy does not see him for himself, but as part of his animal group, someone "other" to her, who could go "savage" despite all the friendship and loyalty he has provided her.

The resolution for Judy comes as she rides the subway.[49] In this public space she sees a bunny mother pull her daughter in closer to her when a tiger sits next to the bunny mother and her daughter. The bunny mother looks at the tiger suspiciously on the subway, and in turn her daughter looks up at the tiger, scared and afraid. In this scene, the film demonstrates that fear of difference is learned, and passed down from parents to children. As Judy looks at a flyer of herself as the face of the Zootopia police department, now that she has used Nick for her own success, the following words pierce her conscience: "Integrity, Honesty, Bravery."[50] In this moment, Judy learns that being a police officer is not about finding the bad guy. That in protecting and defending, she had to examine her own bias first. When she looked at her own reflection in the flyer, she was prompted to examine whether she carried integrity, honesty, and bravery for all citizens she aims to serve and protect. This is the ah-ha moment for *Zootopia*, because when Judy does her own reflection, she is truly able to solve the case and find the real bad guy, someone who looks just like her: Assistant Mayor Bellwether, a sheep. Judy is able to finally look around at how preying on differences was a tool used by a politician she looked up to, in order for that politician to gain higher public office. The resolution echoes critiques about recent political rhetoric, and how social differences can be exploited to divide groups for political gain.

More importantly to the resolution of solving the "whodunit" is that Judy then uses her privilege to truly diversify the Zootopia Police Department. She supports Nick's entrance and successful bid to become a police officer and the two of them work together as equal partners in community policing.

CONCLUSION

Disney uses stereotypical characterization with a narrative plot-twist that subverts the themes of the #BlackLivesMatter social discourse as "edutainment." By using anthropomorphic depictions of various real life racial and ethnic groups, *Zootopia*'s creators are able to lessen "offense" by creating distance for the viewers, who are exposed to an animated message about implicit bias and racial profiling that is unfolded in the story line. Viewers come to love Judy Hopps and root for her. She embodies a young woman, aspiring to break glass ceilings in what society considers a noble profession: policing. However, she turns on her unlikely ally Nick Wilde, and becomes an anti-hero who must self-correct after her own prejudices and prior experiences with foxes sees her use her position of power and privilege to draw her weapon against an ally from a different animal group. It is when Judy does the self-reflection to realize how her biases influence her actions, that she discovers that sometimes the enemy comes from her own kind, Assistant Mayor Bellwether, a sheep, who she looked up to as a role model. All along her journey, as she navigated her new life in a bigger city, she was aided in her goals by animals who didn't look like her and who came from different backgrounds than she did.

This is the discourse of the #BlackLivesMatter movement as its founders outlined. That in correcting "our collective future" and in shaping the Zootopia we all desire, we must affirm and humanize those who do not look like us. Through *Zootopia*, Disney has been able to use its stature as the leading juggernaut in Hollywood for making cultural messages for children to find a politically correct, artistic route to teaching audiences about race and implicit bias. It is through a Disney film that a female police officer from an animal class that is considered as "prey" or the traditional victims, has their sense of honor and integrity questioned in a plot that exposes privilege and bias as much as it exposes a crime. The ultimate resolution for the character is not the solving of the crime of the story line, but that a police officer realizes that their own biases have allowed them to falsely accuse someone who did not look like them, who was in fact their ally, and to take action to correct that wrong.

In seeing this play out through animals, in fiction, *Zootopia*'s cultural impact is that this message is translated in terms that the youngest group in society can learn a lesson about privilege, stereotypes, and the treatments of others who may not look like you. Likewise, parents see how they pass bias and fear onto their children and have a teaching tool to begin to correct it. This speaks to the power of narrative storytelling. More importantly, it shows filmmakers and major studios and production companies do not have to sacrifice profit to make cultural works that appeal to wide audiences, are extremely entertaining, but are rooted in messages that are socially conscious.

NOTES

1. Chris Pallant, *Demystifying Disney: A History of Disney Feature Animation*, London: Continuum, 2011.
2. Ibid.
3. Ibid.
4. Ibid., 123–124.
5. Ibid., 111.

6. M. Keith Booker, *Disney, Pixar, and the Hidden Messages of Children's Films* (Santa Barbara: ABC-CLIO, 2010); Ken Gillam and Shannon R. Wooden, "Post-Princess Models of Gender: The New Man in Disney/Pixar"; Carmen R. Lugo-Lugo and Mary K. Bloodsworth-Lugo, "'Look Out New World, Here We Come'? Race, Racialization, and Sexuality in Four Children's Animated Films by Disney, Pixar, and DreamWorks." *Cultural Studies? Critical Methodologies* 9, no. 2 (2009): 166–178.

7. Annalee R. Ward, *Mouse Morality: The Rhetoric of Disney Animated Film*. Austin: University of Texas Press, 2002; Janet Wasko, *Understanding Disney: The Manufacture of Fantasy* (Malden, MA: Polity Press, 2001, reprint 2013).

8. Johnson Cheu, ed. *Diversity in Disney Films: Critical Essays on Race, Ethnicity, Gender, Sexuality and Disability*.

9. Janet Patricia Palmer, "Animating Cultural Politics: Disney, Race, and Social Movements in the 1990s," PhD diss., Ann Arbor: University of Michigan, 2000.

10. Ibid.

11. Kathy Merlock Jackson, "Introduction. Walt Disney: Its Persuasive Products and Cultural Contexts." *Journal of Popular Film and Television* 24, no. 2 (1996): 84.

12. Neal A. Lester, "Disney's *The Princess and the Frog*: The Pride, the Pressure, and the Politics of Being a First," 294.

13. Alicia Garza, "A Herstory of the #BlackLivesMatter Movement," In *Are All the Women Still White? Rethinking Race, Expanding Feminisms*, edited by Janell Hobson (Albany: State University of New York Press, 2014), 23.

14. Alicia Garza, "A Herstory of the #BlackLivesMatter Movement."

15. Ibid., 23.

16. Ibid., 24.

17. Ibid., 26.

18. Ibid., 26.

19. Ibid., 28.

20. Germain Lussier, "Disney Fixed a Huge Mistake with *Zootopia*, Just One Year Before Release."

21. Oana Leventi-Perez, "Disney's Portrayal of Nonhuman Animals in Animated Films Between 2000 and 2010," Master's Thesis, Georgia State University, 2011, http://scholarworks.gsu.edu/communication_theses/81; David Whitley, *The Idea of Nature in Disney Animation: From Snow White to WALL-E* (New York: Routledge, 2016).

22. Germain Lussier, "Disney Fixed a Huge Mistake with *Zootopia*, Just One Year Before Release."

23. Henry A. Giroux, "When You Wish Upon a Star It Makes a Difference Who You Are: Children's Culture and the Wonderful World of Disney," *International Journal of Educational Reform* 4, no. 1 (1995): 79–83; Peter Trifonas, "Simulations of Culture: Disney and the Crafting of American Popular Culture," *Educational Researcher* 30, no. 1 (2001): 23–28; Andi Stein, *Why We Love Disney: The Power of the Disney Brand*. New York: Peter Lang, 2011.

24. Carmen R. Lugo-Lugo and Mary K. Bloodsworth-Lugo, "'Look Out New World, Here We Come'"? 167; Elizabeth Freeman, "Monsters, Inc.: Notes on the Neoliberal Arts Education," *New Literary History* 36, no. 1 (2005): 85.

25. Henry A. Giroux and Grace Pollock, *The Mouse that Roared: Disney and the End of Innocence*, Lanham: Rowman & Littlefield Publishers, 1999, reprint 2010, 2.
26. Henry A. Giroux and Grace Pollock, *The Mouse that Roared: Disney and the End of Innocence*, 2–3.
27. "Janet Wasko, *Understanding Disney: The Manufacture of Fantasy.*
28. Ibid., 5.
29. Ibid., 152.
30. Ibid., 114.
31. Ibid.
32. Siobhan Elizabeth Smith, "The Portrayals of Minority Characters in Entertaining Animated Children's Programs," Masters thesis, Baton Rouge: Louisiana State University, 2004, 68–76.
33. Daniel Katz and Kenneth Braly, "Racial Stereotypes of One Hundred College Students," *The Journal of Abnormal and Social Psychology* 28, no. 3 (1933): 280–290; and "Racial Prejudice and Racial Stereotypes," *The Journal of Abnormal and Social Psychology* 30, no. 2 (1935): 175–193.
34. Siobhan Elizabeth Smith, "The Portrayals of Minority Characters in Entertaining Animated Children's Programs," 28.
35. Siobhan Elizabeth Smith, "The Portrayals of Minority Characters in Entertaining Animated Children's Programs."
36. Ibid.
37. Walt Disney Animation Studios, *Zootopia*, directed by Byron Howard and Rich Moore, co-directed by Jared Bush, written by Jared Bush and Phil Johnston, 2016, 108 minutes, DVD.
38. Walt Disney Animation Studios, *Zootopia*.
39. Ibid.
40. Ibid.
41. Ibid.
42. Ibid.
43. Ibid.
44. Ibid.
45. Ibid.
46. Ibid.
47. Ibid.
48. Ibid.
49. Ibid.
50. Ibid.

BIBLIOGRAPHY

Bell, Elizabeth, Lynda Haas, and Laura Sells, eds. *From Mouse to Mermaid: The Politics of Film, Gender, and Culture*. Bloomington: Indiana University Press, 1995.

Booker, M. Keith. *Disney, Pixar, and the Hidden Messages of Children's Films*. Santa Barbara: ABC-CLIO, 2010.

Cheu, Johnson, ed. *Diversity in Disney Films: Critical Essays on Race, Ethnicity, Gender, Sexuality and Disability*. Jefferson, NC: McFarland, 2013.

Faherty, Vincent E. "Is the Mouse Sensitive? A Study of Race, Gender, and Social Vulnerability in Disney Animated Films." *Studies in Media & Information Literacy Education* 1, no. 3 (2001): 1–8.

Freeman, Elizabeth. "Monsters, Inc.: Notes on the Neoliberal Arts Education." *New Literary History* 36, no. 1 (2005): 83–95.

Garza, Alicia. "A Herstory of the #BlackLivesMatter Movement," In *Are All the Women Still White? Rethinking Race, Expanding Feminisms*, edited by Janell Hobson. Albany: State University of New York Press, 2014.

Gillam, Ken, and Shannon R. Wooden. "Post-Princess Models of Gender: The New Man in Disney/Pixar." *Journal of Popular Film and Television* 36, no. 1 (2008): 2–8.

Giroux, Henry A. "When You Wish Upon a Star It Makes a Difference Who You Are: Children's Culture and the Wonderful World of Disney." *International Journal of Educational Reform* 4, no. 1 (1995): 79–83.

Giroux, Henry A., and Grace Pollock. *The Mouse that Roared: Disney and the End of Innocence*. Lanham: Rowman & Littlefield Publishers, 1999, reprint 2010.

Jackson, Kathy Merlock. "Introduction. Walt Disney: Its Persuasive Products and Cultural Contexts." *Journal of Popular Film and Television* 24, no. 2 (1996): 50–52.

Katz, Daniel, and Kenneth Braly. "Racial Stereotypes of One Hundred College Students." *The Journal of Abnormal and Social Psychology* 28, no. 3 (1933): 280–290.

———. "Racial Prejudice and Racial Stereotypes." *The Journal of Abnormal and Social Psychology* 30, no. 2 (1935): 175–193.

Lester, Neal A. "Disney's *The Princess and the Frog*: The Pride, the Pressure, and the Politics of Being a First." *The Journal of American Culture* 33, no. 4 (2010): 294–308.

Leventi-Perez, Oana. "Disney's Portrayal of Nonhuman Animals in Animated Films Between 2000 and 2010." Master's Thesis, Georgia State University, 2011. http://scholarworks.gsu.edu/communication_theses/81.

Lugo-Lugo, Carmen R., and Mary K. Bloodsworth-Lugo. "'Look Out New World, Here We Come'? Race, Racialization, and Sexuality in Four Children's Animated Films by Disney, Pixar, and DreamWorks." *Cultural Studies? Critical Methodologies* 9, no. 2 (2009): 166–178.

Lussier, Germain. "Disney Fixed a Huge Mistake with *Zootopia*, Just One Year Before Release." io9 *Gizmodo*, January 20, 2016, https://io9.gizmodo.com/how-disney-fixed-a-huge-mistake-with-zootopia-just-one-1753845684.

Pallant, Chris. "Disney-Formalism: Rethinking 'Classic Disney.'" *Animation* 5, no. 3 (2010): 341–352.

———. "Neo-Disney: Recent Developments in Disney Feature Animation." *New Cinemas: Journal of Contemporary Film* 8, no. 2 (2010): 103–117.

———. *Demystifying Disney: A History of Disney Feature Animation*. London: Continuum, 2011.

Palmer, Janet Patricia. "Animating Cultural Politics: Disney, Race, and Social Movements in the 1990s." PhD diss., Ann Arbor: University of Michigan, 2000.

Smith, Siobhan Elizabeth. "The Portrayals of Minority Characters in Entertaining Animated Children's Programs." Masters thesis, Baton Rouge: Louisiana State University, 2004.

Stein, Andi. *Why We Love Disney: The Power of the Disney Brand*. New York: Peter Lang, 2011.

Trifonas, Peter. "Simulations of Culture: Disney and the Crafting of American Popular Culture." *Educational Researcher* 30, no. 1 (2001): 23–28.

Turner, Sarah E. "Blackness, Bayous and Gumbo: Encoding and Decoding Race in a Colorblind World." In *Diversity in Disney Films: Critical Essays on Race, Ethnicity, Gender, Sexuality and Disability*, edited by Johnson Cheu, 432–449. Jefferson, NC: McFarland & Company.

Ward, Annalee R. *Mouse Morality: The Rhetoric of Disney Animated Film*. Austin: University of Texas Press, 2002.

Wasko, Janet. *Understanding Disney: The Manufacture of Fantasy*. Malden, MA: Polity Press, 2001, reprint 2013.

Whitley, David. *The Idea of Nature in Disney Animation: From Snow White to WALL-E*. New York: Routledge, 2016.

Zipes, Jack. "Breaking the Disney Spell." In *From Mouse to Mermaid: The Politics of Film, Gender, and Culture*, edited by Elizabeth Bell, Lynda Haas, and Laura Sells, 21–42. Bloomington: Indiana University Press, 1995.

17

✢

"It's Good to Be Bad"

Marginalization and Othering in the Descendants *Films*

Shearon Roberts

Four underprivileged teens from the wrong side of the tracks are selected as an experiment to attend an elite boarding school in an extremely privileged, elite community. The four teens come from a place that is poor, lacks proper education, opportunity, and resources. The residents of the affluent town hope that with this benevolence, or scholarship if you will, they can stop four teens from becoming a statistic from the environment they were raised in, and avoid entering into a life of crime.

Only this is not the real world. It is the world of Disney's *Descendants*, its highest watched made-for-TV musical film sequel since it revived the format in the last decade.[1] Other popular made-for-television musical films and their sequels before the *Descendants* films like *High School Musical 1, 2, 3* (2006, 2007, 2008), *Camp Rock 1, 2* (2008, 2010), and *Teen Beach Movie 1, 2* (2013, 2015) have all touched on issues around coming of age. However, the *Descendants* films are the first to delve fully into the subject of evil. More importantly, its appeal comes from its continuity of Disney's popular princess franchise because it imagines a world where the princes and princesses of its popular classic films have had offspring. The stars of the films are not the children of the happily-ever-after. The stars are the children of the doomed villains, whose stories were never fully fleshed out until recent works on the big screen like *Oz the Great and Powerful* (2013), *Into the Woods* (2014), *Maleficent* (2014) and *Maleficent: Mistress of Evil* (2019), *Snow White and the Huntsman* (2012) and *The Huntsman: Winter's War* (2016). On the small screen, Disney-owned network ABC delved further into villain characters in the series *Once Upon a Time* (2011–2018). The ABC series introduced children of the well-known prince and princess characters and transported them into the "real world." Through the *Descendants* films, Disney dives into the complexity of villainy, recasting what good and evil means. This chapter examines how the *Descendants* films tap into Disney nostalgia from its princess franchise films, but flips audiences' perceptions of good and evil through the prism of the children who inherit the decisions and actions of adults.

CHANGE? IN MY LIFETIME?

In one of his final interviews before his untimely death, long-time Disney child actor Cameron Boyce summed up what he and his castmates see as the legacy of the three films. The films' themes taps into many of the issues that marginalize and "other" young people. Boyce states:

> The first movie, it was very much, you know, we have labels and we have designated places for these people that we've placed labels on, and very quickly learn that once you sort of take a label off of someone and just let them sort of thrive in whatever environment that they are in, you can see the best come out of someone.[2]

The work of young activists today echoes generational shifts in tackling social issues. In advocating to end gun violence, the Parkland kids took their community's tragedy and launched the #NeverAgain campaign and #March4OurLives movement that resulted in school walk outs, sit-ins in state and federal buildings, and voter registration and education around gun violence and the gun lobby. Aside from this mass shooting, Parkland, an affluent suburb in South Florida, had not been rocked with gun violence as many inner city, Black and brown communities have had for decades. Yet the Parkland activists, in one of their earliest acts of organizing, invited young African American activists to South Florida to educate themselves about everyday gun violence in communities of color.[3] Those early gestures of solidarity with other children and teens of color brought together young people of different races and economic backgrounds around a shared issue of safety for their generation. It resulted in both white and Black gun control activist teens sharing the same microphones at national rallies, marching together, using social media in solidarity of their distinct organizations' missions, and raising the visibility of each other's fights. In calling on all young people to come together at the 2018 March For Our Lives in Washington, D.C., Parkland activist David Hogg said in his speech, "Now is the time to come together . . . we can and we will change the world."[4]

However, when Hogg and his classmates led the march, they used their privilege to share the stage with Black and brown teens who had been fighting before them, with invisibility, to lobby for gun control and other policies that would end gun violence in their communities. Chicago native, Mya Middleton, also spoke at the 2018 rally with Hogg and shared how she had witnessed her first armed robbery at thirteen. She noted that society had ignored the problem of gun violence until "you see it on kids you know."[5] Edna Chavez, like Middleton, grew up around gun violence in Los Angeles. Chavez, who also spoke at the 2018 March For Our Lives, acknowledged that she "learned to duck from bullets before she learned how to read."[6] She acknowledged that Black and brown children's safety had been ignored by society until mass shootings also affected the safety of white children in schools, shopping malls, theaters and concerts. "It is normal to see flowers honoring the lives of black and brown youth that have lost their lives to a bullet. We need to tackle the root causes of the issues we face and come to understanding of how to resolve them."[7]

This fervor for activism by millennials is something that President Barack Obama tapped into to secure both of his elections as U.S. president.[8] In using the words of their generation, "hope" and "change," Obama noted that young people lacked the cynicism and skepticism of their parents.[9] In a speech after his presidency, he noted that: "The only people that are going to solve that problem are going to be young people. The next generation."[10]

Scholars note today that social justice activism by young people have delved into issues of identity, racism, and dismantling systems of oppression.[11] New media, the platform of their generation, has empowered young people to have voices, even when they cannot vote yet, to place an issue on the agenda that impacts future generations, and to build networks of global solidarity around common challenges. Young people today have led campaigns and movements around anti-bullying, gun violence, racism, beauty standards, climate change, education, and quality of life. More millennials are running for political office than a generation before them,[12] and they are actively engaged in both local and global issues at the forefront of social movements.[13] They see it as the mark of their times to shape their future as the G.I. generation shaped the twentieth century, as scholars Neil Howe and William Strauss note,

> Yes there's a revolution under way among today's kids—a good news revolution. This generation is going to *rebel* by behaving not worse, but *better*. . . . Today's kids are on track to become a powerhouse generation, full of technology planners, community shapers, institution builders, and world leaders. . . .[14]

This chapter examines next how young people *rebel* against power, status quo, and dismantle privilege to bring people together and to make their fairy tale world better for all in the *Descendants* films.

IT'S GOOD TO BE BAD

Swords in their hands, standing in formation like a Destiny's Child trio in the song "Night Falls,"[15] Evie (Sofia Carson) sings to Mal (Dove Cameron) and Uma (China Anne McClain): "We've got bigger fish to fry, put your differences aside, cause right now we're on the same side."[16] At the end of three films the Villain Kids (VKs) had decided they would work together for the good of the Isle of the Lost as they teamed up to protect The United States of Auradon. They were first labeled as outsiders, outcasts. The VKs were split on their purpose for fighting, having never been originally loyal to Auradon, which composed of eighteen regions unified by King Beast who banished all villains to the Isle, stripping them of their magic two decades before the timeframe of the first film.[17] Auradon is its own Disney Fairytale Cinematic Universe.[18]

Mal: An Anti-Hero's Journey

The films are helmed by Mal, the daughter of Maleficent—her very name in Latin, Spanish, and French translates to evil. Children of the Isle grow up in isolation from children of Auradon. They judge each other primarily from what they see on television of the lives of each group, and what is passed down from their parents about their own conflicts between royalty and villains. In banishing the villains and their children to the Isle, the kings, queens, princes, and princesses take away what makes villains powerful—their magic. They create elite schools, castles, and museums to mark the advancement and superiority of Auradon. The Isle is cut off, literally by water, and only the royals can open a bridge resembling the yellow brick road to connect Auradon to the impoverished region. Everything seems to thrive in Auradon. The VKs and their parents are in a form of prison. In fact, some parents, like Hades, can only be transported in heavy chains, with armed escorts. Fairy Godmother's wand helps keep law and order and can bring down the barrier between the Isle and Auradon.

It is the young Prince Ben who is allowed by his parents to make a proclamation ahead of his coronation as king of Auradon. His wish is to embark on an experiment that he thinks will allow Auradon to remain prosperous in the future as united regions. For Ben, there is only one region that poses a so-called threat to Auradon's future, a future where he must rule as King; and that is the Isle. His first gesture in "reforming" the Isle is to grant four children of the Isle the chance to live in Auradon to attend Auradon Prep: Mal, Evie (Evil Queen's daughter), Carlos (Cruella de Vil's son, played by Cameron Boyce), and Jay (Jafar's son, played by Booboo Stewart). It is the ultimate invitation since it is Maleficent, "the Mistress of all Evil," and Mal's mother, whose own story is well-known because she was not invited to Aurora's christening. In *Descendants* (2015)[19] the royals aim to train the four villain kids in goodness. In "Remedial Goodness class" Fairy Godmother drills the original four VKs on what is good, moral, and acceptable behavior. The royals hope that with proper schooling, the VKs can be taught how to conform to society.

Mal resists the "goodness schooling" and spells Prince Ben to fall in love with her so that she can steal Fairy Godmother's wand to bring down the barrier and allow the villains to be free of their wretched lives on the Isle. As the film climaxes, Mal and her friends become conflicted about their evil plan. They decide they want to be both good and "bad," and feel pressured and burdened by their parents to be bad, alone. Mal ultimately makes the choice to confront her own mother about evil and determined that what others considered bad about her can be used for good.

In *Descendants 2* (2017)[20] she struggles to fit in. She sees herself as a traitor to her own background and she is worried that she will not be accepted or that she is not good enough. She opens the film with the original four villain kids singing about "Ways to Be Wicked."[21] They describe that now that they live in Auradon, they want to bring their own backgrounds to shake things up in the conservative kingdom. Evie sings: "A fairy tale can be oh-so overrated. So raise your voices and let's get it activated."[22]

The second film sees Mal run away from Auradon feeling like a misfit and a fraud. She returns to the Isle of the Lost, where she feels at home, unjudged. She faces another confrontation, other villain children who feel abandoned by her when she failed to bring down the barrier in the first film. Her former friend turned rival, Uma (China Anne McClain) reminds Mal that she has turned her back on the Isle, and Uma vows to finish what Mal failed to do in the first film by capturing Fairy Godmother's wand and freeing the villains. Mal rescues Auradon once again at the end of the second film by choosing. In the first film, she defeats her own mother to save Auradon. In the second film, she defeats her childhood friend Uma, to save Auradon, again. However this time, instead of her hiding from who she is, she embraces her full villain form, a powerful dragon, understanding that what others see in her as bad, she has the power to use whichever way she determines.

At the start of *Descendants 3* (2019),[23] Mal has settled that she is both part-Isle and part-Auradon and she returns to the Isle to inspire children that its "Good to be Bad,"[24] or that it is okay to be themselves. The original four villain kids return to the Isle for "VK Day" and take to the streets to celebrate their difference. They sing: "They said that being from the Isle is bad," yet everyone in Auradon wishes they were like the VK kids. The original VK kids call on "lost boys, lost girls" from all corners of the globe and remind them that what makes them different is what makes them special. They sing that "Anybody wanna be like us? Everybody wanna be like us!"[25] The original villain kids reclaim the word "bad," the stigma they inherited from their parents, and encourage other villain kids to be the change they want to see.

> Well, it's good to be bad, and we're proof of that
> Used to be lost, now we're on the map
> Used to steal stacks, now we're giving back. Remember that.[26]

The original four select four new villain kids to attend Auradon Prep. Mal promises the four new VK kids that they will be allowed to visit the Isle, see their parents, and stay in touch with their community when they begin school at Auradon Prep. Not all royals are pleased with the influences that the VKs are bringing to Auradon. The arrival of more and more VKs brings anxiety and jealousy among the royals as early as the first film, who fear that villains bring bad habits, are scoundrels, cheats, murderers, and thieves. They are corrupting conservative royals into dressing differently or having too much fun. Finally, they are dating each other and the head of Auradon will soon be married to a villain kid, the daughter of the most feared villains of the Isle: Maleficent and Hades. Princess Audrey (Aurora's daughter, played by Sarah Jeffery) facing pressure from her grandmother Queen Leah (played by Judith Maxie) because she failed to secure a marriage proposal from Prince Ben, decides she will use evil to defeat what she sees is evil. She steals the queen of Auradon's crown and Maleficent's sceptre from Auradon Museum. In "Queen of Mean"[27] she sings that "I followed all the rules, I drew inside the lines, I never asked for anything that wasn't mine."[28] She explains that because of her privilege, she deserves to rule and "there's no in between."[29] She sings that as a royal she wants "what I deserve, I want to rule the world."[30] Her privilege is clear, and she must fight to preserve it: "if they want a villain for a queen, I'm gonna be one like they've never seen."[31]

Mal now faces three adversaries in the final film: Audrey, Hades, and Uma, who returns with her pirate crew and this time makes it over to Auradon. However, the ultimate villain is herself. For her own personal gain, and for her marriage to Ben where she will rule all of Auradon, including the Isle, she betrays her own people. She tells Uma and her pirate crew that she will bring down the barrier if they help her defeat Audrey. It is a lie. When her deceit is revealed, Uma and her crew, the youngest villain kids, plus her own friends, the original VKs, abandon her. She wrestles with the tensions she faces now that she has access to wealth, privilege, and acceptance in "My Once Upon a Time."[32] As a swan song to Mal's journey she acknowledges why it is up to her generation to speak up for children like her, live her life despite her parent's choices, and use her voice and gifts (magic). She unpacks the notion that life is easy or that people don't make mistakes, but what they do to make things better for everyone is the moral of the story:

> Life is not a storybook but life unfolds in chapters
> Turn the page and start to make amends
> There's no pre-written guarantee of "happily ever after."[33]

Mal ultimately defeats Audrey, but only after Uma shares her magic with her. They are forced to work together, using their "bad" powers for good. The fight hurts Audrey, putting her in a deep sleep. Mal realizes she must save Audrey's life and suggests that her father, Hades, now the most feared villain on the Isle, be brought over to use his dark magic to bring Audrey out of a deep sleep. Hades (played by Cheyenne Jackson) delivers the most poignant line from his generation of older villains to King Beast, who represents the older generation of royals: "When you guys tried to destroy the world it's an error in judgment. But when it is one of us, lock them up, throw away the key."[34]

Mal tells Ben that she cannot be queen of Auradon, alone. She must also be queen to the Isle. She tells the people of Auradon, who are afraid of the people of the Isle: "I've learnt that you can't live in fear. Because it doesn't really protect you from anything."[35] Mal tells Ben and the people of Auradon that: "We are all capable of good and bad, no matter what side of the barrier we come from."[36]

Ben then asks Fairy Godmother to bring down the barrier. As the yellow brick road appears to connect Auradon to the Isle of the Lost, Uma and her crew of pirates lead the children of the Isle onto the bridge. They join Mal, the original villain kids, and the children of Auradon for the final song of the films, "Break This Down."[37] Uma and Mal sing that when barriers are removed "face to face we can see clearly our similarities."[38] As the children dance and sing "bringing it, bringing it down," referring to the barrier that separates "good" and "evil," their parents finally come over from the Isle, briefly, for the first time in twenty years. The last person to be welcomed to the Isle is Hades, the most feared villain. Uma tells Mal she will return to the Isle with the newest four villain children and help her home now that the barrier is taken down. As a final show of love for where they came from the original four villain kids run across the bridge to visit the Isle, their home, now that they can do so freely for the first time.

BUILDING BRIDGES, NOT WALLS

Over the course of three films, the *Descendants* films characters aimed to build several bridges. First, the films build bridges for children without wealth, privilege, or access to opportunity. Prince Ben's granting of a scholarship to four of the most hardened VKs in the first film was his attempt to develop "allyship." He used his privilege to create opportunity for those without access to it. It was also beneficial to him, since as a future king, he saw that having his subjects on the Isle view him favorably would make his reign peaceful. Ben's act of "allyship" was not self-less and this showed when he was quick to agree to close the barrier again for good by the third film. It was his love for Mal, and seeing how important it was for her to bridge both worlds, that Ben ordered the barrier to come down. Therefore, it was love, and not hate, that allowed the characters to put aside fear and work together for the good of all groups.

A second bridge built was a cultural one over the course of the films. The characters alluded to cultural differences between the children of the Isle and those of Auradon. Most of these differences surrounded behavior and comportment, others around notions of good and bad. Initially, Fairy Godmother aimed to train VKs to be good, but over the course of the film, the VKs transformed the community they moved to, filling it with culture, life, and color. The villain's kids learned they did not need to be ashamed of who they were, who their parents were, and the conditions they came from. The privileged royal children learned that they could be just as evil and wicked as the group of people they locked up, stripped of power and resources, and that what they should fear is the actions they take from their own hatred of others.

Lastly, generational divides were addressed in the film. Ben had to confront his parents about who he chose to love and marry, a choice that both Beast and Belle disapproved of, because his girlfriend's parents were their enemies. Mal had to confront both her parents as well. She asked her mother to free her from having to pursue the family business of being evil. She called out her father in "Do What You Gotta Do,"[39] about the "daddy issues" he scarred her with when he abandoned her and forced her to fend for herself. On both sides, all descendants were forced to confront an older generation for the messes they left behind, the personal traumas they had caused, the right to be who they wanted to be, to fall in love with whom they wanted to, and to not live up to their expectations, or be judged by their mistakes.

THERE ARE NO FAIRY TALES

The *Descendants* films do not end with a wedding. In fact, the last action is an open book. The four villain kids, having broken down the barriers that separate them and their community from opportunity decide they will run with hope back to the Isle. However, viewers can assume that they do not see their lives in a place of power, wealth, and access as a reason to be comfortable. In other words, the work has just begun for the characters, and their stories remain open.

In revisiting Disney's classic fairy tales, the *Descendants* films pick away at "happy endings." There is of course reason to celebrate. There is for the while: peace, and villains and royalty have found common ground, and their children have opened their hearts and minds to each other. There is love, but no royal wedding. The work that must be done to bring people together and to fix long unsolved problems is the work of a younger generation, and not their parents. As young people today continue to tackle social issues and are at the forefront of global activism in the current era, the films speak squarely to their audience.

The world of the *Descendants* is also colorless, with a diverse cast on both the villain and royal side. While the films imagine a post-racial world, many of the issues around borders, access to education, wealth-gaps, power, and marginalization of cultures are, in reality, issues where race and racism cannot be ignored. The film takes a class-based look instead around privilege and power, and assumes that the roots of all evil can be attributed to wealth and the spoils of war/conflict, and not necessarily the result of racism.

Yet Disney aims to continue to pursue diversity among it's casting, and takes liberties to cast traditionally white characters as other races to update the white fairy-tale worlds it created in the past. While it reduces understandings around race and racial tensions, it allows children of all races to see themselves on both sides of the spectrum of good and evil, and to see themselves as all being part of a solution.

Finally, the *Descendants* films speak to a "woke" generation to continue "bringing it down," a call to dismantle systems that separate people, marginalize groups, create barriers, lock and imprison some, bully others, shut young people out of opportunity and thus create wars and conflict. In song and dance, the children of Disney's fairy-tale universe sing that: "to make the world a better place, we have to do it face to face."[40] And they are not waiting on their parents to do so; they will lead this work.

NOTES

1. Erik Pederson, "'Descendants 3' Draws 8.3M Total Viewers in L+3 for Disney Channel; Cable's Top Program Since First Sequel in Some Young Demos," Deadline, August 7, 2019, https://deadline.com/2019/08/descendants-3-is-cables-top-program-since-2017-in-some-young-demos-8-3m-total-viewers-in-l3-for-disney-channel-1202663711/.

2. Entertainment Tonight, "Watch Cameron Boyce's Final Descendants Interview," YouTube video, 2:50, posted July 24, 2019, https://youtu.be/KHrmyoZwwo8.

3. Emily Witt, "Launching a National Gun Control Coalition, the Parkland Teens Meet Chicago's Young Activists," *The New Yorker*, June 26, 2018, https://www.newyorker.com/news/dispatch/launching-a-national-gun-control-coalition-the-parkland-teens-meet-chicagos-young-activists.

4. Tim Hains, "David Hogg on Gun Control: "We Are Going to Make This a Voting Issue," Real Clear Politics, March 24, 2018, https://www.realclearpolitics.com/video/2018/03/24/david_hogg_on_gun_control_we_are_going_to_make_this_a_voting_issue.html.

5. Krysten Arneson, "The Best Speeches from the March for Our Lives," *Glamour*, March 25, 2018, https://www.glamour.com/story/best-speeches-march-for-our-lives.

6. Krysten Arneson, "The Best Speeches from the March for Our Lives."

7. Ibid.

8. Ruth Milkman, "Millennial Movements: Occupy Wall Street and the Dreamers." *Dissent* 61, no. 3 (2014): 55–59.

9. Jeff Stein, "Barack Obama Is Betting that Young People Can Save America—and His Legacy," *Vox*, April 24, 2017, https://www.vox.com/policy-and-politics/2017/4/24/15408396/barack-obama-young-people.

10. Ibid.

11. Henry Jenkins, Sangita Shresthova, Liana Gamber-Thompson, Neta Kligler-Vilenchik, and Arely Zimmerman, *By Any Media Necessary: The New Youth Activism*. Vol. 3 (New York: New York University Press, 2018); Darren E. Lund and Maryam Nabavi, "A Duo-Ethnographic Conversation on Social Justice Activism: Exploring Issues of Identity, Racism, and Activism with Young People," *Multicultural Education* 15, no. 4 (2008): 27–32.

12. Nancy LeTorneau, "Millennials Are Stepping Up to Run for Office," *Washington Monthly*, October 18, 2018, https://washingtonmonthly.com/2018/10/18/millennials-are-stepping-up-to-run-for-office/.

13. Helen Fox, *Their Highest Vocation: Social Justice and the Millennial Generation* (New York: Peter Lang, 2012).

14. Cited in Helen Fox, *Their Highest Vocation: Social Justice and the Millennial Generation*, p. 7; originally published in Neil Howe and William Strauss, *Millennials Rising: The Next Great Generation* (New York: Vintage Books, 2000, 7, and 4–5).

15. Walt Disney Records, "Night Falls," *Descendants 3 Soundtrack*, written by Tim James, Antonina Armato, Tom Sturges, and Adam Schmalholz, performed by Dove Cameron, Cameron Boyce, Sofia Carson, Booboo Stewart, China Anne McClain, Thomas Doherty, Dylan Playfair, August 2, 2019, 3:08.

16. Walt Disney Records, "Night Falls."

17. Melissa de la Cruz, *The Isle of the Lost, A Descendants Novel* (New York: Disney-Hyperion, 2015); Descendants Fandom Wiki, "Auradon," accessed June 1, 2019, https://descendants.fandom.com/wiki/Auradon.

18. Melissa de la Cruz, *The Isle of the Lost, A Descendants Novel*.

19. Disney Channel Original Productions, *Descendants*, directed by Kenny Ortega, written by Josann McGibbon and Sara Parriott, starring Dove Cameron, Cameron Boyce, Booboo Stewart, 2015, 112 minutes, Film.

20. Disney Channel Original Productions, *Descendants 2*, directed by Kenny Ortega, written by Josann McGibbon and Sara Parriott, starring Dove Cameron, Cameron Boyce, Booboo Stewart, 2017, 111 minutes, Film.

21. Walt Disney Records, "Ways to Be Wicked," *Descendants 2 Soundtrack*, written by Sam Hollander, Josh Edmondson, Grant Michaels, Charity Daw, performed by Dove Cameron, Cameron Boyce, Sofia Carson, Booboo Stewart, July 21, 2017, 3:38.

22. Ibid.

23. Disney Channel Original Productions, *Descendants 3*, directed by Kenny Ortega, written by Sara Parriott and Josann McGibbon, starring Dove Cameron, Cameron Boyce, Booboo Stewart, Cheyenne Jackson, and China Anne McClain, 2019, 108 minutes, Film.

24. Walt Disney Records, "Good to Be Bad," *Descendants 3 Soundtrack*, written by Tim James, Antonina Armato, Tom Sturges, and Adam Schmalholz, performed by Dove Cameron, Cameron Boyce, Sofia Carson, Booboo Stewart, Anna Cathcart, Jadah Marie, August 2, 2019, 3:09.

25. Excerpts from Walt Disney Records, "Good to Be Bad."

26. Ibid.

27. Walt Disney Records, "Queen of Mean," *Descendants 3 Soundtrack*, written by Tim James, Antonina Armato, Tom Sturges, and Adam Schmalholz, performed Sarah Jeffery, August 2, 2019, 3:09.

28. Walt Disney Records, "Queen of Mean."

29. Ibid.

30. Ibid.

31. Ibid.

32. Walt Disney Records, "My Once Upon a Time," *Descendants 3 Soundtrack*, written by John Kavanaugh and David Goldsmith, performed Dove Cameron, August 2, 2019, 3:48.

33. Ibid.

34. Disney Channel Original Productions, *Descendants 3*.

35. Ibid.

36. Ibid.

37. Walt Disney Records, "Break This Down," *Descendants 3 Soundtrack*, written by Jodie Shihadeh, James K. Petrie, Doug Davis, Ben Hostetler, Nikki Sorrentino, Susan Paroff, Anthony Mirabella, Pipo Fernandez, Ali Dee Theodore, performed Dove Cameron, Cameron Boyce, Sofia Carson, Booboo Stewart, China Ann McClain, Gibson, Sarah Jeffery, Zachary Gibson, Thomas Doherty, Dylan Playfair, Anna Cathcart, Jadah Marie, Mitchell Hope, Brenna D'Amico, August 2, 2019, 3:29.

38. Ibid.

39. Walt Disney Records, "Do What You Gotta Do," *Descendants 3 Soundtrack*, written by Matt Wong, Jamie Jones and Jack Kugell, performed Dove Cameron and Cheyenne Jackson, August 2, 2019, 2:57.

40. Disney Channel Original Productions, *Descendants 3*.

BIBLIOGRAPHY

Arneson, Krysten. "The Best Speeches from the March for Our Lives." *Glamour*. March 25, 2018. https://www.glamour.com/story/best-speeches-march-for-our-lives.

de la Cruz, Melissa. *The Isle of the Lost, A Descendants Novel*. New York: Disney-Hyperion, 2015.

Descendants Fandom Wiki. "Auradon." Accessed June 1, 2019, https://descendants.fandom.com/wiki/Auradon.

Disney Channel Original Productions. *Descendants 2*. Directed by Kenny Ortega. Written by Josann McGibbon and Sara Parriott. Starring Dove Cameron, Cameron Boyce, Booboo Stewart, 2015, 111 minutes, Film.

———. *Descendants 2*. Directed by Kenny Ortega, Written by Josann McGibbon and Sara Parriott. Starring Dove Cameron, Cameron Boyce, Booboo Stewart, 2015, 111 minutes, Film.

———. *Descendants 3*. Directed by Kenny Ortega. Written by Sara Parriott and Josann McGibbon. Starring Dove Cameron, Cameron Boyce, Booboo Stewart, Cheyenne Jackson, and China Anne McClain. 2019. 108 minutes. Film.

Entertainment Tonight. "Watch Cameron Boyce's Final Descendants Interview." YouTube video, 2:50. Posted July 24, 2019. https://youtu.be/KHrmyoZwwo8.

Fox, Helen. *Their Highest Vocation: Social Justice and the Millennial Generation*. New York: Peter Lang, 2012.

Hains, Tim. "David Hogg on Gun Control: "We Are Going to Make This a Voting Issue." Real Clear Politics. March 24, 2018. https://www.realclearpolitics.com/video/2018/03/24/david_hogg_on_gun_control_we_are_going_to_make_this_a_voting_issue.html.

Howe, Neil, and William Strauss. *Millennials Rising: The Next Great Generation*. New York: Vintage Books, 2000.

Jenkins, Henry, Sangita Shresthova, Liana Gamber-Thompson, Neta Kligler-Vilenchik, and Arely Zimmerman. *By Any Media Necessary: The New Youth Activism*. Vol. 3. New York: New York University Press, 2018.

LeTorneau, Nancy. "Millennials Are Stepping Up to Run for Office." *Washington Monthly*. October 18, 2018. https://washingtonmonthly.com/2018/10/18/millennials-are-stepping-up-to-run-for-office/.

Lund, Darren E., and Maryam Nabavi. "A Duo-Ethnographic Conversation on Social Justice Activism: Exploring Issues of Identity, Racism, and Activism with Young People." *Multicultural Education* 15, no. 4 (2008): 27–32.

Milkman, Ruth. "Millennial Movements: Occupy Wall Street and the Dreamers." *Dissent* 61, no. 3 (2014): 55–59.

Pederson, Erik. "'Descendants 3' Draws 8.3M Total Viewers in L+3 for Disney Channel; Cable's Top Program Since First Sequel in Some Young Demos." Deadline. August 7, 2019. https://deadline.com/2019/08/descendants-3-is-cables-top-program-since-2017-in-some-young-demos-8-3m-total-viewers-in-l3-for-disney-channel-1202663711/.

Stein, Jeff. "Barack Obama Is Betting that Young People Can Save America—and His Legacy." *Vox*. April 24, 2017. https://www.vox.com/policy-and-politics/2017/4/24/15408396/barack-obama-young-people.

Walt Disney Records. "Ways to Be Wicked." *Descendants 2 Soundtrack*. Written by Sam Hollander, Josh Edmondson, Grant Michaels, Charity Daw. Performed by Dove Cameron, Cameron Boyce, Sofia Carson, and Booboo Stewart. July 21, 2017, 3:38.

———. "Good to Be Bad." *Descendants 3 Soundtrack*. Written by Tim James, Antonina Armato, Tom Sturges, and Adam Schmalholz. Performed by Dove Cameron, Cameron Boyce, Sofia Carson, Booboo Stewart, Anna Cathcart, and Jadah Marie. August 2, 2019, 3:09.

———."Queen of Mean." *Descendants 3 Soundtrack*, written by Tim James, Antonina Armato, Tom Sturges, and Adam Schmalholz. Performed Sarah Jeffery. August 2, 2019, 3:09.

———. "Do What You Gotta Do." *Descendants 3 Soundtrack*. Written by Matt Wong, Jamie Jones and Jack Kugell. Performed Dove Cameron and Cheyenne Jackson. August 2, 2019, 2:57.

———. "Night Falls." *Descendants 3 Soundtrack*. Written by Tim James, Antonina Armato, Tom Sturges, and Adam Schmalholz. Performed by Dove Cameron, Cameron Boyce, Sofia Carson, Booboo Stewart, China Anne McClain, Thomas Doherty, and Dylan Playfair. August 2, 2019, 3:08.

———. "My Once Upon a Time." *Descendants 3 Soundtrack*. Written by John Kavanaugh and David Goldsmith, performed Dove Cameron, August 2, 2019, 3:48.

———. "Break This Down." *Descendants 3 Soundtrack*. Written by Jodie Shihadeh, James K. Petrie, Doug Davis, Ben Hostetler, Nikki Sorrentino, Susan Paroff, Anthony Mirabella, Pipo Fernandez, Ali Dee Theodore. Performed Dove Cameron, Cameron Boyce, Sofia Carson, Booboo Stewart, China Ann McClain, Gibson, Sarah Jeffery, Zachary Gibson, Thomas Doherty, Dylan Playfair, Anna Cathcart, Jadah Marie, Mitchell Hope, Brenna D'Amico. August 2, 2019, 3:29.

Witt, Emily. "Launching a National Gun Control Coalition, the Parkland Teens Meet Chicago's Young Activists." *The New Yorker*, June 26, 2018. https://www.newyorker.com/news/dispatch/launching-a-national-gun-control-coalition-the-parkland-teens-meet-chicagos-young-activists.

18

No Capes Needed

The Plight of Super Moms

Alexis Woods Barr

WE CAN'T ALL LEAN IN

Work-life balance is an expression generally used to describe comparable time distributed to work and other aspects of a working person's life. This idea of "balance" is problematic for several reasons. To begin with, "work-life balance" suggests that "work" and "life" are somehow separate, but equal forces capable of being balanced. This notion implies that we have to choose between one or the other, as if we can't have both. This is a gross misconception, especially for mothers.

The reality is many working women simply cannot #LeanIn. The movement implies that we as women are responsible for advancing to the top of our careers, and we too often check out or sit on the sidelines. First Lady Michelle Obama, a working mother herself, responded to the Lean In movement: "That whole so you can have it all. Nope, not at the same time. That's a lie. . . . And it's not always enough to lean in, because that s**t doesn't work all the time."[1] The search for balance is something that *The Incredibles*' Helen Parr (the mother) who doubles as Elastigirl, the working crime fighter, navigates over two Disney-Pixar films. In the film's sequel she tells her husband Bob Parr: "You know it's crazy, right? To help my family, I gotta leave it; to fix the law, I gotta break it."[2] In this chapter I explore how our conversation around social expectations of mothers has evolved. I then explore the treatment of familial gender roles as presented in *The Incredibles* franchise.

THE LEAN IN MOVEMENT AND PRIVILEGE

When Sheryl Sandberg, Facebook's chief operating officer, released the book *Lean In: Women, Work, and the Will to Lead* in 2013, it was a huge sensation with the main message of the book being that women need to understand all the forces that work against them in the workplace and then lean up against those things. She promised that women could positively influence their own careers without abandoning the other components of their lives if they just adapted how they approached work, negotiated, and advocated for themselves. In other words, women needed to work harder and imitate their male counterparts in order to have fulfilling careers. This included speaking up in meetings because women tended not to do that. Sandberg suggested that the only way for women to get ahead in their company (i.e., raises and promotions) was to be more assertive.

Many women criticized this idea because it further put the responsibility on women to do all the work of gender equality. It did not force companies to offer more accommodations and show less bias toward women. It did not delve into conversations around equity in the home. This notion completely took the onus off of institutions and society, and placed it all on women to advance themselves. It failed to advocate for the collective movement.[3] Secondly, women noted that it was more difficult to "lean in" when you didn't have the sorts of privileges and supports that Sandberg enjoyed. Many saw Sandberg and her book as elitist. The "working women" she referred to were often white, in white-collar jobs, and were highly educated working women. With Sandberg, being a white, married, wealthy woman, her positionality did not represent the majority of women in America. Most women in the United States are often burdened by the lack of these advantages as well as male dominated work places.

Former first lady Michelle Obama in her own 2018 book, *Becoming*, acknowledged the challenges of balance, as a Black woman in a highly privileged position. She said, "Most of us lived in a state of constant calibration, tweaking one area of life in hopes of bringing more steadiness to another."[4] Obama validated what we knew all along about both race and class, and the ability to fully lean in. For women of color, work-life balance is a different kind of problem. Black and brown women of color's maternal and employment experiences have historically differed from that of white women. For example, Black women have always worked outside the home stemming back to chattel slavery. Since that time, Black and brown women have worked in low-paying jobs that force them to work more than one job.[5] As a result, these women have been driven to value providing financially for their family as opposed to the amount of time spent with their family.[6]

Today, it is increasingly more difficult for families to get by on a single income. As living costs have continued to rise, so have the number of two-income households. A 2015 Pew Research Center report explains that the number of two-income households have increased from 25 percent in 1960 to 60 percent in 2012.[7] It is also important to note the shifts in numbers of women participating in the labor force have increased financial freedom more than ever before and today, women generally feel empowered to continue their careers after childbirth. But for the moment, I will focus on the challenges mothers face in a society that sends countless conflicting messages about motherhood and employment.

Over the past forty years, the rate of mothers participating in the labor force (either working or looking for paid work) has considerably increased from 47 percent in 1975 to over 71 percent in 2018.[8] These participation rates include all mothers who have children under the age of eighteen. For many mothers, going (or going back) to work is a financial necessity compared to decades ago.[9] Major life transitions are key factors to influencing those needs. To give an example of this phenomenon, additions to a woman's family could include welcoming a newborn baby, adopting a child, or receiving another family member into her home to live.

When thinking about parents with newborns, 88 percent of employed mothers in America have no access to paid maternity leave.[10] So, that causes mothers to navigate unpaid maternity leave, which is provided under the Family and Medical Leave Act of 1993.[11] This law provides up to twelve weeks of unpaid job-protection for eligible employees.[12] After all these years, this "legal protection" still isn't always helpful to mothers because of how the law is structured. There are several exceptions and loopholes, making many new mothers ineligible for it. As a result, many of these women are forced to return to work soon after giving birth not only because of the lack of financial assistance, but more importantly, for fear of losing their source of income. Mothers also join the labor force because of other changes in their family structure, including but not limited to, separation or divorce from a spouse leading to single motherhood, family member illness or mounting medical bills, or a spouse being laid off.

In thinking about their return to work, mothers are faced with yet another concern: nonparental childcare, which is the single largest expenditure new parents face before their child begins school.[13] During pregnancy, mothers may not consider this expense because they may focus more on the health of their pregnancy, their company's maternity leave policy, gaining weight, or even what to name their baby. Some of these concerns are exacerbated for Black women and other women of color. For instance, regardless of education, socioeconomic status, income, gestational age, maternal age, and health status, African American women and babies have the worse pregnancy and birth outcomes compared to their counterparts.[14] Additionally, women of color are more likely to work in jobs where they do not possess the cultural capital or job security to call attention to special circumstances like maternity leave. Thus, worrying about childcare may not be high on their priority list during pregnancy. But, when the time does come to think about childcare and parents realize that childcare could cost them up to $21,000 a year, many families decide that it makes financial sense for one parent to stay at home.[15] This is particularly difficult for families that have only one or two working parents earning a modest income. Many times, these families can neither afford to pay for childcare nor allow one parent to stay home. This phenomenon may be more challenging for families where the woman is the main (or only) source of income. In fact, research suggests that more than half of African American households are headed by women, and the labor market discriminates against Black men, resulting in lower earnings and reduced job stability compared to their white counterparts. Consequently, these women don't have the luxury of staying home.

DISNEY AND MOTHERHOOD

In 2018's *Ralph Break's The Internet*, the Disney princesses quiz Vanellope to determine if she was a real princess. Princess Jasmine asks Vanellope:

Jasmine: "Do you have daddy issues?"

Vanellope: "I don't even have a mom."

The princesses: "Neither do we."[16]

For all its content for family, many of Disney's most popular works leave gaping holes in presenting family. In many of its earlier princess classics, the number one missing character, who is often killed off, or dies mysteriously, or is absent or never named are the princesses' mothers. The complexities of motherhood are dismissed as easily as a character who plays one.

More recent Disney works have left mothers' alive for the entire length of the script and given them some screen time. This was the case for Tiana, whose mother Eudora gives her advice, for Merida, Rapunzel and for Moana, whose mother packs her bags for her as she runs away to help her people and save her island. Among the four examples, one Disney/Pixar's *Brave* (2012) goes the furthest, as Merida and her mother Queen Elinor wrestled through the complex nature of mother-daughter relationships. Another instance is briefly touched on through Disney/Pixar's *Inside Out* (2015) as both Riley's parents wrestle with her changes to adolescence. These are recent developments in portraying motherhood in classic Disney works, particularly for princesses, but for many women today, whatever life occurred after "Happily Ever After" as girls/teens progressed to women was rarely explored. *The Incredibles* (2004) and *Incredibles 2* (2018) films distinguish themselves from other animated works for portraying the realities of being a working mother.

The Incredibles: A Mom Who Doesn't Wear a Cape

The Incredibles (2004) and *Incredibles 2* (2018) serve as an example of shifting paradigms of gender roles in the household in this current era of women's empowerment. The first film showed the complexity of the domestic family life and the gender roles within it. It explored a side of superheroes (or supers) that isn't typically shown in traditional superhero movies. In his glory days, Mr. Incredible (Bob Parr) was a popular celebrity. But soon after supers were outlawed, Mr. Incredible became a waning insurance agent that could not handle the pressures of domestic life. He was this gigantic powerful man in a tiny and compact world, being bossed around by an unscrupulous, tiny, loud-mouthed, feeble man and drove a tiny car. But, Bob was the man of the house, who was hyper-masculine and thought to be super strong. Elastigirl (Helen Parr), Bob's wife, was introduced to audiences as a crime-fighting force, who also retreated to domesticity when 'supers' were outlawed. But unlike Bob, she stopped working (crime-fighting), became a mother of three who was trying to keep her superhero family together in a domestic setting. She was a stay-at-home mother who had to stretch herself (literally and figuratively) and be flexible to hold her family together. Their children all possessed a different power, reflective of their personalities. Violet was a repressed teenager who pushed others away and hid her true self by using force fields and invisibility. Dash was an elementary-aged boy who had super speed powers. Finally, there was baby Jack-Jack who we came to learn possessed a multitude of powers. They were combinations of their parents.

This first film showed audiences that Helen was the glue of the family. She embodied the characteristics of womanhood and motherhood. She engaged with each one of her family members in a smart and empathetic way. She was also a vigilante who had superhuman elasticity, permitting her body to stretch to great magnitudes. Elastigirl is so relatable to women because she literally stretches herself thin to save her marriage and her family. In the beginning of the film, it was evident in her interview that Elastigirl always wanted to stay out there saving the world. She was defying the norms, and using her abilities for the greatest good. But, the first film does not follow up on this part of her story until *Incredibles*

2. Much like her husband, Helen really made a very difficult decision in *The Incredibles* to sacrifice these goals for the good of her family. Helen did so willingly with much less apprehension about it than her husband. In a lot of ways, she had a much better sense of perspective than Bob did. Notwithstanding the remarkable strength and ability of Elastigirl, *The Incredibles* highlighted the same old male-controlled, heteronormative structure we were used to seeing time and again. But this may not be unusual considering the film was set in an alternate version of the 1960s. This film brilliantly weaved together traditional superhero themes with a message of the monotonous nature of present-day work and the dangers of pretending to be something that you are not. Although the first film follows Mr. Incredible as he dishonestly returns to a life of adventure, to me Elastigirl is the most important character to the story line. She is the connection between her husband and their children. While Bob became fed up with his mundane life of normalcy, his wife worked hard to build a normal life for their family. When Bob was presented with the opportunity to be a hero again, he took it without informing his wife. Soon Bob's dishonesty caught up with him and he found out that this new adventure was a trap set by a former obsessive fan, now turned nemesis—Syndrome. Elastigirl learned her husband was in great danger shortly after she became increasingly suspicious of his out of town trips. Consequently, it was up to Elastigirl to save the day, along with their two oldest children who stowed away on the plane without her permission.

Between the release of the first film and its sequel, more than a decade had passed. In fact, the second film picks up right where the last film left off on the timeline. Yet the Incredibles' world in the sequel seemed to better reflect the changes in the current social climate that transpired since watching the movie fourteen years before. The sequel presented a closer and realistic depiction of modern day gender dynamics. The creators flipped the domestic gender roles of the first film. It mirrored a decade's shift in parenting in real life. More now than ever, fathers and mothers are rebelling against traditional gender norms and engaging in non-traditional roles where mothers work full-time outside the home and fathers care for the children in the home.[17] More fathers are taking paternity leaves, even those in the tech world as both Mark Zuckerberg and Alexis Ohanian have championed paternity leave. Swapping traditional gender roles in the home was a prominent theme of the sequel. There were notably nuanced agreements on the challenges of balancing a career and child-rearing, the resulting parental strain and the possible joys that come along with that strain. In *Incredibles 2*, the supers were still in hiding, but Mr. Incredible, Frozone, and Elastigirl were offered a chance to spearhead the effort to make super-heroism legal again. The billionaire telecommunications mogul, Winston Deavor, idolized the supers and launched this new legalization effort. He thought that instead of using Mr. Incredible, Elastigirl would make a better face for the campaign to reinstate the public's trust in supers. Before accepting the offer, Elastigirl stated,

> Elastigirl: "You know it's crazy, right? To help my family, I gotta leave it. To fix the law, I gotta break it."
>
> Bob: "You've got to, so that our kids can have that choice [to be supers]."[18]

As any mother faces, Elastigirl took on the assignment, but she did so with much hesitation. The guilt of doing what she loved and leaving the domesticity to her husband weighed on her as a constant tug-of-war. She felt like she was the indispensable part of her family. She navigated the real, yet difficult choices of yearning to return to a fulfilling career while also longing to stay with their children. She still had three young children at home—a teenage daughter in a romantic crisis, a son who was struggling with Algebra, and a baby boy who couldn't even talk. Like most mothers of young children, Elastigirl was happy to work (fighting crime) as long as she was still able to help her children with their issues, be around for their "firsts," and also have a nice dinner with her family each evening. The deciding factor for her was Bob reassuring her that he could handle the task of taking care of the home-front: "I'll watch the kids. No problem. It'll be easy."[19] Like most working mothers experience, this new job opportunity required much more time than she anticipated: she had to leave her family, live in a hotel, and remain on-call twenty-four hours a day. As with any new opportunity, Elastigirl had an initial rush of excitement beginning with her Elasticycle, a simple pleasure of having a "grown-up toy" after several years of not treating herself or owning something "daredevil" as she did when she was single. She was able to focus on something other than the day-to-day tasks of being a stay-at-home mother. She was able to do what she had longed to do for quite some time.

This film did two things very well. One, it allowed Elastigirl to be wrong about Bob being competent enough to fulfill her role at home with the children. And two, even though Elastigirl was literally a superhero, the film never tried to portray her as a stereotypical "do-it-all super mom" who also works. It was very refreshing to see that Elastigirl was saddened to learn that she had missed pivotal moments at home: "I missed Jack-Jack's first powers?"[20] Or, that she couldn't always be present with her children as she wanted to: "Dash, honey, can't talk right now, but look under your bed, OK?"[21] as she rides her Elasticycle along billboards and buildings on the job. The film showed how tough her role was at home juggling three children with every mishap and failing by Bob when he assumed her household duties. It also showed how difficult it was for even the most superb multi-tasker like Helen to give the kids her full attention while solving crime. More importantly it reflected how women wrestle with their own desire to explore their abilities, and to do good in the world, after being transformed by motherhood that innately reorders their lives.

Usually, on-screen mothers are portrayed as frantic, emotional, and unrestrained. Elastigirl was not. The film showed that as a mother, she could still be the best at her job, even better than a man, her own husband. She also supported and loved her family at the same time. This demonstrated that Elastigirl recognized that while protecting the world, she still knew how important her role as a mother was. This pragmatic battle that all mothers face when returning to work also includes having to relinquish and rely on husbands (or significant others) to rise to the occasion in tasks that women traditionally held. For Helen, it was not an easy swap, considering she was initially the primary caregiver. The movie's parental swap normalized discussions about gender equality in the home. Holly Hunter, who voices Elastigirl shared that "Being a member of a family, there are giant responsibilities in raising children, and it's a responsibility that's wonderful if it gets to be shared by two people, whether it's two men, two women, a male and a female."[22] And when it comes to determining just who accomplishes which role, Hunter stated, "Who cares."[23] She is correct, that today, it is more common to encounter stay-at-home fathers, gender no longer determine who completes which family responsibilities. Many fathers echoed actor Ashton Kutcher's soapboxing on social media that men's bathrooms don't have changing station's for dads with small children.[24] And even more fathers posted photos of themselves wearing their babies when host Piers Morgan said actor Daniel Craig had emasculated the image of James Bond for carrying his newborn daughter in a papoose.[25] *Incredibles 2* provided an animated portrayal for children and families that represented these changing norms about parenting, gender roles in the family, and working mothers.

DIVERSIFYING THE CONVERSATION

The Incredibles franchise provides some bright spots in its portrayal of modern families. And while the films had a female co-lead and diversified its treatment and exposition of familial roles, it still lacked representations in other areas. It is important how our current media portrays our world for the impacts it has on social norms.[26] This is important because of historical negative media representations of diverse groups in the past and how it affects perceptions of these groups.[27] The best way to be aware of these biases is to have producers, writers, directors, and storyboard artists that are from the same communities that they are portraying in their content.

Between both *Incredibles* movies, there was little diversity in the directors, writers, producers, and cast members. After waiting fourteen years for the chance to learn more about the off-screen scene-stealer, Honey Best, in the sequel, she remained an off-screen callback joke. Director Brad Bird missed the opportunity to confirm her identity, even many fans assumed Honey to be a sassy Black woman. The story of Honey and whether or not she was also a previous hero would have given the necessary substance to explain Frozone's life and contribution to the Incredibles' story. As we see in both films, Helen is aware of Honey. In fact, it is likely that they are friends, as Helen says to Frozone, "Say hello to Honey for me." But because the director's chose to keep Honey as a background running joke, she never took part in a primary scene in the initial *Incredibles* movie, which set the stage for Mr. Incredible and Frozone's friendship. This could have been the chance to add more diversity to the cast, which currently does not have any Black women in key roles. Brad Bird responded to this criticism by saying:

> She's funnier as a voice. We actually went through all the trouble of designing a character and the design appears in the movie but not as Frozone's wife. We have used her design and she is a hero but there's not a lot of screen time though.[28]

Funnier as a voice? And his use of the word "trouble" is—well, troubling. Were the other characters any trouble to create? The issue is, overall, there's a lack of positive Black characters represented in cinema to date. Add to that, there is even more of a lack of Black women representation. While it is refreshing to see a Black animated superhero—Frozone—in the Incredibles franchise, his role was secondary in the film, regardless of the importance of his presence in the lives of the Parr family. In *Incredibles 2*, Frozone was the only superhero to be called upon to protect the Parr children, though this trust was never explained in the film. Frozone's character has been type casted to be Mr. Incredibles' sidekick. And Honey Best, Frozone's wife, is the only named character that remains off-screen in both movies. Instead, audiences only hear her yelling at her husband from another room in the house. The old belief that women are to be seen and not heard, for Honey, a Black female woman, is exactly the opposite, *heard* but not seen.

This goes to show that characters of color continue to be viewed as comic relief. Audiences were able to see the evolution of a white American super family, in an age of Disney/Marvel's successful dominance and display of diverse super characters. Both *Black Panther* and *Incredibles 2* released in the same year, with the former earning slightly more than the latter at the box office (although both crossed $1 billion).

It would have been easy for Disney/Pixar to have fleshed out Frozone's family and to provide it the dynamic story arch it did for the Parr family in the sequel.

Reflective representation—seeing yourself, your experience, your people's experience in the locations and situations that make a difference in this world—matters for essential civic participation. It gives young children an awareness of the possible, a pathway to pursue, and a more inclusive future to imagine. Reflective representation also helps erase the implicit biases we all have that feed our daily exchanges with others. And all audiences should be able to see and be entertained by a family of color's modern journey, as much as they have for generations been entertained by white families on screen.

NOTES

1. Laurel Wamsley, "Michelle Obama's Take on 'Lean In?' 'That &#%! Doesn't Work,'" *NPR*, December 3, 2018, https://www.npr.org/2018/12/03/672898216/michelle-obamas-take-on-lean-in-that-doesn-t-work.

2. Helen Parr to her husband Bob Parr in Walt Disney Studios Motion Pictures, *Incredibles 2*, written and directed by Brad Bird, 2018, DVD.

3. Leonard Berkowitz, "Social Norms, Feelings, and Other Factors Affecting Helping and Altruism," *Advances in Experimental Social Psychology* 6 (1972): 63–108.

4. Michelle Obama, *Becoming* (New York: Crown Publishing Group, 2018), 201.

5. Kimberly Seals Allers, "Rethinking Work-Life Balance for Women of Color," *Slate*, March 5, 2018, https://slate.com/human-interest/2018/03/for-women-of-color-work-life-balance-is-a-different-kind-of-problem.html; Patricia Hill Collins, "The Meaning of Motherhood in Black Culture and Black Mother–Daughter Relationships," *Gender Through the Prism of Difference* (2005): 285–295; bell hooks, "Revolutionary Parenting," In *Feminist Theory: From Margin to Center* (London: Pluto Press, 2000).

6. Ibid.

7. Pew Research Center, "The Rise in Dual Income Households," June 15, 2016, accessed May 8, 2019, https://www.pewresearch.org/fact-tank/2019/06/12/fathers-day-facts/ft_16-06-14_fathersday_dual_income/.

8. U.S. Bureau of Labor Statistics, "Employment Characteristics of Families—2018," last modified April 18, 2019, accessed May 8, 2019, https://www.bls.gov/news.release/famee.toc.htm.

9. Victoria L. Brescoll and Eric Luis Uhlmann, "Attitudes Toward Traditional and Nontraditional Parents," *Psychology of Women Quarterly* 29, no. 4 (2005): 436–445; Judith S. Bridges and Claire Etaugh, "College Students' Perceptions of Mothers: Effects of Maternal Employment-Childrearing Pattern and Motive for Employment," *Sex Roles* 32, no. 11–12 (1995): 735–751; Tyler G. Okimoto and Madeline E. Heilman, "The 'Bad Parent' Assumption: How Gender Stereotypes Affect Reactions to Working Mothers."

10. U.S. Bureau of Labor Statistics, "Access to Paid and Unpaid Family Leave in 2018," last modified February 26, 2019, accessed May 14, 2019, https://www.bls.gov/opub/ted/2019/access-to-paid-and-unpaid-family-leave-in-2018.htm.

11. U.S. Department of Labor, "The Family and Medical Leave Act of 1993," 1993, accessed November 12, 2017, from https://www.dol.gov/whd/regs/statutes/fmla.htm; U.S. Department of Labor, "Fact Sheet #28: The Family and Medical Leave Act of 1993," 2009, accessed November 12, 2017, https://www.dol.gov/whd/fmla/fact_sheets.htm.

12. U.S. Department of Labor, "Fact Sheet #28: The Family and Medical Leave Act of 1993."

13. Devon Gorry and Diana W. Thomas, "Regulation and the Cost of Childcare," *Applied Economics* 49, no. 41 (2017): 4138–4147.

14. Allan S. Noonan, Hector Eduardo Velasco-Mondragon, and Fernando A. Wagner, "Improving the Health of African Americans in the USA: An Overdue Opportunity for Social Justice," *Public Health Reviews* 37, no. 12 (2016): 12.

15. Alexa Fiander, "Living Expenses in Urban vs. Suburban Neighborhoods," Zillow, March 6, 2017, accessed July 17, 2019, http://zillow.mediaroom.com/2017-03-06-Families-Spend-9-000-More-a-Year-to-Live-in-City-vs-Suburbs.

16. Walt Disney Animation Studios, *Ralph Breaks the Internet*, directed by Rich Moore and Phil Johnston, 2018, Digital Copy.

17. Jessica Fischer and Veanne N. Anderson, "Gender Role Attitudes and Characteristics of Stay-at-Home and Employed Fathers," *Psychology of Men & Masculinity* 13, no. 1 (2012): 16.

18. Walt Disney Studios Motion Pictures. *Incredibles 2*.

19. Ibid.

20. Ibid.

21. Ibid.

22. Kirsten Chuba, "'Incredibles 2' Team Talks Sequel Film's Push for Female Empowerment, Gender Equality," *Variety*, June 5, 2018, https://variety.com/2018/scene/news/incredibles-2-female-empowerment-gender-equality-1202833671/.

23. Kirsten Chuba, "'Incredibles 2' Team Talks Sequel Film's Push for Female Empowerment, Gender Equality."

24. Jack Linshi, "Ashton Kutcher Will Give You a Shout-Out If You Find a Men's Bathroom with a Diaper Changing Station," *Time*, March 10, 2015, https://time.com/3739878/ashton-kutcher-bathroom-diaper/.

25. BBC, "Piers Morgan Mocks Daniel Craig for Carrying Baby," October 16, 2018, https://www.bbc.com/news/uk-45873664.

26. Maryam Raisi, "Representing Model Women in Iranian TV Series (Components of Considering Hijab during Attendance of Strangers)," *International Journal of Humanities and Cultural Studies* 2356-5926 (2016): 2462.

27. Dwight E. Brooks and Lisa P. Hébert, "Gender, Race, and Media Representation," *Handbook of Gender and Communication* 16 (2006): 297–317.

28. Monique Jones, "'The Incredibles' Director on Why We've Never Scene Frozone's Wife, Honey, in the Franchise," *Shadow and Act*, April 16, 2018, https://shadowandact.com/the-incredibles-director-on-why-weve-never-seen-frozones-wife-honey-in-the-franchise/.

BIBLIOGRAPHY

Allers, Kimberly Seals. "Rethinking Work-Life Balance for Women of Color." *Slate,* March 5, 2018. https://slate.com/human-interest/2018/03/for-women-of-color-work-life-balance-is-a-different-kind-of-problem.html.

BBC. "Piers Morgan Mocks Daniel Craig for Carrying Baby." October 16, 2018. https://www.bbc.com/news/uk-45873664.

Berkowitz, Leonard. "Social Norms, Feelings, and Other Factors Affecting Helping and Altruism." *Advances in Experimental Social Psychology* 6 (1972): 63–108.

Borelli, Jessica L., S. Katherine Nelson, Laura M. River, Sarah A. Birken, and Corinne Moss-Racusin. "Gender Differences in Work-Family Guilt in Parents of Young Children." *Sex Roles* 76, no. 5–6 (2017): 356–368.

Brescoll, Victoria L., and Eric Luis Uhlmann. "Attitudes Toward Traditional and Nontraditional Parents." *Psychology of Women Quarterly* 29, no. 4 (2005): 436–445.

Bridges, Judith S., and Claire Etaugh. "College Students' Perceptions of Mothers: Effects of Maternal Employment-Childrearing Pattern and Motive for Employment." *Sex Roles* 32, no. 11–12 (1995): 735–751.

Brooks, Dwight E., and Lisa P. Hébert. "Gender, Race, and Media Representation." *Handbook of Gender and Communication* 16 (2006): 297–317.

Chambers, Deborah. *Representing the Family.* Thousand Oaks: Sage, 2001.

Chuba, Kirsten. "'Incredibles 2' Team Talks Sequel Film's Push for Female Empowerment, Gender Equality." *Variety,* June 5, 2018. https://variety.com/2018/scene/news/incredibles-2-female-empowerment-gender-equality-1202833671/.

Fiander, Alexa. "Living Expenses in Urban vs. Suburban Neighborhoods." Zillow, March 6, 2017. Accessed July 17, 2019. http://zillow.mediaroom.com/2017-03-06-Families-Spend-9-000-More-a-Year-to-Live-in-City-vs-Suburbs.

Fischer, Jessica, and Veanne N. Anderson. "Gender Role Attitudes and Characteristics of Stay-at-Home and Employed Fathers." *Psychology of Men & Masculinity* 13, no. 1 (2012): 16.

Flacking, Renée, Uwe Ewald, and Bengt Starrin. "'I Wanted to Do a Good Job': Experiences of 'Becoming a Mother and Breastfeeding in Mothers of Very Preterm Infants After Discharge from a Neonatal Unit." *Social Science & Medicine* 64, no. 12 (2007): 2405–2416.

Gorry, Devon, and Diana W. Thomas. "Regulation and the Cost of Childcare." *Applied Economics* 49, no. 41 (2017): 4138–4147.

Hays, Sharon. *The Cultural Contradictions of Motherhood.* New Haven: Yale University Press, 1998.

Henderson, Angie C., Sandra M. Harmon, and Jeffrey Houser. "A New State of Surveillance? Applying Michel Foucault to Modern Motherhood." *Surveillance & Society* 7, no. 3/4 (2010): 231–247.

Hill Collins, Patricia. "The Meaning of Motherhood in Black Culture and Black Mother–Daughter Relationships." *Gender Through the Prism of Difference* (2005): 285–295.

hooks, bell. "Revolutionary Parenting," In *Feminist Theory: From Margin to Center.* London: Pluto Press, 2000.

Jones, Monique. "'The Incredibles' Director on Why We've Never Scene Frozone's Wife, Honey, in the Franchise." *Shadow and Act*, April 16, 2018. https://shadowandact.com/the-incredibles-director-on-why-weve-never-seen-frozones-wife-honey-in-the-franchise/.

Linshi, Jack. "Ashton Kutcher Will Give You a Shout-Out If You Find a Men's Bathroom with a Diaper Changing Station." *Time*, March 10, 2015. https://time.com/3739878/ashton-kutcher-bathroom-diaper/.

Noonan, Allan S., Hector Eduardo Velasco-Mondragon, and Fernando A. Wagner. "Improving the Health of African Americans in the USA: An Overdue Opportunity for Social Justice." *Public Health Reviews* 37, no. 12 (2016).

Obama, Michelle. *Becoming*. New York: Crown Publishing Group, 2018.

Okimoto, Tyler G., and Madeline E. Heilman. "The 'Bad Parent' Assumption: How Gender Stereotypes Affect Reactions to Working Mothers." *Journal of Social Issues* 68, no. 4 (2012): 704–724.

Pew Research Center. "The Rise in Dual Income Households." June 15, 2016. Accessed May 8, 2019. https://www.pewresearch.org/fact-tank/2019/06/12/fathers-day-facts/ft_16-06-14_fathersday_dual_income/.

Raisi, Maryam. "Representing Model Women in Iranian TV Series (Components of Considering Hijab during Attendance of Strangers)." *International Journal of Humanities and Cultural Studies 2356-5926* (2016): 2459–2472.

Scovell, Nell, and Sheryl Sandberg. *Lean In: Women, Work and the Will to Lead*. New York: Alfred A. Knopf, 2013.

U.S. Bureau of Labor Statistics. "Access to Paid and Unpaid Family Leave in 2018." Last modified February 26, 2019. Accessed May 14, 2019. https://www.bls.gov/opub/ted/2019/access-to-paid-and-unpaid-family-leave-in-2018.htm.

———. "Employment Characteristics of Families—2018." Last modified April 18, 2019. Accessed May 8, 2019. https://www.bls.gov/news.release/famee.toc.htm.

U.S. Department of Labor. "The Family and Medical Leave Act of 1993." 1993. Accessed November 12, 2017. from https://www.dol.gov/whd/regs/statutes/fmla.htm.

———. "Fact Sheet #28: The Family and Medical Leave Act of 1993." 2009. Accessed November 12, 2017. https://www.dol.gov/whd/fmla/fact_sheets.htm.

Walt Disney Animation Studios, *Ralph Breaks the Internet*, directed by Rich Moore and Phil Johnston, 2018, Digital Copy.

Walt Disney Studios Motion Pictures. *Incredibles 2*. Written and Directed by Brad Bird, 2018, DVD.

Wamsley, Laurel. "Michelle Obama's Take on 'Lean In?' 'That &#%! Doesn't Work.'" *NPR*, December 3, 2018. https://www.npr.org/2018/12/03/672898216/michelle-obamas-take-on-lean-in-that-doesn-t-work.

19

✣

The Women of Wakanda

Black Beauty and Casting

Abeo Jackson

Disney-Marvel's *Black Panther* (2018) was a story with a male protagonist superhero that also managed to center Black female characters. Dark skinned, beautiful, strong, powerful female characters; Okoye, Nakia, and Shuri live-action Disney-Marvel were characters who checked all the boxes for royalty, warrior, and genius, and turned the usual expected Disney "princess" trope entirely on its head.

To understand why the women of Wakanda are unique when it comes to casting it is important to examine casting of Black women before it. To date, the Marvel Cinematic Universe cast the following Black actresses in supporting or co-star roles: Zoe Saldana as Gamora in the *Guardians of the Galaxy* films, Tessa Thompson as the Asgardian Valkyrie in *Thor* and *Avenger* films, Laura Harrier as Liz Allan and Zendaya Coleman as Mary Jane in the *Spiderman* films, Hannah John-Kamen as Ghost in *Ant-Man and the Wasp*, and Lashana Lynch as Maria Rambeau in *Captain Marvel*. Elsewhere around Disney, for Lucasfilm: Crystal Clarke and Femi Taylor were cast in *The Force Awakens* and *Return of the Jedi* respectively, and Thandie Newton in *Solo: A Star Wars Story*. Lupita Nyong'o appeared in both *The Force Awakens* and *Return of the Jedi* as a computer-voice. For Walt Disney Studios, Audra McDonald and Gugu Mbatha-Raw were cast in 2017's *Beauty and the Beast* live-action. Storm Reid was cast as Meg Murry, Gugu Mbatha-Raw was cast as her mother Dr. Kate Murry and Oprah Winfrey was cast as Mrs. Which in 2018's *Wrinkle in Time*. Nico Parker (Thandie Newton's daughter) was cast as Milly Farrier in 2019's *Dumbo* live-action, and Beyoncé was cast as Nala's voice in *The Lion King* (2019).

It is interesting to note in the list of previous Marvel and Disney casting that all the lighter shaded, mixed-race/ethnically ambiguous women are given visibility and may even play the romantic interest of a white male, while those who are darker hued are "de-humanized" in some way; an ever prevalent trend as it pertains to the treatment of the Black female form, particularly those of darker complexion in Hollywood. There is much to unpack and consider with these casting choices, such as the idea of who is an acceptable Black female love interest or child to a white male, or that the only way an audience can accept that a white male Hollywood leading man can fall in love with a Black woman is if she bears some visual proximity to whiteness and Eurocentric ideas of beauty. For instance Chris Pratt's Star-Lord falls for Zoe Saldana's Gamora; Tom Holland falls for two Black girls: Harrier and Zendaya in back to back films, Gugu's husband in *Wrinkle in Time* is Chris Pine and Storm Reid's white male lead Levi Miller, finds her attractive and likes her hair in *Wrinkle in Time*. Nico Parker, Thandie Newton's biracial daughter's father is Colin Farrell in *Dumbo*.

The casting choice of Halle Bailey as Ariel for *The Little Mermaid* live-action remake received much vitriol and backlash against Disney with the #NotMyAriel hashtag. Early digital discourse called for Prince Eric to be white, Latino, or racially ambiguous. We also must consider the constant eroticizing of mixed-race love interests when casting a Black woman in an on screen romance. It begs the question as to why Hollywood has for decades refused to normalize imagery of Black love and has deemed it unpalatable for big budget white audiences.

Oprah being cast in *A Wrinkle in Time* was very literally a quirky new age whimsical take on the Magical Negro that thankfully in some ways was overshadowed by Ava DuVernay being the director. They managed to somehow override the trope because of the nuance both she and Winfrey brought to the character. Arguments can also be made for the fact that DuVernay, being director of such a big budget film, the first non-white woman to direct a live-action film with a budget of over $100 million, and so soon after *Black Panther*, was a gigantic leap for representation despite it being a box office disappointment. There were quite a few who believed the film lacked the signature DuVernay touch and style and it may very well be brought full circle to the manipulation of big studios in the casting and telling of the story. It was a hodgepodge attempt at representation while still pandering to the approval of whiteness, hence its feeling of being generally disingenuous. *Black Panther* worked because of its unapologetic authenticity, while *A Wrinkle in Time* didn't quite seem to hit the right notes and didn't seem to resonate with either Black or white audience demographics.

LACK OF REPRESENTATION THROUGH LACK OF OPPORTUNITY

There are still those who would argue the significance of "representation" in popular culture as the discourse around the casting of a Black Ariel showed. Many Black women online posted in response that for years they had to contend with watching white beauty either as princesses or otherwise on screen. And when they finally got a Black princess she was promptly turning into a frog for over 90 percent of the film. Scholar Shawn Michelle Smith[1] reiterates W.E.B. Du Bois' concept of double consciousness.

> In "The Souls of Black Folk", W.E.B. DuBois describes "double consciousness" as "the sense of always looking at oneself through the eyes of others" and thereby situates a visual model of subjectivity at the center of what he calls "the strange meaning of being black."[2]

Major gatekeepers and stakeholders within Hollywood or Broadway, or as far as West End, continue to passively ignore the perpetuation of colonial racial hierarchies in casting. Black and minority storytellers and actors have had to fight for decades to ensure they are not relegated to fringe players in an industry that was never initially designed with them in mind. There has been an obvious and in many ways understandable lack of funding and promotion of Black and minority stories over the decades and those that have made it to mainstream production were devoid of the nuance that can only come from the agency and actual lived experiences of authentic storytelling. Such projects lacked black and brown folk around the writing tables and as such their voices and stories became marginalized leading to the creation of many damaging tropes and one-dimensional characters. One of the groups who have been most subjected to this phenomenon has been Black women, leading to the pigeonholing and sidelining of Black female actors.

A long line of Black film critics, writers, poets, academics, and theorists have left a legacy of interrogation with regard to our image exploitation, the performance of Blackness and the white gaze, as well as the unpacking of various tropes and stereotypes from the 1920s onward. These scholars[3] have all written extensively about the need for representation, expounding on the reasons why Black creatives must have control of their own narratives. Now as cinema has fast forward to a brand new era of widely successful Black storytellers (Ryan Coogler, Ava DuVernay, Shonda Rhimes, Jordan Peele, to name a few) seemingly having more control over what we as a community create for mass consumption, others cite this as a post–racial Hollywood era. The experiences of Black creatives continue to be living testimony for the continued need for advocacy and creation of opportunities within the community. Elizabeth Reich[4] notes the ever-present reasons for Black film criticism to remain vigilant.

> While black film critics must continue to track the content, aesthetics and methods of new media, and contextualize, theorize, debate their impact, they now also struggle against being rendered moot by the increasingly prevalent belief that we live in a colorblind society. . . . And they have to wage nearly constant warfare against the mainstream media's appropriation and manipulation of black bodies . . .[5]

Today, Black filmmakers continued to expand their own agency. More recently, producer, writer, and director Jordan Peele sparked immense backlash amongst white audiences and quietly white Hollywood when he emphatically stated after his record-setting opening of 2019's *Us*, that he had no intention of making movies starring "'white dudes.' That he has seen that movie."[6] Therefore, as much as the creative forces behind juggernauts like Disney and other major studios like Sony aim to cast diversely or add inclusion riders, until Black creatives control casting decisions and are given freedom by studios to make Black casting choices, it is not enough to trust that the full spectrum of Black representation will make its way on screen. It will mean in the short-run, there may be Black Ariel's or Black MJ's, but they are more likely to look like Zendaya and Zoe Saldana, than Lupita Nyong'o and Letitia Wright.

LIVED EXPERIENCES OF THE BLACK "ACTRESS"

As a Black woman, becoming an actor who achieves even marginal mainstream success is *the* elusive dream. The actual proportion of mainstream leading female actors and the evidence of pay disparity within the industry between Black women and their white majority male and female counterparts compounds this reality. Among the acting community, there has been the recent myth on the London scene that "it is a good time to be a BAME actor in the UK." The same myth also has echoes in Hollywood. Apparently it has become hip for agents to scout Black and Minority Actors because there are "so many more roles" now for Black actors. The opposite still remains true.

In examining casting ratios and averages in the U.K., there are often calls for one role for a Black/Black British/Black Caribbean female actor, playing a character between the ages of twenty-five to thirty. This contrasts with approximately ten to fifteen roles for White/Caucasian female actors of the same playing age. The rationale that "it is a good time to be black" because there are more white counterparts competing for those ten to fifteen roles than there are of Black actors competing for the one role is refuted by the fact that the percentages of aspiring Black actors coming out of drama school has risen steadily over the last decade.[7]

According to a British film industry study between the years 2006 to 2016,[8] there was a paucity of roles for Black actors in contemporary modern British films. Out of 1,172 films included in the study, 59 percent did not feature a single Black actor in a named character role at all. The one film sub-genre that Black actors were in fact featured in, to a staggering 65 percent, was crime-drama. These story lines and character types sideline Black actors and particularly Black womanhood to the ghetto, to some kind of romanticized violence and trauma, to the gag of being the loud best friend with no real featured or developed story line, or to the magical "negro" mama who swoops in to save the day.

It also paints Blackness as a monolith with regard to indigenous cultures to the point of "caricatureship," leaving almost no room for non-U.S. Black women or authentic stories about immigrant experiences that would have helped to build the spaces in which they exist. As Viola Davis said in her speech in 2018 when she became the first African American woman to win the Emmy for Outstanding Lead Actress in a drama series: "The only thing that separates women of color from everyone else is opportunity. . . . You cannot win an Emmy for roles that are simply not there."[9] #OscarsSoWhite would suggest that this lack of opportunity extends more generally.

This movement to Hollywood only floods the U.S. pool of actors, where underrepresentation still remains relatively unchanged. A 2018 University of Southern California study[10] on representation in mainstream Hollywood found that women, and particularly Black women, alongside other minorities such as Asian and LGBT actors, are still grossly underrepresented both on screen and behind the camera. The study spanned from eleven years from 2007 to 2017 and examined the top 1,100 films. The researchers noted that 30.6 percent of characters were female-speaking roles. In 2017, the study noted that forty-three of the top films of that year had no Black female characters. Additionally in 2017, in the thirty-three films that featured women as leads or co-stars, only four of those roles were played by a woman from an underrepresented group. The study's final year findings were unchanged from the year before. The researchers concluded that "The lack of inclusion on screen is matched and exceeded by the exclusion behind the camera," with 4.3 percent of directors being women and 5.2 percent Black over the entire eleven-year study.[11]

The "Gentrification" of Blackness: Hollywood Packaging and Consumption

The data supports the anecdotes both in the U.K. and the U.S. of the struggles of particularly Black female actors who fall to the bottom of the casting food chain as they battle with ideas of Eurocentric concepts of beauty and what is deemed easily marketable for consumption. They still largely have not made the mark for palatability for projections of largely white audiences. In recalling Afro-Caribbean philosopher Frantz Fanon's *Black Skin, White Masks*,[12] scholar Dianca London[13] contemplates the danger of the "white gaze."

> When race is signified via the white gaze, narratives involving people of color are otherized. Their stories become tangential, contingent upon their proximity to or distance from whiteness. When the white gaze is privileged, all other identities are jeopardized, confining marginalized bodies to typecast tokenism or, even worse, erasure.[14]

One such actress who has had to wrestle her way through the trappings of the "white gaze" constraints on Black women's casting is Viola Davis. Scholar Fanta Sylla[15] summarizes well, that despite all her talent, Viola Davis' career had been shaped by how Hollywood perceives a dark-skinned, natural hair, middle-aged Black woman.

> The peculiar situation of an actress like Viola Davis is that much of her job requires/involves a looking relationship with an audience that doesn't want to look at her. Or one that will only concede to look at her under certain conditions: degraded, hypersexualized, ridiculed or bundled up in rehashed caricatures and insipid narratives. An audience that has not been trained to look at her the way she deserves to be looked at. She's working in an industry that is more than complicit, if not the main culprit, in erasing, de-eroticizing and vilifying her body. Indeed, cinematic spaces have historically rejected the (dark-skinned) Black body, constructing it as abject, ugly, expendable and unable to inspire empathy and identification. This is the structure within which Viola Davis tries to exist and be visible.[16]

The debate in the industry today for Black female actors is how can we find a healthy balance that not only accepts or tolerates our differences as artists—like Black physicality, lived experiences, socio-political and socio-economic contexts, and so on, but also celebrates and honestly examines them? How can Black creatives navigate the existing industry and demand that it treats with our individual flaws and shortcomings with the authenticity of human nuance and not as monolithic representations of an entire race?

NEW MEDIA AND A NEW BLACK HOLLYWOOD RENAISSANCE

The current social media and digital landscape has expanded not just the conversation around Black representation, but provided the support for

Black creatives to speak through their work to the Hollywood powers that be. From Tyler Perry to Ava DuVernay, from HBO to Netflix, new platforms and technology have allowed Black filmmakers to begin making our own work, thus gaining more visibility through sharing our stories. We have since begun carving our own creative spaces that over the last decade have started what I have previously described[17] as a new digital "Black Renaissance" of sorts actively intersecting with mainstream Hollywood. Unlike the Blaxploitation film era of the 1970s where Hollywood tried to capitalize on Black film, with stories and characters they believed were geared specifically toward a Black audience, this new Black Creative Renaissance is controlled largely by us. We have boldly started taking creative and financial control of our own narratives and the imagining of our own characters born out of lived experiences. Enter pioneering personalities such as Oprah Winfrey, Tyler Perry, Issa Rae, Shonda Rhimes, and Ava DuVernay who have established themselves as some of the architects of the new Black Hollywood that has begun to undo and deconstruct the damaging aspects of the current existing model.

These showrunners with relatively new financial agency, built-in fandoms and followings, proven box office receipts, and critical acclaim within the industry have all categorically advocated for more producers, writers, and directors of color and more specifically women of color. They have gone so far to make a point of creating and promoting content geared specifically toward that agenda. They have openly called for more Black critics to view and review their work first, before it is subjected to the rest of the industry. This has created a huge shift in the mainstream in the way Blackness is portrayed onscreen and most refreshingly created new work for Black actors, creatives, and academics throughout what is proving to be a hugely profitable, hip-happening, relevant, and innovatively parallel Black Hollywood industry.

With our new visibility facilitated by social and new media as well as the harnessing of financial agency by major Black players in the industry, has come more and more tangible evidence of untapped, or maybe we could venture to say unexploited talent, both in front of and behind the camera. The more we began seeing ourselves as nuanced, multi-dimensional and brilliant, the more other young and previously unheard of talents emerged almost making the continued lack of opportunity with mainstream roles and auditions moot, or at least less daunting. We have in essence started to create our own viable industry that has begun to inextricably weave itself into the very mainstream that had long sought to deny us. This new found exposure also began to challenge established stereotypes particularly as it pertained to one of the long revered and unchallenged cornerstones of mainstream Hollywood: the Eurocentric standard of beauty. This included ideas about the exoticism, over-sexualization, desexualization, and colorism Black female bodies and how Black female actors are viewed and hired.

THE IMAGININGS OF THE WOMEN OF WAKANDA

On examination of the very real phenomenon versus the stereotype of the strong Black woman and how it may or may not manifest in Disney and Marvel's Black utopia, Wakanda, one can surmise two very diametrically opposed perspectives. The first having to do with the suggestion that the story of Wakanda and its warrior heroes is rooted firmly, like much of history dating all the way back to the colonial era, in the idea that Black communities are dependent upon its women to survive, much less thrive. This dependency involves Black women making difficult decisions on their own, often picking up the slack for men, filling their roles when families were forcibly separated, back then by colonial masters, while today it could be anything from incarceration to drug and gang violence or overarching general dysfunction born out of toxic conditioning from societies rooted in a colonial legacy that continues to spawn systemic micro-aggressions against Black men and women. Black women continue to weather these very real-life looming villains, much like the women heroes of Wakanda all for the betterment and survival of their community. The leading ladies of Wakanda are the ones forced to make the hard decisions when things fall apart and the men can't seem to get it together long enough to not consume each other while at the same time annihilating everything in their path.

It was hence easy to understand why audiences around the world fell in love with Shuri, Nakia, and Okoye, because while they were literally "kicking ass" on camera with gadgets and advanced spears and technology, the fact is many Black women truly saw themselves. We recognized the everyday warriors we have always been, managing to fight in the ideologies of the "colonizer" while also holding our men down, loving them fiercely, though many times they seem hell bent on self sabotage and self-destruction. The love stories between Nakia and T'Challa as well as Okoye and W'Kabi, though their relationship was decidedly less developed than the other, clearly demonstrate a dynamic of women who are quite capable of saving themselves and everybody else. Meanwhile the bond between Shuri and her brother T'Challa further and quite literally emphasized the idea of Black women as the brains of the entire operation.

The other perspective one can consider is the very dangerous trope of the independent Black woman: emotionally dysfunctional, exhausted from taking care of everyone around her, and seemingly undeserving of love. At a cursory glance Nakia's refusal to commit to T'Challa and Okoye's defiance and willingness to face off against W'Kabi on the battlefield could lead an audience down the path of depictions of the angry Sapphire archetype and the well used one dimensional narrative of the Black woman's tragic inability to find love without duress. However Coogler managed to shape the stories of these characters in a way that celebrated their independence and prowess on the battlefields all while demonstrating just how fiercely they were capable of loving and deserving of being loved in return. They were capable of disagreeing with each other as women on principle and still respecting each other, ultimately retaining the bonds of sisterhood and loyalty to country. There arguably has not been a more wholly feminist representation of on screen Disney royalty. There is no looking back. *Black Panther* laid a blueprint.

Frog Princess Tiana aside, Nakia, Shuri, and Okoye are finally the "kickass" Black female superheroes which come as close to Black royalty that every young Black, particularly dark-skinned Black girls, have been waiting on since the dawn of on-screen magic and fairy tales. Who needs a waif-like princess when we've always been warriors? Black women's ancestral memory and DNA has never resonated with Snow White and Cinderella or the obsession with vulnerability that centers power on white men; prompting an industry tradition that posits Black female actors as not comparatively attractive, desirable and too aggressive for the affection of a white male lead. We have always needed and wanted our on screen princesses more akin to Yaa Asantewaa and the women of the Mino otherwise known as the Dahomey Amazons.

The industry can no longer ignore Black consumers interests in their visibility. When Danai Gurira's name and character Okoye was left off the official *Avengers: Endgame* poster in March 2019, fans protested. Journalist and critic Jamil Smith tweeted:

> BLACK PANTHER star Danai Gurira is the only actor pictured whose name isn't billed at the top. Her image is larger than some actors who do get that billing. The only one from the franchise's best and most profitable movie, and yet? @MarvelStudios, this isn't difficult. Fix this.[18]

Again Marvel and Disney felt the onslaught of social media backlash and were forced to redo and re-release the poster. Black women and fans had spoken. The recognized financial and creative agency, post-*Black Panther*, is a notch on the belt of every Black female actor walking into a casting. It is the inspiration for Black creatives all across the globe to continue to tell our stories in our own voices and accents, in every language, exploring genres that have otherwise been denied us in mainstream and the impetus for the exploration and investment in new platforms on which those stories can be shared. It also should be noted that the pressure for all our work and stories to be "successful" or a hit is a concept with which we have to grapple. There also must be the same freedoms afforded to our narratives; they cannot be expected to all be monolithic yard sticks and representations for an entire Diaspora. Our stories must be normalized and each piece of work should be able to stand on its own and allowed to authentically exist and be critiqued for what it is, while still celebrating the fact there are now opportunities and spaces for our narratives to thrive. This same freedom to authentically exist in the glare of pop culture must also be given to the Black female form.

To that end, ideally what *Black Panther* and the new Black princess-warrior has done, is further prove to mainstream Hollywood that Black female actors are deserving and nuanced, which is still arguably subjective. The dark-skinned, natural-haired women of Wakanda also served to visibly deconstruct damaging stereotypes pertaining to Blackness and beauty. Especially within our own community where we still struggle with inherited colonial legacies of colorism persistently reinforced through mainstream casting and images. Forget race ambiguity and the eroticizing of lighter-skinned, mixed-raced female actors, Disney-Marvel, through Coogler's genius, has possibly played a major role in setting a new standard of beauty and acceptance in mainstream Hollywood that as an industry is markedly late in coming to the realization that Blackness is inherently beautiful. The women of Wakanda were a proclamation that natural Black hair with a tight kink, or no hair at all on a dark skinned woman is not only "acceptable," but beautiful, and a mark of royalty and strength. It cannot be underscored enough how powerfully that imagery resonated in cinemas around the world.

Mostly and more importantly to the financial bottom-line, it has proven marketability and profitability. There is an audience for badass Black women. We've always known that, even if Hollywood has been purposefully slow on the uptake. Hence the doors may not blast open and seats at the table may not suddenly be made available, but a very heavy wedge has been placed under the door. Okoye, Nakia, and Shuri make it harder for "them" to deny "us." The hope now, is that other mainstream genres are lured in by the magical world of Disney and Marvel profit, thus encouraged to hire more Black showrunners and creatives, investing in our stories, thus creating roles across the board that were not previously an option.

NOTES

1. Shawn Michelle Smith, "'Looking at One's Self Through the Eyes of Others': W.E.B. Du Bois' Photographs for the 1900 Paris Exposition," *African American Review* 34, no. 4: 581–599.

2. Ibid.

3. W.E.B. Du Bois, William Edward Burghardt, and Manning Marable, *Souls of Black Folk* (New York: Routledge, 2015); Frantz Fanon, *Black Skin, White Masks*

(London: Paladin, 1970); bell hooks, *Yearning: Race, Gender, and Cultural Politics* (Boston: South End Press, 1990); Langston Hughes, *Black Misery* (New York: Paul S. Eriksson, 1969); Zora Neale Hurston, *How It Feels to Be Colored Me* (Carlisle, MA: Applewood Books, 2015; 1928).

4. Elizabeth Reich, *The Power of Black Film Criticism* (Ann Arbor, University of Michigan Library, 2016).

5. Ibid.

6. Tonja Renée Stidhum, "Them: A Fake Yet Relevant Film About the White Men Pissed at Jordan Peele for Saying He Won't Make a Film Starring a 'White Dude,'" *The Root*, March 28, 2019, https://thegrapevine.theroot.com/them-a-fake-yet-relevant-film-about-the-white-men-piss-1833633666.

7. Matthew Hemley, "Drama School Stats Challenge Diversity 'Crisis' Complaints," *The Stage*, July 17, 2014, https://www.thestage.co.uk/news/2014/drama-school-stats-challenge-diversity-crisis-complaints/.

8. Melanie Hoyes, "Infographic: The True Picture for Black Actors in the UK Film Industry," *British Film Institute*, December 19, 2016, https://www.bfi.org.uk/news-opinion/news-bfi/features/black-actors-british-film-industry-statistics.

9. Ibid.

10. USC Annenberg, "Happy to Fire, Reluctant to Hire: Hollywood Inclusion Remains Unchanged," *USC News*, July 30, 2018, https://news.usc.edu/147111/diversity-in-hollywood-remains-unchanged-stacy-smith/.

11. Ibid.

12. Frantz Fanon, *Black Skin, White Masks* (London: Paladin, 1970).

13. Dianca London, "'Get Out' and the Revolutionary Act of Subverting the White Gaze," *Medium*, March 9, 2017, https://medium.com/the-establishment/get-out-and-the-revolutionary-act-of-subverting-the-white-gaze-c769cb620496#.nz7a4abb6.

14. Ibid.

15. Abeo Jackson, "A Legacy of Trauma and Perceptions of Vulnerability/Emotional Availability. How Does Generational Trauma Affect the Practice of the Black Female Actor," Master's thesis, Royal Central School of Speech and Drama, 2018.

16. Fanta Sylla, "Anatomy of a Black Actress: Viola Davis–The Toast," *The Toast*, September 29, 2015, http://the-toast.net/2015/09/29/anatomy-of-a-black-actress-viola-davis/.

17. Abeo Jackson, "The New Creative Renaissance," accessed July 1, 2019, https://abeojacksonproductions.wordpress.com/2019/01/09/the-new-creative-renaissance/.

18. Jamil Smith, @JamilSmith, Twitter post, March 14, 2019, 7.59 a.m., https://twitter.com/JamilSmith/status/1106208324154880001.

BIBLIOGRAPHY

bell hooks, *Yearning: Race, Gender, and Cultural Politics* (Boston: South End Press, 1990);

Du Bois, W.E.B., William Edward Burghardt, and Manning Marable. *Souls of Black Folk*. New York: Routledge, 2015.

Fanon, Frantz. *Black Skin, White Masks*. London: Paladin, 1970.
Hemley, Matthew. "Drama School Stats Challenge Diversity 'Crisis' Complaints." *The Stage*, July 17, 2014. https://www.thestage.co.uk/news/2014/drama-school-stats-challenge-diversity-crisis-complaints/.
Hoyes, Melanie. "Infographic: The True Picture for Black Actors in the UK Film Industry." *British Film Institute*, December 19, 2016. https://www.bfi.org.uk/news-opinion/news-bfi/features/black-actors-british-film-industry-statistics.
Hughes, Langston. *Black Misery*. New York: Paul S. Eriksson, 1969.
Hurston, Zora Neal. *How It Feels to Be Colored Me*. Carlisle, MA: Applewood Books, 2015, 1928.
Jackson, Abeo. "The New Creative Renaissance." Accessed July 1, 2019, https://abeojacksonproductions.wordpress.com/2019/01/09/the-new-creative-renaissance/.
———. "A Legacy of Trauma and Perceptions of Vulnerability/Emotional Availability. How Does Generational Trauma Affect the Practice of the Black Female Actor." Master's thesis, Royal Central School of Speech and Drama, 2018.
London, Dianca. "'Get Out' And the Revolutionary Act of Subverting the White Gaze." *Medium*, March 9, 2017. https://medium.com/the-establishment/get-out-and-the-revolutionary-act-of-subverting-the-white-gaze-c769cb620496#.nz7a4abb6.
Reich, Elizabeth. *The Power of Black Film Criticism*. Ann Arbor, University of Michigan Library, 2016.
Smith, Jamil @JamilSmith, Twitter post, March 14, 2019, 7.59 a.m., https://twitter.com/JamilSmith/status/1106208324154880001.
Smith, Shawn Michelle. "'Looking at One's Self Through the Eyes of Others': W.E.B. Du Bois' Photographs for the 1900 Paris Exposition." *African American Review* 34, no. 4: 581–599.
Stidhum, Tonja Renée. "Them: A Fake Yet Relevant Film about the White Men Pissed at Jordan Peele for Saying He Won't Make a Film Starring a 'White Dude.'" *The Root*, March 28, 2019. https://thegrapevine.theroot.com/them-a-fake-yet-relevant-film-about-the-white-men-piss-1833633666.
Sylla, Fanta. "Anatomy of a Black Actress: Viola Davis—The Toast." *The Toast*, September 29, 2015. http://the-toast.net/2015/09/29/anatomy-of-a-black-actress-viola-davis/.
USC Annenberg. "Happy to Fire, Reluctant to Hire: Hollywood Inclusion Remains Unchanged." *USC News*, July 30, 2018. https://news.usc.edu/147111/diversity-in-hollywood-remains-unchanged-stacy-smith/.

20

✢

Culture Wars and the Politics of *Finding Dory*

Prairie Endres-Parnell

"YEP, I'M GAY."

In 1997, stand-up comedian Ellen DeGeneres came out as gay on her sitcom, *Ellen*, and launched herself into the tabloids. ABC affiliates refused to air the sitcom, and sponsors of the show withdrew their support. Despite support from gay-friendly activists, the show was cancelled in 1998 amid a mix of hate mail, bomb threats, and thank you letters.[1] Between 1998 and 2003, DeGeneres struggled to find a balance between her newly ascribed identity as an LGBTQ leader and her role as a public persona in comedy. Rhetorically, DeGeneres aided and abetted the media in assigning her the role of lesbian heroine, appearing on the cover of *Time* with the headline "Yep, I'm Gay."[2] Unfortunately for DeGeneres, that interest came with a response from ABC to attach a parental advisory to *The Ellen Show* due to push back from conservative Christian groups. CNN reported that Disney, who owns ABC, "has been under attack from conservative religious groups over the 'Ellen' coming-out episode"[3] and responded with the following warning: "Due to adult content, parental discretion is advised" and a rating of TV-14.[4]

Ellen was cancelled in 1998, and the actress was out of work in the film and TV industry.[5] In a 2001 interview with Eric Marcus for the "Making Gay History" podcast, DeGeneres recalls:

> Ellen: Yeah. I think so. . . . I don't think it was just ABC. And I don't think it was just Disney. . . . And then when the advisory label came on. . . . Suddenly there was a warning label to put the kids away. You know like, "Don't let

kids see this." And, so . . . I became trouble. . . . And they didn't want that. Especially from a woman. Especially from a gay woman. And I was just too much trouble.[6]

DeGeneres' identity was defined within the context of the Disney-ABC family media company and the 1998 media. In those years between the cancellation of Ellen in 1998, and being cast in *Finding Nemo* in 2000, DeGeneres said, "I went through a phase, whether it was true or not, where my perception was, 'Everyone hates me now.'"[7] *Finding Nemo* director Andrew Stanton consistently said the Dory role was written specifically for Ellen DeGeneres: "without Ellen there is no Dory and it's the most symbiotic role I've ever written."[8]

Research must question, then, how DeGeneres made the jump from discarded and shunned comedian/actress into Disney star, twice over, as well as successful daytime TV host. The brief history provided here sets the stage for a rhetorical examination of the media frenzy surrounding Ellen, the way the media and her own performed persona regained her status as an "acceptable" icon for children and adults. DeGeneres' acknowledged why Dory became symbolic of her own journey: "She just keeps swimming, she just keeps going, she perseveres, and I think that's something that resonated."[9] This chapter will first outline theories of identity, LGBTQ identification in the media, and research into the acceptability of LGBTQ voices within children's discourse. Next, this chapter examines *Finding Nemo* and *Finding Dory* for their long-term impact on American society as it explores issues of identity, belonging, and finding one's place in the world.

IDENTITY: FRAMING ONES' OWN SELF-IMAGE

Research into identity management and presentation throughout the field of communication has grown in the past thirty years. Michael Hecht's Theory of Identity allows us to break Ellen's identity into four types of identity. Hecht reminds scholars that all identity is a communicative process; one that we must understand as being part of an exchange: "These messages are symbolic linkages between and among people that, at least in part, are enactments of identity. Even when identity is largely symbolic, communication rituals are used to create and express it."[10]

Hecht further unpacks his theory through the use of dialectical tensions, narrative, and social demands. These tensions, and the related axioms, create four frames of identity. These frames are the personal, the enacted, the relational, and the communal. These frames allow researchers to understand identity as characteristic of each of these branches of identity. The dialectical tensions reveal the individual identity and the way the identity is revealed through conflict. In a subsequent article Hecht further explicates the four frames identified initially, and the usage associated with each. The first frame of personal identity is the "individual's self-concepts or self-images."[11] The second is enacted identity, which is the expressed identity of the individual. Third is relational identity, and fourth is communal identity:

> first, an individual develops and shapes his/her identity partially by internalizing how others view him/her. . . . Second, an individual identifies him/herself through his/her relationships with others. . . .Third, identities exist in relationship to other identities. . . . The final frame is called *communal identity* and deals with how collectivities define their identity.[12]

Hecht's research into the levels of identity enables this research to define DeGeneres' identity at various points in her career, and to pinpoint the identity ascribed to her by audiences. When we examine Ellen's public persona through the four categories we are able to see how she successfully queers Dory without violating social norms. Through the first frame, DeGeneres presents her own self-concept/self-image as a goofy, happy, casual, friendly girl-next-door. This self-concept, which she reinforces through interviews, on her own TV shows, and through her standup allows her to blend into normative society without challenging her audience as a "flaming" homosexual. When we examine DeGeneres through the second frame, enacted identity, we see her performing good works through charity, communicating and helping with a wide variety of persons on her TV shows, and interacting through social media, and comfortably present with her audiences on her shows. Additionally, we see her history as a quiet but continuous LGBTQ advocate. The third frame of relational identity is what the bulk of this chapter investigates as we examine how others see Ellen. As mentioned earlier in quotes from an interview, Ellen internalized how the audience viewed her after her sitcom and endeavored to change that view in order to gain more acceptance. Once she was accepted in a neutral presentation, as shown through the first frame, she began to show again her connection with diverse cultural groups: LGBTQ persons, persons of color, persons with disabilities, diverse family types, and more. The fourth frame of communal identity is what enables audiences to view Ellen as non-threatening, while the nameless women who may or may not be lesbians within Dory are viewed as threatening to society. Ellen's mantra of "being kind" creates a communal identity that encourages her audiences to get along and support each other. The creation of four layers of positive identity set Ellen DeGeneres up to be an acceptable lesbian in wider popular culture.

AVOWED AND ASCRIBED IDENTITIES

As noted in the research on Hecht's Communication Theory of Identity, individual identities are created both personally and cooperatively. The individual claimed an avowed identity, which Hecht breaks into two parts: the internalization of how others view them and an analysis of relationships with others. This avowed identity is what we prefer to be, what we claim ourselves to be. There can be conflict between the avowed and ascribed identity. An ascribed identity is one that is assigned to an individual. This represents Hecht's third and fourth frames that identities exist in relation to other identities as well as how collectives define and interact with an individual. In this study of Ellen DeGeneres and *Finding Dory*, clarity between these two identities is valuable as it allows the audience to compare the Ellen of activist lesbian status and the Ellen of *Finding Dory*, the safe lesbian. Additionally, using avowed and ascribed identities allows us to track which DeGeneres identity is most similar to our own, enabling further positive identification with her through the concept of consubstantiation.

Identity and Consubstantiation

When discussing identity Kenneth Burke begins simply: "transformation involves the ideas and imagery of identification."[13] This phrase complexly and completely underscores the ways in which identification occurs. Burke's concept of consubstantiality allows us to examine how even the most homophobic, heteronormative audience member believes that DeGeneres is "just like them." Burke writes:

> A is not identical with his colleague, B. But insofar as their interests are joined, A is identified with B. Or he may identify himself with B even when their interests are not joined, if he assumes that they are, or is persuaded to believe so. Here are ambiguities of substance. In being identified with B, A is "substantially one" with a person other than himself. Yet, at that same time he remains unique, an individual locus of motives. Thus he is both joined and separate, at once a distinct substance and consubstantial with another.[14]

Burke uses consubstantiality as an action created by the individual in order to create change. Through the concept of consubstantiality comes the ability for transformation. As long as a viewing audience believes that they are both "joined and separate" with DeGeneres and what the audience has ascribed to her, then she is not a threat.

Impact of Lesbianism in Media

The action of defining ones' sexual identity takes many forms when dealing with media. Yescavage and Alexander argue that Ellen DeGeneres's character of Ellen on her TV show "reinforces some very traditional understandings of sexual orientation, while avoiding more complicated and provocative questions about the role of sexual behavior in human relationships and identity."[15] On the show *Ellen*, the character of Ellen is defined in absence of male attraction, rather than the presence of female sexual moments. The absence of a mate for Dory furthers the idea that Ellen, as Dory, who is perhaps "special needs" and is perhaps queer, can be read as non-threatening. There is no sexual identity, despite the fact that DeGeneres does not hide her marriage and love for her spouse. Indeed, no authors have yet suggested that Dory herself have a sexual identity. Instead, young viewers see singleness modeled in cases of being different.

Adults deal with DeGeneres through her TV shows, HBO and Netflix specials, and standup comedy, while children deal with her through the context of Disney and cameos in children-focused shows. LGBTQ characters in family shows require long-term lead ups that set the stage and prepare the audience for the inclusion of such a character. In the case of Dory, there was no such lead up, and some conservative viewers argued that the potentially lesbian couple shown in the film were an attempt to push a gay agenda. The American Family Association argued:

> Children also notice when something is framed positively or negatively.... If Disney ever begins framing gay relationships in the same way [positively], Christian parents will have to make a decision. Surely they will know their kids will learn the lesson that homosexuality is no different than heterosexuality. But the Bible say [sic] it is different. This contrast in views about sexual orientation will create a struggle for the child. Do they believe the Bible and their parents, or Disney? Which one is telling the truth?
> After seeing how much my granddaughter loves *Frozen*'s Elsa, this is not an insignificant matter. It has grave—and perhaps eternal—consequences.[16]

Similarly, David Roach argues "the more I view Disney shows and movies with my kids, the more I realize they contain elements that seem likely to influence children away from Christian doctrine and morality."[17] He concludes his article for the Baptist Press with a call for "vigilance in monitoring Disney products."[18] In both cases, the representation of LGBTQ persons in film is constructed as a challenge to morality that was snuck in on audiences in order to push a Hollywood agenda. The generic "Christian Right" continues to push against Disney with very limited success. On Disney Junior, a variety of shows targeted at young audiences display gay parents, possibly gay children, and a few deep web articles from disparate sources can be found that comment, briefly and without support, on the "queering" of children's television. Conservative, often religious, groups engaged in other moments of conflict surrounding other recent Disney films including *Frozen* and *Beauty and the Beast*: "In the broader context, the uproar over the possible presence of lesbians in 'Finding Dory' is just another battle in the conflict between liberal advocacy for greater inclusivity and conservative retrenchment against perceived liberal social imperialism."[19] Christian conservatives called for a boycott of the film due to the ascribed lesbian-hood of DeGeneres on social media, which cannot be accurately documented. Briefly trending on Twitter, #BoycottDory, had limited popularity, with responses quick to point out that DeGeneres already *was* a lesbian, regardless of a five second video clip, or the presence of ambiguous female cartoon figures. Consistently, however, the relatively few calls for boycotting the film did not focus on DeGeneres at all, but rather on those two animated women.

A similar boycott call was made again for another Pixar film—*Toy Story 4* included even longer frames of a mixed-race lesbian couple with their daughter at Bonnie's first day of kindergarten.[20] The group One Million Moms launched a petition at Disney for the lack of warning, pointing to gay blogs that celebrated the scene for "normalizing" gay families.[21] The group stated in the online petition that these types of scenes are becoming too common in children's entertainment. One Million Moms specifically argued that children are too young to be "confronted with content regarding sexual orientation."[22] The *Toy Story 4* petition concluded:

> Disney has decided once again to be politically correct versus providing family-friendly entertainment. Disney should stick to entertaining instead of pushing an agenda and exposing children to controversial topics.[23]

However families in the summer of 2019 who went to watch many of Disney's releases have encountered the trailer for the Metro-Goldwyn-Mayer's 2019 *The Addams Family* animated film. The trailer, shown before films like *Toy Story 4* and *The Lion King,* even from a different studio begins with more explicit constructs of family, with sketches of different types of families, including gay families. The trailer's script reads:

> This is an average American family
>
> [image of a white family, father and mother with 3 children]
>
> And so is this
>
> [image of a hetero-African American/Black family]
>
> And so are these
>
> [quickly changes to a family with two white dads, and a lesbian family with two moms—one Black and one white]
>
> Every family is different
>
> [quickly shifts through different combinations of races, adopted families, single-parent families]

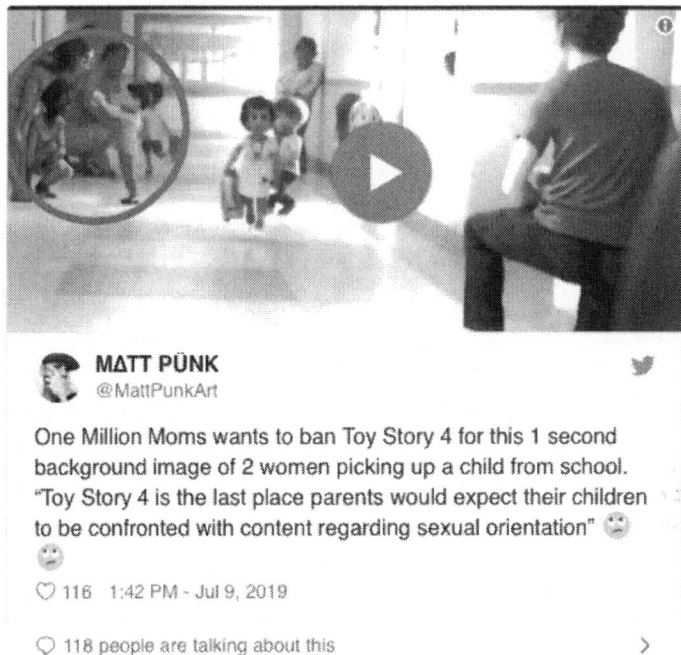

Figure 20.1. Social media reaction to One Million Moms petition of *Toy Story 4* scene.
Tweet in Hannah Lifshutz, "Conservative Christian Group Boycotting Disney and 'Toy Story 4' Over 'Dangerous' Lesbian Scene."

But some families are more different than others

[changes to the Addams family][24]

The entire sequence on types of families in the Addams family trailer lasts fifteen seconds, but its tone is that of a teaching moment. Disney stands in contrast to MGM as an avowed family friendly company; MGM studios does not. However, families who took their kids to watch Disney films in summer 2019 also saw the MGM preview. While advocates praised the MGM trailer for showing gay parents as the "average American family"[25] Disney is arguably held to a much more conservative standard. It is why conservative parents called out Disney for failing to include "warnings" about *Toy Story 4* and *Finding Dory*, because Disney is expected to consider all its families, including conservative ones. Disney grossed over $1.029 billion at the global box office for *Finding Dory* in 2016 because they could market a film that would be entertaining for all while being offensive to few.

Marketing to a wide audience explains why Disney's portrayal of gay parents is featured briefly and in the background. The animosity some parents showed toward featuring two moms in *Finding Dory* could be due to an ascription of romantic connection between the women. As mentioned previously, DeGeneres is held in a sex-less vacuum. She is safe because she is seen as devoid of sexuality. The women in the film are associated with a child, so the assumption could be that they the women are in a relationship in order to create that child. Such rhetorical assumptions on the part of the viewing audience mean that at some point in their own experiences, those audience members noting the women and the avowed sexual identity of DeGeneres, are looking for either consubstantiality, seeing someone "like them" in the film, or are looking to not be consubstantial, seeing someone "dangerous" in the film.

Disney and its team were also careful in how the film was promoted and marketed with DeGeneres as the lead. During the run-up interviews for *Finding Dory*, producers, writers, and actors were all challenged about the sexual identity of the two women revealed in the preview. DeGeneres' public coming out process in 1997 was heralded by a season long negotiation of the character of DeGeneres' identity, a process echoed by DeGeneres' own life. In *Finding Dory*, audiences had no such opportunity to become comfortable with the idea of lesbian parents. Arguably, the audience had no need for such comfort. The women appear onscreen for less than five seconds, and DeGeneres, director Andrew Stanton, and producer Lindsey Collins all said, "They can be whatever you want them to be. There's no right or wrong answer."[26] Some viewers called the two women lesbians due to the hairstyles presented in the film, to which DeGeneres responded: "'One of the women has really short hair. And I have to say, it's not a great haircut because it was really chopped up in the back. . . . I think people assume anyone with a bad short haircut is gay. Robin Wright has short hair. There are a lot of women that are straight that have short hair. It's just not as common.'"[27]

Perhaps a marker of lesbianism is short hair; perhaps, the emphasis should be more about claiming the identity in terms of consubstantiation. Applying the theories of identity explained earlier, we can draw the conclusions that we, the viewing audience, are looking for ways to be more like or less like what we view. We want to see ourselves reflected in our viewing habits.[28]

"JUST KEEP SWIMMING," DORY IN THE SPOTLIGHT

Analysis of *Finding Dory* show multiple opportunities for audience consubstantiation and connection. Ellen DeGeneres as a lead actress invites audiences into the film through her own accepted identity. DeGeneres alone cannot hold the audience in the theater or create a learning environment for the viewer to reflect on their own identity. Disney has long been an expert at allowing audiences to experience emotional connection with characters, whether those characters are human or not. *Finding Dory* is rife with parallels to DeGeneres' own discovery of self. In the film, we see the character of Dory as a fish lost at sea. She is accepted by Nemo and his father, Marlin, which allows her to feel comfortable enough with her own personal identity as it is currently presented. That place of acceptance enables Dory to search for her parents, and her "real" identity. It is not until Dory is happy and settled in with Marlin and Nemo as she ended the first movie, acting as a sister to Nemo, that she begins to remember her original family:

> See, I suffer from . . . short-term memory loss. . . . See, I can remember some things because well, they make sense. I have a family. I-I know, because I . . . You know, I must've come from somewhere, right? Everyone has a family. And I may not remember their names and what they look like. And I may not even be able to ever find them again. But . . . What are we talking about?[29]

Dory's acceptance as part of the Nemo/Marlin family enables her to move forward looking for her own family. This begins the films themes of differences being accepted, longing for acceptance, and diverse cultures. Moving further into the film the plot shows a diverse gathering of sea life. Such diversity models positive behaviors within a community. The group accepts everyone, even when Dory causes trouble, and makes use of the diverse abilities of each individual.

The film embodies DeGeneres' real life mantra to "be kind to one another." Dory speaks whale, Hank the octopus helps with the lengthy escape from the oceanarium, the sea lions help Nemo and Marlin get inside the oceanarium, Dory helps the beluga whale with his echolocation, and more. Each sea creature accepts Dory for who she is, believes in what she claims she can do, and accepts her help gracefully. Through the frames of identity, Dory successfully merges her ascribed identity of "forgetful" with an avowed identity of helpful. Despite the differences, Dory manages to overcome stigma of her "disability" and be accepted as useful. Similarly, the seven-legged octopus Hank is useful because of his disability, not in spite of it, as is Gerald, the "slower" sea lion. In both cases, their differences made them more helpful instead of less. This positive representation enables viewers with different abilities to see themselves represented in the film in a positive light. As mentioned previously, open-ended representations allow for consubstantiation between audience and character, cementing a positive relationship with the film.

When things go south in the film and Nemo and Marlin fail to reunite with Dory, Nemo reminds his father of the importance of their family unit:

Nemo: Dad, stop. She's not coming back.

Marlin: She might. Oorroo.

Nemo: Dad. You made her feel like she couldn't do it.

Marlin: You're not talking about Becky, are you?

Nemo: I miss Dory.

Marlin: Me too. The truth is I'm just so worried about her.[30]

The acceptance of Dory into the family unit despite the trouble she caused reinforces the concept of acceptance and belonging. While Nemo and Marlin are lost in the open ocean, Dory is lost in the pipes of the oceanarium. She encourages the beluga whale Bailey to use his skills in order to save the day. In doing so, the film again underscores the importance of being true to ones' self in order to succeed. While this is not truly a pro-LGBTQ acceptance reading of the text, such detailed examination shows that Disney remains true to a pro-audience message of acceptance and diversity despite any differences or challenges one might have. Marlin vocalizes this in his speech to Dory after they are reunited:

Dory: Do you think my parents will want to see me?

Marlin: What? Why wouldn't they want to see you?

Dory: Because . . . I lost them.

Marlin: Dory. Your parents are going to be overjoyed to see you. They're going to miss everything about you.

Dory: Really?

Marlin: Dory. Do you know how we found you? . . . We were having a very hard time. Until Nemo thought, "What would Dory do?"

Dory: Why would you say that?

Marlin: Because ever since I've met you, you showed me how to do stuff I never dream of doing. Crazy things. Outsmarting sharks and jumping jellyfish. And finding my son. You made all that happened.

Dory: Really? I didn't know you thought that.[31]

Marlin once again demonstrates his acceptance of Dory as herself, something to which Dory is oblivious. By the end of the film, Dory, Nemo, Marlin, and the host of other characters have demonstrated over and again a set of positive, reinforcing behaviors that model acceptance. Throughout the film Disney also provides numerous moments for the audience to identify with each of the characters, allowing the viewer to become consubstantial with the positive emotions that come with achieving one's goals within the film.

While Disney has successfully created a model for promoting behavioral and physical diversity, they remain slow in applying their own model toward overt LGBTQ acceptance. As of 2019, demonstrated LGBTQ acceptance has remained a primarily audience ascribed effort in Disney's works. However, even as I characterize Disney as slow to incorporate LGBTQ characters and behaviors, they are moving more rapidly than many other networks with their attempts at inclusion. Disney is positively aligned with LGBTQ interests. The parks have hosted a pride day, as a workplace Disney ranks positively for LGBTQ employees, and the Disney channel finally has its first openly gay character: Cyrus in the series *Andi Mack*, geared toward tween audiences. Like DeGeneres, the character Cyrus uttered the words "I'm Gay" on a Disney channel episode.[32]

Despite these positives, GLADD rebuked Disney for a lack of LGBTQ characters in 2019, citing limited screen time and lack of diversity in character development.[33] Disney seems to be at an impasse currently; their viewing audience of younger children is a demographic that is typically tightly controlled by parents who remain unsure about allowing LGBTQ characters into their living rooms. For now, the Dory model seems to be the approach by the studio for integrating acceptance into their films thus far through a film's story line, rather than its obvious characterization.

CONCLUSION

Viewing our own identities through the lens of media allows us to engage other identities in safe ways. Reed argues "DeGeneres continues to perform a specifically lesbian identity that speaks to gay and lesbian, or queer literature viewers as well, and thus must challenge heteronormativity at some level."[34] Past research on the impact of Disney on viewing audiences suggests that Disney films are the ideal location to challenge heteronormativity and define lesbianism as the films are "perceived as if they are 'neutral' and 'innocent.'"[35] Consumers must still continue to attempt to define lesbianism in the public eye. DeGeneres' coming out publicly on television paved a path for other coming out stories to be present in mainstream media with fewer negative impacts.[36] The identity that DeGeneres claimed resonated with audiences through terms of "authenticity," "true self," "the authority of experience" and as a "reflection of the real."[37]

DeGeneres' represents a lesbian we can like: "Of course we like Ellen. She's pretty and funny, and doesn't take herself too seriously, so we don't have to either."[38] Ellen as a construct is a concept of lesbianism that allows lesbians to be characters instead of people, keeping them at safe distances from which we, the viewing audience, can pick the parts of the character we like. The LGBTQ community can be consubstantial with a successful, well-liked, lesbian who appears in public to have an avowed and ascribed identity which matches. Hubert suggests that DeGeneres' coming out episode "provides a good measure of what the entertainment industry considers to be both within limits and off-limits for prime-time portrayals of gays and lesbians."[39] Those limits have shifted over time, as audiences become more accustomed to differences in characters.

DeGeneres was the first to define lesbian for an American audience, which set the stage for her acceptability and the acceptability of lesbianism in general. Harris suggests "Ellen's persona might be doing more good for the LGBTQ community/ies than bad . . . even [her] sanitized presence has created a greater comfort with the notion of 'gay' people as normative and powerful."[40] Here we encounter the idea of DeGeneres as a "sanitized presence," one which is acceptable, non-threatening, and who has performed heteronormativity on her TV shows, despite her avowed identity elsewhere. It becomes easy for us to focus on the elements of DeGeneres we desire to identify with. The LGBTQ community works to hold DeGeneres up as an icon of gayness, while a more conservative heterosexual audience views her as a safe icon who is not going to challenge their perceptions, while a third extremely conservative Christian audience views her as a slippery slope into debauchery. DeGeneres stands as a pawn in our own rhetorical construction of her identity. Her identity is simultaneously alike, unlike, safe, and troubled.

Ellen DeGeneres represents an acceptable taste of the LGBTQ culture and lifestyle. Hence she is the only gay person to lead a contemporary Disney film geared toward the smallest of children, and to do so with billion-dollar success. She and her wife reflect "safe" gay consumption: they are beautiful, respectful, funny, charming, and outgoing. Whether those personality traits are performances, or if that really is their personality, is moot to the audience reading their own desires onto DeGeneres. When DeGeneres first came out in public, on national TV and media, the backlash against her attempted performance as a lesbian was negative. Over time, through her own strength of personality, her ability to blend into a crowd, her diverse identity, and the support of the original writer for *Finding Nemo*, DeGeneres recreated her ascribed identity as one of an asexual, non-threatening, non-sexual tomboy next door. That the tomboy liked girls was an element that the general non-LGBTQ focused public could ignore in the light of her other accomplishments and personality. DeGeneres as Dory may pave the way for other LGBTQ actors/actresses to take starring roles in Disney films, but, those actors will need to be a specifically acceptable kind of LGBTQ person.

NOTES

1. Biography, "Ellen DeGeneres Biography," April 2, 2014, accessed March 14, 2019, https://www.biography.com/people/ellen-degeneres-9542420.
2. Bruce Handy, "Yep, I'm Gay," *Time*, April 14, 1997, https://time.com/4728994/ellen-degeneres-1997-coming-out-cover/.
3. *CNN*, "Ellen DeGeneres Angry Over Parental Advisory," October 9, 1997, accessed March 13, 2019, http://www.cnn.com/SHOWBIZ/9710/09/ellens.kiss/.
4. Ibid.
5. Hilary Weaver, "Ellen DeGeneres' Groundbreaking Coming Out: 20 Years Later," *Vanity Fair*, April 18, 2017, https://www.vanityfair.com/style/2017/04/20th-anniversary-of-ellen-degeneres-coming-out.
6. Ellen DeGeneres, "Interview by Eric Marcus," *Making Gay History: Ellen DeGeneres Podcast* February 17, 2001, accessed June 14, 2019, https://makinggayhistory.com/podcast/ellen-degeneres/.
7. Gwynne Watkins, "How 'Finding Nemo' Launched Ellen DeGeneres' Comeback," Yahoo!, June 17, 2016, https://www.yahoo.com/entertainment/how-finding-nemo-launched-ellen-165815366.html.
8. Bill Desowitz, "'Finding Dory' Preview: How Andrew Stanton Found Ellen DeGeneres' Forgetful Blue Tang," Indiewire, April 7, 2016, https://www.indiewire.com/2016/04/finding-dory-preview-how-andrew-stanton-found-ellen-degeneres-forgetful-blue-tang-21793/.
9. Ellen DeGeneres, "Interview by Graeme Kay," *Finding Nemo — An Interview with Andrew Stanton and Lee Unkrich,* IndieLondon, 2003, accessed June 14, 2019, http://www.indielondon.co.uk/film/finding_nemo_stanton_unkrich.html.
10. Michael Hecht, "2002—A Research Odyssey: Toward the Development of a Communication Theory of Identity," *Communication Monographs* 60, no. 1 (1993): 76–81.
11. Michael Hecht and Eura Jung, "Elaborating the Communication Theory of Identity: Identity Gaps and Communication Outcomes," *Communication Quarterly* 52, no. 3 (2004): 272.
12. Michael Hecht and Eura Jung, "Elaborating the Communication Theory of Identity: Identity Gaps and Communication Outcomes."
13. Kenneth Burke, *A Rhetoric of Motives* (Berkeley: University of California Press, 1969).
14. Ibid.
15. Karen Yescavage and Jonathan Alexander, "What Do You Call a Lesbian Who's Only Slept With Men? Answer: Ellen Morgan. Deconstructing the Lesbian

Identies of Ellen Morgan and Ellen DeGeneres," *Journal of Lesbian Studies* 3, no. 3 (1999): 23.

16. Ed Vitagliano, *American Family Association,* March 14, 2017, accessed March 10, 2019, https://www.afa.net/the-stand/culture/2017/03/disney-and-how-children-learn/.

17. David Roach, "First-Person: The SBC's Wisdom About Disney," August 29, 2016, accessed March 10, 2019. http://www.bpnews.net/47463/firstperson—the-sbcs-wisdom-about-disney.

18. Ibid.

19. Karen Frost, "Animated Films' Missing LGBT Characters," November 9, 2016, accessed March 2, 2019, https://www.afterellen.com/movies/515623-animated-films-missing-lgbt-characters.

20. Hannah Lifshutz, "Conservative Christian Group Boycotting Disney and 'Toy Story 4' Over 'Dangerous' Lesbian Scene," *Complex,* July 11, 2019, https://www.complex.com/pop-culture/2019/07/conservative-christian-group-boycotting-disney-toy-story-4-lesbian-scene.

21. One Million Moms, "Disney Blindsides Families With Lesbian Scene in Toy Story 4," June 27, 2019, https://onemillionmoms.com/current-campaigns/disney-blindsides-families-with-lesbian-scene-in-toy-story-4/.

22. Ibid.

23. Ibid.

24. MGM, "The Addams Family, Official Trailer," YouTube video, 1:46, posted April 9, 2019, https://youtu.be/4Z5VUf5x2RY.

25. Daniel Reynolds, "Addams Family Trailer: Gay Parents are an 'Average American Family,'" *Advocate,* April 10, 2019, https://www.advocate.com/film/2019/4/10/addams-family-trailer-gay-parents-are-average-american-family.

26. Rachel Charlene Lewis, "PRIDE: What Sucks about Finding Dory's Lesbian Couple," *Pride,* June 16, 2016, accessed March 8, 2019, https://www.pride.com/movies/2016/6/16/what-sucks-about-finding-dorys-lesbian-couple.

27. Bryan Alexander, "Ellen DeGeneres Laughs Over Possible 'Finding Dory' Gay Couple," *USA Today,* June 9, 2016, https://www.usatoday.com/story/life/movies/2016/06/09/ellen-degeneres-laughs-over-possible-finding-dory-gay-couple/85663136/.

28. Jason Fan, "Queering Disney Animated Films Using a Critical Literacy Lens," *Journal of LGBT Youth* 16, no. 2 (2019): 119–133.

29. Pixar Animation Studios-Walt Disney Pictures. *Finding Dory.* Directed by Andrew Stanton. Starring Ellen DeGeneres. 2016.

30. Ibid.

31. Ibid.

32. Morgan Gstatler, "Disney Channel Airs First Character to Ever Say 'I'm Gay,'" *The Hill,* February 12, 2019, https://thehill.com/blogs/in-the-know/in-the-know/429721-disney-channel-airs-first-character-to-ever-say-im-gay.

33. Daniel Avery, "GLAAD Gives Disney Failing Grade for LGBTQ Characters, Says Studio Has 'Weakest History' of Representation in Film," *NewsWeek,* May 23, 2019. https://www.newsweek.com/glaad-disney-lgbt-fail-1433437.

34. Jennifer Reed, "Ellen DeGeneres. Public Lesbian Number One." *Feminist Media Studies* 5, no. 1 (2005): 34.

35. Quoted in Jason Fan, "Queering Disney Animated Films Using a Critical Literacy Lens."
36. Bonnie Dow, "Ellen, Television, and Politics of Gay and Lesbian Visibility," *Critical Studies in Media Communication* 18, no 2 (2001): 123–140.
37. Ibid.
38. Ibid., 37.
39. Susan Hubert, "What's Wrong With this Picture? The Politics of Ellen's Coming Out Party," *Journal of Popular Culture* 33, no. 2 (1999): 35.
40. Anne Harris, "The Ellen DeGeneration: Nudging Bias in the Creative Arts Classroom," *Australian Association for Research in Education* 40, no. 1 (2012): 82–83.

BIBLIOGRAPHY

Alexander, Bryan. "Ellen DeGeneres Laughs Over Possible 'Finding Dory' Gay Couple," *USA Today*, June 9, 2016. https://www.usatoday.com/story/life/movies/2016/06/09/ellen-degeneres-laughs-over-possible-finding-dory-gay-couple/85663136/.

Avery, Daniel. "GLAAD Gives Disney Failing Grade for LGBTQ Characters, Says Studio Has 'Weakest History' of Representation in Film." *NewsWeek*, May 23, 2019. https://www.newsweek.com/glaad-disney-lgbt-fail-1433437.

Biography. "Ellen DeGeneres Biography." April 2, 2014. Accessed March 14, 2019. https://www.biography.com/people/ellen-degeneres-9542420.

Burke, Kenneth. *A Rhetoric of Motives.* Berkeley: University of California Press, 1969.

CNN. "Ellen DeGeneres Angry Over Parental Advisory." October 9, 1997. Accessed March 13, 2019. http://www.cnn.com/SHOWBIZ/9710/09/ellens.kiss/.

DeGeneres, Ellen. "Interview by Graeme Kay." *Finding Nemo—An Interview with Andrew Stanton and Lee Unkrich.* IndieLondon, 2003. Accessed June 14, 2019, http://www.indielondon.co.uk/film/finding_nemo_stanton_unkrich.html.

———. "Interview by Eric Marcus." *Making Gay History: Ellen DeGeneres Podcast* February 17, 2001. Accessed June 14, 2019, https://makinggayhistory.com/podcast/ellen-degeneres/.

Desowitz, Bill. "'Finding Dory' Preview: How Andrew Stanton Found Ellen DeGeneres' Forgetful Blue Tang." Indiewire, April 7, 2016. https://www.indiewire.com/2016/04/finding-dory-preview-how-andrew-stanton-found-ellen-degeneres-forgetful-blue-tang-21793/.

Dow, Bonnie. "Ellen, Television, and Politics of Gay and Lesbian Visibility." *Critical Studies in Media Communication* 18, no 2 (2001): 123–140.

Fan, Jason. "Queering Disney Animated Films Using a Critical Literacy Lens." *Journal of LGBT Youth* 16, no. 2 (2019): 119–133.

Frost, Karen. "Animated Films' Missing LGBT Characters." November 9, 2016. Accessed March 2, 2019. https://www.afterellen.com/movies/515623-animated-films-missing-lgbt-characters.

Gstatler, Morgan. "Disney Channel Airs First Character to Ever Say 'I'm Gay.'" *The Hill*, February 12, 2019. https://thehill.com/blogs/in-the-know/in-the-know/429721-disney-channel-airs-first-character-to-ever-say-im-gay.

Handy, Bruce. "Yep, I'm Gay." *Time*, April 14, 1997. https://time.com/4728994/ellen-degeneres-1997-coming-out-cover/.

Harris, Anne. "The Ellen DeGeneration: Nudging Bias in the Creative Arts Classroom." *Australian Association for Research in Education* 40, no. 1 (2012): 77–90.

Hecht, Michael. "2002—A Research Odyssey: Toward the Development of a Communication Theory of Identity." *Communication Monographs* 60, no. 1 (1993): 76–81.

Hecht, Michael, and Eura Jung. "Elaborating the Communication Theory of Identity: Identity Gaps and Communication Outcomes." *Communication Quarterly* 52, no. 3 (2004): 265–283.

Hubert, Susan. "What's Wrong With this Picture? The Politics of Ellen's Coming Out Party." *Journal of Popular Culture* 33, no. 2 (1999): 31–36.

Lewis, Rachel Charlene. "PRIDE: What Sucks about Finding Dory's Lesbian Couple." *Pride*, June 16, 2016. Accessed March 8, 2019. https://www.pride.com/movies/2016/6/16/what-sucks-about-finding-dorys-lesbian-couple.

Lifshutz, Hannah. "Conservative Christian Group Boycotting Disney and 'Toy Story 4' Over 'Dangerous' Lesbian Scene." *Complex,* July 11, 2019. https://www.complex.com/pop-culture/2019/07/conservative-christian-group-boycotting-disney-toy-story-4-lesbian-scene.

MGM. "The Addams Family, Official Trailer." YouTube video, 1:46. Posted April 9, 2019. https://youtu.be/4Z5VUf5x2RY.

One Million Moms. "Disney Blindsides Families With Lesbian Scene in Toy Story 4." June 27, 2019. https://onemillionmoms.com/current-campaigns/disney-blindsides-families-with-lesbian-scene-in-toy-story-4/.

Pixar Animation Studios-Walt Disney Pictures. *Finding Dory*. Directed by Andrew Stanton. Starring Ellen DeGeneres. 2016.

Reed, Jennifer. "Ellen DeGeneres. Public Lesbian Number One." *Feminist Media Studies* 5, no. 1 (2005): 23–36.

Reynolds, Daniel. "Addams Family Trailer: Gay Parents are an 'Average American Family.'" *Advocate*, April 10, 2019. https://www.advocate.com/film/2019/4/10/addams-family-trailer-gay-parents-are-average-american-family.

Roach, David. "First-Person: The SBC's Wisdom About Disney." August 29, 2016. Accessed March 10, 2019. http://www.bpnews.net/47463/firstperson—the-sbcs-wisdom-about-disney.

Snetiker, Marc. "Dory: The Untold Story." *Entertainment Weekly*, June 16, 2016. Accessed March 13, 2019. https://ew.com/article/2016/06/16/finding-dory-origin-story-nemo/.

Villareal, Daniel. "GLAAD Gives Disney Failing Grade for LGBTQ Characters, Says Studio Has 'Weakest History' of Representation in Film." *LGBTQ News.* February 10, 2019. Accessed July 1, 2019. https://www.newsweek.com/glaad-disney-lgbt-fail-1433437.

Vitagliano, Ed. *American Family Association.* March 14, 2017. Accessed March 10, 2019. https://www.afa.net/the-stand/culture/2017/03/disney-and-how-children-learn/.

Watkins, Gwynne. "How 'Finding Nemo' Launched Ellen DeGeneres''Comeback." *Yahoo!*, June 17, 2016. https://www.yahoo.com/entertainment/how-finding-nemo-launched-ellen-165815366.html.

Weaver, Hilary. "Ellen DeGeneres' Groundbreaking Coming Out: 20 Years Later." *Vanity Fair*, April 18, 2017. https://www.vanityfair.com/style/2017/04/20th-anniversary-of-ellen-degeneres-coming-out.

Yescavage, Karen, and Jonathan Alexander. "What Do You Call a Lesbian Who's Only Slept With Men? Answer: Ellen Morgan. Deconstructing the Lesbian Identies of Ellen Morgan and Ellen DeGeneres." *Journal of Lesbian Studies* 3, no. 3 (1999): 21–31.

Epilogue

Notes from behind the Camera from a Father of Two Daughters

Varion Laurent

This industry is changing. In my twenty-plus years of working in many facets of television production, I have seen dramatic changes in television and movie making. Among these changes, is the role that women have played. In many regards the production world has not been kind to women. For women, these horror stories are true and I can recall a phenomenal female co-worker of mine who worked in post-production. A supervisor approached her, and he asked if she did any freelance work outside of scheduled hours. She explained to me how he sat behind her as she worked, and after ten minutes he got up and began massaging her shoulders. A cold fear raced through her body as she did her best to divert his attention back to the piece they were working on. It worked, but only briefly. Almost frozen in fear she shut down his advances, but it created a hellish work environment for her from that moment forward.

She only shared this experience to me years after she turned in her resignation for her dream job in Hollywood. Today, women now have a voice in our industry. This is the "#MeToo" era. I've noticed a dramatic change in how men approach their female counterparts in the production world. But for some men, old habits die hard, and navigating the workforce has become dicey. For the vast majority of men that have yet to grasp what changes are being made to this toxic culture it has become increasingly awkward to simply "talk shop" in the workplace out of fear of saying something inappropriate. These simple or intentional slips of the tongue can now lead directly to the unemployment line. Yet while there are men who view the current era of #MeToo as a nuisance, it is important for men in the industry to become allies.

Elsewhere, I see the changes coming rapidly. I was searching on Netflix for something educational for my kids to watch and I noticed that under the genres there is Action, Suspense, Comedy, etc., a new genre in the search engine is called "Featuring a Strong Female Lead." Nowhere to be found is there a "Boys Take the Lead," because it is understood and the norm in our culture that boys and men have always been and still are the default leads. This is how girls and women have been told through the media to understand how their world works. But if this shift in content isn't a window into the future, I don't know what else is.

Index

adultification, 229–31, 236
Aladdin. See Jasmine
*alebrije,*109–10
Anna, 215–18
anthropomorphism, 265, 266, 274
appropriation, 89, 138

Belle 199–207
#BlackGirlMagic, 233-34
#BlackLivesMatter, 23, 24, 265, 271
Black Panther, 19, 21, 83, 238, 239
Black Widow, 60, 63
branding: princess brand, 49–53; rebranding 52, 53; social branding, 23, 25; woke branding, 23, 25, 27

canon. *See* music
Captain Marvel, 60–64
casting, 121, 154, 309–13
catrina, 108
Chase, Leah, xv, 119–21
Coco: Abuelita Elena, 106; Mama Coco, 106; Mama Imelda, 106.
colonialism: 163, 170, 190, 234, 311, 316; settler colonialism 129, 132–33, 141, 144

commoditization. *See* merchandise
consubstantiation, 324, 328, 329. See also identity
controlling images, 229
corporate social responsibility, 22, 23
counternarrative, 231
cultural appropriation 129, 138–40

DeGeneres, Ellen, 321–25
Descendants, 87, 285
Disney, 59, 60, 62, 63, 64, 65, 66, 68
diversity, 22, 303
divine, 101, 250, 251
Dory, 322, 329, 330
#DreamBigPrincess 33

Elena of Avalor, 48, 99–105
Elastigirl, 299
Elsa, 212–15
Enchancia, 44, 47, 50, 51
environmentalism, 129, 134
erasure, 132–45; conceptual, 132, 140; political 133, 140; racial 132, 140; spatial, 132, 140
evil. *See* villain

Feige, Kevin, 21, 62
feminism, 61, 65, 111, 163, 169, 173, 174, 201, 207; Black feminism, 235; Chinese post-feminism 154
flor de cempasuchil, 107
Frozen, 211

Gamora, 63
gender, 32, 33, 199, 200, 202, 203; agency, 188–91; based violence, 181, 190–91; and education 205, 207; empowerment, 188. See also representations
Gerber, Craig, 50
girls, 31, 33, 43, 63, 199; black girls, 228
#GirlPower, 232
goddess, 248

Hamilton, 79–81
Hasbro, 64, 67, 68
Hopps, Judy 266, 268, 274–75
Hurricane Katrina, xiv, 117

#IAMNOTYOURCOSTUME, 137–39, 171
iconography, 246
identity, 321–25, 328, 329, 331, 332; ascribed, 321, 323, 324, 326, 329, 331, 332; avowed, 324, 327, 328, 329, 332; theory of 322–24
Iger, Robert, 22, 133
Inanna, 248
The Incredibles, 295
Indo-Caribbean, 181, 189
islamophobia, 184–86

Jasmine, 49, 184, 187

Kennedy, Kathleen, 65
King Roland, 44, 47, 50, 51, 52
Kingston, Maxine Hong, 147

#LeanIn, 295
Lee, Jennifer, 3, 22, 212, 219
Leia, Princess, 66–67
LGBTQ, 321–25, 330–33

Lucasfilm, 59, 60, 64, 65
Lucas, George, 64–66

Mal, 284
Maleficent, 246, 247, 284
#MAKEMULANRIGHT, 147–57
marginalization, 266, 282, 289
Marvel Entertainment, 59, 60, 68; Marvel *Avengers*, 60, 61, 63; Marvel Cinematic Universe, 59, 68; Marvel Comics, 239
merchandise 63, 67, 137, 228
Mesopotamia, 248
#MeToo, 24, 25, 245–47, 339
Miranda, Lin-Manuel, 79–81
Moana, 129–46
Mulan 136–37, 147–57; *Ballad of Mulan*, 147
music: canon, 81; genre, 79; hip-hop, 80; popular, 81
mythology, 102, 248

New Orleans, 120

Obama, Barack, 283; Michelle, 32, 295
Oceanic Story Trust, 130, 138
ofrenda, 107, 109
orientalism, 169, 183, 192
#OscarsSoWhite, 228, 313

Pacific Islander, 129–46
phenomenology, 171
Pocahontas, 50, 133, 135, 163–75; history of 164–69
Princess and the Frog. See Tiana
princesses, 33–35; franchise, 43, 137, 227

Queen Miranda, 44, 45, 47, 48, 51, 52

race, 27, 28; racial discourse 27–31; racial representations 265
rape, 247, 248
representations, 302; of black women, 229, 303, 310, 311; of gender, 5, 32, 51, 61, 152, 184, 200; LGBTQ, 325
Rey, 64, 66, 67, 68

sacred texts, 230
Shuri, 228, 232–35
Sofia the First, 43–53
Star Wars, 59, 60, 64, 65, 67, 68
stereotypes: Arab, 184; Asian, 151; Black women, 228; Latino, 100; Native American, 163; Pacific Island, 138

Tiana, xiii, 119
transformation, 171, 214, 251

villains, 51; 101, 170, 183, 237, 245, 281

Wakanda, 83, 232, 234, 316
Watson, Emma, 199–200
white gaze, 169, 234, 237, 314
white savior, 147–48, 154–61
whitewashing, 148, 154, 156
work-life balance, 295
womanism, 235, 236
women, Black. See gender, representations.
woke, 22, 25, 27, 33

yellow face, 148, 154, 156

Zootopia, 263–75

About the Editor and Contributors

ABOUT THE EDITOR

Shearon Roberts is an assistant professor of mass communication and affiliate faculty member in African American and diaspora studies at Xavier University of Louisiana. Her research examines media representations and media discourse of race and gender. She is co-author of *Oil & Water: Media Lessons from Hurricane Katrina and the Deepwater Horizon Disaster* and co-editor of *HBO's Treme and Post-Katrina Catharsis: The Mediated Rebirth of New Orleans*.

ABOUT THE CONTRIBUTORS

Jenny Banh is an assistant professor in Asian American studies and anthropology at California State University, Fresno. Her research focuses on Asia/Asian American studies, cultural anthropology, and popular culture.

Alexis Woods Barr earned a PhD from the University of South Florida, with a research focus on breastfeeding behaviors among African American women. Her work focuses on maternal and child health that empowers marginalized populations.

Shaniece B. Bickham is an assistant professor of mass communication at Nicholls State University and a contributing faculty member at Walden University. Her research focuses on influences on student media content, crisis communication, and perceived source credibility.

About the Editor and Contributors

Ahli Chatters graduated from Xavier University of Louisiana with a BSc in psychology, minor in biology, and honors in English. She researches parenting and child development, childhood trauma and its adulthood effects, inner child healing, and the processes of socialization.

Charity Clay is an assistant professor of sociology at Xavier University of Louisiana where she heads the crime and social justice concentration. She researches the impacts of interlocking systems of oppression, the resistance tradition of Black womanhood, hip-hop as post–Civil Rights Black culture, and the significance of HBCUs within the context of Pan-Africanism.

Sarah A. Clunis is the director of the Xavier University of Louisiana Art Gallery and an assistant professor of art. Her research focuses on the history of African art and the display of African objects in Western museum settings, and the influence of African aesthetics and philosophy on the arts, religious rituals, and cultural identities of the African Diaspora.

Veronica Nohemi Duran is a PhD student in the history department at the University of Nebraska–Lincoln. Her research focuses on gender and race in popular culture in the late twentieth century, specifically through bilingual children's programming in the 1970s.

Krystal Ghisyawan holds a PhD in sociology and was a post-doctoral fellow with the Rutgers University Advanced Institute for critical Caribbean studies. Her research interests focuses on the intersections of gender, sexuality, religion, and space.

Susanne R. Hackett is a PhD candidate in Latin American studies at Tulane University. Her research centers on Afro-Cuban mythology, Yoruba moral philosophy, and the role of stories in shaping both national and individual identity.

Sheryl Kennedy Haydel is an assistant professor of public relations at Louisiana State University. Her research examines the role of the Black collegiate press in the Civil Rights era and the use of social media today for both branding and activism.

Abeo Jackson earned a master's degree from the Royal Central School of Speech and Drama, London. She is an award-winning writer, actor, dancer, choreographer, radio and television host, acting coach, creative producer as well as a theater producer.

Varion Laurent is the director of student media at Xavier University of Louisiana. He is a visual artist with over two decades in television production, public broadcasting, film production and post-production.

Leece Lee-Oliver (Blackfeet/Choctaw/Wyandot/Cherokee) is an assistant professor of women's studies and the director of American Indian studies at California State University, Fresno. She is a scholar and activist whose work is dedicated to highlighting the experiences of American Indians, Indigenous peoples, and marginalized peoples.

Sarah Maben is an assistant professor in the Department of Communication Studies at Tarleton State University. Her research interests include experiential learning, public relations, social media, and ethics.

Turon Nicholas earned an MBA from Anglia Ruskin University, U.K. She is an award-winning vocalist with a focus in vocal performance, individual and choral training, vocal technique and style coaching, and choral direction and arranging.

Prairie Endres-Parnell earned an MFA in acting and directing and an MA in communication studies from Texas Tech University. She teaches at Tarleton State University and researches LGBTQ media representations, focusing on transgender identities in pop culture.

Kelsey Ray is a New Orleans native and high school student who attended St. Agnes Middle School, St. Mary Magdalene Middle School, and Temple's Pre-school of Math and Science in the city. She aspires to be a designer.

Daron Roberts earned an MM from Northern Illinois University. He is an award-winning percussionist and recording artist for live and studio albums. He is the Rhythm Project associate director for the Virginia Arts Festival.

Alberto Rodriguez is an associate professor of history at Texas A&M University–Kingsville. His research focuses on race relations in American and Borderland communities with a specialty in Mexican American and African American encounters.

Hannah Shareef is a mass communication and political science major at Xavier University of Louisiana. She is a Chicago native and aspires to be a reporter.

Holly Pate is a masters in mass communications candidate at Kansas State University. She researches credibility of anonymous sources, and gender representation in military media.

Jana Thomas teaches advertising and social media at Kansas State University where she earned a masters in mass communications. She researches adolescent media use, digital citizenship, digital conflict, and social media manager well-being.

Prinsey Walker is a New Orleans native and is pursuing an MFA in film at the University of New Orleans. She has worked in entertainment media and the performing arts in New Orleans.

Rebecca Weidman-Winter is a performer and educator in Fort Worth, Texas. She has researched the musical traditions of the Penitentes of New Mexico. She has taught at Western State Colorado University and the Rocky Mountain Center for Musical Arts.